Praise for
THE BERLITZ TRAVELLERS GUIDES

"Aimed at educated, experienced travellers, the [Berlitz Travellers] Guides capture the flavor of foreign lands."
—*Entrepreneur*

"Filling a needed niche in guidebooks . . . designed to eliminate the cumbersome lists of virtually every hotel and restaurant . . . . Special out-of-the-way places are detailed. . . . The books capture the personality and excitement of each destination."
—*Los Angeles Times*

"There's a different tone to these books, and certainly a different approach . . . information is aimed at independent and clearly sophisticated travellers. . . . Strong opinions give these books a different personality from most guides, and make them fun to read."
—*Travel & Leisure*

"Aimed at experienced, independent travellers who want information beyond the nuts-and-bolts material available in many familiar sources. Although each volume gives necessary basics, the series sends travellers not just to 'sights,' but to places and events that convey the personality of each locale."
—*The Denver Post*

"Just the right amount of information about where to stay and play."
—*Detroit Free Press*

THE CONTRIBUTORS

JULIE WILSON, the author of a book on St. Martin/St. Maarten, is a contributing editor for *Town and Country* and author of nearly 100 articles about the Caribbean for *Travel & Leisure, Food & Wine, Diversion,* and other publications. She was *Connecticut Magazine*'s food critic for many years and is the editorial consultant for this guidebook.

SHARON JAFFE DAN travels the islands extensively as an editor of *Caribbean Travel and Life* and *Latitudes South.* She is the former editor of *Trade Winds.*

ANITA GATES, an author whose work has appeared in *Mademoiselle, Working Woman,* and other magazines, frequently contributes to *Travel & Leisure.* She was also a longtime contributing editor and columnist at *Frequent Flyer.*

JENNIFER QUALE contributes travel-related articles to *Food & Wine, Vogue,* and other major publications. Based in Switzerland, she has lived in the Caribbean and reports on that area frequently.

JESSICA HARRIS specializes in writing about the Caribbean, and Hispaniola in particular. She is the author of *Sky Juice and Flying Fish,* a book on Africa's contributions to New World cooking, and has written for *Caribbean Travel and Life, Essence, Vogue,* the *New York Times,* and other major publications.

J. P. MACBEAN's articles on travel, theater, food, and restaurants have appeared in *Travel & Leisure, Discovery,* and *Going Places* magazines, and in the *New York Daily News* and other newspapers. He is the author of books on Puerto Rico and New York City.

DAISANN McLANE's articles about Caribbean culture, food, and music frequently appear in *Vogue,* the *New York Times,* the *Village Voice, Caribbean Travel and Life,* and *Rolling Stone,* for which she is a columnist. Under the name of Lady Complainer, she spent several years singing calypso in Trinidad.

SUSAN FAREWELL has travelled to the Caribbean for many magazines, including *Vogue España, Metropolitan Home, Travel & Leisure, Caribbean Travel and Life, Child, Bride's,* and *Diversion.*

ROBERT GRODÉ, a journalist, reviewer, and longtime resident of the Caribbean now based in New York City, has written articles on travel and culture for magazines in the United States and abroad. He is the author of a book on the gravestones of St. Eustatius.

THE BERLITZ
TRAVELLERS GUIDES

THE BERLITZ TRAVELLERS GUIDE TO THE CARIBBEAN 1993

ALAN TUCKER
General Editor

BERLITZ PUBLISHING COMPANY, INC.
New York, New York

BERLITZ PUBLISHING COMPANY LTD.
Oxford, England

THE BERLITZ TRAVELLERS GUIDE
TO THE CARIBBEAN 1993

Berlitz Trademark Reg U.S. Patent and Trademark Office
and other countries—Marca Registrada

Published by Berlitz Publishing Company, Inc.
257 Park Avenue South, New York, New York 10010, U.S.A.

Distributed in the United States by
the Macmillan Publishing Group

Distributed elsewhere by Berlitz Publishing Company Ltd.
London Road, Wheatley, Oxford OX9 1YR, England

ISBN 2-8315-1768-0
ISSN 1057-4697

Designed by Beth Tondreau Design
Cover design by Dan Miller Design
Cover photograph by J. Barry O'Rourke/The Stock Market
Consultants: Sherry Marker, Daisann McLane, and Pamela Acheson
Maps by David Lindroth
Illustrations by Bill Russell
Copyedited by Candace Hogan
Edited by Cynthia Sophiea

Printed in the United States of America
1 3 5 7 9 10 8 6 4 2

THIS GUIDEBOOK

The Berlitz Travellers Guides are designed for experienced travellers in search of exceptional information that will enhance the enjoyment of the trips they take.

Where, for example, are the interesting, out-of-the-way, fun, charming, or romantic places to stay? The hotels and resorts described by our expert writers are some of the special places, in all price ranges except for the very lowest—not just the run-of-the-mill, heavily marketed places in advertised airline and travel-wholesaler packages.

We indicate the approximate price level of each accommodation in our description of it, and at the end of every chapter we supply more detailed hotel rates as well as contact information so that you can get precise, up-to-the-minute rates and make reservations.

The *Berlitz Travellers Guide to the Caribbean 1993* highlights the more rewarding parts of the islands so that you can quickly and efficiently home in on a good itinerary.

Of course, this guidebook does far more than just help you choose a hotel and plan your trip. *The Berlitz Travellers Guide to the Caribbean 1993* is designed for use *in* the Caribbean. Our writers, each of whom is an experienced travel journalist who regularly tours the islands he or she covers, tell you what you really need to know, what you can't find out so easily on your own. They identify and describe the truly out-of-the-ordinary resort areas, restaurants, shops, activities, and sights, and tell you the best way to "do" your destination.

Our writers are highly selective. They bring out the significance of the places they *do* cover, capturing the personality and the underlying cultural and historical resonances of a destination—making clear its special appeal.

The Berlitz Travellers Guide to the Caribbean is full of reliable and timely information, revised and updated each year. We would like to know if you think we've left out some very special place. Although we make every effort to provide the most current information available about every destination described in this book, it is possible too that changes have occurred before you arrive. If you do have an experience that is contrary to what you were led to expect by our description, we would like to hear from you about it.

A guidebook is no substitute for common sense when you are travelling. Always pack the clothing, footwear, and other items appropriate for the destination, and make the necessary accommodations for such variables as weather and local rules and customs. Of course, once on the scene you should avoid situations that are in your own judgment potentially hazardous, even if they have to do with something mentioned in a guidebook. Half the fun of travelling is exploring, but explore with care.

ALAN TUCKER
General Editor
Berlitz Travellers Guides

Root Publishing Company
330 West 58th Street
Suite 504
New York, New York 10019

CONTENTS

*The destinations appear in the order in which they lie
in the Caribbean, from the northwesternmost
(the Cayman Islands) clockwise to
the southwesternmost (Aruba).*

THE BERLITZ TRAVELLERS GUIDE TO THE CARIBBEAN 1993

Caribbean

| 0 | miles | 200 |
| 0 | km | 200 |

Miami

Havana

THE BAHAMAS

C U B A

HISPANIOL

Little
Cayman
Cayman
Brac

Grand
Cayman

G R E A T E R

HAITI

JAMAICA Kingston

Port-au-
Prince

A

Caribbean

N

Panama Canal
PANAMA

Maracaibo

COLOMBIA

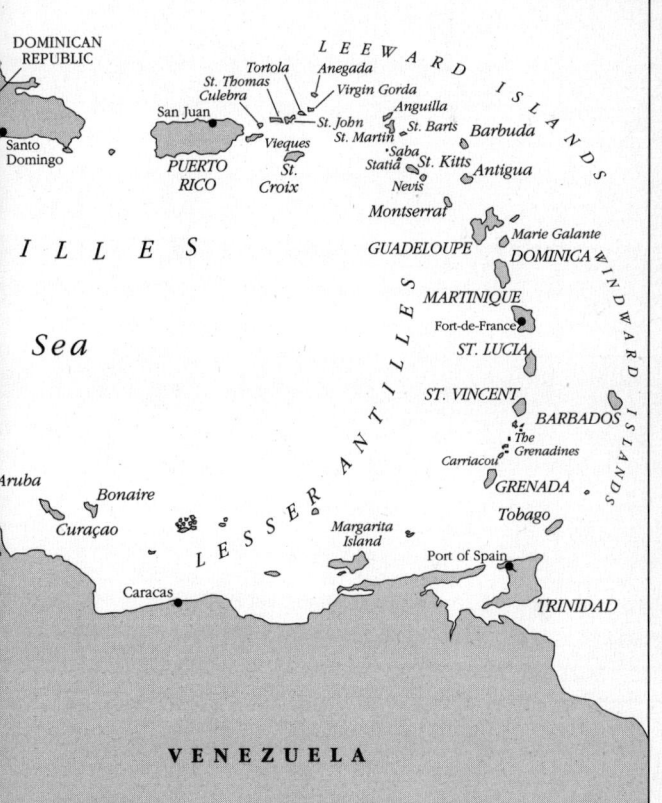

OVERVIEW

By Julie Wilson

Julie Wilson, the author of a book on St. Martin/St. Maarten, is a contributing editor for Town and Country *and author of nearly 100 articles about the Caribbean for* Travel & Leisure, Food & Wine, Diversion, *and other publications. She was* Connecticut Magazine's *food critic for many years and is the editorial consultant for this guidebook.*

In a cold climate, where the winters stretch damp and chill to a distant spring, the most enviable of statements is, "I'm going to the Caribbean." The mental images are immediate and palpable—a blazing tropical sun, warm sand underfoot, the gentle cooling of a trade wind, an infinity of stars in a night sky, coral reefs hiding colorful fish, hummingbirds and yellow birds darting among hibiscus and bougainvillaea, rum punch at sunset, and palm trees stretching as far as the eye can see.

There's nothing wrong with these images; they're all valid. There is, however, something wrong with the enviable statement: The Caribbean is not an entity—it is a collection of separate, politically fragmented islands connected only by navigational charts and airline flight paths. Each island has a distinct personality derived from its own particular history and defined by its geographical blessings and limitations. An island that once grew rich growing sugarcane is different from an island whose economy was based on smuggling and other methods of trade. An island colonized by the French has a different tone from an island colonized by the British or dominated by the Dutch. A flat, beachy island built up of coral has a different feeling from a lush, mountainous, volcanic island. To confuse the issue further, an island can be any, or all, of the above.

Nearly all the Caribbean islands were "discovered" by Christopher Columbus on his four New World voyages between 1492 and 1502. On his first he claimed Cuba, the Bahamas, and Hispaniola (shared now by Haiti and the Dominican Republic). He also made contact with the Arawaks, peaceful Indians who lived in simple compounds and ate roots. On his second voyage he may have wondered why he had been anxious to return—he found not only a lot of other islands but also the Carib Indians, warlike cousins of the Arawaks. The Caribs ate their captives. Nevertheless, Columbus persevered and claimed nearly all of the other islands in the Caribbean. Alonso de Ojeda, who sailed with Amerigo Vespucci, discovered Aruba, Curaçao, and Bonaire in 1499, while Columbus was busy up north. With more foresight than Columbus, Amerigo gave his name to everything on this side of the Atlantic, north and south of the equator.

These islands were on the route to the riches of Mexico and Peru, and—what with countless sheltered harbors and hidden coves—they were a haven for traders, navies, smugglers, pirates, privateers, and buccaneers. The English, French, Swedes, Danes, Dutch, Portuguese—even the Latvians—squabbled over the Caribbean. The islands were treatied away, swapped, sold, fought over, fought on, bloodied, bartered, bargained off—always pawns in someone else's war. History's most romantic heroes and scoundrels sailed here: Sir Walter Raleigh and Sir Francis Drake, Blackbeard, Bluebeard and Captain Kidd, Captain Bligh, Horatio Nelson, and Peter Stuyvesant. Some islands changed hands so often that an eager colonial administrator arriving after a long sea voyage might find that his services were not necessary as the island by then belonged to another government.

The 17th century saw the beginning of the age of the planter, when great fortunes were made growing the sugarcane that Christopher Columbus had introduced to the islands. Since the vast plantations required many workers, ruthless men also made fortunes by "trading around the Triangle." Whether the trader's home base was Europe or New England, the Triangle included a stop in Africa to pick up captured natives; a stop in the West Indies to sell those natives as slaves and pick up molasses, rum, or gold; and a trip back home to realize a fortune. Understandably, those years left a well-deserved legacy of resentment and mistrust. The planters also left the islands an architectural legacy—the colonial West Indian buildings that are today part of the Caribbean charm, and the thousands of stone sugar mills scattered in open fields far behind the beautiful beaches.

With the abolition of slavery in the mid-19th century, agriculture became less lucrative than it had been. Nevertheless, agriculture (with mining and, later, oil refining) persisted as the economic mainstay for the better part of a century, until airplanes, tourism, and political independence shook things up. In the 1950s the Caribbean islands rapidly became a playground for wealthy foreigners, especially North Americans.

As more and more islands moved toward self-government, they became more self-absorbed while, paradoxically, absorbing the characteristics of the latest outsiders into their already separate cultures. Given the financial exigencies of newly independent nations, some of them traded away a newly discovered birthright to an international corporation.

The Caribbean islands now realize that financial independence—and clout—comes through unity, and they are making efforts toward practical regional cooperation.

Besides looking forward (politically and economically), the islands are also starting to look backward and inward, showing an interest in their own cultures and examining why they are who they are—both individually and collectively. Rediscovering their Amerindian heritage, they are protecting archaeological sites and establishing some extremely fine small museums. They are increasingly—and justifiably—proud of their West Indian cuisine and music.

The music of the Caribbean—the lilting, syncopated calypso, born in Trinidad and now universal—is instantly recognizable. Simple, musically unsophisticated, a tuneful narrative of local gossip, calypso is as slangy and catchy as the Caribbean voice, which, of course, varies from island to island. The accepted accompaniment is the steel drum, first hammered out of oil drums by the Trinidadians in the 1940s. Calypso was popularized around the world by Harry Belafonte, singing about banana boats and about Matilda (who took his money and "run Venezuela") in the 1950s. To many the New York–born Belafonte is still the ultimate Trinidadian. By the 1960s, when Bob Marley and other Jamaicans thrust into the public ear the revolutionary reggae (a kind of cross between calypso and rock, with a shuffle beat), West Indian music had crossed over from folk to mainstream popular music. Nevertheless, it still sounds best on its home turf. There are few travellers so jaded that they don't enjoy hearing "Yellow Bird" played on a steel drum on any island— even for the millionth time.

The West Indian, or Creole, cuisine of the Caribbean was for many years confined to home kitchens. As they dined on "Continental cuisine" in hotels, tourists could only imagine what those intriguing aromas wafting from Caribbean homes might promise. Now they know, for West Indian food has become easily available as the natives have discovered that tourists not only like it, they gobble it up. Each island has its own style of cooking, which, like the language, shows the influences of Africa, France, Spain, North America, Portugal, India, the Far Eastern ports of the trading ships—sometimes even the Arawaks.

As with most cuisines, West Indian cooking is based on what is readily at hand—and what is at hand is bountiful. From the sea come spiny langoustes, conch, red snapper, giant grouper, dolphinfish (the fish, not the mammal), and a raft of other fish. From the land come spices, pineapple, coconuts, limes, mangoes, breadfruit, papayas, christophines, eggplants, soursops, bananas, bluggoes, and avocados. From under the earth come sweet potatoes, yams, cassava, and taro (also known as dasheen). Nearly every fruit or vegetable has a different name on each island. The differences among the starchy vegetables are so interesting and subtle that West Indians find the foreigner's preoccupation with the potato quite perplexing. The potato is, to them, unchangingly uninteresting.

Variations aside, West Indian cuisine itself is pretty basic. Consider the ubiquitous hot sauce, a fiery and unsubtle condiment that adds piquancy when used sparingly and could lead to hospitalization if used injudiciously. Or consider the *roti,* a distant, curried cousin of the Cornish pasty that looks like a pillowcase stuffed with laundry. Or the fragrant stews made of goat, pig, sheep, or "free-road" chicken; the variations on rice and peas; the stuffed land crabs; and the vegetable fritters. And remember that whatever the name, and whatever its island of origin, the dish will have been prepared with the uninhibited pleasure typical of the Caribbean.

Caribbean food and music come together at Carnival— the traditional hail and farewell to pleasures of the flesh preceding Ash Wednesday. But Carnival can occur at any time of the year throughout the islands, for it is primarily an island's celebration of itself . . . and an excuse to whoop it up. Many Carnivals are held in summer, when the children are home from school and off-island relatives can return on vacation. On southern islands, such as Aruba and Trinidad, Carnivals are nearly as lavish as Carnival in Rio; on small less-Latin islands they may be very simple, hardly more than glorified bake sales. But almost anywhere, count on costumes, floats, local foods, and a jump-up. Quintessentially Caribbean, a jump-up consists of steel bands swinging down the street, followed by a wild procession of everyone dancing, singing, clapping, and generally having the best time in the world.

But knowing the common culture and the common blessings (sun, sand, sea, and sports) doesn't explain why travellers often love one island above all others. The factors that go into that are as different as the range of human interests and inclinations.

Outstanding Characteristics of the Caribbean Islands

On most Caribbean islands you will find good beaches, plenty of water sports, a nice blend of European and North American cultural influences, West Indian ambience of some sort—in short, a little bit of everything. The following chart emphasizes the *special* strengths of each island, as well as what you should *not* expect to find there.

If an island destination comprises two or more places—as in Trinidad and Tobago—we have assigned numbers to each part. For example, in the shopping category, a number "2" is written in the U.S. Virgin Islands column, indicating that shopping is outstandingly good on St. Thomas—better even than the excellent shopping, say, on St. Croix.

USEFUL FACTS

As the chapter title indicates, these useful facts are merely an overview, pertaining to the Caribbean in general. Specific information about each island (e.g., entry requirements, transportation, local currency) can be found at the end of each individual chapter.

Some islands are coded as follows:

1. Vieques
2. St. Thomas
3. St. Croix and St. John
4. St. Croix
5. Tortola
6. Antigua
7. Barbuda
8. The Grenadines
9. Trinidad
10. Tobago
11. St. Martin
12. St. Maarten
13. Nevis
14. St. Kitts
15. Carriacou

	Cayman Islands	Jamaica	Haiti	Dominican Republic	Puerto Rico	U.S. Virgin Islands	British Virgin Islands	St. Martin/St. Maarten
Big-resort action		●			●			●
Chic and cosmopolitan								
White-sand beaches								●
Black-sand beaches								
No beaches								
Relative quiet							●	
Quiet								
Very low-keyed quiet								
Hiking and dramatic nature			●					
Birdwatching								
Yachting centers						●	●	
Especially good scuba diving	●					4		
Underwater snorkeling trails						3		
Surfing						1	5	
Especially good golf	●	●		●	●	4		
No golf								
Shopping (duty free)						2		●
Island arts and crafts		●	●		●			
Fine dining				●	●			●
Interesting local dishes								
West Indian music		●						
Casinos					●			12
No casinos								11
Spanish influence				●	●			
French influence			●					
Dutch influence								12
British influence		●						
Irish influence								
Luxury resorts on private islands							●	
Known for fine small inns								

St. Barts	Anguilla	Saba	Statia	St. Kitts and Nevis	Antigua and Barbuda	Montserrat	Guadeloupe	Dominica	Martinique	St. Lucia	Barbados	St. Vincent and the Grenadines	Grenada	Trinidad and Tobago	Bonaire	Curaçao	Aruba
•											•						
•	•			13	6								•				
			•	14		•											
		•															
					7			•		•				10			
		•	•	•		•						8					
							•	•		•			•				
								•						9	•		
					6								•				
		•	•													•	
	•													10			
							•				•						
											•						
•	•	•	•		7								15				
									•					9		•	•
•							•		•		•						
								•					•				
									•		•			9			
	•			•													•
•		•	•		7	•							•				
•							•		•								
		•	•												•	•	•
				•	•					•							
						•											
					6								•				
			•	•								8	•				

Local Time

Most Caribbean islands observe Atlantic standard time year-round, which is an hour ahead of eastern standard time and 4 hours behind Greenwich mean time. Exceptions are the Cayman Islands, Haiti, and Jamaica, all of which observe eastern standard time year-round.

Language

English is widely spoken on most islands. On the French islands (especially St. Bart's, Martinique, and Guadeloupe), a knowledge of French is useful, as is a knowledge of Spanish in the Dominican Republic and in parts of Puerto Rico. Every island has its local dialect, or patois, made up—in different degrees—of English, French, Portuguese, Dutch, African, and Spanish.

When to Go

Generally, high season runs from December 15 through April 15. That's when most people want to go where it's 80 degrees and sunny, and consequently the prices are the highest.

The weather in the fall months is likely to be unpredictable. Hurricane season is from August through November. Though hurricanes occur infrequently, when one comes, it's often a humdinger. Airline tickets may be scarce during an island's Carnival week. Unless Carnival falls in February, during the high season, hotel rooms won't be a problem—those fellow passengers on the airplane are going home.

Room Rates and Rate Codes

Unless otherwise indicated, hotel room rates listed in this book are for double rooms, double occupancy; prices given are *projections,* and the range spans the lowest rates in the low season to the highest in the high season. It is always wise to double-check rates before booking. Room rates do not include service charges and taxes, which on some islands can add to the cost by 10 or 15 percent, and sometimes more. Be sure to find out from the hotel about any added charges.

The rate codes listed are as follows: E.P.: European Plan; no meals included. C.P.: Continental Plan; Continental breakfast included. M.A.P.: Modified American Plan; breakfast and dinner included. A.P.: Full American Plan; breakfast, lunch, and dinner included. F.A.B.: Full American breakfast; buffet breakfast plus eggs, pancakes, etc.

What to Wear

Although each island has its own degree of formality (covered at the end of each chapter), the general ground rule calls for loose-fitting sportswear, bathing suits, sunglasses, and a hat. Also sunscreen: The northernmost point of these islands (Port-de-Paix, Haiti) is only 20 degrees from the equator; the southernmost point (Galeota Point, Trinidad) is a mere 10 degrees from the equator.

Currency

Because currency varies among the islands, all prices have been listed in U.S. dollars for comparison purposes unless otherwise specified.

Nightlife

Except on some of the larger, more sophisticated islands, there is not much nightlife. After all that sun and daytime sporting activity, people are usually too bushed to stay up late. Some islands do have casinos, all the big hotels have evening entertainment, and even the smallest inn usually has a steel band playing once a week.

Restaurant Reservations

At the height of the season, it is suggested you make dinner reservations at many of the restaurants we have recommended in this book; at most other times, it won't be necessary. When in doubt, have your hotel make the reservation—its name is better known locally than yours is. Also, if a service charge is not included in the bill (and this varies from island to island and even from restaurant to restaurant), it is appropriate to tip anywhere from 10 percent to 15 percent, depending on the location and the trappings.

Getting from Airport to Hotel

On some islands you can pick up a rental car at the airport. On others you'll have to take a taxi to the hotel, where a rental car will be delivered. On any island it's a good idea to take a taxi first—if only to check out the local driving customs. Ask at the airport what the rate should be. And don't worry about finding a taxi: The drivers know when the planes come in.

Getting from Island to Island

The small interisland airlines have regularly scheduled flights, but they are subject to variables such as weather, darkness, and even the profitability of plane loads. Cancellations are not unheard of, nor are the precipitous departures that occur when enough people show up to fill the plane. Best advice: Buy your ticket in advance and get to the airport early.

Cruise Ships

If you want to go to the Caribbean but don't know where you want to go (aside from someplace warm and sunny), a cruise ship can serve as an island sampler. Cruise ships range, as they say, from the sublime to the gor' blimey, and picking the right one for you is even more important than picking the right island. Once you're on the cruise ship, there's no getting away. Before throwing yourself on the mercy of a good travel agent (which you would be wise to do), here are a few facts to consider.

Most Caribbean cruises are a week long. (On longer cruises, some lines will let you board the ship at a midway port and leave it at another, depending on space available.) Most cruise ships follow each other along a well-travelled route, including stops at such popular ports as St. Thomas, San Juan, Antigua's St. John's, and St. Maarten's Philipsburg. Reasons? Good docking facilities, good shopping, and nautical proximity to major points of embarkation (Miami, Fort Lauderdale, San Juan, Antigua's St. John's, St. Thomas). Some cruise ships leave from Barbados and visit such southern islands as Grenada, St. Lucia, Mustique, Bequia, and other Grenadines.

Cruise ships, like islands, come in different sizes. On a small ship you may have as few as 100 fellow passengers; on a big one you'll share the decks with just over 2,000 people—approximately the number of Wellesley College's entire student body. Some ships attract a younger crowd, some an older crowd, but most have a pretty good mix. As a general rule, the more upscale the ship, the better the chances of having only one seating at mealtimes—which means better food.

When figuring price (which ranges between $1,000 and $7,000 per person per week, double occupancy), remember that the bottom line isn't always an absolute indicator of value at sea. Some of the apparently most expensive ships include in their base price such customarily extra charges as tips, cancellation/travel-delay insurance, even wine with meals.

At the very top of the cruise ship line, the most formal (read "dress for dinner and bring the black tie just in case") are the new *Seabourn Spirit* and *Seabourn Pride,* two small luxury ships with suites rather than cabins. Include, too, the classic Cunards—the *QE2* (big), *Sea Goddess I* (small), and the mid-size *Vistafjord* and *Sagafjord.*

In this same class, but more casual (barefoot elegance, they call it) are the trio of cruise ships with sails—computerized and quite eerie to watch going up and down in unison and in silence. *Windstar* and *Windspirit,* carrying 150 passengers each, were the first of these hybrids. The new *Club Med I* is somewhat larger but carries the same number of sails—yes, it's still sports-oriented Club Med and, yes, it serves free wine with meals.

On the least formal end of the scale are the "fun ships" of Carnival and Costa cruise lines. They are big, they are relatively inexpensive, and they are, in truth, a lot of fun. Especially if you're under 30.

Everything in between includes the Royal Cruise Line's *Crown Odyssey* and *Golden Odyssey,* the Princess Line (of "Love Boat" fame), the Royal Caribbean Line, and the Kloster Cruise Line, whose stately *Norway* was originally the S.S. *France.*

With this précis you are now ready for the help of a good travel agent.

—*Julie Wilson*

BIBLIOGRAPHY

Some of the volumes listed below may be available only in the West Indies. Check with bookshops on the islands you visit for titles dealing with the area, local customs, and history.

General

JAMES BOND. *Birds of the West Indies* (1971). Classic guide to the feathered inhabitants of the latitudes from Port-au-Prince to Port-of-Spain. Lavishly illustrated with sketches detailed enough to make identification a breeze. (And, yes, Ian Fleming copped the author's name when creating the agent-hero of his popular spoofs. When informed of his literary namesake, the ornithologist was reportedly happy as a lark.)

PAULA BURNETT, ED. *The Penguin Book of Caribbean Verse* (1986). Compilation of the works of more than 100 English-speaking West Indian poets. Selections range from 18th-century slave songs to the Rasta-inspired lyrics of Bob Marley and Jimmy Cliff. Copious biographical and explanatory notes as well as a useful glossary of patois words and phrases are included.

QUENTIN CREWE. *Touch the Happy Isles* (1987). This British author takes the reader on a highly subjective tour of Caribbean civilization today.

CARMEN C. ESTEVES AND LIZABETH PARAVISINI-GEBERT. *Green Cane and Juicy Flotsam* (1991). Short stories by an impressive roster of Caribbean women ranging from Jean Rhys to Jamaica Kincaid. The selections include lyrical evocations of island life as well as steely-eyed analyses of women's debased status in a male-dominated society.

PATRICK LEIGH FERMOR. *The Traveller's Tree: A Journey Through the Caribbean Islands* (1950). This richly detailed, insightful, and sensitive account resulted from the prize-winning author's now-classic journey through the Caribbean in the 1940s.

VIRGINIE E. AND GEORGE A. GILBERT. *Down Island Caribbean Cookery* (1991). Comprehensive collection of West Indian recipes reflecting the Latin, French, English, Dutch, East Indian, and African influences that make Caribbean cuisine one of the most varied and exciting in the world.

IDAZ GREENBERG. *The Guide to Corals and Fishes of Florida, the Bahamas and the Caribbean* (1977). Indispensible guidebook to the area's teeming marine life, with color illustrations.

DOROTHY AND BOB HARGREAVES. *Tropical Blossoms* (1960). Golden trumpet or golden shower? Bougainvillaea or bromeliad? You'll find the answers in this brief guide to the flamboyant florals of the islands. Photographs are accompanied by succinct and reliable captions.

JESSICA HARRIS. *Sky Juice and Flying Fish: Traditional Caribbean Cooking* (1991). Authentic West Indian recipes, history of the Caribbean's culinary development, and index of ingredients and where to obtain them. Informed, stylish, and sensitive.

LENNOX HONYCHURCH. *The Caribbean People* (three volumes, 1981). A lively, well-balanced history of the West Indies by one of the leaders of the Caribbean's "New Historians."

IAN KEOWN. *Ian Keown's Caribbean Hideaways* (1992). Guide to the Caribbean's smaller hostelries by a longtime authority on these frequently overlooked tropical inns and guest houses. Up-to-date and reliable.

MARK KURLANSKY. *A Continent of Islands* (1992). Frank and perceptive study of the social, political, historical, and cultural backgrounds of the islands. Required reading for all Caribbean travellers.

PAULE MARSHALL. *The Chosen Place, The Timeless People* (1969). An evocative novel set on a fictional island that may be Barbados. Well-rounded portraits of West Indian haves and have-nots as well as penetrating depictions of visiting off-islanders.

CARYL PHILLIPS. *Cambridge* (1992). Resonantly written historical novel cast in the form of two early-19th-century journals, one kept by an absentee plantation owner's daughter visiting the West Indies for the first time; the other, by a slave convicted of the death of the young woman's lover. Powerful and insightful story-telling.

VIRGINIA RADCLIFFE. *The Caribbean Heritage* (1976). A sensitive, illustrated cultural history, written with an unusual blend of affection and insight.

S. A. SEDDON AND G. W. LENNOX. *Trees of the Caribbean* (1980). A less-than-thorough but handy survey of the more frequently encountered trees of the West Indies. Color photographs add to the usefulness of this compact guide.

BOB SHACOCHIS. *Easy in the Islands* (1985). Short stories that vividly (and sometimes raunchily) capture the vitality and color of the tropics. Winner of the American Book Award for 1986.

KAY SHOWKER. *Caribbean Ports of Call* (1987). Well-researched guide for cruise-ship travellers.

SUZANNE SLESIN AND STAFFORD CLIFF. *Caribbean Style* (1985). Superbly illustrated photographic survey of West Indian domestic architecture from 18th-century estate houses to the hideaways of today's "beautiful people."

ERIC WILLIAMS. *From Columbus to Castro: The History of the Caribbean, 1492–1967* (1970). Scholarly, very thorough chronicle of the West Indies by the former prime minister of Trinidad and Tobago.

HERMAN WOUK. *Don't Stop the Carnival* (1965). Although set in fictional "Amerigo," this novel has attained the status of a classic throughout the Caribbean. Visitors inquiring about expatriate life in the tropics are almost certain to be asked in turn, "Have you read *Don't Stop the Carnival?*" Be prepared.

Aruba
JOHANN HARTOG. *Aruba*. History of the island that also provides valuable pointers on touring Aruba. Illustrated with color photographs.

Bonaire
JOHANN HARTOG. *Bonaire*. An armchair tour of Bonaire, illustrated with 90 pages of photographs by Chris and Donna McLaughlin. In English, Dutch, French, German, and Spanish.

———. *History of Bonaire* (1975). Detailed narrative traces the island's rich past. Black-and-white photographs.

TOM VAN'T HOF. *Guide to the Bonaire Marine Park* (1983). Guide to the park's marine and coral reef ecosystems. Detailed suggestions are given for diving and snorkeling at each site in the park. Photographs and maps.

PEER REIJNS. *Excursion Guide to Washington/Slagbaai National Park* (1984). Nontechnical guide to the park includes descriptions of the sites, plants, and animals to be discovered there.

British Virgin Islands
JOHN ROUSMANIERE. *The Sailing Lifestyle* (1988). Quite technical in its approach, this book should prove indispensible for those intending to explore the islands, cays, and reefs of the B.V.I. by boat.

ROBB WHITE. *Two on the Isle* (1985). Charming autobiographical account of how the author and his wife discovered the British Virgins and set about building a home that eventually became the Marina Cay Hotel.

Cayman Islands

PETER MATTHIESSEN. *Far Tortuga* (1975). Novel that deals with sailors and the sea and has been compared with the works of Conrad and Stevenson.

ROBERT LOUIS STEVENSON. *Treasure Island* (1883). Young Jim Hawkins, Blind Pew, Long John Silver, and all those "Yo-ho-hos."

NEVILLE WILLIAMS. *A History of the Cayman Islands* (1970). Overview of an island group that is as popular with financial types as it is with sun seekers.

Curaçao

TOM VAN'T HOF AND HELEEN COMET. *Guide to Curaçao Underwater Park*. Comprehensive guide to dive sites, along with general information about the park.

GEORGE S. LEWBEL. *Curaçao Underwater*. Scuba and snorkeling guide to the waters along Curaçao's southern coastline.

PEER REIJNS. *Excursion Guide to the Christoffel Park*. Handy suggestions for three driving tours and one on foot, including information about flora and fauna that may be encountered along the way.

JOS DE ROO. *Curaçao—Scenes and Behind the Scenes*. General history of Curaçao, along with suggested walking tours of Willemstad and excursions into the countryside.

Dominica

LENNOX HONYCHURCH. *The Cabrits and Prince Ruperts Bay* (1982). The inside story of the restoration of Dominica's major historical monument.

————. *The Dominica Story: A History of the Island* (1984). Candid, no-holds-barred study by a member of a longtime island family.

JEAN RHYS. *Wide Sargasso Sea* (1982). In this fascinating spin-off of Brontë's *Jane Eyre,* Rhys re-creates in fictional form plantation life in 19th-century Dominica.

ANTHONY TROLLOPE. *The West Indies and the Spanish Main* (1859). What Dominica was like in the mid-1800s; clear-eyed and, predictably, well written.

Dominican Republic

SAMUEL HAZARD. *Santo Domingo Past and Present; with a Glance at Hayti* (reprint, 1982). Originally published in 1873, this book captures the feeling of life in the area during the 19th century. Illustrated with exquisite line drawings.

Grenada

NORMA SINCLAIR. *Grenada, Isle of Spice* (1987). Helpful hints for touring the island, destination by destination. Some general historical and social background.

Guadeloupe

LAFCADIO HEARN. *Two Years in the French West Indies* (1890). Colorful descriptions of life on Guadeloupe and Martinique during the late 19th century.

SAINT-JOHN PERSE (ALEXIS SAINT-LEGER LEGER). *Anabasis* (1924). Modern verse of great emotional power by the Nobel Prize–winning poet born in Guadeloupe in 1887.

Haiti

AIME CESAIRE. *The Tragedy of King Christophe* (1969). Drama depicting the last days of Henri Christophe; required reading for anyone visiting the Citadelle.

HERBERT COLE. *Christophe, King of Haiti* (1967). Biography of Henri Christophe.

GRAHAM GREENE. *The Comedians* (1972). Novel depicting the dark days of the Duvalier regime.

SELDEN RODMAN. *Artists in Tune with Their World: Masters of Popular Art in the Americas and Their Relation to the Folk Tradition* (1982). Forty-page section on Haiti offers a comprehensive look at the "primitive" art Rodman himself did much to encourage.

AMY WILENTZ. *The Rainy Season: Haiti Since Duvalier* (1989). An investigation of conditions since the fall of "Bébé Doc" Duvalier in 1986 by a major new talent who manages, in turn, to be sensitive and outspoken, angry and compassionate. A page-turner.

Jamaica

HANS JOHANNES HOFFER AND PAUL ZACH. *The Inside Guide to Jamaica* (1983). Thorough, illustrated overview of Jamaica's history, people, politics, and culture, with recommendations about what to see and do throughout the island.

LADY MARY NUGENT. *Lady Nugent's Journal* (1939). Intriguing insights into Jamaican life in the early 1800s, when "sugar, slaves, and sin" were as common as "sea, sun, and sand" are today.

Martinique

TRUMAN CAPOTE. *Music for Chameleons* (1975). In the title story, Capote captures in lyrical prose the beauty, strangeness, and sophistication of Martinique.

ANDRE CASTELOT. *Josephine* (1967). Biography of Marie Josèphe Rose Tascher de la Pagerie, better known to the world as "the empress Josephine." Colorful and moving.

AIME CESAIRE. *The Collected Poetry* (1983). Translated by Clayton Eshleman and Annette Smith. Lyric verse by internationally acclaimed Martinique poet and mayor of Fort-de-France. (In French and English.)

EUZHAN PALCY. *Sugar Cane Alley* (*La Rue Cases Nègres*) (1984). Orion Classics film directed and adapted by Palcy from the novel by Joseph Zobl. Filmed in Martinique, a sensitive depiction of a boy's coming of age in the 1920s. (In French, with English subtitles.) Available on videocassette.

GORDON THOMAS AND MAX MORGAN WITTS. *The Day the World Ended* (1969). Riveting account of the events leading up to the Mont Pelée volcanic explosion of 1902 and the destruction of St. Pierre.

Nevis

JOYCE GORDON. *Nevis: Queen of the Caribees* (1985). Guidebook with especially good coverage of the island's intriguing history and its characters—Admiral Nelson, Alexander Hamilton, et al.

Puerto Rico

OSCAR LEWIS. *La Vida* (1966). Poignant account of slum life in the neighborhood called La Perla in Old San Juan.

Puerto Rico: A Guide to the Island of Boriquén. Excellent 1930s WPA-sponsored guide to the island.

Qué Pasa. Superb free seasonal guide produced by the Tourism Office and an essential reference for day-to-day events in music, dance, theater, art, sports, festivals, night spots, and holidays.

CHRISTOPHER RAND. *The Puerto Ricans* (1971). Beautifully written social study of the Puerto Rican people and their lives as new arrivals on the mainland.

KATHRYN ROBINSON. *The Other Puerto Rico* (1987). A New Jersey native who has lived and worked on the island since 1974, Robinson is an adventurous hiker who gives the facts about flora, fauna, waterways, mountain trails, caves, forests, and beaches in such "Out on the Island" spots as El Yunque rain forest, the coffee country in the central mountains, and the off-shore islands of Vieques, Culebra, and Mona.

Saba
JOHANN HARTOG. *History of Saba* (1975). Brief but always intriguing summary of three centuries of Saban life. (Illustrated.)

WILL JOHNSON. *Tales from My Grandmother's Pipe* (1979). Saban lore, charmingly recounted by one of the young leading authorities on the island.

St. Eustatius
YPIE ATTEMA. *St. Eustatius: A Short History of the Island and Its Monuments* (1976). A concise overview compiled by one of the authorities involved in the restoration of Fort Oranje in the early 1970s.

JOHANN HARTOG. *History of St. Eustatius.* Skimpy but interesting, nonetheless. His *Bovenwindse Eilanden* (1964) (only in Dutch, unfortunately) is far more informative.

ELEANOR HECKERT. *The Golden Rock* (1971). Historical adventure novel set during the late 1700s that captures much of the flavor of that boisterous period.

BARBARA TUCHMAN. *The First Salute* (1988). Best-selling history of the American Revolution and St. Eustatius's crucial role in the final outcome.

A. H. VERSTEEG AND F. R. EFFERT. *Golden Rock: The First Indian Village on St. Eustatius* (1986). Slightly stilted but comprehensive survey of pre-Columbian St. Eustatius.

St. Lucia

CHRIS DOYLE. *Exploring the Windward Islands* (1988). The author, a longtime skipper of the islands, provides vital, often amusing—if not the most literate—information on getting around by boat.

HARRIET F. DURHAM AND FLORENCE LEWISOHN. *St. Lucia Tours and Tales* (1971). This homespun volume offers a charming but biased exploration of the island's histories and highways.

St. Maarten/St. Martin

JOHANN HARTOG. *St. Maarten, Saba, St. Eustatius* (1974). Written before tourism reached full flower on St. Maarten, this is somewhat dated in certain areas, yet nonetheless valuable for its historical and cultural background information.

St. Vincent and the Grenadines

BOBOROW AND JENKINS. *St. Vincent and the Grenadines* (1987). Lushly illustrated coffee-table book with informative introduction, plus selected verse by Canadian writer Margaret Atwood, a longtime island enthusiast.

EARLE KIRBY. *Guide to Selected Attractions on the Island of St. Vincent* (1987). The title tells it all; magazine-size scholarly Baedeker to historic sites and other attractions.

Trinidad and Tobago

MALCOLM BARCANT. *The Butterflies of Trinidad and Tobago* (1970). Comprehensive, fully illustrated text contains information on more than 622 species. The author collected butterflies for almost half a century and has bred and crossbred various species.

G. A. C. HERKLOTS. *The Birds of Trinidad and Tobago* (1972). Covers more than 400 species with more than 260 illustrations, most by the author. Essential for visiting birders.

Insight Guide: Trinidad and Tobago (1987). Detailed and beautifully illustrated guide compiled by authorities on various aspects of the islands.

V. S. NAIPAUL. *A House for Mr. Biswas* (1962). Perhaps the best known of the internationally acclaimed Trinidadian author's novels. Set on the island, it sensitively depicts life among the East Indian population.

ERIC WILLIAMS. *History of the People of Trinidad and Tobago* (1964). Written by Trinidad's first prime minister as a gift to the people on the eve of the country's independence (August 31, 1962). First full history of the two islands.

—*Robert Grodé*

THE CAYMAN ISLANDS

By Anita Gates

Anita Gates, an author whose work has appeared in Mademoiselle, Working Woman, *and other magazines, frequently contributes to* Travel & Leisure. *She was also a longtime contributing editor and columnist at* Frequent Flyer.

There's a real sense of privilege about being in the Cayman Islands these days. Apart from the fact that half the people may be here just to visit their money, there's the basic issue of being able to afford the place. Not everything is expensive, of course, but the occasional paperback book with a hardcover price tag might startle a first-time visitor, just as the price of Scotch in Tokyo has taken foreigners aback for years.

The average Caymanian exudes a quiet, take-it-all-for-granted self-confidence, the sort of demeanor Statesiders used to see among 25 year olds who had made a good deal of money on Wall Street. But then Caymanians have many reasons to feel secure. Their economy is strong, their political climate as stable as they come (it's a British Crown Colony), and the 500 or so banks here provide an enviable standard of living for residents as well as an "offshore financial center" (read "tax haven") for outsiders. Tourism is just the icing on the cake.

Scuba enthusiasts have long known the Caymans not only for the finest diving—for people at all levels of expertise—in the Caribbean, but as one of the top diving destinations in the world. In recent years, though, the

25

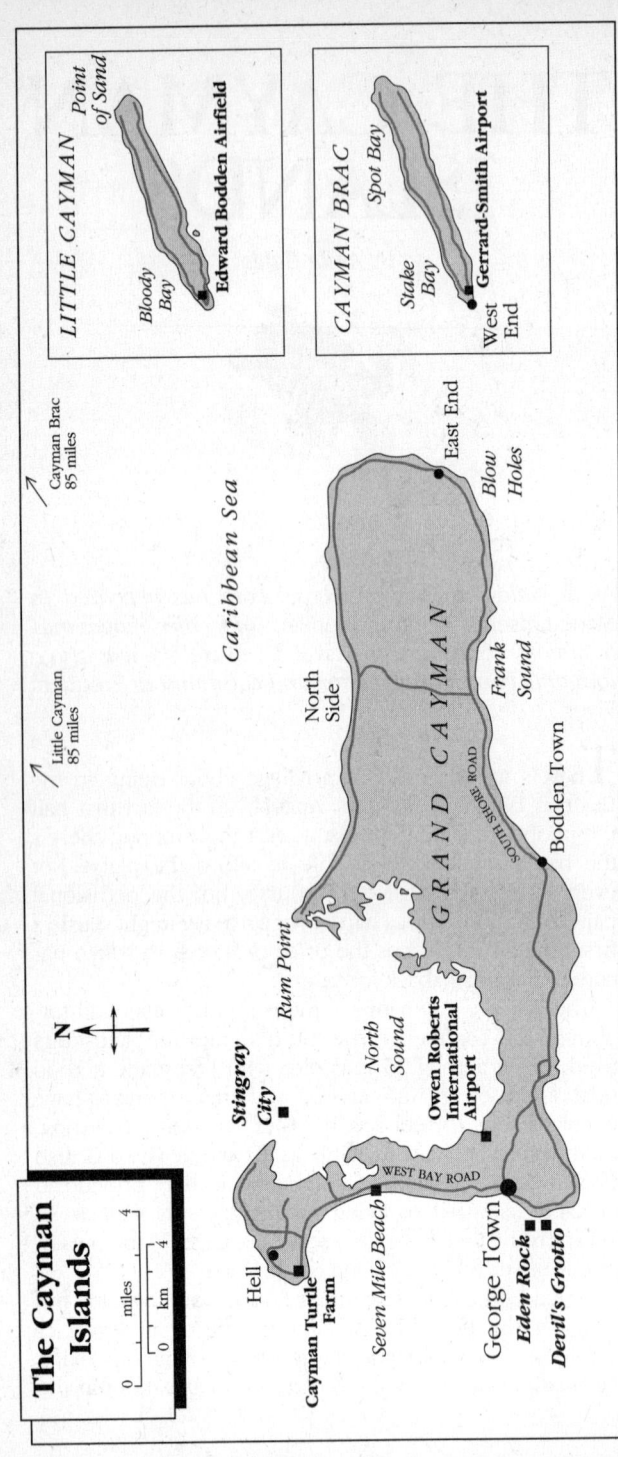

The Cayman Islands

miles
0   4

km
0   4

N

LITTLE CAYMAN

Point of Sand

Edward Bodden Airfield

Bloody Bay

CAYMAN BRAC

Spot Bay

Gerrard-Smith Airport

Stake Bay

West End

Little Cayman 85 miles

Cayman Brac 85 miles

Caribbean Sea

East End

Blow Holes

Frank Sound

North Side

SOUTH SHORE ROAD

Bodden Town

GRAND CAYMAN

Rum Point

North Sound

Owen Roberts International Airport

Stingray City

WEST BAY ROAD

Seven Mile Beach

George Town

Cayman Turtle Farm

Hell

Eden Rock

Devil's Grotto

islands have been luring travellers with many other attractions, from great fishing to superb white-sand beaches.

MAJOR INTEREST

Underwater beauty for divers and snorkelers
Seven Mile Beach's calm, clear waters
Deep-sea fishing
Golf
Stingray City
A very civilized social atmosphere

The Cayman Islands are less than 500 miles south of Miami and about 200 miles northwest of Jamaica. The main island, 76-square-mile **Grand Cayman**, is by far the most popular destination. The two smaller islands, **Cayman Brac** and **Little Cayman**, are favored by serious divers and lovers of ultrasecluded—and that's no kidding—vacations, but everyone should see one or both at least once (each is a half-hour flight away, about $95 round trip, $77 if you book seven days in advance).

The only question seems to be: If you're not a devoted diver or snorkeler, are the Caymans still a destination for you? Underwater there's no argument; these are among the most beautiful islands around. Grand Cayman is actually the top of a huge sunken mountain. Visibility below is 100 to 125 feet year-round, and snorkelers only have to go a few yards out to see some spectacular examples of what the rest of the mountain down here looks like. Diving instruction for beginners is widely available.

But diving has never been the only attraction here, merely the best known. Those who love to fish come for the abundance of tarpon, tuna, wahoo, bonefish, and blue marlin. Tennis players find plentiful courts and golfers one excellent course. And, of course, there's the physical beauty of the place. Grand Cayman is many people's idea of the perfect Caribbean island: white-sand beaches, spectacular sunsets, and crystal-clear water. The palms sway alongside almond, papaya, and sea grape, and gardens of hibiscus, lantana, oleander, and bougainvillaea grace the island's flat terrain. Mangrove swamps harboring all manner of flora and fauna lie inland. It all begins at Seven Mile Beach.

Seven Mile Beach

Back in the 1970s, when tourism was just beginning here, the divers had their dive resorts and their live-aboard boats, and the financial types had their houses and condos. For the sun-and-sand vacationer, there were clean, pleasant hotel rooms—adequate but hardly luxurious. When the Hyatt opened in 1986, all that changed.

The **Hyatt Regency Grand Cayman**, which sits across the road from Seven Mile Beach like a giant Wedgwood-blue sculpture, was the first luxury resort to open its doors on Grand Cayman. Guests have gardens, pools, tennis, golf, a swim-up bar, and restaurants, all set in a grand British colonial atmosphere. The hotel beach club with its restaurant and Red Sail Sports water-sports facility is just across the street.

The Hyatt's first real competition is the **Radisson Resort Grand Cayman**, a five-story oceanfront hotel opened in 1991 on Seven Mile Beach. The atmosphere isn't quite as upscale, but there's a special luxury in being right on the beach. Its other assets include the popular B.W.I. nightclub, restaurants, a pool, water sports, tropical courtyard greenery, and rooms with private balconies.

On a quieter part of Seven Mile Beach, but still within easy driving distance of what passes for the action here, is another new property, **Indies Suites**. It's across the street from the beach and was originally designed to be a condominium complex, so there are only one- and two-bedroom suites (but with full hotel services). Those who prefer an even more secluded, casual setting, but with resort extras such as pool, tennis courts, and sauna, favor the **Cayman Kai**, a resort-and-villa complex on the north-central coast.

The **Ramada Treasure Island Resort**, just off Seven Mile Beach, opened in 1987 and brought a Nashville connection to the Caymans. Country singers Conway Twitty, Larry Gatlin, and Ronnie Milsap were among the original owners; fans are still among the guests. The rooms are more functional than glamorous.

The best reason to go to Treasure Island, however, may be for the shows at **Silver's**. Visiting groups run the gamut in musical style from rockabilly to reggae. Friday night is the time to go. (Because of local Sunday liquor laws, the last Saturday-night drinks are served at midnight.)

Until Silver's came along, Barefoot Man's show at the

Holiday Inn was the essence of island nightlife. It's still the best spot to get a fix of "Montego Bay," "Yellow Bird," and other quintessentially Caribbean fare.

Dining and Shopping

For a fashionable dinner, head back to the Hyatt complex and its beachfront restaurant, **Hemingway's**. Offerings range from veal specialties and blackened or chargrilled fresh fish dishes to jerk chicken. The Grand Pavilion has transformed its French restaurant into the **Living Reef**, a very attractive aquarium-filled setting with a seafood menu. For a Caribbean-romantic atmosphere try **Chef Tell's Grand Old House** (owned by TV chef Tell Erhardt). It's set in the old Petra Plantation, a Victorian house with a big porch and sea views, on South Church Street; Tel: 993-33. Most people also drive out to the northwest tip of the island to **Ristorante Pappagallo** for northern Italian cuisine and seafood served in a thatched-roof Polynesian-style setting. Diners may find themselves surrounded by live (and often very vocal) tropical birds, the owners' house pets. Tel: 934-79.

For a romantic dinner on the beach and under the stars, there's **The Wharf** (Tel: 922-31), which has strolling musicians and what is said to be the island's only bar right on the water. The food is Continental and Caribbean. For Southwest cuisine and Sante Fe style, **Lantana's** at the Caribbean Club on Seven Mile Beach is the place to be; Tel: 740-99. The **Cracked Conch** (just the sort of seafood place it sounds like; Tel: 752-17) and **Santiago's** (for Mexican food and margaritas; Tel: 985-80), both right across from Seven Mile Beach, are more casual restaurants.

It may sound as though everything is within easy walking distance on Grand Cayman, and that's certainly true of the Seven Mile Beach neighborhood. This is the heart of Cayman Islands tourism, its main road lined with hotels, condos, and restaurants. It *can* look and feel a little crowded, yet it's unlikely ever to become a "strip," partly because there is a law against high rises. The pristine white-sand beach is as quiet and laid-back as any escapist could want.

Downtown **George Town** is one possibility for shopping, but the small shopping centers along Seven Mile Beach (among them, the Galleria Plaza and the West Shore Centre) also have everything most visitors will be looking for—from resortwear to local art. The local specialty is black coral, sold mostly in the form of jewelry. This British Crown Colony's wedding present to Prince Charles and Princess Diana was a black coral and sterling silver cutlery set.

Around the Island

Grand Cayman offers limited sightseeing. The best-known spot on the island is probably the "village" of **Hell**, near Seven Mile Beach. A backyard-size landscape of jagged, blackened limestone formations, Hell has its own post office from which visitors can send home postmarked cards inscribed with clever comments ("Came here in a handbasket," "Finally took your advice," etc.).

Nearby is the **Cayman Turtle Farm** (Tel: 938-94), where thousands of turtles are bred for turtle steak and tortoiseshell gift items. If you're a U.S. citizen or just passing through the States on your way home, forget the latter; it's illegal to bring in turtle products. More ecologically responsible visitors can arrange to have a baby turtle or two set free (about U.S. $4 apiece). Sponsors don't actually get to see the hatchlings let loose on the beach to fend for themselves, but they are given Turtle Release Certificates to prove good intentions. The survival rate, researchers say, is pretty good.

One of the most dramatic attractions on Grand Cayman is the 65-foot **Atlantis XI submarine**. The 80-ton submarine, which replaced an earlier 50-foot model, takes 46 passengers down 150 feet for a close-up view of tropical fish, coral, sponges, and undersea cliffs—all in air-conditioned comfort (U.S. $69 per person). There's also a 1,000-foot dive for three people at U.S. $265 per person. The night dives, illuminated by the sub's floodlights, are more colorful than daytime trips. The sub leaves from George Town Harbour; Tel: 983-83.

Scuba divers and snorkelers will find impressive underwater sites all around Grand Cayman. Some maps actually show dive sites—Barrel Sponge Slope, Grand Canyon, Oro Verde, The Maze, Stag Party, Valley of the Rays—instead of streets. Among the best sites: **Eden Rock** and **Devil's Grotto,** both off the southwestern coast just below George Town, and the wall at Little Cayman's **Bloody Bay.** The site known as **Stingray City**, where visitors can swim underwater with and pet the ominous-looking but friendly, velvety-soft stingrays, has become a must for snorkelers.

Fishing, catamaran cruises, swimming, parasailing, windsurfing, and virtually every other water sport are available throughout the island. There are also tennis courts and a golf course where players use the Cayman ball, which only goes half as far as the normal one. Jack Nicklaus designed the Britannia course (part of the Hyatt Regency complex), described as "a tough nine but a forgiving eighteen."

Even the most gregarious of visitors should at least see the secluded but breathtakingly beautiful area of the island around **Rum Point**. It's on the north-central coast, a half-hour-or-so drive from Seven Mile Beach. You'll also find food, drinks, and water sports there.

The **Cayman Islands National Museum** in George Town is a must for those interested in the islands' history and culture. It's in the restored 19th-century courts building. Admission, U.S. $6; Tel: 983-68.

Cayman Brac and Little Cayman

Grand Cayman's smaller sister islands offer dramatically different experiences, although either is only a short 85-mile-or-so flight away.

The larger, Cayman Brac, is 12 square miles of dramatic landscape. There are jagged limestone cliffs (*brac* is Gaelic for "bluff"), junglelike growth, numerous small caves to explore, and as many as 150 species of birds (some living here and some just passing through). The Brac, as all Caymanians call this diver's paradise, has two very popular places to stay. In addition to diving, the 70-room, air-conditioned **Divi Tiara Beach Resort** offers a pool, tennis, and snorkeling. The Divi hotel group is known for its Caribbean informality. The 40-room **Brac Reef Beach Resort** is Caymanian-owned and -operated, and particularly popular with divers.

Seven miles away, Little Cayman is best known for fishing (tarpon and bonefish). This eight-square-mile island offers true seclusion, with unpaved roads, unspoiled beaches, lagoons, and a rookery that shelters a large bird population. The places to stay: either the rustic ten-room **Southern Cross Club** or the eight-room **Pirates Point**, with its authentic island atmosphere. Diving is excellent here, too.

Pirates and Other Influences

The Caymans are one of the most pirate-oriented island groups in the Caribbean—the annual island celebration, originally organized to attract off-season tourists, is Pirates' Week—and the local fascination with buccaneers is based on fact. Sir Henry Morgan first landed here in 1670. Edward Teach, the aforementioned Blackbeard, was doing dastardly deeds at Grand Cayman as early as 1717. As any reader of *Treasure Island* knows, it was Blackbeard who shot and lamed his gunner Israel Hands just for the fun of it. And Neal Walker stored much of his pirate treasure in a cache at Grand Cayman's East End.

A character in Sir Walter Scott's novel *The Pirate* described the mood of the islands in the 1720s: "Is he dead? It is a more serious question here than it would be on the Grand Caymains or the Bahama Islands where a brace or two of fellows may be shot in the morning and no more heard of, or asked about them than if they were so many wood pigeons."

The islands' most famous seafaring tale, however, has nothing to do with pirates. In 1778 ten British ships collided in the Wreck of the Ten Sails, and Cayman citizens rescued all of the survivors. The legend goes that King George III was so grateful he decreed that Caymanians would never have to pay taxes. (In reality, they still don't. The Caymans are virtually free from personal income taxation—and absolute financial secrecy is the law.) The real moral of the story is that Caymanians were, and are, mostly nice folks. Residents brag about the racial harmony here, which, they'll explain, is the result of centuries of intermarriage. When black people with blond hair tell you this, it's convincing.

If Caymanians are tolerant, it is partly because they started out in the 1600s as a racial hodgepodge of settlers—Scots, Welsh, Jamaicans, Africans, and the British from Cromwell's army—who came to the Caymans to start a new life. If Caymanians are sophisticated, it's partly because Cayman men have always been seafarers and brought a certain worldliness back home with them.

Today the Caymans are the picture of domestic tranquillity and the template of a virtually crime-free society. Be advised: The penalty for drug use is stiff. In fact, penalties in general are pretty Draconian. One local homeowner, a transplanted European, tells of being slapped with a $500 fine and five years' probation for a speeding ticket. Once in a while, an example has to be made.

USEFUL FACTS

What to Wear
Summer resortwear is appropriate year-round.

Getting In
Most visitors enter the Caymans via the Owen Roberts International Airport outside George Town on Grand Cayman. Cayman Airways has nonstop flights from New York, Houston, Baltimore, Miami, Atlanta, and Tampa, with charters from several other North American cities during high season. Northwest and American have daily service from Miami. Air Canada has flights from Toronto and Montreal to Miami. Qantas flies from Sydney to Los Angeles and San Francisco, where connections can be made with a U.S. carrier.

Entry Requirements
No passport or visa is required to enter the Caymans. U.S., Canadian, and British citizens need proof of citizenship only.

Local Time
The Cayman Islands are on eastern standard time year-round. This means that when the U.S. east coast moves its clocks forward an hour during daylight saving time, the Caymans no longer are on the same time but are one hour behind.

Currency
Cayman Islands dollar; U.S. dollars are widely accepted. As of this writing the rate of exchange was U.S. $1.00 to 80¢ CI dollars.

Electrical Current
Same as in the U.S. and Canada—110 volts AC, 60 cycles.

Getting Around
Cayman Airways links Grand Cayman with Cayman Brac and Little Cayman. Flights are approximately 30 minutes.
  From the airport it's a U.S. $10–$15 taxi ride to most Seven Mile Beach hotels. To a more out-of-the-way area

like Rum Point, it's almost U.S. $40. Taxi drivers charge flat rates, so fares should be discussed at the outset.

Major car-rental companies have offices here. Unlimited-mileage rates start at about $35 daily off-season. Cars are a necessity only for those staying or touring outside the Seven Mile Beach area. Buses run regularly along the Seven Mile Beach road to and from George Town.

Business Hours
Most businesses and stores operate on a nine-to-five schedule Monday through Friday. Stores in George Town are normally closed on Saturday afternoons.

Festivals
The Cayman's major seasonal events are Pirates' Week, at the end of October, and Million Dollar Month Fishing Tournament, an angling competition that lasts throughout June.

For Further Information
Cayman Islands Department of Tourism, P.O. Box 67GT, Grand Cayman, B.W.I., Tel: (809) 949-0623; **in the U.S.**, 420 Lexington Avenue, New York, NY 10170, Tel: (212) 682-5582; **in Canada**, Earl B. Smith Travel Consultants, 234 Eglinton Avenue East, Toronto, Ontario M4P1K5, Tel: (416) 485-1550; **in the U.K.**, Trevor House, 100 Brompton Road, Knightsbridge, London SW3 1EX, England, Tel: (71) 581-9960.

ACCOMMODATIONS REFERENCE
The rate ranges given here, in U.S. dollars, are projections for fall 1992 through spring 1993, and span the lowest rates in the low season to the highest in the high season. Unless otherwise indicated, rates are for double rooms, double occupancy. As rates are subject to change, it's always wise to double-check before booking. The telephone area code (within the U.S. system) for the Caymans is 809-94.

▶ **Brac Reef Beach Resort.** P.O. Box 56, Cayman Brac, B.W.I. Tel: 873-23; in U.S., (800) 327-3835. $90–$130.

▶ **Cayman Kai Resort.** P.O. Box 1112 GT, Grand Cayman, B.W.I. Tel: 790-56; in U.S., (800) 223-5427. $85–$145 ("sea lodges" and villas).

▶ **Cayman Villas.** P.O. Box 681, Grand Cayman, B.W.I. Tel: 741-44; Fax: 974-71; in U.S., (800) 235-5888. $580–

$7,000 per week. Represents 100 villas, condos, and private homes.

▶ **Divi Tiara Beach Resort.** Cayman Brac, B.W.I. Tel: 873-13; Fax: 873-16; in U.S., Tel: (800) 367-3484 or (305) 633-3484; Fax: (305) 633-1621. $95–$200.

▶ **Hyatt Regency Grand Cayman.** P.O. Box 1698, Grand Cayman, B.W.I. Tel: 912-34; Fax: 985-28; in U.S., (800) 228-9000. $165–$450.

▶ **Indies Suites.** P.O. Box 2070, Grand Cayman, B.W.I. Tel: 750-25; Fax: 750-24; in U.S., (800) 654-3130. $140–$210.

▶ **Pirates Point.** Little Cayman, B.W.I. Tel and Fax: 842-10. $125–$180 per person, including all meals, wine, and diving.

▶ **Radisson Resort Grand Cayman.** West Bay Road, Grand Cayman, B.W.I. Tel: 900-88; Fax: 902-88; in U.S., (800) 333-3333. $148–$299.

▶ **Ramada Treasure Island Resort.** P.O. Box 1817, Grand Cayman, B.W.I. Tel: 977-77; Fax: 986-72. in U.S., (800) 228-9898. $155–$260.

▶ **Southern Cross Club.** Little Cayman, B.W.I. Tel: 832-55; in U.S., Tel: (317) 636-9501 (reservations); Fax: (317) 636-9503. $190–$260, A.P. No credit cards.

JAMAICA

By Jennifer Quale

Jennifer Quale contributes travel-related articles to Food & Wine, Vogue, *and other major publications. Based in Switzerland, she has lived in the Caribbean and reports on that area frequently.*

Jamaica is one of those places where you never want the days to end and you never want to leave. Noel Coward never wanted to say goodbye, so he was buried there. Whenever Ian Fleming had to leave, it was always with a lump in his throat. Even Errol Flynn, despite his self-confessed "wicked ways," remained faithful to the end. And Bob Marley brought it all home. Unlike one-dimensional islands, Jamaica is—as the old advertising campaign claimed—more than a beach. It is a staggeringly diverse country of two million people, the most complex nation in the Caribbean, from its many-sided culture to its distinctive cuisine. The landscape is so varied, so lush, and so beautiful that you can't take your eyes off it. And the people, especially beyond the major tourist centers, are proud, engaging, and full of grave drama. Still, the best reason to go to Jamaica is to be captivated by the seductive rhythms that keep the rest of the world at bay.

MAJOR INTEREST

Classic hotels
Cuisine
Jamaican art and music
The South Coast
Port Antonio area
Firefly, Noel Coward's house

Most first-time visitors land in Montego Bay, the island's primary resort area and second-largest city, to stay in one of the many beachfront hotels strung along the North Coast—the Jamaican Riviera—from Negril to Ocho Rios. But the intrepid traveller who wants more than to bake on a beach might land in Kingston, the country's capital and cultural mecca, cradled in the 7,400-foot Blue Mountain range. From Kingston it's a relatively easy two-hour drive along the coast to Port Antonio in the northeasternmost corner of the island, the niche that Jamaicans refer to as the "real Jamaica." The bare-bones adventurer seeking something completely different, remote even by Jamaican standards, will find it on the South Coast, reached within a couple of hours from Montego Bay. Although in a week's time it's possible to make a clean sweep from Montego Bay west to Negril, down to the South Coast, back to the north to Ocho Rios and Port Antonio, then on to Kingston, such a journey is not recommended. You would never get out of the car. It's best to pick one or two spots and save the rest for the next visit.

The ideal way to get around is by rental car; on the map, distances appear to be short, but roads are often winding, skimpy, and clogged with life of their own (road life, especially in the villages, is the soul of Jamaica). Then, too, many Jamaican hotels and villas are so enticing that you may be loath to leave their confines. Thanks to 300 years of British rule, the tradition of service in Jamaica still holds fast, even though the country has been independent since 1962.

To understand the layout of Jamaica, imagine the island's shape as the profile of a manatee swimming toward the west. (A few of these endangered sea mammals, which fed the sailor's legend of the mermaid, actually survive in a reserve on the island's South Coast.) At the head is Negril, with the South Coast stretching from there down to the flipper; at the top of the tail is Port Antonio. Between Negril and Port Antonio on the North Coast — or cresting the spine—is Montego Bay, with Ocho Rios a little more than half as far as Port Antonio, and Kingston is on the tail's underside.

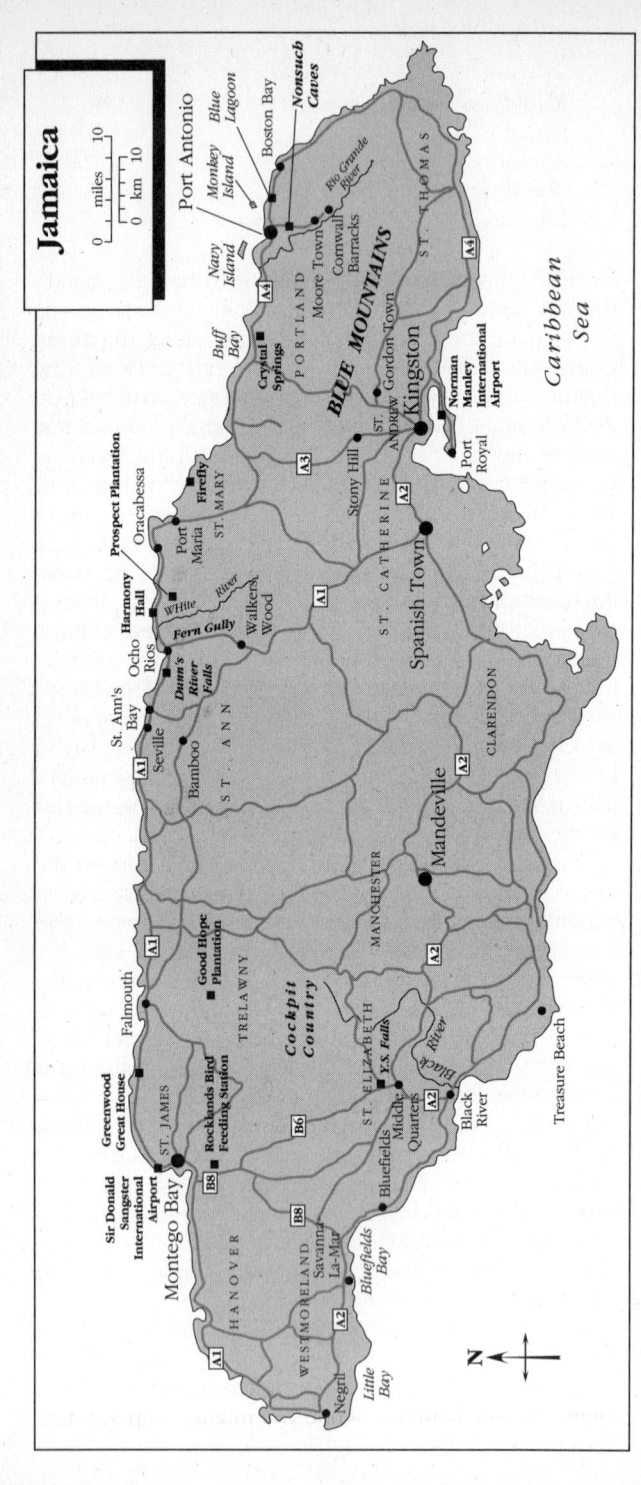

Montego Bay Area

The atmosphere at the airport in Montego Bay (a.k.a. Mobay) sets the tone of this overdeveloped resort town even before you get out of the terminal: A troupe of women in traditional dress singing "Jamaica Farewell" flanks the immigration area, while a welcome bar dispenses lethal rum punches to throngs of eager tourists. There are a few good reasons to stay in Montego Bay; you will then probably push on to the (literally) greener pastures of the North Coast or head down to the South Coast, with a brief stop in Negril.

During the 1950s and 1960s, when the American rich and titled British made Montego Bay their winter place in the sun, the town peaked as the social center of the Caribbean. With jumbo jets and package deals, Montego Bay's highly exclusive status went out with the 1970s. Then, as now, the place to stay was the intimate, magical **Round Hill Hotel and Villas** (about 10 miles/16 km west of town)— unless you preferred the wider open spaces of **Tryall Golf, Tennis & Beach Resort**, 2 miles (3 km) farther west, developed by Texans who felt cramped at Round Hill. (There are people who go to Jamaica just to play golf at Tryall's championship course, possibly the Caribbean's best. Round Hill has no course, but guests may play at Tryall.) If you can't decide between the two, Jamaica's Elegant Resorts offers the unique Platinum Plan at an all-inclusive price with dine-around and sleep-around options (Trident Hotel in Port Antonio is also among them).

Like most of Jamaica's better hotels, Tryall and Round Hill are built on the villa concept; although accommodations can be had in the main buildings, hang the cost, if you can, and go for the private, fully staffed villas, many of which have their own pools (at Tryall some of the villas have two pools—and golf carts for tooling around the 2,200 acres of grounds). Tryall, which suffered considerable damage from Hurricane Gilbert, has completely renovated its clubby great house (recently declared a national landmark) and hotel rooms; but, except for tournament times, Tryall now gives the impression of being a bit groggy. Aside from its private-jet clientele, Tryall has recently bedded down Arnold Palmer, Lena Horne, and Stevie Wonder. In Round Hill's heyday, its loyal cadre of guests included the likes of Noel Coward, Oscar Hammerstein, and Jack Kennedy. While you might bump into Paul

McCartney, Audrey Hepburn, or Goldie Hawn on Round Hill's melon slice of a beach, today's typical guest is more likely to be an American or European tycoon. However, a renewed spirit here seems to be recapturing the flair of the past and a greater share of neon names.

In February, Round Hill—like the rest of fashionable Jamaica—is deluged with the Old Guard, including shareholders of the hotel and a few die-hard colonials who've given up their major holdings on the island. Now they no longer scoff at the hotel rooms, once referred to as "the barracks," since the flamboyant manager Josef Forstmayr redecorated them. During school holidays (particularly summer, now that the hotel stays open year-round), families are in abundance, yet children never intrude on the power-party atmosphere that prevails come nightfall. Some guests never leave the bar, newly redone à la Casablanca by Round Hill's favorite neighbor, Ralph Lauren. No one comes to Round Hill for the food, although it has improved thanks to the new British chef—whose hors d'oeuvres on Beach Party Night are so good you may not have room for dinner.

Guests often venture out to such local restaurants as the new **Norma at the Wharf House** (Tel: 979-2745 or 997-5475), a few miles east on the water. The splendid setting of a converted warehouse and tables on the dock equal the caliber of Norma's inventive—if pricey—blackboard menu (already a proven success at her restaurant in Kingston). When it comes to flair, in food presentation as well as decor, Norma can't be beat.

Even if you don't stay in Mobay, lunch or dinner at the **Sugar Mill Restaurant**, formerly the Half Moon Club House Grill, about 10 miles (16 km) east of town and across from the Half Moon Club Hotel, is worth a detour from anywhere in Jamaica: It's unquestionably the best table on the island (with the new exception of The Restaurant at Temple Hall near Kingston, see below). Chef Hans Schenk, a Swiss expatriate, approaches traditional Jamaican ingredients with a singularly creative spirit, bringing forth such specialties as fettucine tossed with smoked marlin (a North Coast catch), bouillabaisse with lime and hot peppers, or wine-poached snapper with an ackee-yogurt sauce, and show-stopping desserts that make the most of the fine, local Appleton rum and liqueurs. Everything is fresh, even the hearts of palm from the Sugar Mill's plantation grounds, and the expanded wine cellar is remarkable for the Caribbean. The moderately expensive restaurant caters to *soigné* but casual patrons who may linger on the candlelit terraces long after the last cup of perfect Blue Mountain coffee is poured. (Ironically, Jamaica produces the world's most expensive, exquisite coffee, but the bulk of it is shipped to Japan, making a good cup hard to find on the island.) Reservations, except for lunch, are essential here; Tel: 953-2314. Like many fine restaurants in Jamaica, the Sugar Mill offers complimentary transportation within a radius of 5 miles (8 km) or so.

While Haiti has always been considered the Caribbean hub of primitive art, Jamaica's own Intuitive (a.k.a. naïve) vision has finally come to canvas. Until recently, the art scene was confined to Kingston's hallowed museums and schools, but now galleries of all sorts (including bamboo shacks on the roadside) flourish along the North Coast. The best of these is **The Gallery of West Indian Art**, on Orange Lane opposite the parish church in downtown Mobay, which carries, here and at its tiny branch at Round Hill, works of the leading artists of Jamaica as well as of Haiti. Often the artists are self-taught, as is the case with Hyacinth. The gallery owner helped Hyacinth, an erstwhile laundress, parlay her sense of color and embroidery into a dazzling output of painted cedar sculptures—now a major cottage industry, with shipments exported as far as Japan. When enthusiasts of folk art see this Noah's Ark of whimsical creatures, they want to buy out the lot—along with as many pieces as they can carry from the collection of irresistible pottery created by the owner's daughter, Nicola, sponge-painted and finished off with pointillistic or Impressionist flowers. Recent additions include crocodile coffee tables and award-winning cedar chairs with hand-carved goats' heads for armrests.

You might combine a visit to the gallery (which occasionally closes at lunchtime) with lunch next door at the pubby **Town House Restaurant**, a spot that is deservedly popular with locals. Another worthy coupling of art and cuisine lies two blocks away on Orange Street, at the **Images Gallery** and **The Georgian House Restaurant** (their coconut pie will leave you begging for more). The new **Bay Gallery** in St. James Place exhibits serious paintings and sculpture by island artists. The fine line between Jamaican arts and crafts is drawn at the **Things Jamaican** shop on Fort Street, where you can pick up anything from hand-tooled chess sets to the beautifully packaged array of "Busha Browne's" chutneys, jellies, and sauces.

A few miles west of Montego Bay, the **Reading Reef Club**, quite a find with its pleasant beach and pool, attracts low-key types who prefer to skirt the frills and high tariffs of Round Hill and Tryall. The cheerful restaurant (Tel: 952-7217) overlooking the sea also draws a steady clientele (e.g., Lady Sarah Churchill) for its crayfish specialties and pasta alla cruda. Owner Joanne Rowe, a New York–born Italophile, brings in cognoscenti and chefs on their nights off with such creations as pasta seasoned with fresh ginger.

Opposite the Reading Reef, route B 8 (Long Hill Road), which follows the railroad, leads to the **Rocklands Bird Feeding Station**. In Jamaica 252 species of birds have been recorded, 24 of them endemic. The doctor bird, the country's national bird (Jamaica makes much ado of her many national attributes), is one of the species that has never been found elsewhere. The most likely explanation for this hummingbird's name is that its twin streamer tail resembles a doctor's stethoscope. Normally rather shy and elusive, the doctor bird turns genial host in the Rocklands setting. Daily bird feeding for visitors begins afternoons at 3:30, although crusty naturalist Lisa Salmon, who established the sanctuary 30 years ago, welcomes card-carrying bird-watchers any time of day (no children under five admitted).

About two miles farther inland on B 8, just after the Mount Carey Health Clinic, **The Antique Furniture Shop Ltd.** houses not antiques but stunning reproductions in native mahogany, as well as the small factory that makes them. Paulette Jackson, matriarch of the family operation, will make anything to order ("as long as it's wood") and will ship anywhere.

To see Montego Bay's rural inland environs, take the **Hilton High Day Tour** (Tel: 952-3343)—named for the modest plantation house it visits—that stages a luncheon of roast suckling pig and home-style accompaniments. The genteel hosts of this unusual tour pick up participants in a van wherever they're staying in Mobay.

Negril

The 50-mile (80-km) drive west from Montego Bay to Negril is far more interesting than the town of Negril itself, which consists of little more than a ramshackle shopping mall. Just beyond Tryall, the ruins of Kenilworth Estate recall the opulent era when sugar was king and when even the mills took on the dimensions and details, among them Palladian windows, of the planters' great houses. (By the mid-18th century, the island boasted some 400 sugar estates, making it the world's largest sugar producer and England's richest colony.)

Now every Jamaican has a stake in the tourism-based economy, as the proliferation of one-man shops — sort of bamboo lean-tos — along the road suggests. Enterprising and persistent to a fault, the Jamaican vendor will run after your car with merchandise in hand if you happen to make eye contact. Works of art in themselves, many of the shanty shops are painted in contrasting neon pastels and polka dots. One worth stopping at is **Bigga's Dwarf Factory**, where a pungent aroma wafts over the hand-carved and hand-painted statues inspired by the eccentric English artist Jonathan Routh.

When the numerous fruit stands along the road give way to chockablock tee-shirt shacks, you know you're in Negril, primarily recognized for its evolution from a haven for hippies in the 1960s to its present status as Jamaica's self-styled center of hedonism. Negril's bow to yuppies premiered three years ago with the Grand Lido Resort and its "Power Vacation"; it's the first hotel you'll encounter along this overwhelming stretch of development.

Unless you like nude volleyball, the most agreeable activity in Negril is walking the not-quite-seven-mile-long beach in the early morning while the hedonists sleep. (Hedonism II, yet another of Jamaica's packaged holiday "camps," now stages a weekly circus with guests as fledgling performers.) Gone is the Sundowner Hotel, Negril's first guest house, where Norman Rockwell used to stay in the 1950s. In its place sprawls Sandals, one of the island's numerous all-inclusive resorts. Artists today are more apt to stay on the western, cliff side (vs. the beach side) of Negril, perhaps at **Love Solution Guest Cottages**, formerly Tensing Pen. This enchanting cluster of thatched-roofed rondavels on stone pillars is situated in a garden on a rocky ledge overlooking a labyrinth of seaside grottoes and rock pools. With their primitive decor, the cottages could have been designed by Crusoe himself—although the new American owners have installed a breakfast-only restaurant, along with hot running water. A short walk down the road leads to **Café au Lait**, a satisfying bistro on the sea with genuine French bread, all manner of crepes, and good *vins du table*. Farther on, little-known **Chicken Lavish** draws west-end habitués for quick, hearty lunches, and the **Blue Cave Castle** oddity attracts patrons for its wonderful pizza and pastries.

For years everyone has gone to nearby Rick's Café to see the celebrated Negril sunset and the rare Green Flash—those atmospheric fireworks on the horizon just as the sun disappears. But after Hurricane Gilbert, Rick's opted for glitz in its renovation and expansion, denuding the landmark of its once rakish charm. A better flavor of Negril might be captured with a French-flair lunch and a swim at the bourgeois **Charela Inn** or **Tanya's** at Seasplash—both on the beach—or at the low-down **Cosmo's**, a local hangout with good *escovitsch* (a marinated fish, grilled or baked) near Negril's as-yet-undeveloped east end.

The South Coast

Travelling southeast from Negril, you feel as if you are the first foreigner to encounter the strange, windswept plains here. In its southernmost reaches, the arid landscape conjures up images of East Africa. If you want a beach to yourself, head to **Little Bay**, about 8 miles (13 km) southeast of Negril.

Masses of sugarcane fields flank the inland road connecting Negril with Savanna-La-Mar, which is still a vital port for raw sugar exports. From here the main road, referred to as A 2 on the map (don't depend on infrequent road signs), follows the coast along Bluefields Bay. In the forested hills near the police station, the old Bluefields Guest House overlooks the wide bay. (Philip Gosse stayed at the guest house in the 1840s while researching his books *A Naturalist's Sojourn in Jamaica* and *The Birds of Jamaica.*) Now the only place to spend a night here is **Wilton on the Sea**, a gracious five-room guest house named for the hometown of the wealthy woman from Wilton, Connecticut, who built it. The Jamaican social presence who now presides over Wilton, awhirl in caftans and tales of the former prime minister, Edward Seaga, makes her guests feel as if they were personally invited rather than the paying sort. (Go now before she retires—although it's certain a kindred spirit will take over when she does.) This is a fine place to turn in early and get up with the birds. However, if the idea of staying a week or more in this area appeals to you, you might be happier at nearby **Bluefields Bay Villas**, a quartet of tightly run villas with a tennis court, pool, and other diversions. For interested guests, the villas' American owner will arrange tea or cocktails at the ancestral home of his eloquent neighbor, one of the vanishing breed of British colonials. A visit to this private, hilltop great house—one of the few that hasn't been restored (there's no electricity) and commercialized—is definitely worth a trip.

A cheerful addition to the South Coast, **Natania's** sits on the sea just 6 miles (10 km) southeast of Bluefields. This family-owned guest house and seafood restaurant is popular with families and adventurous, budget-minded travellers who know to ask in advance for a room facing the sea.

Beyond Bluefields, the first town of note is **Black River**, with its Georgian-cum-gingerbread architecture that epitomizes the Jamaica of the 1920s. In fact, this entire parish, St. Elizabeth, seems to be frozen in time. While Black River may have been the first town on the island to put up electric lights, it has been among the last to harness tourism energy. In 1989 **South Coast Safaris Ltd.** (Tel: 962-0220 or 965-2513) "came on stream," as they say, at the Black River Bridge, with its Evinrude-powered boat trip on Jamaica's longest river. Knowledgeable environmentalist Charles Swaby takes the helm, pointing out crocodiles basking among the lily pads and shrimpers paddling Arawak canoes through the bulrushes, as well as endless species of flora and fauna indigenous to the swampy wetlands. Swaby, who has conducted Audubon Society tours for years here, can also steer visitors to nearby **Y.S. Falls**, the most stunning, least-spoiled venue of waterfalls on the island. The family who owns the property has recently organized a jitney service for the 20-minute jaunt across the fields to the falls. (Be sure to go before 3:00 P.M.) Y.S., also called Wyess, borders on Cockpit Country, an interior region distinguished by volcanic, tree-studded mounds and dips and a history of runaway slaves who once hid among them.

Farther south in this tropical outback the local people, supposedly descended from buccaneers, have blondish hair, blue eyes, and a skin tone earning them the nickname "Red Man." There are few places to stay except a rather bizarre villa in Treasure Beach (forget about its lone, spooky hotel). Known as **Folichon**, the Art Deco curiosity, with fishermen for neighbors, has been a well-kept secret among the German visitors and Kingston colonials who take its cure of utter seclusion. It sits amid a coconut grove on a barren black-sand beach, with extraordinary views of the sunset. The housekeeping at Folichon is not what Jamaicans would call "up to standard," but for the ridiculously low price you can't expect the Ritz.

To return to Montego Bay from Black River on the A 2 road, pick up the B 6 10 miles (16 km) north at **Middle Quarters**, known as the shrimp capital of Jamaica. Middle Quarters's spindly ladies with scarved coifs sell little bags of fiery hot river shrimp that go down just fine with a bottle of Red Stripe beer and a hunk of hard dough bread. Just east of Middle Quarters lies **Bamboo Avenue**, one of the island's loveliest sights: a three-mile stretch of towering bamboo that forms an arched canopy over the little-used road.

Ocho Rios Area

Until the late 1960s Ocho Rios was the proverbial quiet fishing village. Then developers saw the biggest fish in the sea: the tourists trickling over from crowded Montego Bay. Along with its shopping arcades, attractions, and helicopter tours, Ocho Rios entrepreneurs now offer day jaunts to Cuba. The port town itself appeals largely to day-trippers off cruise ships (six per week), to families with active children, to Japanese honeymooners, and to those travellers who staunchly refuse to stay anywhere but at their favorite hotels—Jamaica Inn, Sans Souci, and Plantation Inn. These three hostelries were in existence here before the high rises, and even now sightseeing seldom figures on their guests' agendas. The regulars are content to stay within the hotels' hermetic domains and wouldn't dream of joining the daisy chain of tourists climbing the 600-foot Dunn's River Falls—Jamaica's most highly touted attraction.

In many ways the **Jamaica Inn** *is* Jamaica as it used to be, with a staff that never dies but just gets older and still bows to every idiosyncrasy of its guests. The polo-playing Morrow brothers, Peter and Eric (sons of the original co-owner), now preside, but, as on the old transatlantic ocean liners, an effortless elegance prevails here. On Saturday nights in season gentlemen don black tie and ladies long gowns (just as they would at home), and dine and dance under the stars to the accompaniment of "civilized" music. Once a private estate, the inn comprises a main house and two wings, done in an architectural style that might be called Jamaicanized Greek revival and painted in a sort of tropical Wedgwood blue. Situated on the finest beach in Ocho Rios, the hotel's most favored rooms are in the refurbished west wing, where, in the White Suite, Winston Churchill used to work on his watercolors. (A request for the White Suite usually ends up on a waiting list as long as its private terrace.) Each room here has its own balustraded balcony jutting out over the seaside coral ledge: an idyllic spot for sunset cocktails or proper English breakfasts (with bangers and broiled tomatoes). On an island where buffets are a highly regarded barometer of good taste, Jamaica Inn's, with Chef Batista still running the show, comes out on top.

If the Jamaica Inn is Old Jamaica, the **Sans Souci Hotel & Spa,** just east of town, is Updated Jamaica, perhaps now unrecognizable to patrons of the recent past. The guests here tend to be younger than those at the Jamaica Inn, and more trendy (as opposed to tweedy)—the right sort of people for Sans Souci's spring-fed mineral pool and state-of-the-art spa facilities. You don't have to enroll in the spa program to take an aerobics class or at least have a massage on the gazebo-sheltered stone slab overlooking the sea. And if you stray from the spa menu at the hotel's Casanova Restaurant, a day's healthful efforts can be wiped out in a single dinner. Architecturally, Sans Souci clings to a beach-bottomed hillside in a tiered labyrinth of spacious (though dark) rooms and terraces that looks like a huge mocha-pink wedding cake. Last year a change in owners brought about massive sprucing up along with 36 new beachfront rooms beside the tennis courts, a zippy beach bar, and an oddly formal restaurant featuring French and Jamaican cuisine. Although it's easy to get lost here at first, come nightfall all guests eventually find their way to the **Balloon Bar,** where Delroy Stephens, a Sans Souci institution and Jamaica's answer to Bobby Short, presides over the baby grand piano.

Somewhere in between, **Plantation Inn,** with its white-columned porte cochere, four-story beach wing, and impressive art collection, draws a mixed crowd (more gracious in winter) who dote on one of the island's finest wine cellars and who hope the neighboring disco falls flat on its needle.

Jamaicans revere their traditions with a steadfastness left over from the British. For instance, while the **Hibiscus Lodge Hotel** has shed its homey pension image in a knockout renovation and expansion—with new tennis courts, alfresco Jacuzzi, piano bar, and gardens—it's still the place for colonials who've sold their island houses to hang their old planter's hats. The price is right and, moreover, everybody—from locals to visiting celebrities—goes to the inn's open-air **Almond Tree Bar** (with bar stools suspended from the thatched roof) **and Restaurant**, especially for its roast suckling pig and pineapple beignets.

What used to be the Disneyesque theme park of Carinosa Gardens has now been transformed under the auspices (and part ownership) of the former prime minister into an all-inclusive hotel. Despite the Miami motel–style rooms in concrete blocks tucked up on a hillside, **The Enchanted Garden** evokes a vaguely Southeast Asian mood with its Thai silks and open tearoom–style architecture spilling over 20 lush acres. Tiptoeing through the botanical gardens and jungles leads to the stylish spa (with homegrown aromatherapy treatments) or twittering aviary, the treehouse pasta bar or the restaurant (one of five) that could pass for a Thai temple. The seaquarium with coffee shop and games room could have been flown—tented ceiling, spangles, and all—straight from Rajasthan, while Annabella's nightclub takes you back to Miami. Guests who aren't content to loll around the waterfall gushing down these slopes of inland Ocho Rios can sign up for a multitude of daily activities, from the "sunrise power walk" to lessons in patois.

When anything new opens in Jamaica the whole island is set atwitter, especially when native son Chris Blackwell has a hand in it. Blackwell, descended from a landowning Jamaican-Irish family, founded Island Records and put Bob Marley on the musical map. With **Evita's** restaurant (Tel: 974-2333) occupying Blackwell's old Mantalent Inn on Bower Road, he brings a tropical dolce vita to Ocho Rios. High on a hill overlooking town, this is a fashionable and delectable place to dine in the area. Eva, the blond, transplanted-Venetian hostess, adds a humorous twist to the menu with such dishes as jerk spaghetti and Rastafarian lasagna. Start with the gratis *focaccia* and finish with *dolce di noci di palma* (a sublime coconut and chocolate creation). More casual eating is good at the new, bustling **Forever Café** on Main Street and the tarted up **Double V Jerk Centre**, near the Pineapple Place mall.

For daytime sightseeing take a leisurely stroll through the old **Shaw Park Gardens**, a serene oasis with bird sanctuary and botanical grounds a mile off the road to Fern Gully.

Be sure to go in the late afternoon, when the cruise-ship day-trippers have departed and you might have the place to yourself. Don't bother with a guide—markers identify the flora.

The jitney (or horseback) tour of **Prospect Plantation,** a working agricultural estate just east of the White River and a mile inland, affords an excellent education in how the island's garden grows. A visit to the **Bromley Estate,** 8 miles (13 km) beyond Fern Gully, gives a glimpse of life as it's lived now on a small plantation. Although primarily a private home with the occasional room to let (but only to kindred spirits), Bromley is also in the business of making marmalade, guava jelly, fudge, and bottled "jerk" seasoning (more on jerking in the Port Antonio section). The kindly owners of Bromley, in the noblesse-oblige tradition, also operate a woodworking shop in the nearby village of Walkers Wood that sells some of the finest carved bowls in Jamaica.

Plantation life on a grand scale exists now only in memory and in great houses that have been converted to museums (the most authentic being **Greenwood,** the ancestral home of Elizabeth Barrett Browning, 10 miles/ 16 km west of Falmouth). The possible exception will be Good Hope Plantation, about 10 miles inland from Falmouth, when and if it reopens. Once the island's premier treasure house, its Irish aristocratic owner, Patrick Tenison, died in 1990 shortly after he sold his home-cum-hotel. The new owner, a prominent Jamaican, plans to refurbish the great house, set amidst a 2,000-acre cattle and coconut plantation. Among its paying guests, James Michener found ample fodder here for his *Caribbean* tome, inspired by a huge Kidd landscape in the parlor that depicts Good Hope as it was 150 years ago: the quintessential West Indies plantation. Some of the out-buildings may now be in ruins, but the aura remains. Ornithologists, historians, and culture buffs who flocked to Good Hope as if it were their private sanctuary yearn to return—along with visiting equestrians who felt as if, out on the trails, they could trot through that Kidd painting into another era. (And now, at least, the riding stables have reopened; Tel: 954-3289.)

As in the old American South riding expertise was essential to Jamaica's plantocracy. In addition, because of Jamaica's British heritage, polo became the planter's primary sport. Saturday afternoon polo matches, open to the public, are still played at Drax Hall near St. Ann's Bay. The international set holds tournaments at **Chukka Cove**, about 20 minutes west of Ocho Rios. (In fact, it's just around the bend from Seville, the site of the first Spanish capital, where archaeologists are still digging for remnants of the old city and Columbus's ships. Across the road, on the inland side, you can peek in the windows at the startling original interior of the empty Seville Great House.)

The only equestrian facility of its caliber in the Caribbean, Chukka Cove offers instruction and riding holidays that include accommodation in seaside villas. Nights on the trail are spent up in the hills near the village of Bamboo at the newly restored **Lillyfield**. When Arnold Bertram, former cultural minister under Michael Manley in the 1970s, decided to open a guest house, he came back to his native village and bought the long-deserted pimento, coffee, and ginger plantation. Last year Bertram and his wife, Claire, parlayed their high-mountain coffee prowess into the island's first and only museum devoted to the history and production of the precious bean. Although Lillyfield feels more like a suburban inn than a 17th-century manor house, the Bertrams's enthusiastic welcome and wonderful home cooking make Lillyfield a treat.

About 10 miles (16 km) west of Chukka Cove, the old Trelawny Country Club has leased a new life as the **Runaway Bay H.E.A.R.T. Academy** hotel and restaurant, a training ground for resort skills. The earnest, eager-to-please staff combined with the sweet setting (a pawpaw-and-cream-colored Georgian affair overlooking the golf course and sea) and absurdly low prices provide ample cause to stop—if for nothing else, a slice of banana cream pie—in otherwise grotty Runaway Bay.

Port Antonio Area

The trip to Port Antonio, just 60 miles (96 km) east of Ocho Rios in the parish of Portland, takes a good two hours—and that's without stopping, which is almost impossible. For example, some of the island's best crafts and paintings are for sale at **Harmony Hall**, an old gingerbread-y manor house 4 miles (6½ km) east of Ocho Rios. Unless you enjoy haggling with aggressive vendors at the ubiquitous crafts markets elsewhere, shopping is much more pleasant here, and the goods (such as indigenous alabaster sculpture and painted wood-fruit carvings) are of higher quality.

During the Thanksgiving, Easter, and Independence

(August 6) holidays, Harmony Hall stages lively crafts fairs on the spacious grounds. Along with high-priced local artists, Jonathan Routh, the outrageously whimsical English painter who has become Jamaican society's somewhat off-color darling, shows his works in the upstairs gallery. Routh's canvases, with his imaginary dwarf-tossing and Queen Victoria motifs (he likes to depict her in such bizarre contexts as swinging from a vine), hang in the lobbies of the island's best hotels. On occasion, Routh hosts the hilarious International and Inter-Island Dwarf-Tossing Championships here, with proceeds from the judge's bribe-box benefitting local charities. For a small fee competitors can rent a (wooden) dwarf to toss in the contest.

James Bond fans will want to pay a moment of homage at Goldeneye, once author Ian Fleming's home in the sun. It's about 7 miles (11 km) beyond Harmony Hall, on the old coast road in Oracabessa—and the only estate with neon-blue gateposts. Now rented out by the week, the sparsely furnished, boxy white house—not officially open to the public—is nothing special, but the setting of seven untamed, lush acres leading down to a private beach is. You can drive in and no one will mind; if the house isn't rented, ask the housekeeper for a look inside and proffer a small tip. Whenever he would set to work (the character of James Bond, named after a visiting ornithologist, was created here), Fleming would close the window louvers to avoid the temptation to look at his favorite scenery. In the living room his desk, dusted daily, seems to await his pen.

It was after having rented Goldeneye back in the early 1950s that Noel Coward decided to build his own Jamaican retreat. He bought three seaside acres, just a few miles down the road outside of Port Maria, from the Blackwell family. In short order, the estate called Blue Harbour, a.k.a. Coward's Folly, drew a steady stream of houseguests. For his private life Coward built another house on the hill 1,000 feet up from Blue Harbour. He left Firefly to the people of Jamaica, and it opened as a museum a few years ago. His former housekeeper, Ima Jean, gives "personalized" tours from 10:00 A.M. to 4:00 P.M. daily. The concrete bungalow commands one of the island's most spectacular views of the sea below and the misty Blue Mountains beyond. But what truly makes it memorable are the touches of Coward's design for living:

pianos, books, and clothing, left much as they were the day he died, and his studio in the basement, still faintly redolent of paints.

Just down the coastal road toward Port Maria, the old **Casa Maria Hotel**—still operating in a 1950s time warp—offers a winsome spot for lunch at its seaside bar and grill, **Kokomo's**. Along with good jerk chicken, they make the best lime squash on the North Coast. If you spend the night (there's always room at this basic, somnolent place) you can wake up to saltfish and ackee, the national dish (ackee is a fruit that looks and tastes like scrambled eggs). For the truly adventurous palate, try liver and banana.

One of Coward's favorite pastimes in the tropics was to "plant something, stand back, and watch it grow." About 20 miles (32 km) farther east of Firefly, you can do just that—almost—at the flourishing gardens of **Crystal Springs**, just beyond Buff Bay on Skibo Road. A few years ago botanist Paulette Stuart started transforming the overgrown acreage of an old plantation with the island's loveliest orchid nursery and other indigenous flora. Along with meticulous landscaping, this tranquil spot offers a lunch-only café (try the curried goat), a spring-fed pool, and a few modest bungalows to let on former grounds of the Spring Garden Estate. The nearby private great house was once the scene of grand entertainments for planters en route by horse and carriage to the playground of Port Antonio.

Ever the magnanimous mistress, Jamaica has always courted more than her share of notable suitors. Errol Flynn, for one, fell in love with Port Antonio and, while building his empire there, brought swashbuckling to the Rio Grande, the island's largest river, about 6 miles (10 km) west of town. Flynn took the bamboo rafts traditionally used to ferry bananas down to the coast, added backbreaking seats for two, and trained his local followers to pole his pals (and, later, tourists) through the jungle-skirted rapids. Although **rafting** has turned into big business by local standards, it is nonetheless one of the most exotic interludes to be had in the Caribbean. Don't be put off by the swarm of would-be rafting escorts who may swamp your car as you approach the bridge over the Rio Grande; the raftsmen, licensed by the government, are merely vying for your patronage. At the end of the two-and-a-half-hour ride, the Jamaican-style gondoliers deposit passengers at a dock studded with red-and-white-striped gondola hitching posts (the restaurant and bar here at **Rafter's Rest** serves a nice, simple alfresco lunch and tea).

The wildly incongruous Venetian effects foreshadow things to come farther down the road, in the vague atmosphere of fantasy that characterizes Port Antonio. Indeed, where else but in Portland Parish would you encounter Robbie's Seaview Beach Joint and Jerk Centre (just beyond Ken Jones Airport, where cows lounge on the lone runway next to the one-room terminal)? Robbie is the beaming local lad in black tie and chef's hat who tends to his spicy chicken on the shoulder of the road. When Robbie is off-island, his mother and her in-law Lydia preside over the dueling grills, now enclosed in wood shacks.

The seeds of Portland fantasy were planted at the century's turn when New Englander Alfred Mitchell built a 60-room version of the Parthenon on a rolling peninsula just east of Port Antonio's twin harbor. According to legend Mitchell painted everything white and imported monkeys, dogs, horses—all white—and his Tiffany-heiress bride (who loathed the place). Known as "Folly," the structure soon started to crumble from faulty masonry. Mrs. Mitchell fled, leaving her husband and house to wither. These days graffiti-splashed gateposts lead to an eerie, roofless ruin.

More follies show up a few miles down the road in the form of fallen hotels, along with a Rhine castle put up in the early 1980s by an ambitious German baroness. Left unfinished, the castle fell into the hands of its neighbor Earl Levy, Jamaica's foremost architect of whimsy and the owner of the **Trident Villas & Hotel**. Levy transformed the castle into a hotel annex nonpareil (affordable only to the ultrarich), tantamount to another monument to fantasy. Instead of lions guarding the entrance, Levy installed two great stone alligators; in the banquet hall a gesso frieze depicts not the usual cornucopia of grapes, but local fruits such as bananas and pawpaw (papaya). A helicopter from Kingston occasionally flutters onto the lawn beside the castle's chapel, depositing guests who don't want to waste a minute getting here. But then the Trident hotel itself is pretty improbable, too, with its white-gloved service in a baronial dining room and its resident peacocks strutting about the impeccable gazebo-studded grounds. In fact, this place feels like a tropical Castle Howard, of *Brideshead Revisited* fame. It's pure theater and not the least bit stuffy, although you may find Princess Elizabeth of Yugoslavia taking high tea on the verandah. Here even royalty goes barefoot, and the staff treats every guest as if he or she were a member of a royal family.

Each room is fit for the occasional king, with luscious four-poster or canopied beds (even in the less expensive rooms in the main hotel), but the most idyllic suites are in the villas strung along the rocky seaside. By day Trident's offerings include a small beach with water sports (beware of the undertow), a pool, and tennis. But come twilight in season, Trident becomes a midwinter night's dream: The resident calypso combo—The Jolly Boys (now enjoying a summer of fame from a recent European tour)—plays softly on the terrace while guests enjoy cocktails before dinner by candelabra light. Afterward the castle may host an entertainment. Or, if the mood suits, guests might be whisked off to the **Roof Club**, Port Antonio's dark and booming reggae disco in the heart of town.

For the most part the town of **Port Antonio** itself remains blissfully oblivious to the occasional tourist, who tends to think it a bit shabby anyway. The few foreigners you see are likely to be villa owners or renters who appreciate Port Antonio for its resistance to change, or the crusty sailors who hang out at the **Huntress Marina** across from Navy Island (Errol Flynn's old haunt), an unlikely spot for great pizza. Everyone— dreadlocked Rastafarians, old ladies carrying fringed umbrellas for shade, crisply uniformed schoolchildren, shoeless street urchins, sidewalk trinket vendors, somber-faced farmers balancing bananas or whatever atop their heads—gathers in the town square (pay heed to the belching buses) to talk about politics and the price of saltfish. They go to the Victorian-vintage Musgrave Market across the street, where Miss Martha, queen of Portland "higglers"— women vendors—presides over the produce stand of choice; to the rank but requisite Cheapside grocery store; to the old courthouse with its wigged judges to see who's on trial; to Mr. Stewart's (the able town artist now located in a white shack at Clear Spring, across from the castle) for conversation if not a canvas depicting a local scene; to the Coronation bakery for hard dough bread and the spicy meat turnovers Jamaicans call patties (pronounced potties); and to the hole-in-the-wall newsstand to pick up the *Daily Gleaner*. Indeed, the beauty of Port Antonio is that you can feel you're a part of Jamaica here and not just another face on a tourism brochure.

Ironically, though no evidence of it survives, Port Antonio was the island's first center of tourism. Once Yankee Captain L. D. Baker had established the town as the world's banana capital, he began filling the empty banana boats returning from Boston with well-heeled travellers who stayed at the Titchfield, the hotel he built on "the Hill" in 1905. The Titchfield burned, but the old, flaming-red-brick **DeMontevin Lodge** carries on amid a profusion of so-called guest houses. Flynn's cook used to preside over the kitchen, now revitalized and serving up its best island dishes when you call ahead (Tel: 993-2604). The dark, turquoise dining room, bedecked with stern pictures of British royalty, still plays host to titled Brits ensconced in local rental villas looking for a lark at a modest price.

On the much higher Richmond Hill behind the town is one of the island's oldest operating hotels, erected in the 1940s. Seedy for years, the **Bonnie View Plantation Hotel** parlayed Hurricane Gilbert's wrath into a blessing with extensive refurbishing and a new wing of rooms with great views of the harbor and the Blue Mountains. That's just what Europeans and New Yorkers of a creative nature like here, along with affordable rates, a bush-horse riding stable, hiking tours, and a respectable, if eclectic, menu.

If the one-time German baroness, now Mrs. Fahmi, has her way, Port Antonio will resurrect its glory days as the island's exclusive hotel hub. Just up the road from Trident's castle, her Jamaica Palace Hotel rises on a knoll that once served as the site of a nondescript shopping plaza. Designed by a German architect with Palladian notions, the immense, blinding-white building with its endless columns and ornate interiors gives off an air of European formality. Indeed, Robin Leach, of "Lifestyles of the Rich and Famous" fame, dubbed it "a baby Buckingham Palace." But the New World staff and the soft-reggae/calypso band, plus the huge pool in the shape of Jamaica and Patrice Wymore Flynn's (Errol's widow) boutique-cum-art gallery (and maybe an impromptu tour of the Flynn ranch) all put it undeniably in Port Antonio. The Jamaica Palace appeals to groups (the Fred Astaire Dance School swung here recently) and occasionally draws locals for fine poolside lunches. While the menu changes daily, you can always expect baked Alaska at dinner. And with the place put on the auction block last spring, the Palace may come to be known as Mrs. Fahmi's Folly.

Food enthusiasts who want a steady diet of real Jamaican cooking would be happiest staying in a rental villa, where every cook is queen of the island cuisine. Lady Sarah Churchill, who lives near Mobay, maintains that the best restaurants are, in effect, the villas; nowhere else can a visitor get such local delicacies as stamp'n'go (codfish fritters) or authentic pepperpot soup. At the most desirable **Port Antonio Villas**, those situated along the "strip" between Monkey (Pellew) Island and the Blue Lagoon, you can dine or dive at whim off the sensational seaside terraces. Local fishermen pull up in their rickety boats alongside the villas, proffering the daily catch, and snorkeling off the coral reef can't be equaled anywhere in Jamaica. Besides wonderful meals, the staffs of these villas provide pampering their guests will never forget. (Peter O'Toole stayed in one of these villas, and the houseman now sports his black cigarette holder.) Nearby **Goblin Hill Villas at San San** combines a bit of the privacy and staff of villa life with such hotel-style amenities as a pool, two lighted tennis courts, and a video/games room. There's no restaurant at Goblin Hill, but with its small, row house–styled villas, a cook for each (guests buy their own food), and the **Blue Lagoon Restaurant** a short walk down the hill, no one seems to mind.

The supposedly bottomless **Blue Lagoon** (also called Blue Hole) ranks among the more seductive settings in Jamaica. Rudyard Kipling sang its praises, Robin Moore once owned it, and the Aga Khan kept a house near it. When Warner Brothers transformed its shore into a Robinson Crusoe–type film set, an enterprising local parlayed the place into a water-sports and rafting center along with a snappy bar and jerked-chicken restaurant.

The cradle of jerk—not jerky but a precursor to the New Orleans invention of "blackened" foods—is in **Boston Bay**, 3 miles (5 km) east of Blue Lagoon. Until a few years ago Boston Bay was the only place in Jamaica to buy the highly spiced meat, but now this regional cooking wave has flooded the island with jerk stands. Ever since Columbus discovered allspice here back in 1494 (he thought it was pepper), Jamaicans have been known for their tongue-searing cuisine. Jerking could likely be traced back to the Arawaks, but it was the Maroons, the island's early runaway slaves, who perfected the method of marinating wild pig with pimento—what Jamaicans call allspice—hot peppers, and scallions. (Descendants of the Maroons still live in the Portland hilltowns of Cornwall Barracks and Moore Town and in the Cockpit Country south of Montego Bay.) Next to the bay in Boston, with its rolling surf, the old jerkers fire up huge smoking barbecues of green pimento sticks at dawn, and orders by the handful are ready at lunchtime. But if your tastes run to sit-down settings, head to **Frenchman's Cove**—once the Caribbean's most exclusive hotel (Liz Taylor and Richard Burton honeymooned here) and still the site of the best beach in Portland—where waiters serve jerked specialties and accompaniments on your table in the sand.

Off the beach and up in the hills beyond the hamlet of Sherwood Forest, spelunkers and botanists find bliss at **Nonsuch Caves**, tucked below Athenry Gardens. A local farmer discovered the remarkable caves not long ago when his baby goat was trapped at the entrance. The half-hour trek through the stalactite-dripping realms makes you feel like Indiana Jones—bats and all. Outside, the views extend from Portland to the Blue Mountains. An inexpensive and charming villa, **Blue Moon**, on neighboring Pimento Hill captures the essence of hilltop serenity.

Deeper in and higher up in the hills of Portland, a bold young couple from the Louisiana bayous has recently organized a downhill biking tour (no pedalling) with pit stops for a *beignets* breakfast and a Jamaican-style jambalaya lunch at their cliffside Papillon café. Tel: 993-2240 or 0-997-7637 (cellular).

Kingston

Despite all the bad press it gets, Kingston is nonetheless important culturally—not only to Jamaica but to the whole Caribbean community. (After all, Jamaica is the largest English-speaking country in the West Indies.) Ignoring the capital would be like avoiding New York's Museum Mile because of its proximity to some tough spots in nearby Harlem. Granted, there is crime in Kingston, but it's mostly in the rougher sections that a visitor would not encounter in the course of a stay; caution should be exercised here as in any developing country. Not that anyone would necessarily want to spend a week-long holiday in Kingston, but to miss its considerable high points altogether would be a mistake.

Although Kingston's population is less than a million, its chaotic urban sprawl, fanning out from the enormous harbor to the foothills of the Blue Mountains, makes the city seem much bigger. Up to a dozen years ago the old colonials used to canter through the city's open spaces, but all available ground has been gobbled up by housing developments that seem to have deafening reggae bars on every corner. This is not a walking city.

If you want to be close to the cultural pockets, i.e., downtown, the place to stay is the sophisticated **Jamaica Pegasus Hotel**, with its V.I.P. floors, cable TV, and a swimming pool the size of a cricket pitch. Some business travellers prefer the **Wyndham Kingston Hotel,** a recently refurbished salmon-and-cream high rise with a health club and noted live entertainment, just steps away from the Pegasus and a bit less formal. One alternative is to head for the hills, to the cozy **Ivor Guest House and Restaurant**. In fact, Ivor could be Kingston's best-kept secret and bargain: Its verandah, nudging a terraced cliffside, overlooks the city and, come nightfall, makes the 20-minute drive 2,000 feet up a small price to pay. Good home-cooked Jamaican dishes have a Scottish flair, compliments of the Scottish owner. (Note the curling stones used for doorstops.) By early morning, the Blue Mountains peek through a cosseting mist behind the 1870s hilltop retreat, bird-watchers awaken, and the glistening lawn awaits its first croquet match.

The other alternative is to flee to the sea, especially if you're flying out the next day. Try **Morgan's Harbour Hotel and Yacht Marina**, in Port Royal just ten minutes from the airport. Almost uninhabitable a few years ago, the hotel was transformed by a sympatico Swiss-Italian management duo drawn by a setting that sang to them of the Italian lakes; it is now run by a Frenchman. Come evening Kingston sparkles across the harbor, with the dark Blue Mountains hovering close behind. You could sit out all night at the dockside restaurant, savoring the scene—unless you prefer the indoor lights of the newly installed disco.

Don't come to Kingston on a weekend, when the city is dead and many of the museums close, unless it's to climb the **Blue Mountain** peak. This is a sublime experience, best arranged through the hospitable owners of the Pine Grove Guest House halfway up the mountain (see below).

Like much of Kingston, the **Institute of Jamaica** may surprise you. Founded in 1879 to foster cultural and scientific growth, the East Street complex serves as a sort of Smithsonian Institute. (If you're really serious about Jamaica's heritage, subscribe for a farthing to the Institute's quarterly, *Jamaica Journal.*) The national schools of art and music, drama, and dance operate under its well-respected auspices, drawing students from all over the Caribbean. History scholars spend days in the stacks at the National Library, formerly known as the West Indian Reference Library, which houses the foremost research collection in the Caribbean. The **National Gallery**, a few blocks away in a contemporary building of impressive proportions on the waterfront, exhibits the definitive collection of Jamaican artists past and present. Particularly interesting are the 19th-century scenes of plantation life (such as Belisario's); the sensitive sculpture of the late Edna Manley, who was a primary force in the development of local arts; and the work of such visionary artists as Albert Artwell, who depicts the growth of the Rastafarian movement in Jamaica. The best selection of paintings (as well as old maps) to buy is at **Bolívar Bookshop and Gallery**, on Grove Road less than a mile from the Pegasus (don't miss the West Indian room in the attic). For antique objects and furniture, such as museum-quality tortoiseshell combs dating from the 17th century, go to **The Antiquarian and Trading Co.** between Devon House and Jamaica House (offices of the prime minister) at number 30 Hope Road.

Jamaica's reputation for excellence in the performing arts is borne out at such revered venues as the **Ward Theatre** (the oldest theater in the Western Hemisphere) and even in the tourist outposts of Ocho Rios and Mobay, where the off-season happenings encapsulate the formidable array of talent. It's worth visiting Kingston in July, August, or December just to attend a performance at the **Little Theatre**, where folkloric dance becomes avantgarde, with brilliant costumes and lighting that would bring even Twyla Tharp to her knees.

Still, Jamaica's most famous export is reggae, the rocksteady Caribbean soul music born in the slums of Kingston and spread like gospel according to Bob Marley. You don't have to be a reggae fan to enjoy the museum that was both Marley's home and the Tuff Gong recording studio; there's even a wax statue of Marley, complete with the musician's guitar and dreadlocks of silk, donated by Madame Tussaud's.

Just down Hope Road from Marley's erstwhile throne is **Devon House**, the 19th-century mansion of Jamaica's first black millionaire—the kind of place that Rastas and reggae rail against with egalitarian fervor. The stately museum complex showcases life as it was when Jamaica was rich—and offers one of the best spots in town for shopping (at **Things Jamaican**) and lunching.

Eating well in Kingston often means leaving town—and calling ahead—for such enchanting aeries as Ivor (see above; Tel: 977-0033) and the **Blue Mountain Inn** (Tel: 927-1700), once the great house of an old coffee plantation on the Gordon Town Road, 20 minutes from Kingston's hotel district. Kingstonians call it their Maxim's, with the moderately expensive fare ranging from shrimp and lobster fettucine to rich Continental-style dishes and selections from the flambé trolley.

One of Jamaica's early governors, who built 18th-century Temple Hall plantation as his cool country retreat, would surely rise up and cheer the newest eatery on the Kingston scene. Called simply **The Restaurant at Temple Hall** (Tel: 942-2340 or 926-5556), it combines the aura of a colonial estate house with outstanding food grown and raised on the back forty. The Italian-Swiss proprietors offer courtesy transportation to the estate, 30 minutes outside of Kingston in outlying Stony Hill.

Norma's nouvelle Creole cuisine gives good reason to stay in town, or, in fact, to visit Kingston on a Thursday or Friday just to dine on her stylish, tented patio. If you can't manage dinner, try lunch Monday through Friday. Those who can't get enough of Norma Shirley's cooking sign up for one—or a series—of her classes on Monday and Wednesday evenings. Call ahead for details as well as reservations (Tel: 929-4966) at this tiny restaurant on Belmont Road (number 8) in a pleasant section of midtown.

From here it's all uphill—to the mysterious Blue Mountains, with their pine-crusted ridgebacks that could easily be mistaken for Tuscany. In the mountains you can stay at the old **Pine Grove Guest House**, a chalet that's short on taste and long on grace (try to overlook its tacky rooms for the warmth of the owners and its *Sound of Music* setting). Here you can only imagine the profound beat of reggae several thousand feet below.

USEFUL FACTS

What to Wear

Ascots rather than ties suit many gentlemen staying at the posh resorts, which normally require a jacket and neckwear for dinner. In Kingston ladies are better off wearing a dress or skirt, day or night. Otherwise, casual cottons are most comfortable. For mountain climbing bring a heavy sweater, windbreaker, and suitable shoes.

Getting In
Airlines serving Jamaica include American, Continental, Air Jamaica, Air Canada, British Airways, Northwest, Balair, Key Air, and BWIA. Nonstop flights (some of them charter) are available from many major U.S. cities including New York, Newark, Los Angeles, Denver, Chicago, Atlanta, Boston, Baltimore, Orlando, Washington, and Philadelphia. Trans Jamaican Airlines operates flights within Jamaica. Have your island destination in mind when you choose the Jamaican airport you'll use.

Entry Requirements
All visitors must supply proof of citizenship, either a passport or a birth certificate.

Local Time
Jamaica is on eastern standard time year-round. This means that when the U.S. east coast moves its clocks forward an hour during daylight saving time, Jamaica is no longer on the same time but is one hour behind.

Currency
The Jamaican dollar, although U.S. dollars are accepted nearly everywhere. Banks are plagued with endless queues, so you should change money at the airport upon arrival. Save J $100 for the departure tax. To change Jamaican money back to other currencies, remember to save exchange receipts. At press time the rate of exchange was U.S. $1 to J $25.

Electrical Current
In most cases, same as in the U.S. and Canada—110 volts AC, but 50 cycles.

Getting Around
Once out of the airport you will be besieged by taxi drivers; chances are you won't need one, but if you do, look on the taxicab door for the JUTA sticker, which signifies the most reliable transportation association. Most rates are government-fixed, but determine before taking off if the price quoted is in Jamaican or U.S. dollars.

If you are planning to rent a car, the stress-free route is

to prearrange transfer to your ultimate destination (hotel or villa), then have the car delivered the next day. Otherwise, go immediately *before* claiming your luggage to the Jamaica Tourist Board counter to pick up the free Discover Jamaica map (you'll be helpless without it) and then proceed on to the airport car-rental offices. If the J.T.B. is out of maps, get one from the car-rental company; failing that, try a gas station. It's wise to book a car well in advance since they're often in short supply, but the process is usually such a time-consuming ordeal that you'll wonder why you bothered. With all the taxes, insurance, etc., the basic rate quoted back home seems to double. All of the big-name rental agencies operate franchises here; local companies such as Sunshine, Jules Dave, Ltd., and Island Car Rental maintain good reputations. Driving is on the left and gas costs a fortune (cash only). Beware of hell-bent drivers and those who stop in the middle of the road for a chat with pedestrians.

Business Hours
Usual business hours are from 8:30 A.M. to 4:30 P.M., Monday through Friday (tourist shops stay open on Saturdays); banks are open Monday through Thursday from 9:00 A.M. to 2:00 P.M. and on Fridays from 9:00 A.M. to noon and from 2:30 to 5:00 P.M. (try to avoid banks on Fridays—it's payday).

Festivals and Events
Reggae Sunsplash, an international festival (concerts) held annually since 1977 in Mobay for five days in mid- to late July; Port Antonio International Marlin Tournament, the oldest and most prestigious fishing tournament in the Caribbean, in October; the Johnny Walker World Championship of Golf played at Tryall in late December; Jamaica Sprint Triathlon in Negril in January; Miami/Montego Bay Yacht Race in February; Carnival Week starting Easter Sunday; Accompong Maroon Festival in early January in the parish of St. Elizabeth.

Meet the People, an ongoing program that really works, puts together visitors and locals with common interests, from birds to beeswax. Simply contact the nearest Jamaica Tourist Board office.

Departure
Save enough cash to pick up some of the fine local products at the duty-free airport shops, including JABLUM

or Mavis Bank Blue Mountain coffee (don't settle for any other brand), Jamaican cigars, Appleton rum, Tia Maria, and fine chutneys. Should your flight be delayed, hire a licensed taxi and head for **Port Royal**, about 10 minutes from Kingston's airport, to stroll around the ruins of what was once the "wickedest city on earth," the bastion of Caribbean pirates such as Henry Morgan—who later became governor of Jamaica.

For Further Information
The Tourism Centre, 21 Dominica Drive, P.O. Box 360, Kingston 5, Jamaica, W.I., Tel: (809) 929-9200 or 9219, Fax: (809) 929-9375; **in the U.S.**, The Jamaica Tourist Board, 866 Second Avenue, 10th Floor, New York, NY 10017, Tel: (800) 223-5225 or (212) 688-7650, Fax: (212) 759-5012; **in Canada**, 1 Eglinton Avenue East, Suite 616, Toronto, Ontario M4P 3A1, Tel: (416) 482-7850, Fax: (416) 482-1730; **in the U.K.**, 111 Gloucester Place, London W1H 3PH, England, Tel: (71) 224-0505, Fax: (71) 224-0551.

ACCOMMODATIONS REFERENCE
The rate ranges given here, in U.S. dollars, are projections for fall 1992 through spring 1993, and span the lowest rates in the low season to the highest in the high season. Unless otherwise indicated, rates are for double room, double occupancy. As rates are subject to change, it's always wise to double-check before booking. The telephone area code (within the U.S. system) for Jamaica is 809.

▶ **Bluefields Bay Villas.** P.O. Box 5, Westmoreland Parish, Jamaica, W.I. In U.S., Tel: (703) 549-5276; Fax: (703) 549-6517. From $130–$275 per person per day on a weekly basis, all-inclusive depending on size of group and season.

▶ **Blue Moon Villa.** c/o Dr. and Mrs. Micha Valenti, Pimento Hill Farm, P.O. Box 208, Port Antonio, Jamaica, W.I. Tel: 993-2135. Inexpensive, negotiable.

▶ **Bonnie View Plantation Hotel.** P.O. Box 82, Port Antonio, Jamaica, W.I. Tel: 993-2752 or 2862; Fax: 993-2862; in U.S., Tel: (800) 448-5398; Fax: (509) 547-1265. $72–$80; M.A.P. available. Call hotel directly for special packages.

▶ **Casa Maria Hotel.** P.O. Box 10, Port Maria, Jamaica, W.I. Tel: 994-2323; Fax: 994-2324; in U.S., (800) 222-6927 or (509) 545-0670. $60–$115.

▶ **Chukka Cove.** P.O. Box 160, Ocho Rios, Jamaica, W.I.

For reservations and riding details, Tel: 972-2506, or 974-2593 or 2239; Fax: 974-5568. Two-bedroom villas from $1,380 to $1,725 per week; otherwise, rates vary according to length of stay and type of package, e.g., $200 per person for two-day riding trek, including meals, drinks, and overnight accommodation at Lillyfield.

▶ **DeMontevin Lodge**. P.O. Box 85, Port Antonio, Jamaica, W.I. Tel: 993-2604. $74, C.P.

▶ **The Enchanted Garden**. Ocho Rios, Jamaica, W.I. No children under 14. Tel: 974-1400; Fax: 974-5823; in U.S., Tel: (800) 654-1FDR; Fax: (516) 223-4815; in U.K., (81) 908-1516. $185–$250 per person per night (three-night minimum stay), includes everything.

▶ **Folichon**. c/o Arthur Sutton, Marshall's Pen, P.O. Box 58, Mandeville, Jamaica, W.I. Tel: 962-2260. The villa sleeps eight and costs $90 per night, including maid service; two-night minimum.

▶ **Goblin Hill Villas at San San**. San San, Port Antonio, Jamaica, W.I. Tel: 993-3286 and 925-8108; Fax: 925-6248; in U.S., (800) 423-4095. One-bedroom villa from $1,795 to $2,080 includes basic car rental and housekeeper (without car, $1,370–$1,570).

▶ **Hibiscus Lodge Hotel**. P.O. Box 52, Ocho Rios, Jamaica, W.I. Tel: 974-2676; Fax: 974-1874; in U.S., (800) 526-2422. $62–$80, C.P.

▶ **Ivor Guest House and Restaurant**. Jacks Hill, Kingston, 6, Jamaica, W.I. (includes breakfast plus transportation to and from Kingston). Tel: 977-0033; Fax: 926-7061. $90.

▶ **Jamaica Inn**. P.O. Box 1, Ocho Rios, Jamaica, W.I. Tel: 974-2514; Fax: 974-2449; in U.S., (800) 243-9420 or (804) 460-2343; in U.K., (71) 730-7144. $210–$400, M.A.P. in low season; $350–$600, A.P. in high season. No children under 14.

▶ **Jamaica Pegasus Hotel**. P.O. Box 333, 81 Knutsford Blvd., Kingston, 5, Jamaica, W.I. Tel: 926-3691; Fax: 929-5855; in U.S. and Canada, (800) 225-5843; in U.K., (71) 567-3444. $175–$550.

▶ **Lillyfield**. See Chukka Cove for reservations.

▶ **Love Solution Guest Cottages**. P.O. Box 13, Negril, Jamaica, W.I. Tel: 957-4417. $125–$150.

▶ **Morgan's Harbour Hotel and Yacht Marina**. Port Royal, Jamaica, W.I. Tel: 924-8464; Fax: 924-8146; in U.S., (800) 526-2422. $120–$150 (ask about the "Airport Special").

▶ **Natania's Guest House and Seafood Restaurant**. Little

Culloden, White House P.O., Westmoreland, Jamaica, W.I. Tel and Fax: 957-4335 or 969-5213. $70.

▶ **Pine Grove Guest House.** Reservations c/o 62 Duke Street, Kingston, Jamaica, W.I. Tel: 922-8705; Fax: 942-9848. From $63; M.A.P., $20 extra per person.

▶ **Plantation Inn.** P.O. Box 2, Ocho Rios, Jamaica, W.I. Tel: 974-5601; Fax: 974-5912; in U.S. and Canada, Tel: (800) 237-3237 or, in Miami, Tel: (305) 666-3566; Fax: (305) 665-3163. $150–$460. Ask about optional meal plans.

▶ **Platinum Plan.** Tel: (800) 237-3237 or (305) 666-3566; Fax: (305) 666-7239. From three- to seven-night programs.

▶ **Port Antonio Villas.** Jean Paterson & Associates, P.O. Box 276, Port Antonio, Jamaica, W.I. Tel: 993-3009; Fax: 993-2143. $1,000–$2,200 per week per villa.

▶ **Reading Reef Club.** P.O. Box 225, Reading P.O., Montego Bay, Jamaica, W.I. Tel: 952-5909; Fax: 952-7217. $75–$185 (includes water sports).

▶ **Round Hill Hotel and Villas.** P.O. Box 64, Montego Bay, Jamaica, W.I. Tel: 952-5150; Fax: 952-2505; in U.S. and Canada, (800) 237-3237 or, in Miami, (305) 666-3566. $190–$620 including tax and service (highest rates are for villas with pools). Ask about special programs and meal plans.

▶ **Runaway Bay H.E.A.R.T. Academy.** P.O. Box 98, St. Ann, Jamaica, W.I. Tel: 973-2671; Fax: 973-2693; in U.S., (800) JAMAICA. $60–$85, M.A.P.

▶ **Sans Souci Hotel & Spa.** Box 103, Ocho Rios, Jamaica, W.I. Tel: 974-2353 or 2354; Fax: 974-2544; in U.S., Tel: (800) 654-1FDR; Fax: (516) 223-4815; in U.K., (81) 908-1516. $203–$616, M.A.P. optional. Ask about the spa program.

▶ **Trident Villas & Hotel.** P.O. Box 119, Port Antonio, Jamaica, W.I. Tel: 993-2602; Fax: 993-2590; in U.S. and Canada, Tel: (800) 237-3237 or, in Miami, (305) 666-3566; Fax: (305) 665-3163. $150–$500, depending on meal plan, size of accommodation, and season. Ask about helicopter or air charter arrangements.

▶ **Tryall Golf, Tennis & Beach Resort.** P.O. Box 1206, Montego Bay, Jamaica, W.I. Tel: 952-5110 through 5113; Fax: 952-8637; in U.S. and Canada, Tel: (800) 237-3237, (800) 336-4571 for villas, or in Miami, (305) 666-3566; Fax: (305) 665-3163; in U.K., (71) 730-7144. From $165–$460, M.A.P. optional in hotel suites at $66 per person. One- to five-bedroom staffed villas from $2,400 to $8,500 per week. Ask about special golf and tennis programs.

▶ **Wilton on the Sea.** P.O. Box 20, Bluefields, Westmoreland, Jamaica, W.I. No phone. $150, M.A.P.

▶ **Wyndham Kingston Hotel.** 77 Knutsford Boulevard, P.O. Box 112, Kingston, 10, Jamaica, W.I. Tel: 926-5430; Fax: 929-7439; in U.S., (800) 822-4200; in Canada, (800) 631-4200. $125–$145.

▶ **Villa rentals** throughout most of the island: Villas and Apartments Abroad, 420 Madison Avenue, New York, NY 10017. Tel: (800) 433-3020 or (212) 759-1025. With an overall range of $600 to $12,000 per week for one- to seven-bedroom villas, a fully staffed, three-bedroom villa averages about $1,900 per week.

HAITI

By Jessica Harris

Jessica Harris specializes in writing about the Caribbean, and Hispaniola in particular. She is the author of Sky Juice and Flying Fish, *a book on Africa's contributions to New World cooking, and has written articles for* Caribbean Travel and Life, Essence, Vogue, *the* New York Times, *and other major publications.*

Haiti, beautiful, battered, and perhaps the most controversial of the Caribbean islands, would seem today to be suffering under one of its own voodoo spells cast by a malevolent priest. Already buffeted by the growing spectre of Duvalier politics, human-rights violations, and the precipitous departure of "Bébé Doc" Duvalier, the country was plunged into political chaos by the failure of the much-awaited 1987 elections. Up until recently Haiti was witness to a danse macabre that could be called the "dance of the generals." Coups d'état have succeeded each other at an alarming rate. It was hoped that the election of Jean-Bertrand Aristide, the frail but feisty priest who was the country's first democratically elected president in decades, would bring peace, progress, and prosperity. However, those hopes were dashed with another coup. As we go to press, the situation fluctuates daily. Be sure to check with your government as to the advisability of vacation travel in Haiti before making your plans. Even if there is no advisory warning, you may not feel comfortable being in the country as things currently stand.

Now only the most adept voodoo priest would attempt to foresee what's in store for this country, which was the second republic to be established in the Western Hemisphere and the first black nation in the New World. Haiti

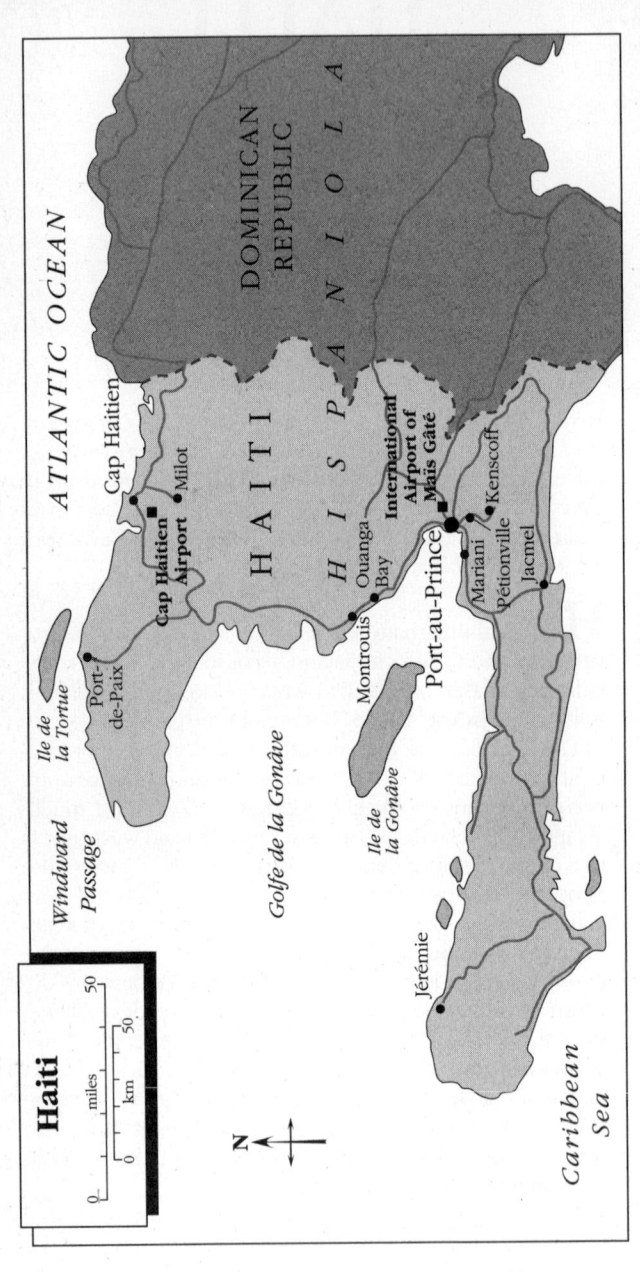

aficionados, and a staunch and faithful lot they are, have but one wish: that this time it will all turn around so that the country can go back to being one of the most fascinating of all Caribbean destinations.

Haiti has never been a country to leave observers indifferent. Partisans praise a people whose creative force and vitality have decorated rickety buses, created masterpieces on canvas, invented a unique cuisine, and above all maintained an air of great goodwill toward visitors despite all the tricks of history. Detractors see poverty and, of course, political unrest. The only way to know how Haiti will affect you is to come here—when the political climate settles down. Those who have find that this western part of the island of Hispaniola offers no large resorts and very few important sights. Its beaches are fine but are not the primary reason for visits either. What the country does offer is a chance to get in touch with the most African of the Caribbean islands and to spend some time in a truly fascinating place.

MAJOR INTEREST

Strong African influence
Naïve art
Creole cuisine

Port-au-Prince and Pétionville
Panthéon National d'Art Haitien
Art galleries

Cap Haitien
Citadelle La Ferrière
Sans Souci palace

Elsewhere
Jacmel (beaches)

Visitors usually arrive at the international airport, a half-hour drive from Port-au-Prince. The capital city and its hillside suburb of Pétionville house most of Haiti's hotels and are the bases for most excursions. The more adventurous visitors make a trip with car and driver (or on one of the infrequent flights) to the northern city of Cap Haitien to see what some have classified as one of the wonders of the world: the Citadelle La Ferrière, the fortress built by King Henri Christophe. Those determined to have their time at the beach take a southern route and head for Jacmel.

Travellers who come to Haiti in search of art find it everywhere. The many galleries in the capital sell paintings that range from the ridiculous to the sublime, priced for every budget. There are several museums and art centers in Haiti, most of them in Port-au-Prince, and it seems that hawkers selling paintings and mahogany sculpture occupy every street corner. For those for whom art extends beyond painting or sculpture to all of life, Port-au-Prince and the rest of the country provide many a lesson in the very Haitian art of living. It is an education to watch the merger of the Haitian sense of commerce and the all-too-real need of many Haitians to earn a living. Few hands are idle in this country, which could teach the rest of the Western world a great deal about recycling: Old tires are transformed into sandals, orange peels are saved and used to make a liqueur, and evaporated-milk tins become oil lamps.

But this is only a part of Haiti. In the Port-au-Prince suburb of Pétionville, for example, things take a slower pace, and the French influence is more evident, especially in the elegant restaurants.

Columbus, who arrived in 1492 and set up a temporary settlement at La Navidad, named the island Hispaniola. In 1697 the Spanish granted the western part of the island to the French, and they transformed it into Saint Domingue, "the Pearl of the Antilles." The colony was so rich in tobacco, cane, and coffee that the world reeled when the shock waves of the French Revolution led first the planters, then the mulatto class, and finally the slaves to revolt in what would culminate in the declaration of independence of 1804, which made Haiti the world's first black republic. The revolution brought Toussaint-L'Ouverture, Jean-Jacques Dessalines, Alexandre Pétion, and Henri Christophe to fame; their names are touchstones in the country even today.

Following the brilliance of the glory days of independence, Haiti and the Dominican Republic were one country. In 1844 the two became separate entities. Thereafter, Haiti's fortunes seesawed: rule by an emperor, occupation by U.S. Marines, and 30 years of oppressive rule by the Duvalier family—which ended in February 1986 and paved the way for the current turmoil.

Voodoo

No traveller comes to Haiti without wanting to witness a bit of voodoo. Folkloric shows at all of the hotels oblige with sometimes chilling accuracy. Those in search of the real thing will probably not find it unless they are fluent in Creole and have the confidence of a Haitian friend. Until recently a good substitute was the demonstration at the *peristyle* (voodoo temple) in Mariani, a small village on the outskirts of Port-au-Prince. This show was run by Max Beauvoir, a *houngan* (voodoo priest) and lawyer who writes scholarly articles on a computer. The complex has closed, but you can find Beauvoir if you're diligent—and serious about your interest in voodoo.

Port-au-Prince

The Victorian gingerbread houses of Port-au-Prince lean precariously and seem to be ready to topple at the first strong wind. They are as much a testimony to the Haitian will to survive as anything. The traveller is sure to spot one or more memorable examples while passing through the city.

Works by the old masters of Haitian art can be seen at the Episcopal Cathédrale de St. Trinité on the corner of the rue Monseigneur Guilloux and rue Pavée; murals depict the life of Christ in Haitian naïve style. Visitors who are intrigued by the intricacies of Haitian history should not miss the **Panthéon National d'Art Haitien**, on the Champs de Mars in front of the National Palace. Exhibits include an anchor from the *Santa Maria* and Papa Doc's physician's satchel, as well as a selection of Haitian art. Have your hotel check for opening hours.

Le Plaza Holiday Inn is nearby. Favored by business-people with in-town activities (most leisure travellers prefer the calmer Pétionville suburbs for lodging), the hotel offers a downtown oasis of calm. Holiday Inn–type rooms are set in low-rise buildings around a lush internal courtyard, in the midst of which businesspeople can catch a few rays while waiting for the next appointment.

A visit to the Marché de Fer (Iron Market) takes you right into the fray of Haitian life—and is not for the weak of heart. A photographer's dream and an agoraphobe's nightmare, the area has always been best visited only by those who want a true baptism of fire. Merchants jostle and cajole, children harass and surround, and the Haitian wheels of commerce grind inexorably onward. Crowds are intense, and for most tourists this area of wall-to-wall activity and bustle is best avoided.

Instead, a leisurely visit to some of the capital's galleries will give the visitor a good look at Haitian art. Galleries to seek out include **Galerie Nader** (Tel: 22-00-33 or 69), downtown on rue Magasin de l'Etat, and **Issa's** (Tel: 22-32-87), on the rue du Chili. **Claire's Gallery**, in the same neighborhood, is run by Aubélin Jolicoeur, a Haitian institution himself and formerly a fixture at the airport, where—in an impeccable white suit and carrying a mahogany cane—he would greet all arrivals.

Many of the art galleries also sell original handcrafted items such as hand-carved wooden salad bowls, embroidered pillows, crocheted wares, ceramics, and the like. The best can be found at **Ambiance**, at 17 avenue M, **Gingerbread** (Tel: 45-36-98), 52 avenue Lamartinière, and **Zin d'Art** (no phone), 86 John Brown, in the Port-au-Prince/Pétionville area, and at the **Galerie Trois Visages** (Tel: 62-09-38) in Cap Haitien. Near Claire's Gallery and Issa's, on the place St. Gérard, is the **Grand Hotel Oloffson**, immortalized in Graham Greene's novel *The Comedians*. A stop for a drink at the mahogany bar of this Victorian gingerbread wonder, a gathering place for the country's literati and artistic visitors for years, is obligatory for all. The world-famous hotel was closed briefly before reopening in November 1987. Today a few antiques-furnished guest rooms are available, and others will be opened as tourism on the island improves.

Haitian cuisine differs from that of the rest of the French-speaking Caribbean; when in Port-au-Prince, try such unique dishes as *riz au djon djon* (rice with black mushrooms), *griots de porc* (spicy pork bits), and *soupe au giraumon* (pumpkin soup) at restaurants such as **Le Récif** (Tel: 46-26-05) on Delmas Road or **Le Rond Point** near the Exposition grounds, or in some of the hotel dining rooms.

When things are packed tighter than the proverbial sardines in downtown Port-au-Prince, life in Pétionville moves at a more relaxed pace. Located on the mountainside overlooking downtown Port-au-Prince, this affluent suburb is more sophisticated than its seaside sister. In Pétionville, visitors can find comfortable hotels and excellent restaurants such as **Chez Gérard** (Tel: 57-19-49), **La Souvenance** (Tel: 57-76-88), and the **Steak Inn** (Tel: 57-21-

53), which could easily be in the South of France. La Cascade, which was destroyed in a fire a few years ago, has reopened as **Les Cascades** (Tel: 57-67-04). Numerous art galleries, most notably the **Galerie Marassa** (Tel: 57-19-67) and a branch of **Galerie Monin** (Tel: 57-44-30), are here, too, in adjacent buildings on the rue Lamarre.

"Las Vegas goes Haitian" is the best way to describe the **El Rancho** hotel in Pétionville. A nightclub and casino keep things jumping at night, while twin pools, complete with a waterfall and swim-up bar, and an indoor/outdoor dining room are centers of activity during the day. High rollers used to frequent the hotel in the 1950s, but today's guests are more apt to be attracted by the slightly kitschy decor.

The **Villa Créole**, a family-run property also in Pétionville, is the favorite Haitian roost of members of the press and businesspeople. One of the big attractions of the moderately priced hotel is breakfasting under the poolside almond tree. Most hotel activities take place poolside, including the Monday night barbecues. Manager Roger Dunwell can usually find visitors a tennis game on one of the hotel's two courts if he's too busy to play himself. The hotel also offers beach excursions and other activities for guests. Best of all, the welcome of the owners is as warm as the Haitian sun.

The stalwart can make a trip to the **Jane Barbancourt Castle** on the road to Boutilliers and Kenscoff. This establishment, a tasting room for the Jane Barbancourt rum distillery, offers a wide assortment of rum liqueurs flavored with everything from coconut to hibiscus. The excursion might continue to **Boutilliers**, with its panoramic view of Port-au-Prince, and beyond to **Kenscoff**, a village in a pine forest high in the hills, where many wealthy Haitians have weekend homes. Kenscoff is degrees cooler than Port-au-Prince, and its weekly Monday market is a photographer's delight.

Cap Haitien

It is hard to believe that Cap Haitien, previously known as Cap Français, was once the richest French city in the New World. Today, for most visitors, a major reason to go to the sleepy town that Cap Haitien has become is the **Citadelle La Ferrière**, a massive fortress atop a 3,000-foot-high mountain. On the way there many take time to stop at Milot, site of the ruins of King Henri Christophe's palace, **Sans Souci**. The ascent to the fortress that the security-conscious Christophe built far above his palace is by car, on mule, and on foot, and is not for the feeble. The view from the top, however, is breathtaking. Little imagination is required to appreciate the fact that 200,000 men were needed to build it—and that 20,000 of them died in the process. The task took 15 years and was completed in 1817, a year before the king took his own life. This monument to megalomania never saw battle and today is covered with moss.

A perfect spot from which to explore these memories of Haiti past is the **Mont Joli Hotel**. This small, moderately priced hotel epitomizes the quiet charm of Cap Haitien, with antique furniture in the public rooms and the caring attention of everyone, from the owners to the chambermaids.

Elsewhere in Haiti

Those in search of the ultimate beach resort won't find it in Haiti. Instead, they will find a family-oriented resort, Kaliko Beach and Scuba Club, at Ouanga Bay, and Moulin sur Mer, the weekend roost of the Haitian fast set, in Montrouis. **Kaliko Beach and Scuba Club** offers comfortable Haitian/Creole-decorated motel-style rooms set in low-rise buildings by the sea on the 15-acre property. Most guests are attracted by the hotel's scuba activities and its variety of dive packages. **Moulin sur Mer**, a more sophisticated resort, centers around a restored plantation mill and offers accommodations in two-story units near a small strip of beach. Haitian families drive out for weekend stays and relax on Sundays over lengthy luncheons at **Les Boucaniers**, the seaside barbecue restaurant. Afterward, it's tennis, miniature golf, water sports, or simply sunbathing. Currently closed, the Club Med Magic Isle, also in Montrouis, was known to provide that company's all-inclusive type of vacation with a Haitian flair and had rapidly become one of the company's best-loved clubs in the Caribbean. At this writing a reopening date has not been announced.

Jacmel, a coffee boomtown of the late 19th century, is another alternative for beach lovers. The town itself has a gray-sand beach, but secluded coves a short drive away are more enticing. Ask someone at the hotel desk to explain to your taxi driver how to get to these private spots; they're quite difficult to find. Of the few hotels in Jacmel, the best is the beachfront **La Jacmelienne**—somewhat like a fancy Stateside motel with artistic touches.

USEFUL FACTS

What to Wear
Although French chic is evident in some of Pétionville's restaurants after dark, those planning to spend any time exploring the downtown area or perhaps riding on a tap-tap (a gaily decorated local jitney) should think of dressing comfortably.

Getting In
American has regularly scheduled flights from New York and Miami; ALM also flies from Miami and Air Canada flies from Montreal. There are no direct flights from London.

Most visitors to Haiti arrive at Port-au-Prince's Maïs Gâté International Airport. A three-man band plays Haitian songs to help visitors pass the time as they wait in line for immigration. Then it's out into the crowds. Haitian taxis include the good, the bad, and the ugly. Pick one that looks as if it has working shock absorbers and brakes and, because taxis are not metered, negotiate the rate in advance (the cost from the airport to most Pétionville hotels is about U.S. $15). The driver should carry a card spelling out the rates set by the government.

Entry Requirements
U.S. and Canadian citizens must have a valid passport, birth certificate, or naturalization papers. British subjects need only a valid passport; Australian citizens need a passport and a visa issued by a Haitian consulate. An ongoing or return ticket is also required of all non-Haitians. A tourist card is issued on arrival. Currently there is a U.S. $20 departure tax, payable in U.S. dollars; this, though, is scheduled to be lowered.

Local Time
Haiti is on eastern standard time year-round. This means that when the U.S. east coast moves its clocks forward an hour during daylight saving time, Haiti is no longer on the same time but is one hour behind.

Currency
The basic unit of currency is the Haitian gourde, which has been pegged to the U.S. dollar since 1919. Five gourdes are equal to one dollar. Presently, the need for

dollars has boosted the exchange rate, which seems to be floating. However, dollars and gourdes are interchangeable throughout the country. Canadian money and other currencies are not accepted.

Electrical Current
Same as in the U.S. and Canada—110 volts AC, 60 cycles.

Getting Around
Driving in Haiti is only for the initiated or the masochistic. Haitian roads, with the exception of the road to Jacmel and the road to the beaches outside of Port-au-Prince, are neither well marked nor well lighted, and are patrolled by cows, donkeys, and pedestrians who tend to dart out into traffic. Haitian drivers are used to all of this and know how to use their horns to clear a path. If driving is an absolute must, a valid U.S., Canadian, or international driver's license is required.

Taxis are available at all of the hotels and can also be rented by the hour or for the day.

Business Hours
They vary. Check with the hotel desk or phone ahead.

Festivals
On Sundays between Epiphany (January 6) and the beginning of Lent, the island celebrates Carnival. Dancing crowds wind their way through the streets from morning until well past dark. During the Easter season they also celebrate Rara; small bands of people parade in the streets to music and stop occasionally to perform acrobatic feats.

ACCOMMODATIONS REFERENCE
The rate ranges given here, in U.S. dollars, are projections for fall 1992 through spring 1993, and span the lowest rates in the low season to the highest in the high season. Unless otherwise indicated, prices are for double rooms, double occupancy. As rates are subject to change, it's always wise to double-check before booking. The telephone country code for Haiti is 509.

▶ **Grand Hotel Oloffson.** 60 Avenue Christophe, P.O. Box 260, Port-au-Prince, Haiti, W.I. Tel: 23-40-00 or 23-41-01; Fax: 23-09-19. $50–$100, C.P.

▶ **La Jacmelienne Beach Hotel.** P.O. Box 916, Port-au-Prince, Haiti, W.I. Tel: 22-48-99. $98, M.A.P.

▶ **Kaliko Beach and Scuba Club.** P.O. Box 338, Port-au-Prince, Haiti, W.I. Tel: 22-80-40. $98–$134.

▶ **Mont Joli Hotel.** P.O. Box 12, Cap Haitien, Haiti, W.I. Tel and Fax: 62-03-00. $69–$92, F.A.B.

▶ **Moulin sur Mer.** Montrouis, Haiti, W.I. Tel: 22-18-44, 22-19-18, or 22-76-52; Fax: 45-20-85. $60–$100.

▶ **Le Plaza Holiday Inn.** 10 rue Capois, P.O. Box 1429, Port-au-Prince, Haiti, W.I. Tel: 23-98-00; Fax: 22-08-22. $69–$150.

▶ **El Rancho.** P.O. Box 71, Port-au-Prince, Haiti, W.I. Tel and Fax: 57-20-80. $60–$145.

▶ **Villa Créole.** P.O. Box 126, Port-au-Prince, Haiti, W.I. Tel: 57-15-70 or 71; Fax: 57-49-35. $77–$110.

DOMINICAN REPUBLIC

By Jessica Harris

Without the Dominican Republic there might be no Caribbean vacations; it was here that Christopher Columbus, or Cristóbal Colón as he's known here, first set foot ashore in the New World. Located on the eastern portion of the island of Hispaniola—which it shares with Haiti—the Dominican Republic offers the best of two Caribbean worlds to its visitors. History lovers are sure to enjoy the majestic Spanish Renaissance buildings of Old Santo Domingo, while beach buffs will find more than enough secluded white sandy beaches and elegant resort facilities on the southern, eastern, and northern coasts of the country to suit their fancies.

MAJOR INTEREST

Spanish influence

Santo Domingo
Colonial Santo Domingo
Plaza de la Cultura

La Romana
Casa de Campo resort
Altos de Chavón replica colonial town

Punta Cana
Punta Cana Beach Resort

Puerto Plata
The beaches of the area

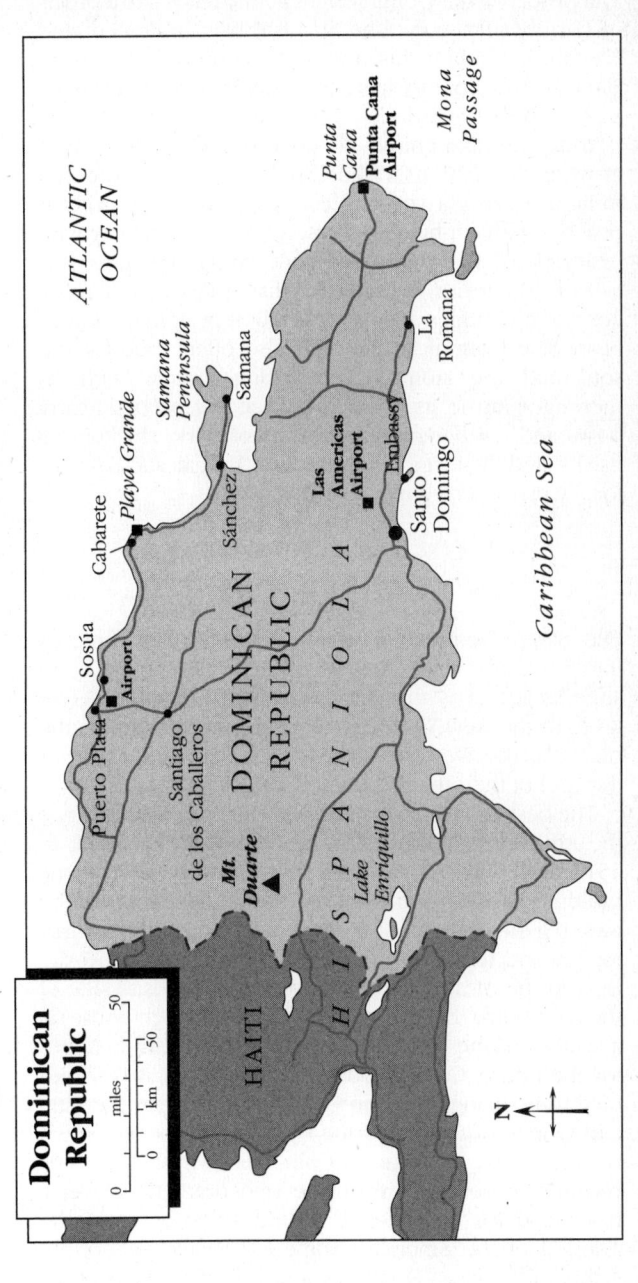

The history of the Dominican Republic reads like a précis of Caribbean history: The Spanish, British, French, and Haitians battled for this land. Self-determination came in 1844, and the country has been independent—except for a brief Spanish interlude—ever since.

Today the Dominican Republic is one of the fastest-growing destinations in the Caribbean. It greets almost a million tourists a year, welcoming them to its pristine beaches with sophisticated resorts, to its capital city with restored colonial monuments and vibrant nightlife, and to its lush interior with lagoons that are home to flamingos and crocodiles and with the tallest peak in the Caribbean. The Dominican Republic also offers food for the soul and the stomach, entrancing visitors with its merengue music, its cuisine—such as *sancocho* (a hearty stew) and *chicharrones* (fried bits of pork, chicken, or fish)—and the three B's: Bermudez, Brugal, and Barcelo, locally produced rums.

Santo Domingo

Old Santo Domingo, elegant and providing glimpses into the past of the New World, can be spoken of in superlatives: It is the first permanent European settlement in the New World, for one, and its cathedral is the oldest in the Western Hemisphere. The colonial city is the soul of the capital, indeed of the country.

The best way to see the colonial city is on foot. Begin at the **Alcázar**, also known as the Casa de Colón. Built in 1510 and restored in 1957, the two-story hewn-stone building has furnishings of the period and seems to be awaiting the return of Don Diego Columbus, son of Christopher and the first Spanish viceroy of the New World. Behind the Alcázar, on a hilltop on the opposite side of the Río Ozama, El Faro a Colón (Columbus Lighthouse) is a symbol of the country's glorious history and its hopes for the future. Currently under construction, it is scheduled to be inaugurated on October 12, 1992, by the King and Queen of Spain and the Pope. Once opened, you'll be able to pay homage to Columbus, whose tomb was recently moved here from the cathedral. (Controversy has raged for centuries as to the actual grave of the Admiral of the Americas. Some say Seville, others the cathedral in Santo Domingo, and still others Cuba. Current opinion disallows the Cuban claim and compromises on the notion that some of the bones are indeed in Spain and some in the Dominican Republic.)

The **Atarazana**, across the plaza, was a colonial arsenal. Shops selling jewelry of amber and larimar (two Dominican specialties), art galleries, and restaurants now occupy the 16th-century buildings.

A short walk away is the **calle las Damas**, named for the Spanish ladies who once promenaded here in the evening. The cobbled street, lined with imposing Spanish Renaissance carved façades, still evokes images of conquistadores and their ladies. The street is lined with museums, including the **Museo de las Casas Reales**, which houses artifacts from life in colonial Santo Domingo.

Those wishing to stop for a drink or to spend a night or two in historic splendor will enjoy the **Hostal Nicolás de Ovando**, a small, inexpensive government-owned hotel on calle las Damas in the restored house of a colonial governor.

It would be inconceivable to leave colonial Santo Domingo without stopping at the **Catedral de Santa María la Menor**, the first cathedral in the New World and an imposing example of Spanish Renaissance architecture.

The confirmed history lover can linger for days in the colonial city visiting museums, marveling at the carved-stone cord of St. Francis's habit on the façade of the 1503 Casa del Cordon (the first stone house built in the Americas), peeking into courtyards, or straining for glimpses behind half-closed doorways. Others may decide to hop into a taxi and find some local color and a few souvenirs at the **Mercado Modelo**, where bargaining is the watchword and stalls offer everything from voodoo powders to amber and gold jewelry. Those wishing to shop with a bit more tranquillity will find the same items, minus the voodoo powders and double the price, at the **plaza Criolla** on avenida 27 Febrero.

Shoppers will find that style is a hallmark of Dominican goods. You see it in the silk, linen, and chiffon clothing of designers like **Jenny Polanco** (Tel: 541-5929), whose boutique in the lobby complex of the Sheraton is a necessary stop for fashion mavens. Handmade Dominican furniture and decorative items are available at **Nuebo**, 36 Fantino Falco (Tel: 562-3333). **Tu Espacio**, at 102 Cervantes Street, two blocks behind the Sheraton, offers antiques and sophisticated handicrafts in an old colonial house; Tel: 686-6006. On the avenida Maximo Gómez, the **Gran Hotel Lina and Casino** offers 220 rooms with terraces as well as a casino, two pools, tennis, and a gym where visitors can work off the effects of the food served at the excellent adjoining restaurant of the same name (see below).

A few blocks to the south, property belonging to Generalíssimo Trujillo (ruler of the Dominican Republic from 1930 to 1961) has been transformed into the **plaza de la Cultura**, a complex housing the Teatro Nacional (the country's national theater), the public library, and several museums. Those wondering what happened before Columbus are well served by the exhibits in the **Museo del Hombre Dominicana**. Bring a dictionary, though, because almost all of the exhibit captions are in Spanish.

Nearby in one of the city's exclusive residential districts (El Embajador) are numerous embassies and the *grand dame* of Dominican hotels, Trujillo-built **El Embajador**. Two excellent restaurants, a casino, large rooms, and attentive service characterize this property, which is much loved by Dominicans.

A walk on the **Malecón** by day allows visitors to enjoy sea vistas and stop for lunch at one of the small cafés and restaurants. Also known as the avenida George Washington, the seaside promenade is the location of many of Santo Domingo's luxury hotels. The current star of the Malecón is the **Ramada Renaissance Jaragua**, a 14-acre, 355-room tropical-pink extravaganza. With grounds including tropical gardens, waterfalls, and a lagoon with swans and ducks, this is an in-town resort. The casino is one of the largest in the Caribbean, the tennis center has four clay courts and stadium seating for international tournaments, and most rooms have spectacular ocean views. There are five restaurants, which feature a variety of cuisines including nouvelle, Latin American, and Asian. Menu selections range from gazpacho with lobster to pork spare-ribs lotus. When you tire of all the luxury, there's the modern European spa where facials, massages, and loofah scrubs are available at low Dominican prices.

Overlooking the water, on the avenida Independencia, the hotel **Santo Domingo** was one of the first properties to mark the new boom in Dominican tourism. Interiors designed by Oscar de la Renta, a large pool, and three tennis courts lure the flashy, mostly Stateside crowd that flocks to the hotel and its luxurious **El Alcázar** restaurant.

In the evening diners looking for Dominican specialties head for **El Buren**, on Padre Billini. **Aurora**, on calle Hermanos de Ligne near Santiago, offers late night *sancocho* in an outdoor garden. **El Conuco** (Tel: 686-0129), on calle Lea de Castro, and **Meson de Bari**, on calle Hostos one block north of El Conde, are other good choices for Dominican cuisine. The latter draws a writers-and-artists crowd for lunch. **Jai Alai** (Tel: 685-2409), on avenida Independencia, places an accent on seafood.

Aside from Dominican the favorite cuisine seems to be Spanish—such as that served at **Lina's Restaurant,** near the plaza Criolla. (Try the *zarzuela de mariscos,* a seafood dish.) Lina, who was Trujillo's cook, came from Spain, and her restaurant has become famous. **El Meson de Castillo**, 8 calle Dr. Baez (Tel: 688-4319), is another Spanish favorite, complete with Castilian wines. Of the several Italian restaurants, **Vesuvio**, on the Malecón, is particularly good. For Italian food on the go, try one of the many branches of **Pizzarelli**; they're all over the city. **El Jardin de Jade**, a marvelous Chinese restaurant in El Embajador hotel, serves Peking duck and dim sum at prices way below those of any Western capital.

The activity doesn't stop when the sun goes down. **Drake's Pub** (Tel: 687-8089) in the Atarazana and **Raffles** on avenida Hostos are both English-style pubs located in colonial buildings. The truly underground **La Guacara Taina**, a club and disco, is located in the Parque Mirador del Sur in a cave. Fans of Latin music will head for **El Patio de Joseito**, an open-air club in the west end of Santo Domingo for merengue and **Le Vieja Habana** on Maximo Gómez for mambo. (There are no real addresses for either club. Have someone inform your taxi driver of your destination. Once in the area, he'll stop and get his bearings.)

Discos and nightclubs abound, particularly on the Malecón. The street is a sight in itself, pulsing with activity as the Dominicans parade nightly. On Saturdays beer and rum are sold from containers on tailgates, mixers appear miraculously, and suddenly everyone is dancing to the merengue or whatever else is blaring from what seems to be hundreds of car radios turned up to full blast. For those who prefer their merengue indoors, there's the **Omni Disco** at the Sheraton, with dancing to the hottest bands.

La Romana

First there was a sugar plantation at La Romana, a two-hour drive from Santo Domingo at the eastern end of the island.

Then there were Gulf & Western and Oscar de la Renta, who together created a 7,000-acre luxury resort called **Casa de Campo** and gave it international cachet. Today, minus Gulf & Western, the resort is a well-run complex that offers two 18-hole Pete Dye golf courses, 17 tennis courts, six pools, abundant water sports, horseback riding, beaches, and for the truly affluent, polo. Eight different restaurants ensure that taste buds will find as much diversity as the rest of the body. Casa de Campo tends to appeal to U.S. executives, international jet-setters, vacationers on special golf and tennis packages, and conventioneers.

Another attraction in the area is **Altos de Chavón**, a modern rendering of a 16th-century European city. Altos has a small Taino Indian museum, gift shops that sell sophisticated but pricey examples of local craftsmanship, and restaurants; unfortunately, the most interesting among the last are closed at noon and not available to those taking day trips from Santo Domingo. But if you're here at night, **Casa del Río** is picture perfect, perched on the edge of a gorge overlooking banana plantations and a sinuously curving river below. Only 15 minutes from Casa de Campo by shuttle bus, Altos de Chavón is a good place for resort guests to spend the day or evening.

Punta Cana

Punta Cana, an area on the Dominican Republic's east coast, is best known for its fine sand, its crystal-clear water, and its **Club Med**, a 600-bed resort village that boasts a miniclub for children two to eleven years old. A sandy, coconut tree–lined beach, a wide range of activities from water sports to tennis (with ten courts) to circus training, two pools, a disco, and lavish buffet meals are offered in traditional Club Med style.

Punta Cana's newest star is the **Punta Cana Beach Resort**, which centers around a 2,200-foot stretch of powder-white-sand beach. The resort offers tennis on ten clay courts, horseback riding, and numerous water sports, and will soon boast a Robert Trent Jones 18-hole golf course.

Santiago de los Caballeros

One hundred and fifty-five miles (248 km) north of Santo Domingo on the road to Puerto Plata is Santiago de los Caballeros, the country's second city and the cultural center of the Dominican Republic. Founded by Bartolomeo Colón (the admiral's brother), it has a long tradition of history and art. The city's claim as the birthplace of the merengue is based on its being home to an astonishing 1,000 nightclubs—one for every taste. In addition to dancing, there's plenty to do in the city. Stop by the **Museo del Arte Folklorico Tomas Morel**, located in a Victorian house, and the **Museo del Tobacco**, which offers the history of the leaf from seed to cigar. Or take a ride in a horse-drawn carriage to view the city's colonial buildings from the 18th and 19th centuries.

Because the city is off the tourist track, the hotels are either city-center business types like the Hotel Camino Real or old-style Dominican like the Hotel Matum. For dining the **Pez Dorado**, 43 calle el Sol (Tel: 582-2518), is a local landmark for Chinese specialties and seafood. **Restaurant Osteria**, avenida 27 de Febrero (Tel: 582-4165), is considered the best in town for Italian food—especially pastas.

Puerto Plata and the North Coast

The "silver port" of the Dominican Republic's north shore, 215 miles from Santo Domingo, is rapidly becoming a tourist mecca. Its largest development, the **Playa Dorada**, is a complex of hotels that offer lodging in every price range. Here the watchwords are beach, beach, and more beach. The **Dorado Naco**, with its large condominium apartments, lures families; pleasant service, golf, riding, and an excellent beach nearby are part of what makes this hotel a favorite of travellers from the United States and Canada. The **Eurotel Playa Dorada**, a cluster of low-rise buildings with five lighted tennis courts, a cascading freshwater pool, and a casino, stretches down to the beach and boasts European-style luxury, while the **Jack Tar Village** has a plan that includes all meals, drinks, and sports—sort of like a budget Club Med—in the price of a room.

Those in search of more secluded beaches can head for the seemingly endless strip of coconut palm–fringed strand at **Playa Grande**, a one-and-a-half-hour drive east from Puerto Plata. The drive takes you through the town of **Sosúa**, where German refugees from Nazi persecution set up dairies before tourism proved more profitable, and through **Cabarete**, a sleepy village that has turned into a windsurfer's paradise and a haven for French-Canadian visitors. The road is dotted with tourist accommodations and small villages where pig farmers gather at weekly markets. There are no facilities yet at Playa Grande, only a unisex outhouse cum changing room without even a door. Dominicans set up grills and cook fish and lobster and sell beer and piña coladas to the beach crowd here. However, development is on its way.

Samana Peninsula

The Samana peninsula on the island's north coast has long been sleepy backwater. The peninsula, with its mountainous spine, boasts some of the island's most lush scenery and exquisite beaches. Peaceful fishing villages like Las Terrenas add to its charm. Don't miss **Sanchez**, a 19th-century railroad terminus, now a sleepy hamlet of Victorian buildings.

The coastline here once provided a haven for smugglers and a home for resettled freedmen and escaped slaves from the United States. Today that past lives on in the English still spoken by some, complete with antebellum southernisms, and in foods like Johnny Cakes, a local specialty. In Las Terrenas, French-owned **Casa Paco** serves dishes like grilled goat and mousse of langostino, while **Diny** offers great drinks and Dominican specialties at moderate prices. Hotel choices are few and range from small hotels like the 20-room Las Terrenas Club, in the town of the same name, to the El Portillo Beach Club, an all-inclusive hotel. This year the opening of several world-class hostelries is sure to draw Samana peninsula reluctantly into tourism's 21st century.

USEFUL FACTS

What to Wear
Summer cruise–type clothing is de rigueur. However, the Spanish influence has imposed an air of formality on the island. Men are required to wear jackets at night in better restaurants, and women may want to bring something with an extra bit of flair. Shorts are fine in resort areas but are frowned upon in cities.

Getting In
American, Dominicana, and Continental fly to Santo Domingo and/or Puerto Plata from New York and Miami. Flights are also available from San Juan. American Eagle flies to the new airport at La Romana from San Juan, and

most Punta Cana resorts have charter flights to the Punta Cana International Airport included in their packages. Air Canada flies weekly from Toronto. There are no direct flights from London.

Most visitors to the Dominican Republic enter either at Santo Domingo's Las Americas Airport or, in the north, at Puerto Plata. Strangely, there are no regular flights from the capital to the north coast, and itineraries should be routed so you can visit one coast and then transfer (by convenient air-conditioned bus, car with driver, or rental car) to the other.

Tourist cards (see Entry Requirements), if necessary, should be purchased at a kiosk next to the tourism booth prior to getting in the immigration line, which moves more rapidly than expected. Baggage claim is daunting, but for a small tip someone will locate your luggage and carry it to customs, which for most travellers is perfunctory.

Entry Requirements
Citizens of the United States and Canada need only a tourist card, which costs U.S. $10 and is purchased at point of entry upon presentation of a passport (valid or expired), voter-registration card, or birth certificate. The limit of entry with a tourist card is 90 days, and the card must be presented upon departure. British subjects need a valid passport (entry visa is not necessary); entry is for 90 days. There is also a $10 departure tax, payable in U.S. dollars.

Local Time
The Dominican Republic is on eastern standard time year-round. This means that when the U.S. east coast moves its clocks forward an hour during daylight saving time, the Dominican Republic is no longer on the same time but is one hour behind.

Currency
The basic unit of currency is the Dominican peso. Its dollar-sign symbol can be confusing, so travellers should always double-check prices. The exchange rate fluctuates daily. Exchange establishments abound in most tourist areas, and hotels and many shops will accept foreign currency and traveller's checks—though some are reluctant to take Canadian money. As of this writing the rate of exchange was U.S. $1.00 to 12.55 pesos.

Electrical Current
Same as in the U.S. and Canada—110 volts AC, 60 cycles.

Getting Around
Any visitor with a valid foreign license or international driver's license may drive rental vehicles for up to 90 days. Driving is on the right. Roads are not well marked and a knowledge of Spanish is a must outside of cities. Taxis, unmetered, are relatively inexpensive and for most tourists are the preferred means of transportation in Santo Domingo.

Business Hours
Shops are open from 8:00 A.M. to noon and 2:00 to 6:00 P.M. Most banks are open from 8:00 A.M. to 2:30 P.M. Other businesses are usually open from 8:00 A.M. to 6:00 P.M., and government offices follow a 7:30-to-2:30 schedule. When in doubt, call ahead.

Festivals
All of Santo Domingo is transformed into a ballroom during the latter part of July as that city celebrates Merengue Week.

For Further Information
Tourism Promotion Council, Desiderio Arias, Bella Vista, Santo Domingo, Dominican Republic, W.I., Tel: (809) 535-7757; **in the U.S.**, Dominican Republic Tourist Information, Tel: (800) 752-1151.

ACCOMMODATIONS REFERENCE
The rate ranges given here, in U.S. dollars, are projections for fall 1992 through spring 1993, and span the lowest rates in the low season to the highest in the high season. Unless otherwise indicated, rates are for double rooms, double occupancy, and are subject to tax and service charges that amount to an additional 21 percent. As rates are subject to change, it's always wise to double-check before booking. The telephone area code (within the U.S. system) for the Dominican Republic is 809.

▶ **Casa de Campo.** P.O. Box 140, La Romana, Dominican Republic, W.I. Tel: 523-3333; Fax: 523-8548; in U.S., Tel: (800) 877-3643 or, in Florida, Tel: (305) 856-5405; Fax: (305) 858-4677. $130–$270.

▶ **Club Med Punta Cana.** Punta Cana, Alta Gracia, Dominican Republic, W.I. Tel: 687-2767; Fax: 687-2896; in U.S., (800) CLUB MED. $1,249–$1,470 per week including airfare, depending on gateway. Excluding airfare: $699–$980 per week, all meals and most activities included. (These rates are per person for double occupancy.)

▶ **Dorado Naco.** P.O. Box 162, Puerto Plata, Dominican Republic, W.I. Tel: 586-2019; Fax: 320-3608. $60–$110.

▶ **El Embajador.** 65 Avenida Sarasota, Santo Domingo, Dominican Republic, W.I. Tel: 221-2131; Fax: 532-4494; in U.S., (800) 457-0067. $85–$115.

▶ **Eurotel Playa Dorada.** P.O. Box 336, Puerto Plata, Dominican Republic, W.I. Tel: 586-3663 or 4333; Fax: 320-4858. $100–$270.

▶ **Gran Hotel Lina and Casino.** Avenida Maximo Gómez esquina 27 de Febrero, P.O. Box 1915, Santo Domingo, Dominican Republic, W.I. Tel: 689-5185; Fax: 686-5521. $60–$130.

▶ **Hostal Nicolás de Ovando.** 53 Calle Las Damas, Old Santo Domingo, Dominican Republic, W.I. Tel: 687-7181; Fax: 688-5170. $45–$55.

▶ **Jack Tar Village.** P.O. Box 368, Puerto Plata, Dominican Republic, W.I. Tel: in U.S, (800) 999-9182, (214) 586-3557, or (214) 891-9000; Fax: (214) 363-9825. $120–$130 per person, all inclusive.

▶ **Punta Cana Beach Resort.** P.O. Box 1083, Punta Cana, Dominican Republic, W.I. Tel: 688-4032; Fax: 687-8745. $125–$180, M.A.P. Rates include most land and water sports.

▶ **Ramada Renaissance Jaragua.** P.O. Box 769-2 Centro de los Heroes, Santo Domingo, Dominican Republic, W.I. Tel: 221-2222; Fax: 686-0503; in U.S. and Canada, (800) 228-9898. $80–$210.

▶ **Santo Domingo.** P.O. Box 2112, Santo Domingo, Dominican Republic, W.I. Tel: 221-7111; Fax: 535-4050; in U.S., Tel: (800) 877-3643 or, in Florida, (305) 856-5405; Fax: (305) 858-4677. $118–$155.

PUERTO RICO

By J. P. MacBean

J. P. MacBean's articles on travel, theater, food, and restaurants have appeared in Travel & Leisure, Horizon, Discovery, *and* Going Places *magazines and in the* New York Daily News *and other newspapers. He is the author of books on Puerto Rico and New York City.*

Puerto Rico (Rich Port) has been receiving visitors for five centuries—ever since 1493, when Christopher Columbus set foot on the island's west coast.

Ponce de León established Puerto Rico's first Spanish settlement (Caparra) in 1508, a foothold that was to remain firm for almost 400 years. Although the English made attempts to take the island—Sir Francis Drake failed miserably in 1595—it was not until 1897 that Luis Muñoz Rivera, the "George Washington of Puerto Rico," won from Spain the charter that gave the island autonomy. Shortly thereafter, as a result of the 1898–1899 Spanish-American War, Puerto Rico passed into U.S. hands. Today it enjoys commonwealth status, although there are movements advocating complete independence (unlikely) or statehood (a possibility in the near future).

Though it is the smallest of the Greater Antilles (after Cuba, Hispaniola, and Jamaica), Puerto Rico is by far the most affluent, diverse, sophisticated—and the most visited. Its capital, San Juan, is considered the hub and unofficial capital of the Caribbean, and its international airport and bustling harbor are centers both of tourism and business traffic. Those who have not visited the island

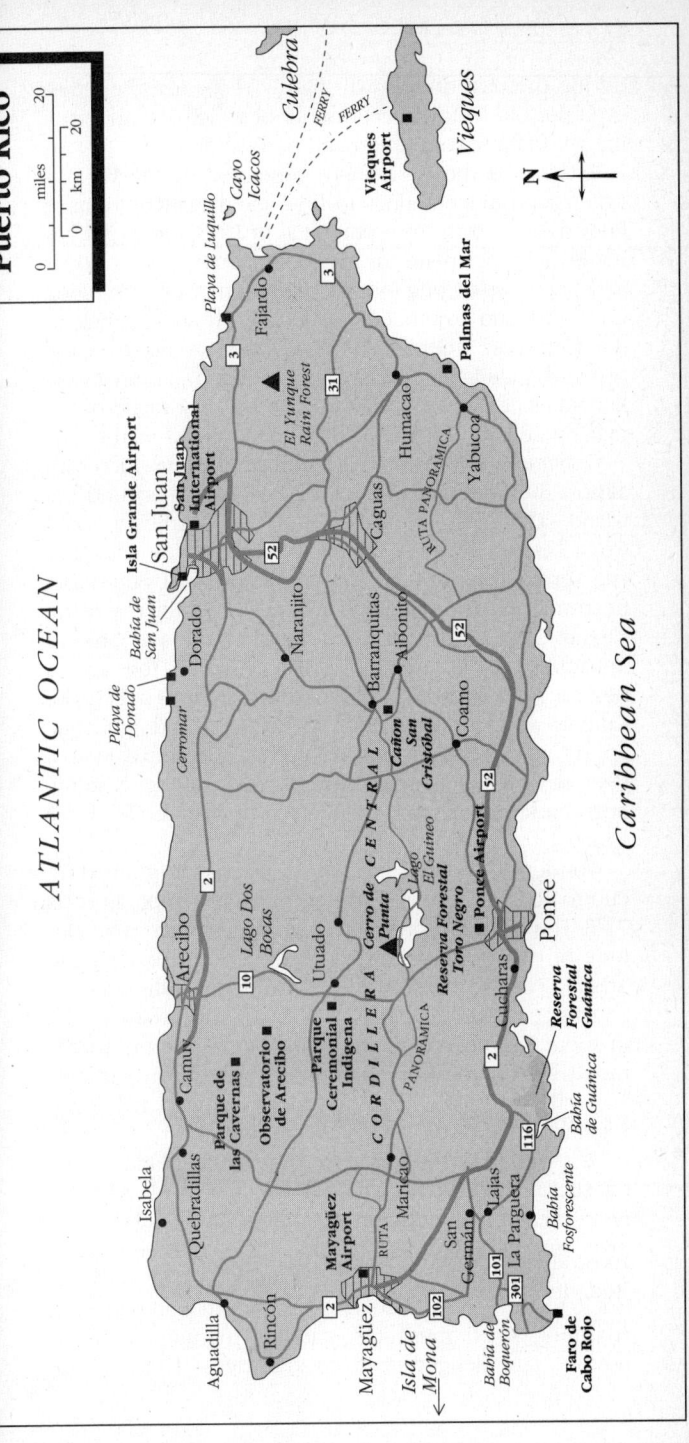

during the past decade will hardly recognize the cities, even the old historic sections, all of which are undergoing painstaking restoration and renovation.

Because of the excitement generated by the U.S.A.'s Columbus quincentennial in 1992 and the celebrations of Puerto Rico's own quincentennial in 1993, the island has made ambitious plans for the prolonged festivities. Roads and highways throughout the commonwealth are being improved and expanded—especially in and leading to the northwest, where Columbus landed (somewhere between Aguadilla and Añasco, near Rincón), an area now known as "Discovery Coast." Much is being made of the many wonders of this area, both natural and man-made.

Geography and nature have endowed Puerto Rico with almost 300 miles of fine, sandy beaches all around the island. The most popular are on the northeast "Gold Coast," especially those connected with the Condado and Isla Verde strips in San Juan, the resorts at Dorado and Cerromar, and the magnificent Playa de Luquillo east of the capital. The northwest coast beaches, in and around Aguadilla, Isabela, and Rincón, are considered the island's best for surfing; diving and snorkeling are tops in Fajardo, Culebra and Vieques islands, La Parguera, and Aguadilla. Sports include golf and tennis (on championship courses), deep-sea fishing (from charter boats), sailing, boating, horseback riding, and, of course, all manner of water sports.

Wonderful weather is almost taken for granted in Puerto Rico, where the average annual temperature is 77°F. The central mountain range, which reaches an altitude of over 4,000 feet, divides the coastal regions; the Atlantic (north) coast of the island is generally greener and more humid than the Caribbean (south) coast, which in spots resembles a desert. March and April are usually the driest months, but the thunderstorms of the summer and fall are usually brief (afternoon showers fall pretty regularly in the west, so plan accordingly).

Yet it would be rather sad to come to this island just for the sea and sun, dazzling though they may be. It is Puerto Rico's vitality—in addition to its diversity of culture, climate, and geography—that attracts the cultivated traveller as well as the seeker of fun and sun. There is Old (Viejo) San Juan, with its restored colonial architecture, charming small museums, national monuments, town houses, and delightful shops and cafés. There is the world-renowned **Casals Music Festival**, founded in 1957, and staged in San Juan every June. A thriving art colony commands international attention, and the commonwealth boasts two of the oldest theaters in the Western Hemisphere, the **Tapia** in Old San Juan and the **Yagüez** in Mayagüez, plus the recently restored 1940 Teatro La Perla in Ponce.

These theaters, "out on the island," as the Puerto Ricans refer to anything beyond the San Juan city limits, are just the beginning of attractions outside of the capital. In a 3,500-square-mile territory that includes mountain peaks, sandy beaches, a tropical rain forest, and vast underground caves lies the "other" Puerto Rico. Besides a wealth of natural beauty it offers *paradores* (country inns) located in settings ranging from coffee plantations and thermal springs to surfing beaches and beautifully restored little colonial towns; Indian ceremonial grounds; phosphorescent bays; and unspoiled offshore islands. In short, visitors to Puerto Rico find far more than a tropical resort: They find a miniature continent.

As in most Latin lands, Puerto Rico's pulse picks up after the sun goes down. In San Juan—in both the old and new sections—nightlife is centered in the big hotels, with their floor shows, discos, and casinos. Out on the island hotel nightlife is limited to the resorts at Dorado, Cerromar, Palmas del Mar, the Mayagüez Hilton, and to the *paradores,* where some kind of local entertainment may be provided on weekends. But there are many other forms of Puerto Rican entertainment—folk festivals, carnivals, crafts fairs, dances, concerts, and art exhibitions, celebrating the people and their roots.

Puerto Rico's population of 3.5 million, a third of which lives in the San Juan area, includes descendants of the Taino Indians (the island's original inhabitants) and the Spanish colonists, along with Africans, South and Central Americans, immigrants from other Caribbean islands, and, finally, North Americans. Although Spanish is the leading language, English is widely known and used, especially in the cities. Another 2.5 million Puerto Ricans live in the United States (most of them in the New York City area), and, as they shuttle back and forth to the mother island visiting friends and relatives, Puerto Rico becomes more Americanized every year. Nevertheless, the roots of native culture are deep and dominant. Island life moves to a very definite southern rhythm, and the stress of northern urban centers will probably remain a foreign malady, no matter how industrialized the commonwealth becomes.

Manners are warm and relaxed in Puerto Rico, and human contact is effortless, even unavoidable. Dignity, pride, family loyalty (especially love of children and respect for older people), proper behavior (the traditional Latin importance of the *La Bella Figura* concept)—all are virtues here.

There's a reason people have gravitated to Puerto Rico for 500 years. Visitors find what they're seeking here, whether it's action or atmosphere, history or vitality, solitude or the social life.

MAJOR INTEREST

Old San Juan
Forts: El Morro and San Cristóbal
La Fortaleza and Puerta de San Juan
Catedral de San Juan
Casa Blanca
Plaza San José: Iglesia de San José, Convento Dominicano, Museo de Pablo Casals, Casa de las Contrafuertes
The port area
Shopping and dining

New San Juan
The Condado Strip/Isla Verde (casinos, nightlife, dining, shopping, beaches, deep-sea fishing, water sports)

Out on the Island
El Yunque rain forest
Ponce: cathedral, Parque de Bombas, museum
San Germán: churches
Bahía Fosforescente (Phosphorescent Bay)
Nature preserves: Guánica and Toro Negro
Mayagüez: central square, theater, gardens, and zoo
Faro de Cabo Rojo (lighthouse)
Observatorio de Arecibo (Arecibo Observatory)
Parque de las Cavernas (Río Camuy caves)
Parque Ceremonial Indígena (Caguana Indian Ceremonial Park)
Cañon San Cristóbal
Ruta Panoramica
Beaches, water sports
Resorts and paradores

The Offshore Islands
Natural beauty
Crowd-free beaches
Peace and quiet

Because no one could ever cover Puerto Rico's leading sights in one visit (as you can in, say, Barbados or Curaçao), you should probably first decide what type of vacation you wish to have and where you would like to establish your base of operations. If a city visit is your preference, you will probably decide upon a stay in San Juan's lively beachfront areas: Puerta de Tierra, Condado, or Isla Verde, where the prime hotels, casinos, discos, shops, restaurants, and night spots are situated. If you want to be near the action, yet submerge yourself in the culture, charm, and history of old Puerto Rico, Old San Juan is the perfect spot. Those to whom golf, tennis, and water sports are the ingredients of an ideal vacation in the sun regard the self-contained resorts of Dorado, Cerromar, and Palmas del Mar as tailor-made. And if your dream is to "get away from it all"—yet not be *too* far away from civilization and its pleasures—one of Puerto Rico's *paradores,* preferably in the mountains or overlooking the coast, would do the trick, as would a stay on one of the offshore islands, Culebra and Vieques, with their small inns and guest houses.

Although it is possible to make day trips from San Juan to many of Puerto Rico's "out on the island" attractions, another option is to settle for a few days in one spot—such as Ponce, Mayagüez, Quebradillas, Jayuya, or Fajardo—and make forays to nearby sights from that home base.

We begin our coverage of these and other areas with Old San Juan.

OLD SAN JUAN

The old section of the city of San Juan (Saint John) is contained within a long peninsula that pokes out into the Atlantic Ocean, separated from the mainland by the Bahía de San Juan and the Laguna de San José. As you approach by air, your first glimpse of the city is the triangular headland of tiny Viejo (Old) San Juan, capped by the enormous fortress of El Morro. The small, congested old quarter of the city is a historic landmark district, the

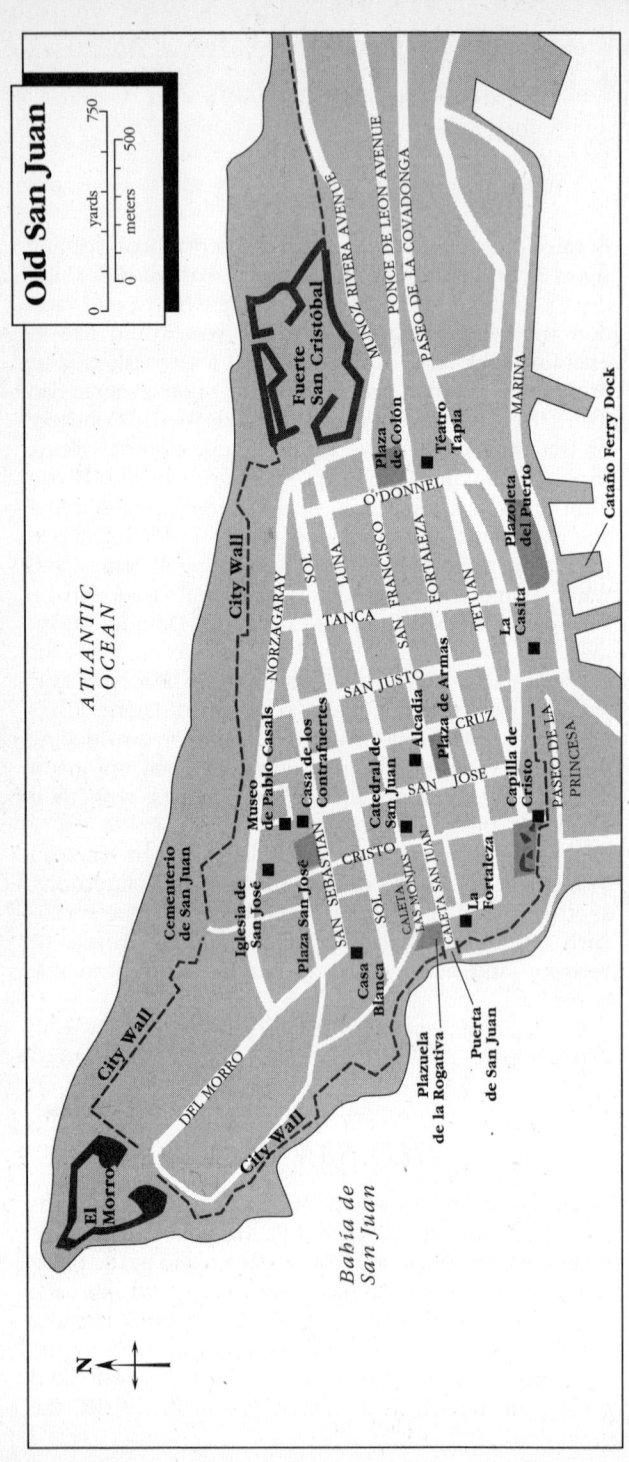

Old San Juan

0 yards 750
0 meters 500

ATLANTIC OCEAN

Bahía de San Juan

N

El Morro

City Wall

DEL MORRO

City Wall

Cementerio de San Juan

City Wall

Museo de Pablo Casals

Casa de los Contrafuertes

Iglesia de San José

Plaza San José

SAN SEBASTIAN

Casa Blanca

SOL

CRISTO

NORZAGARAY

Catedral de San Juan

SAN JUSTO

TANCA

SOL

LUNA

O'DONNEL

SAN FRANCISCO

FORTALEZA

Plaza de Colón

Téatro Tapia

MUÑOZ RIVERA AVENUE

PONCE DE LEON AVENUE

PASEO DE LA COVADONGA

MARINA

Plazoleta del Puerto

Cataño Ferry Dock

TETUAN

La Casita

FORTALEZA

SAN

CRUZ

Plaza de Armas

Alcaldía

JOSE

Capilla de Cristo

PASEO DE LA PRINCESA

CALETA SAN JUAN

LAS MONJAS

CALETA DE LAS MONJAS

La Fortaleza

Puerta de San Juan

Plazuela de la Rogativa

Fuerte San Cristóbal

second-oldest European settlement in the New World (after Santo Domingo in the Dominican Republic).

This compact area of narrow cobblestone streets—you can easily walk its length or width in 10 or 15 minutes—is lined with two- and three-story colonial town houses and their wrought-iron-gated passageways. (Legend has it that the brick-shaped cobblestones were once used as ballast in ships, though the tale cannot be proved. The bluish color of the stones comes from the slag used in making the bricks.) The old quarter's colorful gardens, quaint shops, art galleries, cafés, bars and restaurants, small parks, churches, and historic sites fill a seven-square-block district, which is laid out in a grid plan. Traffic is discouraged—especially on weekends, when access is limited—and no high rises or modernized exteriors are permitted.

The district has been undergoing a painstaking restoration of its town houses and public buildings, including the conversion of a 17th-century mansion into Casa San José, the first new hotel in Old San Juan in years (discussed below). Near plaza de San José and below El Morro fortress, a large area is being rehabilitated for the celebration of the Columbus quincentennial; when completed (finishing touches are expected early this year), there will be the renewed Cuartel de Ballajá (military barracks), the plaza del Quinto Centenario (Quincentennial Square), a museum of the Americas (celebrating the entire Western Hemisphere, Alaska to Antarctica), the restored Asilo de Beneficiencia (a former welfare home and now the new headquarters of the Institute of Puerto Rican Culture), and a vast underground parking garage (sorely needed to control the old city's traffic).

Before you begin exploring the old quarter, arm yourself with a copy of *Qué Pasa*, an invaluable guide to the pleasures of Puerto Rico and to finding your way around San Juan and the rest of the island. This seasonal publication by the Tourism Company is a font of information, including listings of cultural events, festivals, restaurants, hotels, and tour and charter companies. Another helpful source for local happenings is the Thursday edition of the *San Juan Star*. Ideally, one day in Old San Juan should be spent enjoying the sights and another shopping or browsing.

A Walking Tour
of Old San Juan

Begin your exploration of the old quarter at its highest point, **El Morro** (The Headland). One of the most important historical monuments in Puerto Rico, Fuerte San Felipe del Morro is an intimidating fortress that juts into the Atlantic from a rocky promontory on the old city's northwest tip. Rising more than 140 feet and covering more than 200 acres, El Morro's wide decks and battlements with cannon emplacements surround an inner core that holds munitions rooms, barracks, prisons, and assembly areas. Built in stages by the Spanish between 1540 and 1783 to protect the harbor and guard the city from foreign invasion, El Morro was remarkably successful in repelling major attacks by both the British and the Dutch. It fell only twice—first in 1598 to the earl of Cumberland, whose victory lasted only until dysentery drove him from the fortress, and finally to the Americans in 1898.

Leaving El Morro, you face wide sloping fields that lead down to the old city, grounds enjoyed by San Juañeros and visitors alike for strolling, picnics, and other frivolities. To the right of the recently restored Escuela de Artes Plásticas (School of Fine Arts), at the bottom of the hill, a path skirts the Bahía de San Juan and leads you past Casa Blanca. However, there will be no access from this path to the historic structure (discussed below) until the construction projects are completed. Continue instead to **plazuela de la Rogativa** (small plaza of the religious procession), dedicated to the bishop and a group of women who, by singing and carrying torches, supposedly frightened away British troops, who mistook them for a marching army. From this park high above the city walls you can enjoy one of the finest views in all Puerto Rico. On your left is the 17th-century **Puerta de San Juan**, the last remaining gate of six in the old sandstone walls (*las murallas*). On your way to the gate take time to stop at the **Museo Felisa Rincón de Gautier** at 51 caleta San Juan; the town house of the former mayor contains Doña Felisa's collection of fans.

The 16th-century fortress that rises beyond the gate is **La Fortaleza**, which once served as the official residence of the Spanish colony's governors and now serves as the

Western Hemisphere's oldest executive mansion still to be used for that purpose. Guided tours of the old fortifications (weekdays except holidays, in Spanish and English) take you to the dark prison cells, as well as through the mansion's state rooms and formal gardens where guests are entertained. Crystal chandeliers, gilded mirrors, stairways of polished West Indian mahogany, floors paved with Genoan marble and Moorish tile, and a banquet hall furnished with Chippendale and Hepplewhite antiques embellish this gleaming white palace. Go early, if possible, to avoid hordes of schoolchildren and cruise-ship passengers.

Two of Viejo San Juan's most beautiful small streets, **caleta las Monjas** and **caleta San Juan**, lined with pastel-colored colonial town houses, lead out of plazuela de la Rogativa. Both end at the Catedral de San Juan a block away. (If you take caleta las Monjas to the cathedral you will pass by the only two "step streets"—*escalinatas*—in the old city.) The elaborate Gothic edifice of the **Catedral de San Juan** dates from the 19th century, although other religious structures on the spot date back to the early 1500s. The remains of Ponce de León, which for centuries lay in the nearby church of San José, were moved here in 1913.

Behind the cathedral is the 16th-century **plaza de Armas**, the central square in Viejo San Juan, named for the military drills formerly held here. The spacious plaza embraces a fountain with four statues (representing the seasons) and a bandstand, and is faced on the north side by the restored 1789 **Alcadía** (City Hall), which contains a tourist information center and an arts gallery.

Heading south from the cathedral, back toward the Bahía de San Juan, you reach the **Capilla de Cristo**, a small indoor/outdoor chapel. On one side of the chapel is the small Parque de las Palomas, which, as its name implies, is carpeted with pigeons (and tourists posing with them). On the chapel's other side are two of Puerto Rico's most important small museums, the **Fine Arts Museum** and the **Casa del Libro**. (Both are currently closed and no opening dates have been announced.) The former features occasional special exhibits of prints, paintings, sculpture, and photographs. The latter, which is of exceptional interest, is devoted to the art of printing and bookmaking. It houses an outstanding collection of incunabula, two cedulas signed by Ferdinand and Isabella mentioning Puerto Rico, and the first map showing the island. Tel: 723-0354.

Proceeding north from the cathedral up calle Cristo and then left (or west) on calle San Sebastián is the best way to reach **Casa Blanca** while construction continues. Puerto Rico's "White House" was built in the early 16th century for Juan Ponce de León but was never occupied by him; according to legend he was wounded in Florida searching for the Fountain of Youth and died in Cuba before making it back home. Casa Blanca remained in his family for more than 250 years, after which it served as a residence for Spanish and then U.S. military commanders.

Today the restored building holds two **museums**. The first floor represents family life in the 16th and 17th centuries and includes a weapons room with dungeon (Casa Blanca was also part of the city's fortifications), a colonial kitchen, and a "throne room" with 16th-century armchairs for use by visiting royalty.

Upstairs you'll find the **Taino Indian Museum** (memorabilia of Puerto Rico's first inhabitants), with its model of a Taino village and several odd-looking *cemíes* (godlike idols carved from stone and shaped like two-headed hammers). A map shows the extent of Taino settlements in 1508 Borinquén, Puerto Rico's Taino name, and a model recreates the Taino ceremonial park at Caguana (see The Northwest, below). In addition, the second floor features special exhibits such as the recent Christopher Columbus biographic/historic display and a photo exhibit on indigenous cultures in South American countries. To the right and left of Casa Blanca are gardens and long reflecting pools with fountains and benches for relaxing.

A short walk northeast of Casa Blanca (on calle San Sebastián) will bring you to plaza San José, with its statue of founding father Juan Ponce de León, shipmate of Columbus; the statue was forged from British cannon captured during a failed attack in 1797. At his back the **Iglesia de San José** offers a cool refuge from the sun. This church has a sparely adorned look; its soaring Gothic arches (patterned after Spanish churches of the 16th century), white walls, and red-tile floors are accented by an altar covered in gold leaf, a mid-16th-century crucifix, and the Stations of the Cross in blue and white tiles. Adjoining the church is the handsome, early-16th-century **Convento Dominicano**, now the headquarters of the Instituto de Cultura Puertorriqueña. Arcaded galleries surround the two-story convent's interior cloister, where cultural events are held frequently; the galleries themselves hold art exhibits on occasion.

Across from the church is the previously mentioned underground parking garage, which is currently under construction. To the right (or east) of the church is the **Museo de Pablo Casals** (Tel: 723-9185), a two-story town house celebrating the life and art of the founder of Puerto Rico's annual Casals Festival (in June). Here you'll find memorabilia of the master musician, including photographs, music manuscripts, videotapes and recordings (available for your enjoyment), his cello, and a smattering of awards received during his long life. Casals left his native Spain in 1936, protesting the regime of Francisco Franco; in 1956 the cellist moved to Puerto Rico, his mother's birthplace, where he lived until his death in 1973. Also nearby is the **Casa de las Contrafuertes** (House of Buttresses), said to be the oldest domicile in Viejo San Juan. It contains two museums: the **Museo del Grabado Latinoamericano** on the second floor and the reproduction of a 19th-century drugstore on the first. The upstairs museum recently exhibited the works of such noted photographers as Sandra Reus, Nitza Luna, Victor Vázquez, and Hector Mendez Caratini. Tel: 724-5949.

To the east (with the ocean at your left) rises the impressive **Fuerte San Cristóbal**, built in the late 18th century to supplement El Morro's defenses and to protect against inland attack. The formidable fort consists of a main structure and five separate battlements (connected by tunnels and dry moats), looming 150 feet above the sea and covering 27 acres. From these grounds you can look down on La Perla, the ramshackle community of wood and tin shanties, nestled on the beach between the sea wall and the ocean. Oscar Lewis vividly depicted La Perla in his 1965 book, *La Vida.*

Plaza de Colón, southwest of the fort, contains, as you'd expect, a statue of Columbus on a pedestal, newly refurbished for the 500th anniversary of his discovery.

A fine way to end a walking tour of Old San Juan is to stroll along the waterfront esplanade of San Juan's bay-side port, the most active in the Caribbean. An ongoing expansion and renovation project has turned a once seedy, rowdy, and disreputable area into a spacious promenade, the **Paseo de la Princesa**, with a municipal crafts center, fountains, and refreshment kiosks. Plans for the waterfront project include a 230-room Wyndham Hotel and residential condominiums. Giant cruise ships—sometimes eight at a time on weekends—line up at the piers like whales at feeding time, and across the waterfront drive new restaurants and shops have opened. Of special interest is the **plazoleta del Puerto**, a courtyard filled with shops and boutiques selling fashions, local crafts and ceramics, art works (including antique and modern *santos,* described below), and souvenirs.

La Casita, a "little house" information center near Pier One along the waterfront, provides literature on the area's sights and services.

Before you leave the port area, take advantage of one of the world's most reasonable and scenic cruises. A ride on the ferry across the Bahía de San Juan to Cataño and back (a dime each way) is essential, not only to enjoy the sweeping views and sea breezes but also to watch the other passengers. Cataño, an industrial/residential area, is noted chiefly as the site of the Bacardi Rum Plant, which offers guided tours of the distillery, the bottling plant, and a museum that traces the history of the corporation.

Staying in
Old San Juan

With the opening in December 1991 of **Casa San José**, 159 calle San José, Old San Juan gained its first new hotel in almost 30 years. This small (only ten rooms and suites) inn occupies an impressive 17th-century town house said to be one of the oldest structures in the old city. All rooms and suites on the three floors open up on an interior patio with a fountain. The rooms are furnished with handwoven folk rugs and plush, four-poster beds that reach almost to the rustic beamed ceilings; watercolor landscapes and 19th-century prints decorate the walls. Breakfast is the only meal served at San José. Next door, and running the entire length of the mansion's second floor, is the Grand Salon, overlooking the street, where drinks are served in the early evening. Staying in Casa San José is like being a guest in a fine private home only steps away from everything.

Another lodging option in the heart of Old San Juan is the much larger (100-room) **Gran Hotel El Convento**, down the street from Casa San José at the corner of Cristo and Monjas. Although not as polished or well run as it used to be (there is talk of a takeover and subsequent renovation), El Convento offers a unique experience. Formed from a 17th-century Carmelite convent and facing a small park with ancient trees, flower beds, and inviting benches, it wins the favor of cruise-ship guests docking in the nearby harbor. All the rooms open onto galleries surrounding an inner courtyard that was once the convent's cloister. Today the atrium contains the hotel's restaurant and small swimming pool. Although the hotel has no beach, transportation to one along the Condado Strip is provided daily.

The **Gallery Inn**, in an 18th-century house at 204–206 Norzagaray, overlooking the sea, offers six rooms and suites built around a lush courtyard. The house is home to Jan D'Esopo and her Galería San Juan (for more detail, see Shops and Galleries, below).

Dining in Old San Juan

Because San Juan is an international city you will find all of the world's major cuisines. A recent explosion of new restaurants—serving Japanese, Mexican, Greek, and German food—has made the city even more of a culinary capital. Naturally, however, you'll want to sample local specialties, which reflect the island's four major influences: Spanish, Latin American, African, and Indian. Pork (especially succulent roast pig, *lechón asado*) and chicken are the popular meats, and fish is plentiful in coastal regions. Beans, rice, and bananas (including plantains, which are fried, baked, mashed, and worked into numerous pastries) provide the ubiquitous side dishes, and fruits (pineapples, oranges, limes, grapefruit, coconuts, papayas, guavas, and avocados) are put to a thousand uses. A favorite staple is *mofongo,* in its most basic form mashed plaintains with pork, lard, crackling, and garlic, but creative variations on the theme abound.

Two oft-used, highly seasoned marinade mixtures found in many dishes are *sofritó* (garlic, onion, peppers, tomatoes, coriander, and lard or annatto oil from the native achiote seed) and *adobo* (garlic, salt, pepper, spices, oil, and lemon). Flan and *natilla* (a vanilla cream) are the most popular desserts, along with guava shells or guava paste and cream cheese. Puerto Rican coffee is strong and aromatic; if you ask for Spanish coffee you'll get it laced with liquor and topped with whipped cream.

If you are a newcomer to Puerto Rican cuisine, here are a few dishes to get you started. Roast suckling pig, as mentioned, is a must, as is *asopao* (a wet rice stew, redolent with flavors and spices), which can be made with seafood, chicken, beef, pork, or veal. Dried salt cod, a Friday specialty, is prepared *en casserole* with sliced potatoes, pimentos, peas, garlic, onion, and herbs. Rice and beans (the beans—black and delicious—are spooned *over* the rice) provide the perfect accompaniment to the cod. Key lime pie, made with the local small, thin-skinned, yellow limes, and coconut-pumpkin pudding make sumptuous departures from the usual flan. Spanish wines and local beer (ask for Medalla) are your best bets in Puerto Rico.

Among the most romantic and atmospheric restaurants in the Viejo San Juan area is the rather sizable **La Zaragozana** (Tel: 723-5103), at 356 San Francisco; it is somewhat formal but certainly not stuffy, and service is attentive and unobtrusive (try the seafood asopao). **El Patio de Sam** (Tel: 723-1149), opposite the Iglesia de San José at 102 San Sebastián, is a bar/restaurant/local hangout that looks as if it's been around forever. Bogie and Bacall would have loved this place (indeed, it seems as if they just left), and you should go at least for a beer or piña colada at the bar. Next door to Sam's, at number 104, is **El Boquerón** (Tel: 721-3942), a Spanish restaurant (open for dinner) serving such specialties as shrimp in garlic sauce, fried squid, and fresh goat's milk cheese. Next in line comes **Amadeus** (Tel: 722-8635), which serves *nuevo* Puerto Rican cuisine (olive oil instead of lard, and more fish and vegetables than meat) amidst sleek, modern decor at number 106. **La Mallorquina**, 207 San Justo, possibly the oldest restaurant in Puerto Rico (1848 is the date on the plaque), is a bit shabby these days, but its authenticity is unquestioned; go for lunch and stick to soups, salads, or one of the house asopaos. Tel: 722-3261.

The restaurant currently considered the best in the old city is **Il Perugino**, located in a small shopping arcade (Gucci and Benetton are here) at 202 calle Cristo; try one of the fresh northern Italian pastas followed by a shrimp or fish entrée. Tel: 722-5481. Another "in" place—this one more informal, more fun, and less expensive—is **Bistro Gambaro**, down a long entranceway at 320 calle Fortaleza. The waiters, young bilingual students, give you your choice of seating in the open-air patio, bar, or the area in between; specialties include pumpkin-plantain soup, chicken breast in mint sauce, and apple crisp; Tel: 724-4592. After dinner drop by **Café Violeta**—a dark, romantic, plant-filled bar and patio at 56 calle Fortaleza—

for a nightcap and some soulful guitar (weekends only);
Tel: 723-6804.

On the corner of calle San Sebastián and calle Cristo is
a lively bar called **el pub en los balcones**, whose rooms,
doors, sidewalks, and upstairs balconies are filled with a
young crowd in the evening.

Shops and Galleries
in Old San Juan

Over the past few decades Puerto Rico has developed
into a thriving art colony whose galleries and exhibitions
represent not only local artists but many from throughout
Latin America. Dozens of galleries are found in Old San
Juan, with satellite shops in the major Condado and Isla
Verde hotels. The Biennale of Latin American Art, one of
the major events in the Caribbean art world, is held here;
the next will take place February 26 to May 30 of this year
at El Arsenal.

Calle Cristo is a prime street for gallery hopping, especially for **Galería Palomas** and **Galería Botello**, two of the
most notable. Botello sells original *santos,* those small,
hand-carved wooden religious figures that are now such
sought-after collector's items. But don't overlook calle
San José, from plaza San José down to plaza de Armas.
Here you will find, among others, **Fenn Gallery**, at number 58, with colorful oils, pastels, and prints of Old San
Juan scenes by artists such as David D. Howlett; **Galería
Coabey** (Tel: 723-1018), at number 101, which recently
exhibited the still-life oils of Félix Rodríguez Báez; **El
Taller de Lyzette** (Tel: 722-7831) across the street, and
actually two galleries: one for prints and painted whiskey
bottles, the other for paintings; **Corinne Timsett** (Tel:
724-1039), next door at number 100, featuring marble
sculptures, prints, and pastels of San Juan scenes; and the
Galería San Juan Bautista in the City Hall on plaza de
Armas, which has staged an exhibit of fanciful Puerto
Rican scenes in acrylics by Santurce artist Pablo Romero.

Antiques—furniture, mirrors, porcelains, silver, china,
candlesticks, and jewelry, including items from Old San
Juan houses and collections—are available from **El Alca-
zar Galería Antiquedados**, 103 calle San José, and from
Antiques, at the northwest corner of calle San José and
calle Sol.

Galería San Juan, 204–206 Norzagaray (overlooking the sea, near the fort of San Cristóbal), provides a chance to see first-rate modern art in an 18th-century setting. This 1750 house (and inn, see Staying in Old San Juan, above) is home to owner Jan D'Esopo, as well as a gallery for her own work and that of others. The gallery does not keep regular hours, so Tel: 722-1808, 725-3829, or 723-6515 for an appointment. With advance notice special lunches and dinners can be arranged in rooms overlooking the patio.

Drop by **The Butterfly People Gallery**, upstairs at 152 Fortaleza, to see thousands of butterflies mounted in Plexiglass cases. The place also serves a light lunch on a balcony overlooking its inner courtyard. For crafts, including top-notch modern art works and *santos,* don't miss **Puerto Rican Arts and Crafts** at 204 Fortaleza. Books in both Spanish and English are sold at the **Book Store**, 255–257 San José. Local spices for those Puerto Rican recipes you plan to try await you at **Spicy Caribbee**, 202 calle Cristo.

For discount shopping in the old quarter try **Ralph Lauren Polo Factory Outlet**, on Cristo just below the cathedral, or the **London Fog** boutique, catercorner. **N. Barquet** and **Gastón Bared**, both on pedestrians-only Fortaleza, are two of San Juan's largest and finest jewelry stores, and each also offers china, crystal, porcelain, and other gift items.

NEW SAN JUAN

For the visitor, New San Juan means the chic beachfront areas of Condado and Isla Verde with their large, seaside hotels and rows of small, modest guest houses along the side streets. The Condado Strip is lined with fashionable shops and boutiques, and a number of the city's finest restaurants, casinos, and discos are found here and in nearby Miramar, many of them in the hotels.

As you leave Old San Juan on your way to Condado, Miramar, or Isla Verde, you will come to the large and fashionable **Caribe Hilton International**, ensconced on its own spit of land (17 acres)—which includes old Fuerte (Fort) San Jerónimo—in **Puerta de Tierra**. Even if you don't stay here, do tour this paradise within a paradise. Its largest restaurant, **Il Giardino Rotisserie** (Tel: 721-0303), has long been considered one of Puerto

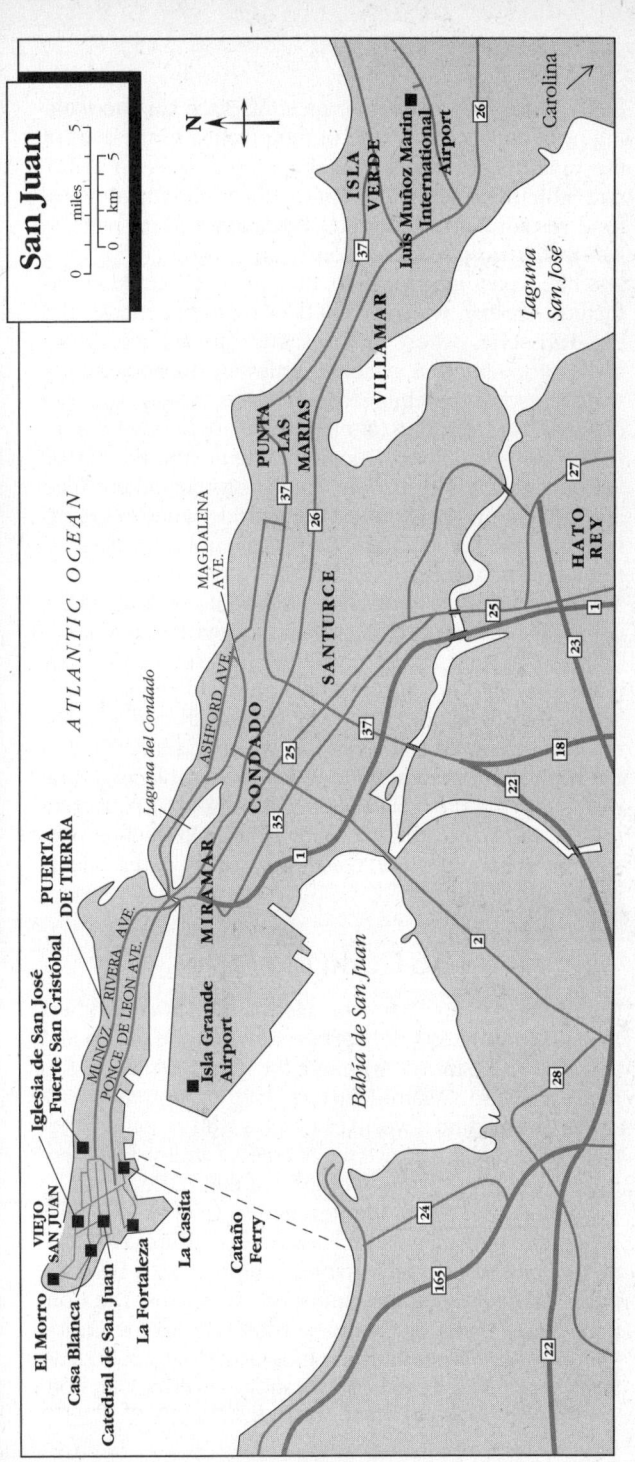

Rico's finest, and its popular meeting-place bar overlooking pool and ocean is one of the putative birthplaces of the piña colada. There is a shopping arcade, an elaborate athletic program and sports department, and a seafood restaurant, **El Batey del Pescador**. And despite the fact that it hosts package tours, the Caribe Hilton feels less like a package-tour hotel than many. Other additions include **Caribar**, which offers dancing to live music, and the **Patisserie**, where pastries and fanciful ice cream dishes are served. A concrete walkway, overlooking the wide crescent beach, leads to a reef where you can observe fish frolicking (at night there are floodlights).

The ship-shaped Art Deco building next to the Caribe Hilton is the old Normandie Hotel, restored and unveiled as the **Radisson Normandie**. Originally designed in 1939 to resemble the French ocean liner, the repolished architectural gem now contains 180 rooms, most of them suites. The hotel has a very small elevated pool overlooking the ocean, a small crescent beach, and its own restaurant.

If you happen to be travelling on business, you may choose to stay in **Miramar**, a fashionable inland area across the Laguna del Condado, with small, well-run hotels (one example is the Clarion, which has a casino and the rooftop restaurant, Windows of the Caribbean). Miramar is also the site of a local favorite, **Augusto's** restaurant (Tel: 721-7400) in the Excelsior Hotel. Although expensive at night, this fine restaurant serves a reasonably priced lunch buffet.

The Condado Strip

Cross the Puenta Los Dos Hermanos (Two Brothers Bridge) from Puerta de Tierra and the Caribe Hilton and you are on Ashford Avenue—the Condado Strip, San Juan's answer to Miami Beach.

Here you'll find a world of glitz (as well as some rather tacky stretches) on an avenue of hotels standing like sentinels along the Atlantic Ocean shoreline. The Condado Plaza Hotel & Casino, the Regency, La Concha, Condado Beach, and the Ambassador Plaza Hotel—all are very modern, reliable, and comfortable, equipped with beaches, pools, shops, restaurants, and sports programs. The **Condado Plaza Hotel & Casino**, second only to the Caribe Hilton in size, is certainly the most active of the Condado Strip hotels, and its strategic location—overlooking both sea and lagoon—is a definite advantage. It also contains one of the island's largest casinos, a lively disco (Isadora's), three pools, a well-equipped health club and sports program, and a lobby filled with shops and crafts boutiques.

A classical Spanish beauty painted peaches and cream, the **Condado Beach Hotel** (built by Cornelius Vanderbilt in 1919 and lovingly preserved and restored) seems to reflect another, more graceful, era. Swimmers can choose between the secluded third-floor pool, with its flowering plants and waterfall, and the palm-fringed beach, where experts give scuba and snorkeling lessons. The lobby, its double staircase curving to the second-floor ballroom, presents a chic cocktail lounge and the hotel's restaurant, **El Gobernador**, overlooking the ocean. Not surprisingly, it is the Condado Beach to which Puerto Rico's wealthy citizens often come for their charity balls, anniversary celebrations, and bridal receptions.

Among and between the big hotels are some of San Juan's most notable shops and restaurants—plus a smattering of small guest houses, of which **El Canario Inn** is the gem. The inn, which was completely renovated in 1988, resembles a large Condado town house of Spanish-influenced architecture. A friendly, extremely popular place with 25 rooms and a devoted following, it's often fully booked months ahead, especially over holidays and peak periods. Although not directly on the beach, the inn is only one and a half blocks away from the ocean, and has a small backyard pool and sundeck. **El Canario by the Sea**, near the inn at 4 Condado, also has 25 rooms, but it is not as personal or personable as its more attractive cousin. Although the rooms are small and the services minimal, it is a clean, comfortable, well-run bed-and-breakfast stop, with complimentary morning fare of fresh baked goods, coffee, and juice.

For shopping **Level 1**, at 1004 Ashford, features the best in women's fashions, and **Nono Maldonado**, at number 1051, has the latest in both men's and women's wear. Courrèges, Ungaro, and Valentino designs can all be found at **Bugatti (Paris)**, 1126 Ashford. A fine book store, **Bell, Book, and Candle**, at 102 De Diego in the Santurce section (south of Condado), is open every day; it stocks books in both Spanish and English and even sells the *New York Times*. (It also happens to be right next door to a 24-hour Pueblo supermarket.) Newcomers on the Condado Strip include the **Cartier** boutique at 105 Ashford and

Benissimo, at number 884, a most attractive gift shop specializing in both imported and local china, pottery, and ceramics.

You'll find most of Condado's better restaurants in the large hotels: El Gobernador (the Condado Beach), Lotus Flower and Capriccio (the Condado Plaza), and the Greenhouse (an airy, informal, plant-filled restaurant in the Dutch Inn & Towers). By far the most unusual and ambitious restaurant to open recently in the Condado area is **Ramiro's,** 1106 Magdalena Avenue; Tel: 721-9049 or 9056. The setting is a red-tiled Spanish-style house just south of Ashford Avenue. Here, in softly lit plush rooms trimmed with dark wood, a young culinary wizard named Jesús Ramiro produces Italian and Spanish specialties; he calls his work "creative cuisine." The dishes are served on fanciful ceramic platters resembling palettes, and some courses look as if they had been painted or sculpted: succulent lamb-stuffed ravioli in Chardonnay sauce; halibut filet in a sea of tamarind sauce; and crumb-encrusted "fried ice cream" in a swirling moat of strawberry sauce, crème anglais, and whipped cream.

One of the finest introductions to the *cocina criolla* (native Puerto Rican cuisine) is the new and warmly welcoming **Criollísimo** (Tel: 767-3343) at 300 avenida Franklin Delano Roosevelt (Route 23), in the Hato Rey section (Hato Rey is south of Santurce, below the estuary of the Laguna de San José). This simple restaurant is owned by Adrian Marrero, who will eagerly describe the menu's offerings. For dessert try the house specialty: *delicados de limón* (a truly lemony tart). For a firsthand look at the ingredients of *cocina criolla* visit the public marketplaces in the districts of Santurce and Río Piedras (south of Hato Rey); directions and traffic can be tricky, so take a taxi or get exact directions from the Tourism Company; Tel: 791-1014 or 722-1709.

An old standby and one of a chain of restaurants, **The Chart House** is located in a magnificent old home replete with shaded verandahs, manicured lawns, gardens, and even a treehouse. The restaurant, known for its steaks, serves an early-bird dinner of good value; Tel: 728-0110. Other eateries to look for in Condado include **Panache,** 1127 Seaview, for light lunches and dinners overlooking the sea; **Kasalta** (Tel: 727-7340), 1966 McCleary, for cholesterol-bomb sandwiches and snacks; and, in Santurce, **La Casita Blanca,** 351 Tapia Street, for a nice country atmosphere (Tel: 726-5501).

Isla Verde

Isla Verde, the beachfront strip beyond Condado near the airport, has experienced such a renaissance in the past few years that it is giving the Condado Strip fierce competition. The **El San Juan Hotel & Casino** and the **Sands Hotel & Casino**—both renovated from top-to-bottom and now transformed into posh self-contained resorts—have joined the well-established **ESJ Towers** and **Empress Oceanfront Hotel** to create a new gold coast. A long crescent beach joins all of the hotels, and the calm waters here, even on breezy days, make for delightful swimming.

Although next-door neighbors, the El San Juan and the Sands—both large properties offering attractive package plans—are quite different in atmosphere. The El San Juan's grounds and gardens resemble a tropical paradise; within the hotel's dark interior crystal chandeliers cast a soft glow on the elaborately carved mahogany ceiling and paneling; 24-hour security enables parents to give their children the run of the place; and the staff, inspired perhaps by a popular incentive program, could not be friendlier or more courteous. Five restaurants serve cuisines ranging from *criolla* to Continental, with the honors for atmosphere going to **Back Street Hong Kong**, the excellent Chinese restaurant situated in a setting that was part of the last New York World's Fair.

The grounds at the Sands are also well kept, but not nearly as spectacular as the El San Juan's, and the Sands' public rooms are bright and cheery rather than awe-inspiring. Both of these renovated hotels draw a varied but basically energetic clientele of families, young marrieds, and jazzy singles, while the quieter, more contemplative crowd gravitates toward the ESJ Towers or the much smaller Empress, with its inviting deck bar overhanging the sea.

Popular activities offered to guests of the Condado and Isla Verde hotels are deep-sea fishing trips (or you can arrange your own excursion through an outfit like that of Mike Benítez at the Club Náutico de San Juan at the marina in Miramar; Tel: 723-2292 or 724-6265), year-round thoroughbred horse racing at **El Comandante Racetrack** (Tel: 724-6060) in the Carolina area, southeast of the Laguna de San José (tours leave from all hotels), or the full spectrum of water sports, including scuba diving, snorkeling, windsurfing, water skiing, boating, and sailing (contact Mike Benítez, listed above, or Carib Aquatic Adventures, San Juan Bay Marina, Miramar; Tel: 724-1882, or 765-7444 in the evening).

THE RESORTS

These self-contained vacation areas are ideally suited for those whose main interests are sports (particularly golf and tennis) and quiet, away-from-it-all relaxation.

The elegant and sedate **Hyatt Dorado Beach**, on a former seaside grapefruit and coconut plantation 30 minutes west of San Juan on the northern coast was developed by Laurance S. Rockefeller, who preserved and enhanced the site's natural beauty. Exquisitely landscaped, the rambling, 1,000-acre compound consists of 296 rooms in rows of two- or three-story beach houses or rows of one-story *casitas* that face the pounding surf on one side and the resort's secluded pool on the other. There are two Robert Trent Jones 18-hole golf courses, seven tennis courts, a full sports and athletic program (including a fitness course), water sports, bicycling, lawn games, dinner-dancing, and casino gambling. Dining is a delight at Dorado, whether at the outdoor patio for breakfast/brunch, the main dining room overlooking the sea, or the charming **Su Casa Restaurant** located in the old plantation's hacienda.

Hyatt Regency Cerromar Beach—Dorado's larger, livelier, and much more commercial next-door neighbor—is an eight-story, 504-room high rise built in the shape of a double Y. It, too, has twin 18-hole R.T. Jones golf courses, and guests can exercise privileges at the Dorado courses if traffic jams develop here. There are 14 all-weather championship tennis courts, a health club with sauna, and a beach at the end of a gigantic lawn. The latest addition (1986) is a most unusual swimming pool, a "water complex" fashioned into an artificial river with currents and a waterfall (great for families with children). Conventioneers and youngbloods out for action can look to the resort's disco, casino, restaurant/nightclub, and several bar/hangout spots. (Note: Because Dorado and Cerromar are sister establishments, guests at either resort enjoy privileges at both, and there is regular jitney service between the two.)

Renovated and updated over the past few years, **Palmas**

del Mar, on the island's southeast coast, has a championship golf course, a tennis complex with 20 courts (several lighted for night play), deep-sea fishing, horseback riding along the beach, and water sports (including snorkeling, scuba diving, sailing and sailing yacht cruises, surfing, and windsurfing). There are children's and teens' activities—Palmas is an ideal spot for families—nature and bike trails, a casino, and ten snack bars and restaurants. (Those staying in kitchen-equipped villas may shop either in the nearby town of Humacao or in the on-premises commissary.) The six freshwater pools (one for lap swimming) come in handy when the currents along the three-and-a-half-mile beach run too strong for ocean bathing.

Currently under renovation near Fajardo in Puerto Rico's northeast corner, the old El Conquistador will soon appear as a 950-room resort, complete with 16 restaurants and lounges, six swimming pools (in addition to ocean swimming), casino, full-service spa and rooftop jogging track, 18-hole golf course, eight tennis courts, children's camp, private "fantasy island" for water sports, marina for guests with boats, and the largest meeting and exhibit facilities in the Caribbean. A fall opening date is expected.

OUT ON THE ISLAND

Driving around the island is the best way to experience the real Puerto Rico. You can set a leisurely pace (food, drink, and rest are only minutes away no matter where you find yourself) and trust the Puerto Rican people to be friendly and eager to help. Feel free to ask questions, even if you speak only *un poquito* Spanish—the Puerto Ricans are great communicators. A few words of advice: Equip yourself with good up-to-date road maps because the highways and byways, while in generally good condition, are often poorly marked. They are also undergoing a great deal of construction—especially the stretch from San Juan to Aguadilla and Mayagüez. To avoid traffic jams around San Juan, stay off the road during the morning or evening rush hours, 7:00 to 9:00 A.M. and 4:00 to 7:00 P.M. Driving at night over unlighted roads is hazardous—especially on twisting mountain byways—and you haven't really driven in the rain until you get swamped by a tropical downpour (so pay attention to weather reports). Before venturing out make sure you've got a copy of *Qué Pasa* in hand, not only for cultural events and other happenings in Puerto Rico but for its listings of traditional restaurants out on the island that are recommended by Mesones Gastronómicos, a tourism-sponsored program denoting quality establishments.

If you are a first-timer on the island, you may prefer to take a few of the guided day trips and half-day trips out of San Juan, just to get the feel of the countryside with expert guidance. Tours are available to the rain forest, Playa de Luquillo, El Comandante Racetrack, Ponce, and the Río Camuy caves by such companies as **Borinquen Tours**, Tel: 725-4990 or 722-1745; **Gray Line**, Tel: 727-8080; and **Normandie Tours**, Tel: 722-6308 or 725-6990. These and other tour companies, which also will guide you through Old San Juan, can be contacted through the tour desk of most of the San Juan hotels. **Exclusive Tours, Inc.**, (Tel: 728-0079 or 792-4945) is run by two efficient German women living in San Juan; they tailor outings in English, German, French, and Spanish.

You may want to take a guided tour of **El Yunque Rain Forest**, the lush, dense, 28,000-acre Caribbean National Forest and the only tropical rain forest in the United States National Forest System. The area is vast, the trails are numerous and often confusing (even with the free map available at the visitors' center), and unless you're an expert in the flora and fauna and the topography and geology of the rain forest you may miss the highlights. They include **La Mina Falls**, spectacular views from El Yunque Trail and the observation tower, and **El Toro** (the highest peak, 3,532 feet). El Yunque, named for the benevolent Indian spirit Yuquiyú, receives an annual rainfall of more than 100 billion gallons. It boasts some 240 tree species; flora such as Sierra palms, fingernail-size orchids, and air plants that grow on branches; and fauna such as the endangered Puerto Rican parrot and millions of tiny *coquí* frogs (listen to the sound and you'll hear the name).

Those who wish to take in these sights without guides should contact the Sierra Palm Visitor Center on Route 191, about an hour (depending on traffic, which can be heavy) due east of San Juan. The center, open daily from 9:30 A.M. to 5:00 P.M., schedules talks and programs by appointment; you can also call the Catalina Field Office at (809) 887-2875 or 766-5335, or write to the Caribbean National Forest, Box B, Palmer, PR 00721.

Playa de Luquillo, about 30 miles (48 km) from San

Juan and just north of El Yunque on the northeast coast, is one of the Caribbean's most exquisite strands of sand. It is open daily (except Mondays) from 9:00 A.M. to 5:00 P.M., and dressing facilities and parking are available at nominal rates. To avoid crowds go on weekdays. Pack a picnic lunch from your hotel or snack at one of the many food stands along the road (Highway 3) leading to the beach.

Ponce and the South Coast

Ponce, in the middle of the south coast, is Puerto Rico's second city, a prosperous, steadily growing commercial center. A Ponce stay is suggested for those who wish to concentrate on the south coast attractions: the phosphorescent bay, 17th-century San Germán, Indian ceremonial centers, and spacious beaches with calm waters.

As you choose your route to Ponce from San Juan, consider heading south on the twisting mountain road that will take you through such out-of-the-way villages and towns as **Naranjito** and **Barranquitas**. (If you visit Ponce as a day trip, you may want to return on the infinitely faster, less taxing superhighway, Route 52; the long route could take you up to five or six hours, whereas you can cover the 70 miles/112 km from Ponce to San Juan on the *autopisto* in two.) Although the hill villages and their surrounding red-clay farms contain no attractions that demand a stop, passing through them provides an excellent introduction to rural Puerto Rico.

Ponce, whose nickname is "Pearl of the South," was named for the family of early settlers that included Juan de Ponce de León, the island's first governor. The town's spacious central square, **plaza de las Delicias**, is the crown jewel of this lovely, relaxed southern city. Transformed by an ongoing reclamation project that has restored and painted houses, buried electric wires, and installed gas lights, it is landscaped with flower beds, splashing fountains, benches, statues, and India-laurel fig trees. Set in the plaza are two of Ponce's most famous landmarks. On the west side of the square is the **Cathedral of Our Lady of Guadalupe**, its twin towers blazing white in afternoon sun. Behind the cathedral on the east side of the plaza is the fanciful red-and-black-striped **Parque de Bombas**, the city's famous firehouse. Originally designed to house the Exposition Fair of 1882, the Moorish-style wooden pavilion was designated a firehouse in 1883 and painted in the city's official colors. Also a museum, the Parque de Bombas displays antique fire-fighting equipment.

Casa Alcaldía, Ponce's colonial city hall and still an operating government building, dominates the central plaza's south side; take time for a stroll around the inner patio after picking up tourism brochures in the entranceway. Free 30-minute tours of the two-story 1898–1901 private **Casa Armstrong,** facing the plaza's west side, are conducted on an irregular schedule (Tel: 844-8240 or 840-5695). Although its furnishings are not original, its distinctive turn-of-the-century architecture (stained glass, highly polished woodwork, louvered shutters on high Romanesque windows) has been faithfully restored. The mansion's exterior, white with orange-red trim, is decorated with balconies (both stone and iron grillwork), caryatids holding up pilasters, and ornamental rooftop urns. The **Teatro La Perla,** a classic Greek revival structure at Mayor and Cristina streets, has been a performing arts center since 1864—a fact illustrating that it was Ponce, not San Juan, that took the early lead as Puerto Rico's cultural hub. It now presents programs of music, dance, and drama; Tel: 843-4080. Nearby, at 70 Cristina, is the new **Museum of Puerto Rican Music,** which exhibits musical instruments ranging from primitive to modern; the **Casa Seralles,** at Cristina and Salud, is a museum devoted to the plastic arts.

Allow several hours to visit the estimable **Ponce Museum of Art** (Tel: 848-0511 or 0505), in the southern part of the city on avenida Las Américas across from Catholic University. Designed by Edward Durell Stone and built in 1965, the two-story museum is composed of seven interconnected hexagons. The collection, consisting of some 1,000 paintings and 400 sculptures, covers the major European schools from the 14th to the 20th century—including such renowned artists as Bronzino, Rubens, Gainsborough, Murillo, and Van Dyke—and is particularly strong in the 19th-century Pre-Raphaelite and Italian Baroque schools. Works on display include Lucas Cranach's *Christ,* Ferdinand Bol's portrait of *Hendrick Trip,* and Cristóbal Ruiz's *Pablo Casals* (showing the master cellist on the beach with his umbrella). There are also works by such Puerto Rican artists as Francisco Rodón and scenes of Ponce and the Puerto Rican countryside. (Closed Tuesdays.)

When it's time to eat, try **Ambert,** A-11 calle Ferrocarril (Tel: 840-6434); **Ancla,** 9 Hostos (Tel: 840-2450); or **Pito's,**

Route 2, Cucharas (Tel: 841-4977), all of which are cited by Mesones Gastronómicos for their quality traditional foods.

For accommodation, the **Meliá Hotel**, located a half-block off the main square, is a modest establishment frequented by business travellers; its lobby restaurant is a popular meeting place for locals. Ponce's **Holiday Inn**, situated outside the city's center on Route 2, is for those who want more modern accommodations. The new La Guancha Hilton, overlooking the port, is scheduled to receive guests sometime in 1993, but as of this time no opening date has been announced.

Just north of the city on Route 503 is the **Centro Ceremonial Indigena** (Tibes Indian Ceremonial Center), the oldest cemetery in the Antilles, where human remains of the Igneri culture (A.D. 300) were excavated in 1975. The site also contains pre-Taino (A.D. 700) ball courts and dance grounds and a recreated Taino village; Tel: 840-2255. **Hacienda Buena Vista**, about 10 miles (16 km) northwest of Ponce on Route 10, is a restored 19th-century coffee plantation with functioning coffee and corn mills. Tours of the estate are given Friday through Sunday, 8:30 A.M. to 3:30 P.M., by reservation only; Tel: 722-5882.

You can visit San Germán and the phosphorescent bay in the southwestern part of the island from either Ponce or Mayagüez (there are no tours there from San Juan), but it's probably better to make an overnight stop outside these cities. (The phosphorescent bay is a nighttime excursion and it's best to avoid driving back to Ponce or Mayagüez over dark or poorly lighted roads.) Two possible lodging choices (see The Paradores and Accommodations Reference below) are San Germán's Parador Oasis and **Lajas's Parador Villa Parguera**, from which cruises of the bay can be arranged.

San Germán, 35 miles (56 km) east of Ponce, was the second urban center created by the Spanish in Puerto Rico. Today a great deal of its original colonial charm is preserved in the compact center of town. There are two plazas, one dominated by the simple, whitewashed **Iglesia Porta Coeli** (Gate of Heaven Church), now a museum of religious art (Mexican colonial paintings and wood sculpture of the 18th and 19th centuries); the other square contains the elaborate **Iglesia San Germán de Auxerre**, noted for its chandeliers and trompe l'oeil ceiling. Maps suggesting what to see in town—houses and art galleries—can be picked up at the **Parador Oa-**

sis, a converted colonial town house with a patio restaurant and bar. Another choice for respite is **La Botica** restaurant, 33 Dr. Veze, in the old pharmacy in the town center; Tel: 892-5790.

From San Germán it's an easy trip south to **Bahía Fosforescente,** La Parguera's phosphorescent bay. This natural wonder, best experienced on the darkest nights, when it puts on its most dramatic show, is not to be missed. Launches take visitors out on the water to watch the "theater of dancing lights." Whenever the surface of the bay is disturbed (by boats or the hands and feet of swimmers), showers of shimmering lights—like millions of lightning bugs—illuminate the waters. The bioluminescence is caused by the bay's large population of dinoflagellates, a form of microscopic marine life that produces sparks of light when agitated.

Also near Ponce (to the west) is Guánica, where U.S. troops first landed in 1898 during the Spanish-American War. Not only a historic site, Guánica is also the site of the **Reserva Forestal Guánica,** the largest tract of tropical dry coastal forest in the world and an International Biosphere Reserve. Here you'll find the nesting grounds of the greatest number of bird species on the island.

Mayagüez and the West Coast

Situated in the center of the island's west coast, Mayagüez—a thriving fishing center—is the logical stopping place for a leisurely examination of the region's unusual attractions. These include some of Puerto Rico's most spectacular (and uncrowded) beaches, especially the one at Boquerón; rustic fishing villages; superb deep-sea fishing; excursions to the wild, uninhabited island of Mona; a celebrated surfing beach at **Rincón** (site of the 1988 World Surfing Championships); the tropical gardens of the U.S. Department of Agriculture's research station; Puerto Rico's only zoo; the eerie topography of the island's southwest corner, with its limestone boulders; salt flats; and the Cabo Rojo lighthouse, crowning the crest of a promontory.

Mayagüez makes a convenient home base for explorations of such attractions as San Germán and the phosphorescent bay (see Ponce section, above). Unlike Ponce, Mayagüez cannot be easily negotiated in a day trip from San Juan (unless you fly), and the area is so seductive that you will want more time.

Downtown Mayagüez is not a fascinating place for the visitor. It was almost completely leveled by a 1918 earth-quake, which accounts for the dearth of historic structures—and the fact that you can cover its attractions easily in an hour. Ficus trees border its handsome **central square**, the centerpiece of which, a magnificent statue of Columbus, stands mounted on a globe and surrounded by a fountain. A government building dominates one end of the square, a fine church graces the other. A block from the main square is the 1920 **Teatro Yagüez**. Along the Mayagüez waterfront on Route 102, a rather bleak-looking area, you'll see docks, tuna-processing plants, and shipping warehouses. The building here that stands out among them is the pink Customs House built in the 1920s.

The city's tropical gardens and the zoo will appeal to students of flora and fauna. Established almost 100 years ago on a former plantation, the lush **gardens** are main-tained by the U.S. Department of Agricultural Research Station (Tel: 831-3435). On your own you can see some 2,000 exotic species of plant life, including Panama canoe trees, traveler's palms, Ceylon cinnamon, pink torch gin-ger, and bowers of orchids. The gardens (closed on week-ends) are located on Route 65, next to the campus of the University of Puerto Rico at Mayagüez and across from Parque Los Próceres (Patriots Park). The **Mayagüez Zoo**, on Route 108 at Barrio Miradero, supports a splendid collection of wildlife, including Bengal tigers, Andean condors, and huge rats called *capybara*. The grounds, which include a children's playground, display the ani-mals in a landscaped setting of small islands, accented by tropical plants and a lake; Tel: 834-8110.

One possible choice for accommodations is the reno-vated **Hilton International Mayagüez**, which now includes a casino and the Vista Terrace, with nightly entertainment. A sophisticated resort hotel on a hillside overlooking the Mayagüez harbor, the Hilton offers tennis and pool swim-ming on its lush 20-acre grounds, and can arrange golf at nearby nine- and 18-hole courses, skin diving at prime spots along the coast, fishing trips from the Mayagüez Marina (15 minutes away), and day trips to Playa Boque-rón. If weather and sea conditions permit—and if the price is right—boats can be chartered for the often rough crossing to Isla de Mona, halfway between Puerto Rico and the Dominican Republic.

Uninhabited **Isla de Mona** is an arid, rugged, "outback"

place recommended only to backpack adventurers, naturalists, and lovers of the offbeat. (Bring water.) Small chartered planes also cross the Canal de la Mona, rumored to be a great spot for whale watching, to land on the island's primitive airstrip. Inquire at the Mayagüez Hilton or call the Department of Natural Resources, Tel: (809) 724-8774.

Part of the delight of a west coast stay is visiting—and eating at—one of the simple, almost ramshackle fishing village restaurants on the coastal road, Route 102, about 15 miles (24 km) south of Mayagüez near Cabo Rojo. **Casona de Serafín** (Tel: 851-0066); **Perichi's** (Tel: 851-3131); and **Tino's** (Tel: 851-2976) all specialize in seafood and are included in the Mesones Gastronómicos program.

Few Puerto Rican beaches rival **Playa Boquerón** (only Luquillo in the northeast and Sombé on the island of Vieques come to mind)—a golden crescent stretching several miles along the Bahía de Boquerón. The waves are gentle, the waters calm and perfect for swimming, and the sands are packed at water's edge for beach hiking. As you face the sea you can see the sheltering "arms" of the bay, Punta Guaniquilla to the right and the low hills of Boquerón state forest to the left. A government-regulated beach, Boquerón offers comfortable cabins, showers, and toilet facilities, and it is, as you'd expect, a fine place for a picnic.

South of Playa Boquerón, Route 301 (which branches off Route 101) will take you to the extreme southwestern tip of Puerto Rico—a rugged landscape of salt farms and arid wasteland. At the end of Route 301 you'll arrive at a flat-topped, two-pronged peninsula, its steep cliffs plunging into the sea. Crowning the promontory is the **Faro de Cabo Rojo**, a lighthouse built a century ago by the Spanish colonial government. Behind you loom the oldest mountains in Puerto Rico, and, if you arrive during the summer or fall rainy season, you'll probably witness spectacular lightning storms. In the early evening during clear weather, you may be lucky enough to witness one of the world's most glorious sunsets.

About 25 to 30 miles (40 to 48 km) north of Mayagüez (there is no direct route, and a number of roads in this area are under construction or repair), you'll find Puerto Rico's most famous surfing beaches, just north of **Rincón** and its **Parador Villa Antonio**. As with all the small inns and hotels in this area, it can be rambunctious and noisy, especially on weekends, when the surf's up and crowds of young people descend on the beaches.

Ten miles (16 km) north of Rincón, on the coast near Aguada, you'll discover a concrete boat monument marking the spot where Columbus is said to have landed in 1493 on his second voyage to the Caribbean.

A very special place to stay is the small (24 suites) and elegant **Horned Dorset Primavera** hotel, near Rincón. Located amid palms and flowering plants on a hillside overlooking the sea, this Spanish colonial resort is a rest-inducing place—it feels more like a private home than a hotel—and one that serves renowned multicourse dinners in a gracious hacienda-style dining room. (If you do not stay at the hotel, at least make reservations for lunch. Dinner is also available to outsiders, but remember: You'll have to negotiate the poorly marked, poorly lighted nighttime roads—a real challenge after seven courses with drinks and wine.) Although the Horned Dorset's beach is meager, a more generous (and virtually private) strand lies only a short walk away.

The Northwest

The **Observatorio de Arecibo** and the **Parque de las Cavernas** (a.k.a. the Río Camuy caves) in the northwest section of the island can be taken in as a day trip from Mayagüez or San Juan. The observatory has the largest radar/radio telescope in the world, a 20-acre "dish" set into a karst sinkhole, enabling scientists to scan the solar system and monitor natural radio emissions from distant galaxies.

The Río Camuy caves, a series of immense, still largely unexplored underground caverns, is one of the most impressive, most intelligently interpreted wonders in the U.S. park system. Trolleys take visitors from the Information Center, where an introductory film is shown, to the mouth of the main cavern; from there a guide leads 40-minute tours on foot through the caves. The trail passes through imaginatively lighted, vaulted "cathedrals," around dripping stalactites and stalagmites and oddly shaped formations, and over natural bridges hundreds of feet above the rushing Río Camuy.

The observatory is open to visitors from 2:00 to 3:00 P.M. Tuesday through Friday and from 1:00 to 4:30 P.M. on Sundays; tours, given in the mornings, must be arranged in advance; Tel: (809) 878-2612. The caves are open Wednesday through Sunday from 8:00 A.M. to 4:00 P.M. (though they sometimes close without warning and long waits are not unknown), and a weekday visit is strongly advised; call the caves' park office, Tel: (809) 898-3100, or the San Juan number, Tel: (809) 756-5555, for up-to-date information. If you're coming from San Juan, allow plenty of time; although no more than a 60-mile (96-km) trip, traffic and road construction can make the ride seem much longer. (Few tours from San Juan include these two places.)

Accommodations in the area include the **Parador El Guajataca**, ideally situated on a lovely, uncrowded crescent beach at the foot of rugged hills, and a relatively new parador in Utuado, **Casa Grande**, nestled in the central mountains near the **Parque Ceremonial Indigena** (Caguana Indian Ceremonial Park), which the Taino Indians used as a site for games and religious ceremonies some 800 years ago. Cobblestones border the ten courts (*bateyes*), and stone monoliths, some etched with petroglyphs, outline the lengths of several of the courts. The 13-acre site is a profoundly peaceful, unadorned, unspoiled spot, planted with indigenous trees such as guavas and royal palms. Unclouded by any trace of modern civilization, it offers a rare peek into another time.

Although not particularly rugged or physically taxing experiences, visiting the observatory, the caves, and the ceremonial park requires comfortable clothing, caps or hats, and rubber-soled shoes or sneakers. Bring your own picnic lunch, too.

The Center of the Island

Other sights and excursions—and these are for the adventurous visitor—include **Cañon San Cristóbal** (San Cristóbal Canyon) and **Reserva Forestal Toro Negro**, both roughly northeast of Ponce in the center of the island. The 700-foot canyon, the deepest gorge in Puerto Rico, lies between the hill towns of Aibonito and Barranquitas. Rivers, waterfalls, and pools (not recommended for swimming because of the danger of bilharzia-infected snails that can cause a severe disease resembling typhoid) mark the area, which is an experienced hiker's paradise. Although the region is not yet developed for tourists, intrepid explorers can learn how to negotiate the terrain by reading Kathryn Robinson's authoritative book *The Other*

Puerto Rico (see Bibliography). Robinson, an indefatigable hiker, also guides her readers through the wonders of the dense, tropical Toro Negro forest, smack in the middle of the **Cordillera Central**, the central mountain range. Here are the **Lago El Guineo** reservoir, Puerto Rico's highest lake; **Cerro de Punta**, the island's tallest peak at 4,390 feet, with spectacular views of both the Atlantic Ocean to the north and the Caribbean Sea to the south; and the multiple cascades of the **Río Inabón**.

Traversing the center of the island, from Mayagüez on the west coast to Yabucoa and Maunabo on the southeast coast, is the **Ruta Panoramica**. Visitors should know that this "route" along the Cordillera Central is not a scenic superhighway but rather 165 miles of interlocking roads, often poorly marked and lighted (if at all) and frequently twisting and turning. Those who seek the real Puerto Rico should travel at least part of it, especially if on the way to one of the coffee-plantation paradores: **Casa Grande**, in the mountains near Utuado, northeast of Mayagüez, or **Hacienda Gripiñas**, in the mountains above Ponce near Jayuya and the Caguana Indian Ceremonial Park. If you'd like to travel its length, set aside two days at the very least (more would be better), with an overnight stop midway (Hacienda Gripiñas is a logical choice). Passing through dense tropical vegetation on the way you will see mountains aflame with flamboyán trees, hillside houses perched on stilts, chicken ranches, rivers and reservoirs, forest preserves—startling views at every turn. For a not-too-arduous taste of the Ruta Panoramica, pick up the route at Mayagüez and drive to Hacienda Gripiñas (take time for a meal at **El Dujo** restaurant in Jayuya). You would then be near such attractions as the Caguana Indian Ceremonial Park and the Toro Negro forest. After your stay at the parador, return to the north coast via Route 10, another scenic stretch through forest preserves, over rushing rivers, and alongside one arm of **Lago Dos Bocas**, one of Puerto Rico's largest lakes.

The Paradores

Some 15 small inns (ranging in size from seven to 64 rooms) are scattered about the island and operated by Paradores Puertorriqueños, an organization sponsored by the island's tourism association. Each parador has a distinctive personality yet shares in common these attractive traits: small, unpretentious size and homelike style;

proximity to historic, scenic, or cultural sites; and bargain rates (recent listings ranged from $45 to $95 per room, per night). No one who prefers the creature comforts of a sleek, modern high-rise hotel over personal charm and friendly service would be interested in a parador experience. But for those who do not expect constant pampering and entertainment, the paradores can be a joy and an adventure.

Pick your parador for the type of visit you wish to have or for the region you wish to explore—that's why these country inns were selected in the first place. For a beach vacation, consider **Boquemar** (on the wildly beautiful southwest coast), **Vistamar** or **El Guajataca** (perched on a hill above or on the beach below the equally impressive northwest coast; see The Northwest section, above, for El Guajataca), or **Martorell** (at Luquillo, described above, one of the world's finest strands). For the cool and calm of the interior mountains, select either of the above-mentioned coffee-plantation paradores with their lush vegetation, nature trails, and access to Indian ceremonial centers. There is even an in-town parador, the colonial **Oasis**, with its interior patio restaurant, located in the heart of historic San Germán near Mayagüez (see Ponce section, above). A thermal spa near Ponce, **Baños de Coamo**, known to the Indians and thought by some to be a fountain of youth, is where Franklin Roosevelt, Thomas Edison, and Alexander Graham Bell used to "take the waters." For an offshore island retreat (see below) situated on an old sugar plantation, go to Vieques. **La Familia**, in Fajardo, the fishing village and boating/sailing center in Puerto Rico's northeast corner, is one of the newest paradores, having opened in 1989. (From Fajardo you can catch the ferries for the offshore islands of Culebra and Vieques.)

Although not all paradores are located on beaches, all offer swimming pools or easy access to a nearby beach. Meals—hearty local fare—are available at all paradores, and all have bars, some with local entertainment on weekends.

THE OFFSHORE ISLANDS

Once Puerto Rico has captured your heart and you want to see and know it *all,* you are ready for an island adventure.

Both Culebra and the much larger Vieques lie off the eastern coast and are easily reached by a flight from San Juan or by ferry from Fajardo; both islands provide simple and inexpensive accommodations in guest houses (five to 32 rooms) and on Vieques there is a parador. Island vacations and visits are not for those who feed on the Condado Strip's casinos, discos, and international restaurants, but if feasts of nature's wonders sustain your spirit, the offshore life is for you. The beaches on both islands are superb, and after days filled with such activities as swimming, surfing, sailing, snorkeling, and scuba diving, nights without casinos and floor shows can be a relief.

Vieques, where the original, 1963 *Lord of the Flies* was filmed, is to many the more interesting of the two main offshore islands. There is a small hotel, **Ocean View**, and a guest house, **Sea Gate**, plus a most unusual (and highly recommended) guest mansion, **Casa del Francés**. Looking for all the world like a kissing cousin of Tara in *Gone With the Wind,* the del Francés offers accommodations in both the mansion itself and in a modern annex. Once the manor house of the sugar plantation, La Casa is perhaps the place to stay for the first-time Vieques visitor. The spacious rooms in the main house have high ceilings, revolving ceiling fans, and louvered French doors opening onto wide porches. Elaborate and creative evening meals are served by candlelight on the open-air patio, or you can retreat to the funky fishing village down the hill for burgers and fresh fish at such harborside hangouts as **Bananas** (also a guest house). La Casa is run by the owner/manager team of Irving Greenblatt and Frank Celeste as if it were a private home for special friends. They will happily smother you with attention or leave you absolutely alone to enjoy complete privacy if you wish. A 15-minute stroll from La Casa is the vast, gently curving **Playa Sombé** (Sun Bay Beach), one of the most extravagantly beautiful spots on earth—and still, if you hurry, comparatively uncrowded and underappreciated.

Culebra, a former gunnery site for the U.S. military, is a small, rustic island of 2,000 residents who are just waking up to their island's tourism potential. The beaches are pristine and dazzlingly white, their crystal-clear waters laced with unspoiled coral reefs. The entire island—and numerous surrounding islets—teems with wildlife (protected in the Culebra National Wildlife Refuge) such as red-billed tropical birds, sooty terns, and laughing gulls.

There are no tennis courts, golf courses, nouvelle cuisine restaurants, discos, or casinos, and there is no nightlife—unless you fancy after-dark turtle-watching (great leather-neck *and* green turtles), from mid-April through much of June.

Available guest-house rooms on Culebra number fewer than 100, and most visitors stay in one of three places, the most upscale of which is **Club Seabourne**, a hillside home with the island's only swimming pool. For more rustic accommodations try **Villa Boheme**, located in the center of Dewey, the island's principal town, or **Punta Aloe Villas and Cielo y Mar**, a complex right on the bay (Ensenada Honda) that resembles a well-run camp.

USEFUL FACTS

What to Wear
Loose-fitting, washable cotton clothing and comfortable walking shoes, sneakers, or sandals are the hard-and-fast rule. For dressy evenings women may want a long skirt, and men will be fine in dark slacks, a light jacket, or, to be very Puerto Rican, one of those long-sleeved, fancy dress shirts called *guayaberas*. (Casinos and leading restaurants appreciate these touches of evening formality.)

Getting In
Puerto Rico's Luis Muñoz Marin International Airport, the busiest in the Caribbean, receives direct flights from major U.S. cities via American Airlines, Delta, and TWA. Recently USAir introduced nonstop flights from Baltimore, Pittsburgh, Philadelphia, and Charlotte, N.C., and United runs a daily nonstop flight from Washington, D.C. Carnival now offers several weekly nonstop flights to Aguadilla and Ponce, and Braniff operates six weekly nonstops from New York, Newark, and Miami to San Juan. Because there is no scheduled direct flight service from Canada to Puerto Rico, most Canadians fly to New York and then proceed directly to San Juan (Toronto's Wardair offers nonstop charter service). From Europe, Air Portugal, British Airways, Iberia, and Lufthansa have recently introduced service to the island. Virtually all Caribbean cruise ships make San Juan a principal port of call, and combination cruise-in/fly-out plans can be arranged.

The airport, recently expanded, is a model of speed and efficiency. Just outside the luggage area you'll find taxis and hotel limos; inexpensive buses make the rounds of the hotels in Isla Verde, Condado, and Old San Juan; limos take you to the resorts of Dorado, Cerromar, and Palmas del Mar (inform these places *in advance* that you will be using their transportation); and *públicos* (a public taxi service) take passengers (up to four or five) from town square to town square—simply go to the main plaza and hop into the next available car leaving for your destination.

Entry Requirements
U.S. and Canadian citizens need proof of citizenship (a passport is best but a driver's license will suffice), and British subjects need both a passport and visa.

Local Time
Puerto Rico is on Atlantic standard time year-round, one hour ahead of the U.S. east coast except when the east coast moves its clocks ahead an hour during daylight saving time. Then the two keep the same time.

Electrical Current
Same as elsewhere in the U.S. and Canada—110 volts AC, 60 cycles.

Getting Around
Transportation around Puerto Rico is easily managed via rental cars, American Eagle Airlines (which has recently expanded its services), or licensed públicos.

Culebra and Vieques islands, off the east coast, are easily reached by air from San Juan's convenient, inner-city Isla Grande Airport (call Vieques AirLink, 809/722-3736, or Flamenco Airways, 809/725-7707, for arrangements), or by ferry from Fajardo, which is easily reached from Luis Muñoz Marin International via taxi or público. The ferry for Vieques (an 80-minute trip) departs weekdays at 9:30 A.M. and 4:30 P.M.; weekends and holidays at 9:00 A.M., and 3:00 and 6:00 P.M. The ferry ride to Culebra takes an hour and leaves Monday through Thursday at 4:00 P.M., Fridays and Saturdays at 9:00 A.M. and 4:00 P.M., Sundays and holidays at 8:00 A.M. and 2:30 P.M. Cars may be transported on the cargo ferry by calling, one week in advance, Tel: (809) 863-0705 Monday through Friday. Because flights to Vieques and Culebra are so swift and scenic (you fly low over shimmering waters and lush vegetation) and so inexpensive ($50 round trip), they have a decided edge over the longer, more arduous ferry crossings. However, if rides on very

small planes make you squeamish (or panicky), take the
ferry.

Many people fly over to Charlotte Amalie on St.
Thomas for a day of duty-free shopping. (San Juan is not a
duty-free port, in spite of all the advertised bargains.)
There are frequent flights from Luis Muñoz Marin International Airport.

Business Hours
In tourist areas, such as Old San Juan and the Condado
Strip, stores and shops will often stay open late. Evening
restaurant hours tend to follow the Spanish custom of late
dining at around nine or ten.

Currency
The U.S. dollar.

Festivals
Almost every town and village in Puerto Rico has its festivals and saint's days celebrations, which are listed in the
free seasonal guide *Qué Pasa*. San Juan's ongoing, year-
round LeLoLai festival is the island's best introduction to
native song and dance. Dances, music, presentations,
films, cruises, and fiestas take place at different locations.
The Institute of Puerto Rican Culture Theater also spon-
sors frequent concerts, religious festivals, and folkloric
evenings. Festival Casals (held every June), the Fine Arts
Center Festival Hall in New San Juan's Santurce district,
and Old San Juan's historic Tapia Theater (the New World's
oldest theater in continuous use) offer performances in
classical and modern music, dance, and drama. Ponce's
Carnival (late February, early March) features parades with
floats, street parties, dances, and the rhythms of the African
plena. The city also stages a "Bomba y Plena Festival" every
June to celebrate with music and dance the island's
African-American heritage.

For Further Information
Tourism Company of Puerto Rico, P.O. Box 4435, Old San
Juan Station, San Juan, Puerto Rico 00905, Tel: (809) 721-
2400, Fax: (809) 725-4417; tourism booths in San Juan can
be found at Luis Muñoz Marin International Airport, Tel:
791-1014 or 2551; the City Hall (Alcaldía) on Plaza de
Armas in Old San Juan, Tel: 724-7171; and La Casita, near
Pier One, Old San Juan, Tel: 722-1709; **in the U.S.**, 575
Fifth Avenue, New York, NY 10017, Tel: (800) 223-6530 or,

PUERTO RICO   129

in New York, (212) 599-6262; **in Canada**, 380 Ontario
Street, Toronto, Ontario M5A 2V7, Tel: (416) 969-9025,
Fax: 969-9478; **in the U.K.**, 67–69 Whitfield Street, London
W1P 5RL, England, Tel: (71) 636-6558.

ACCOMMODATIONS REFERENCE
*The rate ranges given here, in U.S. dollars, are projections
for fall 1992 through spring 1993, and span the lowest
rates in the low season to the highest in the high season.
Unless otherwise indicated, rates are for double rooms,
double occupancy. As rates are subject to change, it's
always wise to double-check before booking. The telephone area code (within the U.S. system) for Puerto Rico is
809.*

▶ **El Canario by the Sea.** 4 Condado, **San Juan**, PR
00907. Tel: 722-8640; Fax: 725-4921. $55–$95.
▶ **El Canario Inn.** 1317 Ashford Avenue, **San Juan**, PR
00907. Tel: 722-3861; Fax: 722-0391. $70–$90.
▶ **Caribe Hilton International.** P.O. Box 1872, **San Juan**,
PR 00903. Tel: 721-0303 or (800) 468-8585; Fax: 725-8849.
$195–$385.
▶ **Casa San José.** 159 San José Street, **Old San Juan**, PR
00901. Tel: 723-1212; Fax: 723-7620. $140–$170.
▶ **Condado Beach Hotel.** P.O. Box 41226, Minillas Station, **San Juan**, PR 00940-1226. Tel: 721-6090 or (800) 468-
2775; Fax: 722-5062. $130–$250.
▶ **Condado Plaza Hotel & Casino.** 999 Ashford Avenue,
San Juan, PR 00907. Tel: 721-1000 or (800) 468-8588; Fax:
721-4613. $140–$360.
▶ **Empress Oceanfront Hotel.** 2 Amapola, **Isla Verde**, PR
00979. Tel: 791-3083 or (800) 678-0757; Fax: 791-1423.
$88–$148.
▶ **ESJ Towers.** P.O. Box 2200, **Carolina**, PR 00979. Tel:
791-5151 or (800) 468-2026; Fax: 791-5888. $135–$245.
▶ **The Gallery Inn.** 204 Norzagaray Street, **Old San Juan**,
PR, 00901. Tel: 722-1808; Fax: 724-7360. $95.
▶ **Gran Hotel El Convento.** 100 Cristo Street, **Old San
Juan**, PR 00902. Tel: 723-9020 or (800) 468-2779; Fax: 721-
2877. $95–$200.
▶ **Hilton International Mayagüez.** Route 2, **Mayagüez**,
PR 00709. Tel: 831-7575 or (800) 445-8667; Fax: 265-3020.
$170–$300.
▶ **Holiday Inn.** Route 2, **Ponce**, PR 00731. Tel: 844-1200
or (800) 465-4329; Fax: 841-8085. $125–$170.

▶ **Horned Dorset Primavera.** Apartado 1132, **Rincón**, PR 00677. Tel: 823-4030; Fax: 823-5580. $190–$350.

▶ **Hyatt Dorado Beach.** Route 693, **Dorado**, PR 00646. Tel: 796-1234 or (800) 228-9000; Fax: 796-2022 or (402) 593-9838. $155–$555 (high-season rate includes mandatory M.A.P.).

▶ **Hyatt Regency Cerromar Beach.** Route 693, **Dorado**, PR 00646. Tel: 796-1234 or (800) 228-9000; Fax: 796-4640 or (402) 593-9838. $135–$380.

▶ **Meliá Hotel.** 2 Cristina Street, **Ponce**, PR 00731. Tel: 842-0260 or 0261; Fax: 841-3602. $65–$70.

▶ **Palmas del Mar.** P.O. Box 2020, **Humacao**, PR 00661. Tel: 852-6000 or (800) 468-3331; Fax: 850-4844. $115–$270.

▶ **Radisson Normandie Hotel.** Call Box 50059, **San Juan**, PR 00902. Tel: 729-2929 or (800) 333-3333; Fax: 729-3083. $115–$220.

▶ **El San Juan Hotel & Casino.** 187 Isla Verde Road, **Isla Verde**, PR 00913. Tel: 791-1000 or (800) 468-2818; Fax: 253-0178. $215–$385.

▶ **Sands Hotel & Casino.** P.O. Box 6676, Loiza Station, **Santurce**, PR 00914. Tel: 791-6100 or (800) 443-2009; Fax: 791-8525. $165–$315.

PARADORES AND GUEST HOUSES
The general number for parador information and reservations is (809) 721-2884 or (800) 443-0266 (except for those in Culebra); Fax: (809) 721-4698. Call between 8:00 A.M. and noon and 1:00 to 4:30 P.M.

▶ **Parador Baños de Coamo.** Route 546 off the super-highway from San Juan to Ponce, P.O. Box 540, **Coamo**, PR 00640. Tel: 825-2186 or 2239; Fax: 825-4739. $50–$68.

▶ **Parador Boquemar.** P.O. Box 133, Boquerón, **Cabo Rojo**, PR 00622. Tel: 851-2158; Fax: 851-7600. $60–$75.

▶ **Casa del Francés.** P.O. Box 458, **Vieques**, PR 00765. Tel: 741-3751; Fax: 741-0717. $75–$89 (high-season rate includes mandatory M.A.P.).

▶ **Parador Casa Grande.** Route 612, P.O. Box 616, **Utuado**, PR 00761. Tel: 894-3939. $55–$65.

▶ **Club Seabourne.** P.O. Box 357, **Culebra**, PR 00645. Tel: 742-3169; Fax: 742-3176. $65–$110.

▶ **Parador La Familia.** Route 987, **Fajardo**, PR 00648. Tel: 863-1193; Fax: 860-5345. $60–$80.

▶ **Parador El Guajataca.** P.O. Box 1558, **Quebradillas**,

PR 00742-1558; Tel: 895-3070 or 2204; Fax: 895-3589. $67–$84.

▶ **Parador Hacienda Gripiñas.** Route 527, P.O. Box 387, **Jayuya**, PR 00664. Tel: 828-1717; Fax: 828-1719. $50–$70.

▶ **Parador Martorell.** P.O. Box 384, **Luquillo**, PR 00673. Tel: 889-2710; Fax: 889-2710. $45–$60.

▶ **Parador Oasis.** Luna Street, P.O. Box 144, **San Germán**, PR 00753. Tel: 892-1175; Fax: 892-1175, ext. 200. $55–$60.

▶ **Ocean View.** Plinio Peterson, P.O. Box 124, **Vieques**, PR 00765. Tel: 741-3696. $40–$50.

▶ **Punta Aloe Villas and Ciclo y Mar.** P.O. Box 292, **Culebra**, PR 00645-0292. Tel: 742-3167 or (207) 882-5203. $295–$395 (fully equipped studio for two) or $450–$595 (villa for four).

▶ **Sea Gate.** Barriada Fuerte, P.O. Box 747, **Vieques**, PR 00765. Tel: 741-4661. $35–$50.

▶ **Parador Villa Antonio.** Route 115, P.O. Box 68, **Rincón**, PR 00743. Tel: 823-2645; Fax: 823-8380. $60–$90.

▶ **Villa Boheme.** P.O. Box 218, **Culebra**, PR 00775. Tel: 742-3508. $45–$65, E.P.

▶ **Parador Villa Parguera.** Route 304, **Lajas**, PR 00667. Tel: 899-3975; Fax: 899-6040. $70–$80.

▶ **Parador Vistamar.** Route 113, **Quebradillas**, PR 00742. Tel: 895-2065; Fax: 895-2294. $55–$80.

THE UNITED STATES VIRGIN ISLANDS

By Susan Farewell

Susan Farewell has travelled to the Caribbean for many magazines, including Vogue España, Metropolitan Home, Travel & Leisure, Caribbean Travel and Life, Child, Bride's, *and* Diversion.

"**D**o you take American money?" a cruise-ship passenger inquired at a jewelry shop in Charlotte Amalie on St. Thomas. The woman behind the counter had heard it many times before. She responded kindly, "Of course, dear, this *is* part of the United States."

This—and variations on the same theme—is not an uncommon scenario on St. Croix, St. Thomas, and St. John, the three main islands that make up the United States Virgin Islands. The United States bought this family of Caribbean islands (a total of 68, most of them uninhabited) from Denmark in 1917 to help guard the Panama Canal. Still, their status as a U.S. Territory doesn't quite fully register with Statesiders. Somehow, the tropical climate, the lilting Caribbean accent, and the water (which

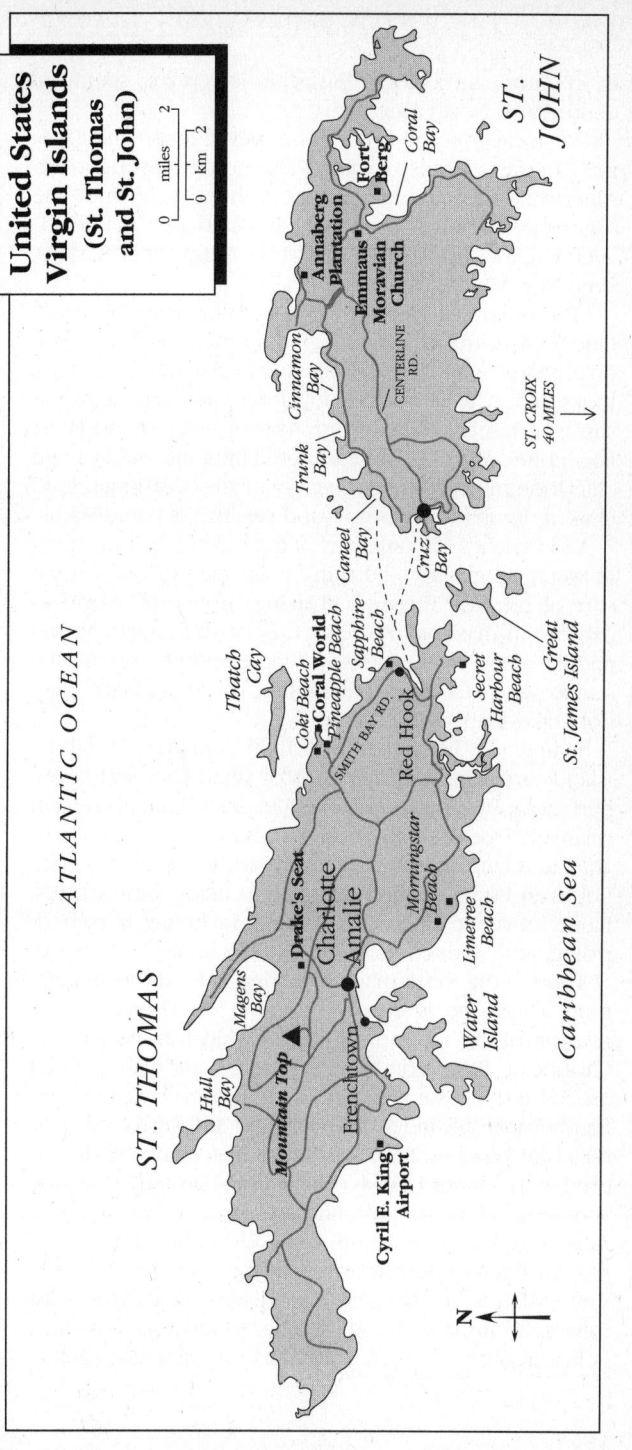

United States Virgin Islands (St. Thomas and St. John)

is, in places, the color of pistachio ice cream) seem too exotic to be North American.

The locals, on the other hand, never forget their U.S. ties. In fact, license plates—attached to proud-to-be-American cars—are emblazoned with the nickname "The American Paradise." You see signs of the "mainland" everywhere: fast-food restaurants, mega-supermarkets, even New York–style delis.

"The American Paradise" is not a misnomer, however. One look at the beaches encircling the islands and you understand why. They're absolutely flawless: The sand looks as if it were washed in bleach, the water laps the shore in rainbow hues from clear-as-a-window to lapis-lazuli blue. Add to this the sculpted hills and wind-carved cliffs looming up behind them—with the occasional cloud chasing its shadow below—and yes, this is paradisiacal.

And beaches are only part of the picture. Just offshore, in water so clean you'd think it dripped through some sort of purifier, there's a thriving submarine world to explore in mask, snorkel and fins, or scuba gear. As you paddle along in the dense silence, bubbles rise to the surface and seascapes resembling Disney's Magic Kingdom take shape around you.

Sailing, too, is a major recreation in the U.S.V.I. All the islands are edged with dozens of small bays and coves, perfect for dropping anchor. Wide, deep channels remain relatively free of tricky reefs, winds prove generally reliable, and land stays almost always within sight. You need not even be an amphibious type to enjoy these islands. Plenty of other diversions abound, including horseback riding, golf, and tennis at some of the hotels and resorts.

Though the three major U.S. Virgins have lots in common, each one is clearly different. **St. Thomas** is the liveliest of the lot and the biggest duty-free port in the Caribbean. It's very hilly, covered with lush tropical greens and blossoms (including bougainvillaea, hibiscus, flamboyants, oleander, and orchids) and surrounded by beautiful beaches. **St. Croix** offers history (to be discovered in its former Danish capital, Christiansted), duty-free shopping, very fine golf, and scenic landscapes (rolling hills dotted with sugar mill ruins, cliffs plunging into the sea, an Edenesque rain forest in the northwest). Of the three islands, it's the most sophisticated and the least touristy. **St. John** feels like one big national park—which is just about what it is. Thanks to Laurance Rockefeller, who bought up large hunks of the island in the 1950s and turned it over to the U.S. National Park Service for safe-keeping, more than two-thirds of it is, indeed, virginal. Most of its visitors are day-trippers from next-door St. Thomas.

Perhaps the most satisfying way to visit the U.S.V.I. is to divide your time among the three islands. You can easily travel between St. Thomas and St. John by ferry or take one of the daily flights between St. Croix and St. Thomas. The best way to get around on the islands is by rental car. If you prefer, taxis are readily available and fairly inexpensive; they also may be hired for tours.

The big hotels on all three islands serve up a combination of after-dark activities including steel bands, calypso shows, limbo contests, and fire-eating performances. There are also discos and other dance floors at local establishments. For the most up-to-date happenings, pick up a copy of *St. Thomas and St. John This Week* or *St. Croix This Week,* free local publications available on the islands.

MAJOR INTEREST

St. Thomas
Charlotte Amalie (shopping)
Mountain Top (views)
Coral World
Beaches and water sports (especially good snorkeling and scuba diving)

St. Croix
Christiansted
More shopping
Buck Island National Park
More beaches and water sports (especially snorkeling and scuba diving)
Botanical Gardens
Whim Great House
Frederiksted

St. John
Beaches, snorkeling, and scuba diving
Undeveloped national parkland
Cruz Bay area

ST. THOMAS

This Virgin Island is the furthest from being "virgin." It does covet its share of empty beaches, among them some of the most beautiful in the world, and it's not completely developed . . . yet. St. Thomas is a rapidly growing—or should we say "progressing"—island. Condominiums seem to be sprouting up everywhere, and traffic has become an uncombatable problem. Still, the island is a favorite for many return visitors, and it is just a boat ride away from dozens of unspoiled isles and cays, a consolation for lifelong residents.

In spite of the signs of progress, St. Thomas has managed to retain much of its native charm. Along with the fast-food places, there are open-air shacks serving West Indian dishes (some of the seediest-looking joints have the best cuisine and prices). And though there are several could-be-anywhere hotels and condo communities, the enormous variety of accommodations on St. Thomas offers something for everyone, from big sea-front hotels (with every kind of water sport imaginable, restaurants, children's programs, and nighttime entertainment) to condominiums that can be rented by the week or small inns where guests are made to feel part of the family.

Charlotte Amalie

You can see all of St. Thomas in about five hours, spending two of them weaving your way through the labyrinth of streets in Charlotte Amalie (ah-MAHL-yah). The capital of the U.S.V.I., this bustling town—centered around two main streets connected by alleyways—is crammed with architecture influenced by the Danes, the British, the Italians, and the French, but adapted to the West Indian climate. Throughout the day it's packed with both locals and visitors from around the world; at night, but for a few restaurants, it shuts down. One look at its main street, Dronningens Gade, and you'll understand why it has a reputation for being the biggest duty-free port in the Caribbean: One jewelry store gleams next to another, interspersed with linen and leather shops. There is also shopping at Havensight, where the cruise ships dock, about a five-minute taxi ride away.

Just outside the main shopping area in town—you

can't miss it—is **Fort Christian** (Tel: 776-4566), a cranberry-red bastion built by the Danes in 1617. It now houses a small museum with a modest collection of Arawak and Carib Indian artifacts and a couple of displays depicting the island's early Danish history. The **Senate Building** (Tel: 774-0880) stands on the harbor side of the fort. Completed in the 1870s as a Danish marine barracks, today it houses the Virgin Islands legislature.

You need strong legs to venture elsewhere in Charlotte Amalie, because most of the city is built on three steep hills. The climb up the steps of Government Hill to the **Government House** (Tel: 774-0001) on Kongens Gade is a must. Built in 1867 as a meeting place for the Danish Colonial Council, the house is now the governor's official residence. Inside are several historical murals as well as a collection of paintings by local artists, including the Impressionist Camille Pissarro, who was born in St. Thomas. Also on Kongens Gade, you'll find the Hotel 1829, a European-style inn built by a French sea captain; Fiddle Leaf, a highly regarded restaurant serving contemporary Caribbean cuisine (see Dining on St. Thomas below); and the Street of the 99 Steps (one of the few remaining streets of the old Danish town).

The **Frederik Lutheran Church**, at the foot of Government Hill, was built in 1826 on the site of the island's first Lutheran church. Its 18th-century ecclesiastical silver, brought over from Denmark, is still used today. The **Synagogue of Berecha V'Shalom V'Gemilath Chasidim** (blessing and peace and loving deeds) perches atop the neighboring **Synagogue Hill**. Built by Sephardic Jews in 1833, it is said to be the Western Hemisphere's second-oldest synagogue still in use. (The oldest is in Curaçao.)

Hotel 1829 and Blackbeard's Castle are not on the water, but they make up for it with charm. The **Hotel 1829**, a St. Thomas landmark with rooms overlooking a bougainvillaea-draped central courtyard and an exceptionally good restaurant, has antique four-poster beds, high wood ceilings, and Haitian artwork throughout. On top of the hill is **Blackbeard's Castle** (not to be confused with the larger Bluebeard's Castle Hotel on a nearby hilltop). It proffers a lovely pool and an excellent restaurant—both with harbor views. Blackbeard's is quite small (20 rooms) and elegantly run by co-owners Bob Harrington and Henrique Konzen. The decor speaks tasteful simplicity.

Dining on St. Thomas

The U.S.V.I. are not exactly known for their outstanding cuisine, but several restaurants (especially on St. Thomas) are noteworthy. In Charlotte Amalie the handful of commendable restaurants include the one at **Hotel 1829** (Tel: 776-1829), which prepares a wonderful Caribbean rock lobster (and nonpareil desserts); **Virgilio's** (Tel: 776-4920), highly regarded all over the island for its Northern Italian cuisine; the aforementioned **Fiddle Leaf** (Tel: 775-2810), which combines stunning harbor views with such inventive dishes as seared sea scallops with mango relish and coconut sauce and papaya and brie quesadilla; and **Entre Nous** (Tel: 776-4050) at Bluebeard's Castle, for French cuisine and another terrific view of the harbor.

Just west of Charlotte Amalie on the waterfront is **Frenchtown**, a small enclave settled by descendants of French refugees who fled the Swedish invasion of St. Barts in the late 18th century. Here you'll find a little pocket of exceptionally good restaurants, including **Alexander's Café** (Tel: 776-4211), where the soups (hot and chilled) are celestial; **Famous at Johnnycakes** (Tel: 776-2466), which prides itself on spanking fresh seafood and fish dishes; and **Café Normandie** (Tel: 774-1622), French cuisine in a tiny notice-me-yellow building.

For the best West Indian food on St. Thomas (and possibly in all of the U.S.V.I.), head over to **Eunice's Terrace** (Tel: 775-3975), at the eastern end of the island on Smith Bay Road. The catch of the day—broiled, boiled, sautéed, or fried—is accompanied by heaping servings of spicy rice, fungi (a mixture of cornmeal and okra), and breadfruit (an island staple). The "oldwife fish" can't be beat, especially if it's offered as the catch of the day. A Caribbean fish, oldwife is tender, tasty, and mild, usually served with fresh tomato and island spices.

Out on the Island

St. Thomas is not very big—just 32 square miles—so you are never far from Charlotte Amalie or from some of the island's most beautiful natural spots and beaches. Spend at least one afternoon driving over its steep, high hills, making stops at Coral World, a truly worthwhile underwater observatory; Drake's Seat, a scenic overlook; Magens

Bay, an immaculate, though often crowded, mile-long beach; and **Mountain Top**, the island's highest point.

Coral World (Tel: 775-1555), on the northeastern side of the island at Coki Point, does not fall into the seen-one-you've-seen-'em-all aquarium category. It's a very conscientiously assembled and maintained marine park and submarine observatory devoted to safeguarding the reefs around St. Thomas. In its three-story observatory, guests descend right down to the ocean floor and get a 360-degree view of submarine life in its natural state. **Magens Bay** is one of the island's most beautiful beaches, with calm, glass-clear water and powdery white sands. **Pineapple Beach**, at the Stouffer Grand Beach Resort (see below), has every water sport imaginable, and lessons are available there, too. Daily sailings (half day or full day) to St. John on a trimaran pull in right at the Pineapple Beach dock. Other beaches worth finding include **Coki Beach** on the northeastern shore (crowded on Sundays; a magnet for snorkelers) and **Sapphire** on the eastern end. At both you can rent snorkeling gear and pollywog about in unbelievably clear water. **Hull Bay** on the northern shore has good surfing conditions.

Several dive sites ring St. Thomas. One of the most popular is the **wreck of the Major General Rogers**, a Coast Guard vessel purposely sunk nearly 20 years ago to establish a fish habitat. At nearby **Thatch Cay** a series of underwater tunnels and passageways teem with fish; huge boulders and lava archways characterize **Congo Bay**. Diving companies include **Aqua Action** (Tel: 775-6285) and **Caribbean Divers** (Tel: 775-6384). In addition, there's good snorkeling right off several of the island's beaches, including Coki Beach, Hull Bay, and Secret Harbour.

Sportsfishing can be arranged through several island companies including **Island Holiday** (Tel: 775-6500) and the **St. Thomas Sport Fishing Center** (Tel: 775-7990), or ask at **American Yacht Harbor** (Tel: 775-6454).

If it's sailing you love, you can charter a bare boat or hire a yacht with a crew for a day, a week—however long you like. The Virgin Islands Charteryacht League publishes a color brochure each year featuring member yachts and their crews, and can also recommend bareboat charter companies (there are dozens). Write to them c/o Flagship, Anchor Way, St. Thomas or call (800) 524-2061 or (809) 774-3944 for information.

There's not much in the way of land sport on St. Thomas, with the exception of a little golf and tennis. The best place for both is **Mahogany Run Villas** (Tel: 775-5000), a golf/tennis/condo community on the north shore. Its 18-hole course overlooks the Atlantic, and two courts are lighted for night play. Several other hotels on the island have tennis courts, including Sapphire Beach, Stouffer Grand Beach Resort, Limetree, Bluebeard's Castle, and Frenchman's Reef. All properties mentioned above serve non-guests as well as guests.

At night steel-band and calypso shows liven up many of the island's larger hotels. If you're not up for watching limbos, bottle dancing, and fire eating, your best bet might be a leisurely dinner before settling down on chaise longues around your hotel's pool with a couple of fruity concoctions. If you must go out, consider the highly regarded **Agave Terrace** at Point Pleasant Resort (near Pineapple Beach), which hosts steel bands Thursdays, a guitarist Saturdays and Sundays, and jazz bands every full moon. If you've still got energy to burn, try one of the island's top dance clubs: **Green House** (Tel: 774-7998), which features live bands almost every night of the week, or **Club Z** (Tel: 776-4655), with live bands and disco music.

If seclusion and privacy spark your idea of a romantic, getaway vacation, consider staying at **Pavilions & Pools** on Smith Bay Road. The hotel's 25 private villas, each with its own pool and patio surrounded by jungly greens, includes a kitchen, a living room, and a bedroom with TV and VCR (some have "garden" showers). **Point Pleasant Resort** would be another fine choice for peace and quiet. Built into a bluff, its attractive suites look out over the sea and outlying islands, and each has a fully equipped kitchen and balcony. There are three pools, a tennis court, wooded trails for strolling, a private beach, and the above-mentioned Agave Terrace, offering a view and a touch of low-key nightlife.

Right down the hill—smack dab on the beach—is the **Stouffer Grand Beach Resort**, a complex of brown-gray shingled units and motorized buggies whizzing about. It's a large, has-everything (including a health-and-fitness room) luxury resort and attracts lots of honeymooners. Farther over on the eastern end of the island, you'll find several condominium communities, among them the **Sapphire Beach Resort and Marina**. The Sapphire Beach features single- and two-story condo units, all with private balconies facing the beach, huge living rooms, sleeping accommodations for two to six adults, and full kitchens (with microwave ovens). There's also a full array of water sports and beach activities. It's a good choice for families and groups of friends.

ST. CROIX

Hurricane Hugo, which squalled over St. Croix on September 17, 1989, left the island in ruins. Stretches of beach were swept to sea, long-trunked palm and huge mahogany trees toppled over like toothpicks, and the rain forests practically disappeared. Though the island took a real beating, it has had an amazing recovery, thanks to a tremendous group effort by local residents. Today's visitor finds a spanking new island with rebuilt homes, hotels, and businesses.

Christiansted

The most famous and most visited place on St. Croix, Christiansted is a warren of narrow streets lined with Easter egg–colored buildings. Fortunately, its 18th-century Danish structures (including a small, unforbidding fort) all survived Hugo's wrath. The Visitors Bureau in the old Scalehouse building will provide you with a brochure outlining a self-guided walking tour of the area.

It seems that every visitor to St. Croix spends at least one day shopping, and cruise ships—they dock across the island in Frederiksted—send passengers over by the busload. Bargains can be found if you are up to dealing with the throngs.

Most of Christiansted's restaurants occupy second floors above shops and hotels. A popular breakfast spot is **Antoine's** (Tel: 773-0263) over the Anchor Inn. You can have endless mugs of strong coffee and your choice from more than a dozen omelets while watching the action on the wharf, which is especially busy in the morning. Snorkel boats gear up to take amphibious types out to nearby Buck Island (see below), suntanned blonds scrub down sailboats, and local partygoers exchange stories about the previous night. If you're in the mood for a simple lunch, try the **Banana Bay Club** for a burger, a basket of shrimp, or a chicken salad. It, too, sits on the water; Tel: 778-9110.

One of the favorite dining spots on the island is the **Club Comanche** (Tel: 773-2665), with ceiling fans, peacock chairs, and servings big enough for two. The fish of the day cooked Cruzan style (spicy and tomatoey) is always a good choice. At lunch be sure to try the West Indian conch, which is served with corn bread and fungi. Club Comanche is also a charming West Indian inn, complete with four-poster beds, old chests, and mahogany mirrors. And the location—in the heart of Christiansted—is super if you want to be near everything. **Top Hat** (Tel: 773-2346) is a small, elegant spot that prides itself on its Danish dishes—split pea soup, *frikadeller* (meatballs with red cabbage), and herring platters. **Kendrick's** (Tel: 773-9199) has three dining areas off the lobby/bar entrance that are separated by etched glass panels and island-fabric print curtains. The menu includes a variety of fish, beef, chicken, duck, and pasta dishes. Try the pork satay appetizer for starters and one of the homemade desserts—pecan-honey-crunch pie, perhaps—to finish.

If you're in the mood for something Italian, try **Tutto Bene** (Tel: 773-5229), a casual (read "inexpensive, but good") Italian restaurant or **Dino's** (Tel: 778-8005), well respected on the island for its pasta, made fresh daily by the chef/owners. The **Cultured Pelican Café** (Tel: 773-3333) has a satiating selection of seafood dishes, as well as soups, salads, and sandwiches. And **Anabelle's Tea Room** (Tel: 773-3990) is a family-owned affair featuring Cuban cuisine.

Dinners can be topped off with a nightcap at any of a number of bars in and around town. The **Moonraker Lounge** (Tel: 773-1535), at the Lodge Hotel on Queen Cross Street, spotlights a new guitarist from the States every six weeks. Or head over to **Hondo's** (Tel: 773-5855), a popular nightclub with live music above **Hondo's Backyard** restaurant, where you can sample Tex-Mex specialties, fried chicken steak, and sandwiches and burgers. On Saturday nights one of the island's most highly regarded saxophone players—Jimmy Hamilton—plays at the **Terrace Lounge** of the Buccaneer Hotel, just outside of town; Tel: 773-2100.

Of the several small, attractive inns in Christiansted, one of the best is **Pink Fancy**, a restored 18th-century Danish town house that was once a private club for wealthy planters. Each of its 13 rooms is named after one of the island's old plantations (Upper Love, Jealousy, Sweet Bottom) and handsomely decorated in white, except for the Mexican terra-cotta tiled floors and the Brazilian imbuia doors. Pink Fancy was popular among well-known performers, writers, and painters in the 1950s,

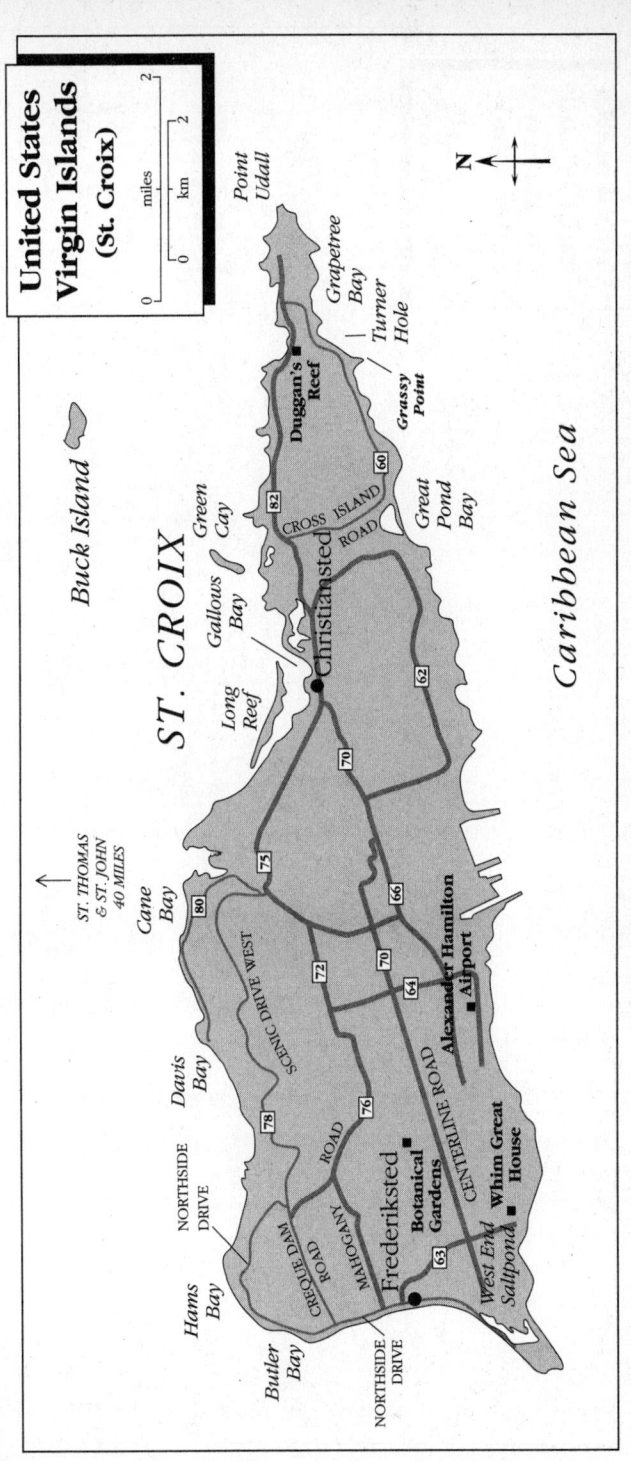

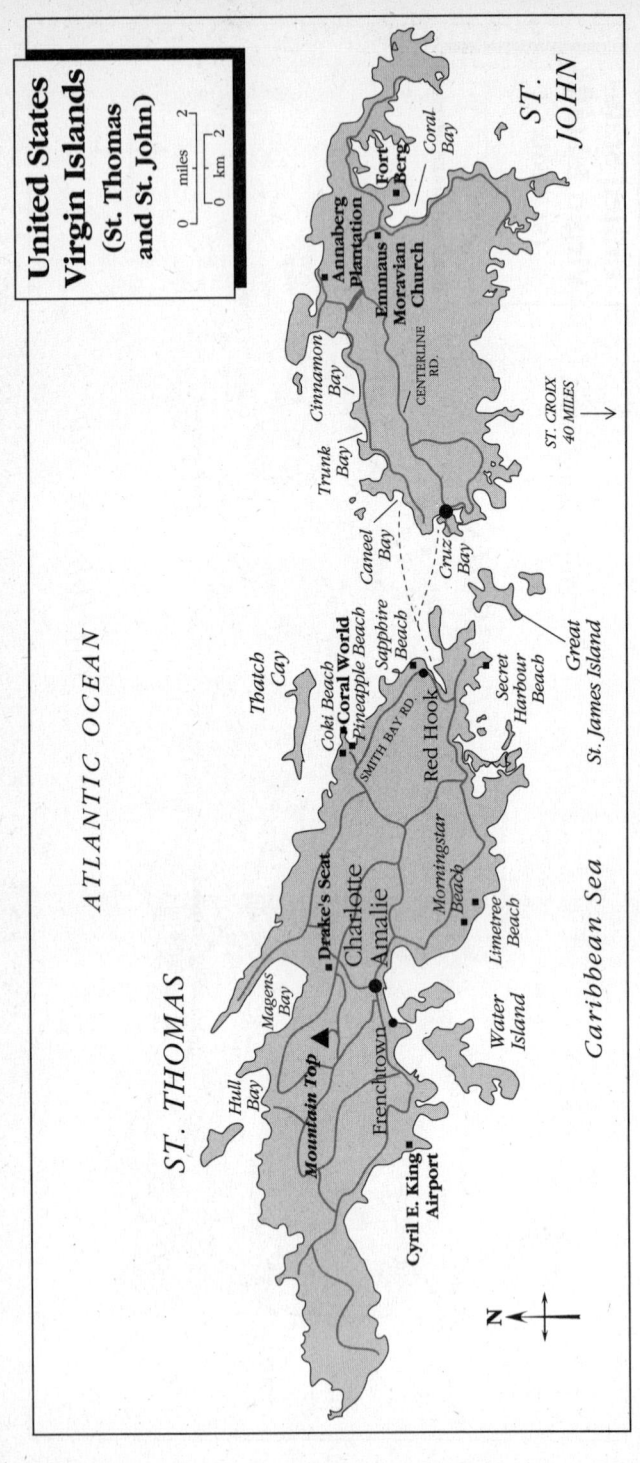

United States Virgin Islands (St. Thomas and St. John)

ST. THOMAS

ST. JOHN

ATLANTIC OCEAN

Caribbean Sea

Hull Bay

Magens Bay

Mountain Top

Drake's Seat

Charlotte Amalie

Frenchtown

Cyril E. King Airport

Water Island

Morningstar Beach

Limetree Beach

Red Hook

Thatch Cay

Coki Beach

Coral World

Pineapple Beach

Sapphire Beach

SMITH BAY RD.

Secret Harbour Beach

St. James Island

Great

Cruz Bay

Caneel Bay

Trunk Bay

Cinnamon Bay

CENTERLINE RD.

Emmaus Moravian Church

Annaberg Plantation

Fort Berg

Coral Bay

ST. CROIX 40 MILES

N

and today attracts professionals seeking peace and quiet. There's a pool on the premises and an open bar, and breakfast is served each morning.

Another good in-town find is the **King Christian Hotel**, which occupies a convenient wharfside location. (Rooms 201 and 301 offer the best views and balconies facing the wharf.) The hotel, which has a pool and a branch of the **Chart House Restaurant** chain on the premises (Tel: 773-7718), attracts many repeat guests, frequently nautical types. The beach is a short ferry ride away.

If you're interested in going out to snorkel or dive the reef at the mesmerizingly beautiful **Buck Island National Park**, sign on for a boat trip right at the Christiansted dock (you can't miss the signs). Catamarans and glass-bottom boats leave a couple times a day carrying first-time snorkelers as well as certified divers. A designated U.S. National Monument, the reef is clearly marked with blue signs along the ocean floor directing you through the forests of staghorn coral that swarm with metallic-looking fish. Some of the boat trips include a picnic lunch on the island, which is ringed by blinding-white beaches.

The East End

The setting of **The Buccaneer Hotel** is absolutely glorious—its grounds sprawl down a hill above Christiansted harbor. Part of the Buccaneer's now flamingo-pink main building was originally built for a Knight of Malta in 1653. Then the French bought the place, and later the Danes turned it into a residence for the island's first governor, Baron von Prock. Guests can stay in the Danish colonial rooms in the main house or in the more modern beachside suites and rooms. Sports include tennis and golf, and there's a spa and a private beach with scuba diving, snorkeling, swimming, sportsfishing, you name it—all are big at the Buccaneer. It's also one of St. Croix's most popular night spots, with live bands and dancing at the alfresco bar.

Many of the island's nicest beaches are carved out of the eastern end of the island. Follow the road that clings to the coast and pull over whenever you see an appealing strand. All beaches are public, including those in front of hotels, which are open to all visitors, sometimes for a small fee. Just ten minutes outside of town is **Duggan's Reef**, one of the island's best. And nearby **Villa Madeleine** is one of the island's most elegant accommodations. It's a beautiful collection of one- and two-bedroom villas with complete kitchens, oversized marble baths, intricate woodwork, and mahogany French doors. Each one has a private patio with its own pool and a view of the sea in the distance. Its restaurant—**Café Madeleine**—is just as appealing, with an ever-changing menu of fresh seafood and Italian dishes served in a traditional West Indian plantation house high above Teague Bay. Diners can choose between the canopied terrace overlooking the sea or the air-conditioned dining room, beautifully appointed with antiques and plants. Dinner reservations are necessary; Tel: 778-7377. The southeast coast along Turner Hole is especially beautiful, and at its best at **Grassy Point**, with views of the sea stretching off in a carpet of blues and greens. And it's not just the beach that will capture your attention—the lush scenery of the interior is glorious, too.

To Frederiksted

Centerline Road, the oldest on the island, runs in a more or less straight line to connect Christiansted with Frederiksted. There are two notable stops along the way: the **Botanical Gardens** (Tel: 772-3874) and **Whim Museum and Great House** (Tel: 772-0598). The gardens grow around the ruins of a 19th-century sugarcane workers' village; the great house was built in 1794 on a sugar plantation and has been carefully restored by the Landmarks Society. Tours of Whim conclude with a sampling of St. Croix's famous johnnycakes, baked in the plantation's cookhouse.

Frederiksted

Cruzans consider Frederiksted the "West Indian" town of St. Croix. Cruise ships tie up at its deep-water port, but most passengers are whisked through town to Christiansted, considered by islanders to be more cosmopolitan and more Danish. As a result, Frederiksted has an undiscovered air about it. Although most of the town's original Danish colonial buildings were destroyed by fire and replaced by wooden Victorian gingerbread, some of its landmarks date back to the 1700s. Pick up a copy of the walking-tour guide at the Customs House and wander around to see Fort Frederik (1760); the Market Place, operating since 1751; the Old Danish School, designed by Danish architect Hingelberg in the 1830s; and the town's four historic churches. Also worthwhile is a tour of the **St. Croix Aquarium** (Tel: 772-1345), led by a marine biologist.

A handful of restaurants in town include **Blue Moon**, a bistro serving Cruzan dishes along with nightly jazz (Tel: 772-2222 for reservations), and **Le St. Tropez** (Tel: 772-3000), which specializes in French and Mediterranean dishes. At the end of the day, make your way to one of the beach bars on the water's edge for rum punches and a sunset you'll never forget.

The Northwest

Northside Drive follows the coastline up from Frederiksted, passing one elegant great house after another. Among them is **Sprat Hall Plantation**, the oldest continuously lived-in great house in St. Croix. It dates back to the French occupation of 1650 to 1690, when it was built to duplicate an original in Brittany. It is now an inn with dining room run by owners Judy and Mark Young, whose families have been on the island since the 1700s. The dining room occupies the original ballroom and specializes in old island recipes. Most guests come for the horseback riding; the guided rides twist through the rain forests, up to scenic hilltops, down to Danish ruins, and along the west coast beaches. If you're not staying at Sprat Hall, you can still go riding there. Be sure to call ahead, though; Tel: 776-2627.

To immerse yourself in some of the island's most intensely beautiful scenery, consider taking a four-wheel vehicle on nearby **Creque Dam Road**, which meanders through virgin rain forest just off the Northside Drive.

ST. JOHN

All too often you return to a cherished island and discover that what was once your favorite view is now the site of a mega-resort, or that a shopping mall has sprung up next to the house you've been renting for years. Not so on St. John. Due to the foresight of Laurance Rockefeller, there's no chance of such things happening here.

Today much of the island enjoys the protection of the National Park Service and you can walk miles and miles of undisturbed wilderness over well-marked trails. Tourists, armed with beach bags, snorkeling paraphernalia, and video cameras, ferry over daily to Cruz Bay from Red

Hook on St. Thomas. Everyone comes to see the scenery and to lie on the beaches, which are lovely and plentiful.

St. John is a curvaceous little island; precipitous mountain edges give over to stunning views; greenery and flowers smell so sweet they are almost asphyxiating at times. It is easy to explore on your own in a rented Jeep or Suzuki, but you still might want to take one of the island's guided tours, which are exceptionally good. Most of the guides are native St. Johnians who take you to such sites as the **Annaberg Sugar Plantation**; **Trunk Bay**, known for its underwater trail frequented by snorkelers; and a number of scenic overlooks. Another standard tour follows the Danish Centerline Road to **Coral Bay**, the site of the first permanent Danish settlement on St. John. You have plenty of time to walk around the ruins of Fort Berg (scene of a major slave revolt from 1733 to 1734) and the Emmaus Moravian Church. Tours usually end in Cruz Bay, the island's hub. The National Park Service also offers tours, led by well-informed rangers. For more information, stop by the park's Visitors Center (across from Mongoose Junction in Cruz Bay). There, you can also pick up a free map of the island.

For all-out beaching on St. John, head straight over to Trunk Bay or to **Cinnamon Bay**, both of which are part of the Virgin Islands National Park. Both have chaise longues and snorkeling gear for rent as well as changing rooms, showers, and snack bars. And both are about as beautiful as beaches get. You can also spread out your towels on just about any inviting stretch of sand that happens to catch your eye as you drive around the island.

The Cruz Bay Area

Cruz Bay is a picturesque town that always seems to have an air of carnival. All types of characters abound: beach bums (usually college kids from the States down for extended visits), honeymooners, permanent hippies, and camera-toting day-trippers from St. Thomas. Most of the latter immediately gravitate to **Mongoose Junction**, an assemblage of shops that some would call a mall, but it's far too attractive to be given such a label. Its shops purvey island fashions, funky aquatic accessories and necessities, and locally crafted jewelry and pottery. **Wharfside Village** also houses several clothing stores, jewelers, and a gift shop, as well as such eateries as **Beni Iguana's Sushi Bar** (Tel: 779-4068) and **Pusser's** (Tel: 774-5489) for seafood.

If you're interested in sea kayaking, stop by the **Big Planet** shop. These adventure outfitters take novices and experienced kayakers out on paddling excursions to nearby islands right from the Cruz Bay dock area. Trips start at U.S. $45 for four and a half hours. Tel: 776-6638 for reservations.

The grande dame of places to stay on St. John is **Caneel Bay**, which locals refer to as "Larry's Place." Caneel Bay is the first of several resort properties developed by Laurance Rockefeller in the Caribbean. Sprawling over 170 acres on a peninsula within the designated national park area, it has an air of clubbiness and attracts plenty of affluent couples—both newlyweds and those who have been coming here for 25 years. Guests have a choice of seven beaches for lounging, snorkeling, or sailing. There's also a pool, 11 tennis courts, and nature trails.

Although Caneel Bay has been the longtime favorite, there's a new kid on the block: the **Hyatt Regency St. John at Virgin Grand Resort**. Its 264 rooms all have terraces and patios with views of the sea. Not quite as exclusive as Caneel Bay, the Hyatt offers its guests a pool, tennis courts, a whole array of water sports, and three restaurants on the grounds.

Gallows Point condominiums provide an alternative to staying in a hotel on St. John. Located on a hill up from Cruz Bay, the four-unit buildings offer great views of the sea and St. Thomas in the distance. The "units" (really apartments) have kitchens, ceiling fans, and terrarium-like bathrooms.

St. John is home to two campgrounds that are ideal for those wanting to get very close to nature. Both the **Cinnamon Bay Campgrounds** (run by the National Park Service) and the **Maho Bay Camps** are on beaches and offer cottages for rental. Maho Bay's cottages have stoves, beds, and linens, but no TVs, phones, or running water. Cinnamon Bay also has bare campsites and some with tents, cots, and other provisions.

There are some very good restaurants on the island, including those at Caneel Bay and the Hyatt, and **Paradiso** (Tel: 776-8806) at Mongoose Junction. The latter—which offers a varied menu with French, American, and pasta dishes—is always busy; make sure to call ahead to reserve. More casual finds include **Lime Inn** (Tel: 776-6425), which is locally famed for its Wednesday night all-you-can-eat shrimp feast (be prepared to wait); **Shipwreck Landing** (Tel: 776-8640), specializing in West Indian and

American cuisine; and **Fish Trap** (Tel: 776-9817), for flawlessly grilled fish dishes.

USEFUL FACTS

What to Wear

Dress is casual all over the U.S.V.I., but it is against the law
to wear bathing suits away from the beach. The only place
where you will need a jacket is Caneel Bay. Nights can get
a bit cool, so pack a sweater or two.

Getting In

American Airlines flies nonstop from New York to both St.
Thomas and St. Croix. American also flies direct to both
from Miami and Raleigh/Durham. Delta Air Lines has
daily direct service from both Orlando and Atlanta to St.
Thomas, continuing on to St. Croix. Continental flies daily
from Newark to St. Thomas and on to St. Croix.

   From Europe, it's usually necessary to stay overnight in
San Juan, Miami, or New York.

   Passengers bound for St. John fly into St. Thomas, taxi
to Red Hook, and take the 20-minute ferry over to Cruz
Bay or Caneel Bay, or water-taxi over from the waterfront
in Charlotte Amalie.

Entry Requirements

U.S. citizens need only proof of residency (a birth certificate or voter-registration card). Citizens of other nations
must have passports. There is no departure tax.

Local Time

The U.S.V.I. is on Atlantic standard time year-round, one
hour ahead of the U.S. east coast except when the east
coast moves its clocks ahead an hour during daylight
saving time. Then all keep the same time.

Electrical Current

Same as elsewhere in the U.S. and Canada—110 volts AC,
60 cycles.

Getting Around

Ferries run between St. Thomas and St. John. SUNAIRE
offers frequent flights daily between St. Thomas and St.
Croix. The flight is usually crowded with commuters
(they're 16-seater planes), so passengers must arrive one-

half hour early to get on the flight. American Eagle also offers service between the two islands.

The best way to get around on the individual islands is by rental car. Otherwise, taxis are readily available and fairly inexpensive; they are also available for tours of the islands.

Business Hours
Shops are customarily open from 9:00 A.M. to 5:00 P.M. daily, except Sundays. When cruise ships are in port, many will stay open late and even open on Sundays. Check the *St. Thomas Daily News* for ship arrival and departure times.

Holidays
In addition to the standard U.S. holidays, the Virgin Islands observe January 6 (Three Kings' Day); March 31 (Transfer Day, celebrating the transfer of the Danish islands to the U.S.); May 1 (Children's Carnival parade); May 2 (Grand Carnival parade); June 18 (Organic Act Day); July 3 (Emancipation Day, commemorating the freeing of the slaves in 1848); July 25 (Hurricane Supplication Day); October 17 (Hurricane Thanksgiving Day); November 1 (Liberty Day); and December 26 (Boxing Day).

For Further Information
United States Virgin Islands Division of Tourism, P.O. Box 6400, Charlotte Amalie, **St. Thomas,** U.S.V.I. 00804, Tel: (809) 774-8784, Fax: (809) 774-4390; P.O. Box 4538, Christiansted, **St. Croix,** U.S.V.I. 00822, Tel: (809) 773-0495, Fax: (809) 778-9259; P.O. Box 200, Cruz Bay, **St. John,** U.S.V.I. 00830, Tel: (809) 776-6450; **in the U.S.,** 1270 Avenue of the Americas, New York, NY 10020, Tel: (800) USVI-INFO or (212) 582-4520; **in Canada,** 33 Niagara Street, Toronto, M5V 1C2, Tel: (800) 465-8784 or (416) 362-8784; **in the U.K.,** 2 Cinnamon Row, Plantation Wharf, York Place, London SW11 3TW, England, Tel: (71) 978-5262.

ACCOMMODATIONS REFERENCE
The rate ranges given here, in U.S. dollars, are projections for fall 1992 through spring 1993, and span the lowest rates in the low season to the highest in the high season. Unless otherwise indicated, rates are for double rooms, double occupancy. As rates are subject to change, it's always wise to double-check before booking. The tele-

phone area code (within the U.S. system) for the U.S. Virgin Islands is 809.

St. Thomas

▶ **Blackbeard's Castle**. P.O. Box 6041, Charlotte Amalie, St. Thomas, U.S.V.I. 00804. Tel: 776-1234; Fax: 776-4321; in U.S., (800) 344-5771. $95–$140, C.P.

▶ **Hotel 1829**. P.O. Box 1567, Charlotte Amalie, St. Thomas, U.S.V.I. 00804. Tel: 776-1829; Fax: 776-4313; in U.S., (800) 524-2000. $60–$170, E.P.

▶ **Pavilions & Pools**. Route 6, St. Thomas, U.S.V.I. 00802. Tel: 775-6110; Fax: 775-6110; in U.S., (800) 524-2001. $175–$255, C.P. (C.P. available winter only).

▶ **Point Pleasant Resort**. Estate Smith Bay, St. Thomas, U.S.V.I. 00802. Tel: 775-7200; Fax: 776-5694; in U.S., (800) 524-2300. $175–$350, E.P.

▶ **Sapphire Beach Resort and Marina**. P.O. Box 8088, St. Thomas, U.S.V.I. 00801. Tel: 775-6100; Fax: 775-4024; in U.S., (800) 524-2090. $190–$295, E.P. (M.A.P. available.)

▶ **Stouffer Grand Beach Resort**. P.O. Box 8267, St. Thomas, U.S.V.I. 00801. Tel: 775-1510; Fax: 775-3757; in U.S., (800) 233-4935 or (800) HOTELS-1 (reservations). $195–$415, E.P. (M.A.P. available.)

St. Croix

▶ **The Buccaneer Hotel**. P.O. Box 25200, Gallows Bay, St. Croix, U.S.V.I. 00824-5200. Tel: 773-2100; Fax: 778-8215; in U.S., Tel: (800) 223-1108; Fax: (914) 763-5362. $140–$325, E.P.

▶ **Club Comanche**. 1 Strand Street, Christiansted, St. Croix, U.S.V.I. 00820. Tel: 773-0210; Fax: 773-0210. $70–$100, E.P.

▶ **King Christian Hotel**. P.O. Box 3619, Christiansted, St. Croix, U.S.V.I. 00822-3619. Tel: 773-2285; Fax: 773-9411; in U.S., (800) 524-2012. $80–$135, E.P.

▶ **Pink Fancy**. 27 Prince Street, Christiansted, St. Croix, U.S.V.I. 00820. Tel: 773-8460; Fax: 773-6448; in U.S., (800) 524-2045. $75–$150, C.P.

▶ **Sprat Hall Plantation**. Route 63, P.O. Box 695, Frederiksted, St. Croix, U.S.V.I. 00841. Tel: 772-0305; in U.S., (800) 843-3584. $80–$160, E.P. (main house).

▶ **Villa Madeleine**. P.O. Box. 3109, Christiansted, St. Croix, U.S.V.I. 00822. Tel: 773-8141; Fax: 773-7518; in U.S., (800) 548-4461. $300–$425, E.P.

St. John

▶ **Caneel Bay.** Caneel Bay, P.O. Box 720, Cruz Bay, St. John, U.S.V.I. 00831-0720. Tel: 776-6111; Fax: 776-2030; in U.S., (800) 223-7637. $200–$535, E.P.; A.P., $80 per person extra per day.

▶ **Cinnamon Bay Campgrounds.** Cruz Bay, St. John, U.S.V.I. 00830. Tel: 776-6330; Fax: 776-6458; in U.S., (800) 223-7637. $14 (bare sites), $40–$62 (tents), $53–$79 (cottages).

▶ **Gallows Point.** P.O. Box 58, Cruz Bay, St. John, U.S.V.I. 00831. Tel: 776-6434; Fax: 776-6520; in U.S. (800) 323-7229. $125–$295.

▶ **Hyatt Regency St. John at Virgin Grand Resort.** Great Cruz Bay, St. John, U.S.V.I. 00830. Tel: 776-7171; Fax: 779-4500; in U.S., (800) 233-1234. $155–$475, E.P.

▶ **Maho Bay Camps.** P.O. Box 310, Cruz Bay, St. John, U.S.V.I. 00830. Tel: 776-6226; Fax: 861-6210; in U.S., (800) 392-9004. $50–$75 (cottages).

THE BRITISH VIRGIN ISLANDS

By Susan Farewell

The writer Lawrence Durrell wrote about a disease not yet classified by medical science that he called "islomania," which afflicts "people who find islands somehow irresistible."

You couldn't find an archipelago that is more fitting for islomaniacs than the British Virgin Islands. There are about 50 islands in the B.V.I.—only 16 of them inhabited—clustered together like croutons in soup. These islands were formed through volcanic activity and therefore are—with the exception of Anegada, a flat coral atoll—very hilly, surging steeply out of the sea, their hillsides densely colonized by leafy greens, including frangipani, banana, and mango trees. All the islands are well endowed with long white-sand beaches washed by the clearest of Caribbean water and backed by clusters of sea grapes and palm trees.

For years these islands have been well known among yachtsmen, who come from all over the world to explore the small bays and coves scalloped out of the shores. But the appeal of the B.V.I. extends beyond the deck of a sloop. Probably the biggest draw is the fact that the islands have not sprouted into a tourist mecca. They are somewhat more difficult to reach than some Caribbean

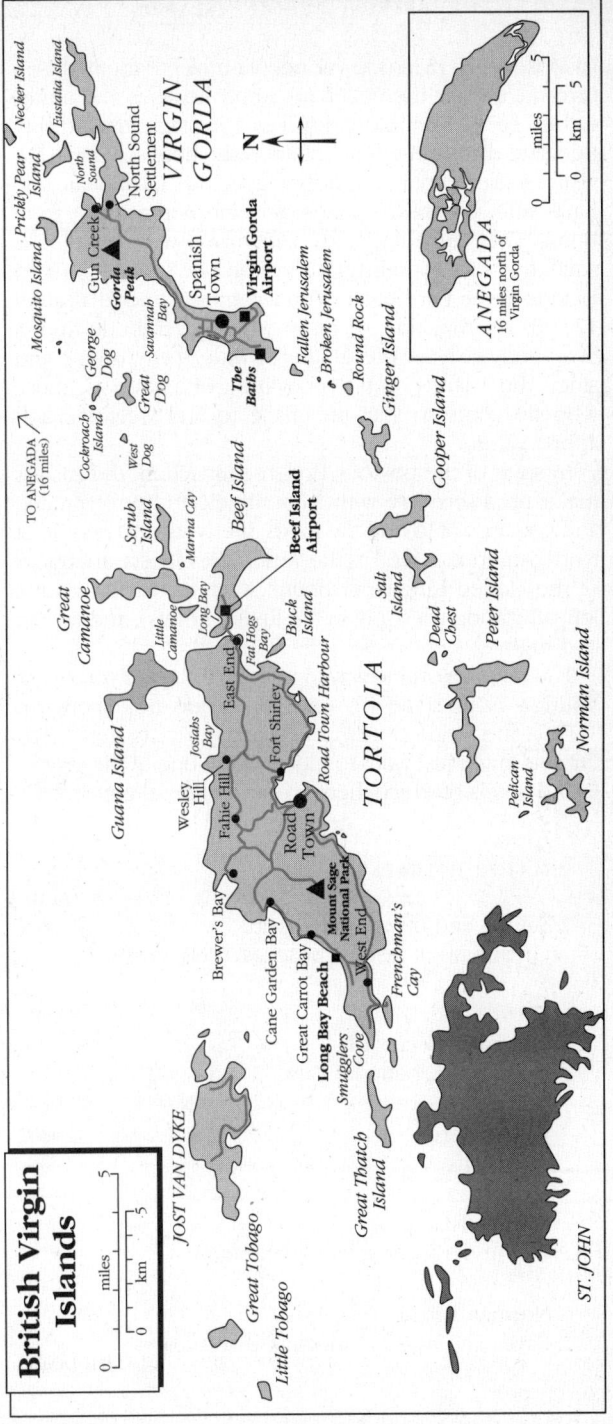

islands, which means fewer people travel to them; this in turn means that there still are empty beaches and undisturbed reefs. Nightlife is low-key, revolving around dinners and drinks in open-air bars at the hotels. Many B.V.I. visitors grew up island-hopping in the Caribbean and have selected these islands as their home away from home. They come back year after year, usually to sail. The small-town feel you'll find here can't be found on many islands in the Caribbean. With a combined population of 12,000, it's the kind of place where everybody knows everybody else. As a result there's little, if any, crime. And since the islands aren't "crawling" with tourists, those who do come to visit are made to feel welcome and appreciated.

In spite of the obvious British connection, the islands make up a territory with a locally elected government, and you are apt to find the foods, lifestyles, and people of North America as well as the West Indies. There are traces of the United Kingdom, though, such as driving on the left, afternoon tea (only in the luxury hotels), and cricket and rugby.

The most enjoyable way to visit the B.V.I.—if you're not sailing—is to settle on one (or divide time between Tortola and Virgin Gorda) and take day trips to the others. Or you might just want to hide away at one of the private island hotels of which there are several excellent choices.

MAJOR INTEREST

Sailing and other water sports
Great natural beauty: beaches, reefs, coves

Tortola
Quiet and seclusion
Mount Sage National Park

Virgin Gorda
The Baths

Off Salt Island
The underwater wreck of the *Rhone*

Norman Island
Caves and nearby "Indians" dive sites

TORTOLA

Tortola, the hub around which the B.V.I. radiate, seems meant by nature to be a sailor's world. Perfect little coves lie scooped out of its coastline, and coral reefs segregate rough seas from smooth waters. On land there are craggy peaks, mountaintop vistas all around, pure white-sand beaches, and remains of a primeval forest. Tortola is home to Road Town, the capital and only "real" town in the British Virgin Islands. (It is also the most populated, with 10,000 year-round residents.) Tortola, however, is a small island, a mere ten square miles, which makes the scale of things reassuring. Within the span of one or two days, you can visit all of its beautiful natural spots and historic sites.

Road Town

The tiny capital of Road Town is the nucleus of all commercial and political activity in the B.V.I. Even so, it takes less than ten minutes to walk from one end of town to the other, past traditional Virgin Islands houses that have been painstakingly restored and past the town's eclectic mix of shops, banks, restaurants, and government buildings. There are a handful of decent restaurants in town, including **Spaghetti Junction** (Tel: 448-80), which serves by-the-book Italian (dinners only); **The Virgin Queen** (Tel: 423-10), where boaties crowd in for shepherd's pie, bangers and mash, and all-around spirited pub atmosphere; and **Pusser's Co. Store and Pub** (Tel: 424-67), for meat pies and deli sandwiches. Upstairs is **The Outpost** (Tel: 441-99), which serves steaks, chops, and seafood in a more formal setting.

If you want to try some exceptionally good local food, hire a taxi to take you to the impossible-to-find-on-your-own **Aries Club** (Tel: 433-29). Locals crowd in, especially during weekday lunch hours, for some of the island's best fish, accompanied by ample servings of rice, potatoes, plantains, and vegetables. Try *mauvy* (or *maube*), a sweet nonalcoholic drink made from bark.

For more serious dining, try **Brandywine Bay** (Tel: 523-01), east of town, where you can feast on flawlessly grilled local fish, or **Skyworld** (Tel: 435-67), about ½ km (¼ mile) above Road Town on Ridge Road. At the latter listen for the hum of satisfaction from diners enjoying West Indian and Continental food as they gaze out upon the mountains and sea around them.

If you'd like to stay near town, choose **Treasure Isle**, into a hillside overlooking Sir Francis Drake Channel, about a ten-minute walk from the town center. In addition to standard hotel rooms, suites (with kitchenettes) are available; all are air-conditioned and equipped with TVs, phones, and verandahs. There are tennis courts, a pool, and an open-air bar and restaurant. The Offshore Sailing School operates from Treasure Isle, so you're sure to see many boaties.

You'll find more nautical types over at the **Moorings Mariner Inn**, a five-minute cab ride out of town. Its open-air bar and restaurant are always packed with sailors sporting honey-gold tans that make them look as if they were slowly roasted on a spit. The conversation is 100 percent sailing talk (winds, anchorages, the 51-foot this, the 37-foot that). Occasionally, a proud skipper dog wearing a bandanna trots through, claws clicking on the red-tile floor. Rooms are very Caribbean: no air-conditioning, just lazy ceiling fans and tepid sea breezes wafting in with reliable consistency. Furnishings are simple—you'll never feel guilty flinging your damp towels down. All rooms have terraces, and some look out over the marina. The inn has a pool and a tennis court.

Out on the Island

From Road Town a steep, curving road wraps around the hills of **Mount Sage National Park**, where you can hike to the top of Mount Sage—at 1,780 feet, the highest spot for miles around—for an impressive view of the sea and the other British Virgin Islands. Blanketing this park is the remaining vegetation from ancient forests that once covered much of the island's ridges. Though not a rain forest per se (it gets less than 100 inches of rain a year), it grows many of the same plants and trees you'd find in a rain forest, including enormous elephant ears and philodendrons, ferns, massive mahogany trees, and tangled vines. Follow the marked trails.

From Mount Sage continue over to **Cane Garden Bay**, northernmost of some of the island's best beaches, which line this shore, inviting you to try their white sands, snorkeling, and body surfing. Make your way down the coast sampling such other favorites as Apple Bay, Long Bay, and Smugglers Cove.

Mrs. Scatliffe's Restaurant (Tel: 545-56) in Carrot Bay is unquestionably geared to tourists but nonetheless an experience not to be missed. As you sit on the terrace, audience to a symphony of whistling tree frogs and the fruity scent of flowers, Mrs. Scatliffe and her family (kids, grandchildren, in-laws) serve artfully prepared West Indian dishes and serenade you with songs from their well-rehearsed repertoire.

If you want to stay on this coast, consider **The Sugar Mill**, owned by Jinx and Jeff Morgan, a U.S. writing-and-cooking team. The main building, across the street from the beach, is a 300-year-old sugar distillery that now houses a restaurant and an art gallery specializing in Haitian paintings. The food is unfailingly good, with such dishes as grilled boned quail with mango and papaya sauce, Caribbean bouillabaisse, and grilled scallops with red-pepper sauce. The inn's rooms are done up in soft tropical pastels and include kitchenettes and terraces. Just down the road is the more casual **Long Bay Beach Resort**, a group of villas set back into a hillside and on the beach. Long Bay Beach, sweeping along for about a mile, is without question the resort's focal point. There are also tennis courts and a pool. Guests at both the Sugar Mill and the Long Bay hotel tend to be seclusion-seeking professionals.

You can also rent a villa on the northwest coast through **Rockview Holiday Homes**. All 25 of their houses are tastefully decorated, meticulously maintained, and magnificently situated.

Stop at **Pusser's Landing** (Tel: 545-54) in West End for a good cold drink. Lunch (burgers, sandwiches) is nothing extraordinary but certainly acceptable, and as you eat you can watch sailboat crews stock up on ice and provisions.

For travellers who prefer accommodations on the western end of the island there is **Frenchman's Cay**, a collection of co-op villas, each with one or two bedrooms, a sitting room, a fully equipped kitchen-cum-dining room, and a terrace. Catering to a professional, quiet crowd, Frenchman's Cay offers a restaurant and bar, pool, man-made beach, tennis courts, and snorkeling.

The remarkably small Fort Recovery stands on what are now the grounds of a hotel along the southern coastal road. You aren't permitted to climb up, but you are welcome to admire it from sea level. The fort, about 45 feet in diameter and 30 feet high, was built by the Dutch in 1660 to protect the island from pirates. Just a short distance away (there's no sign) is an overgrown path leading to the so-called Dungeon. This seaward battery, probably built in the mid-18th century, was dubbed the Dungeon because its underground cell once housed prisoners. Many of its walls and staircases still stand beneath a tangle of growth. Another ruin stands nearby on an unmarked road in Pleasant Valley—the thick, vegetation-covered stone walls of William Thornton's House. (Thornton, born in the B.V.I. in 1761, designed the U.S. Capitol.)

The eastern half of Tortola centers on the East End Settlement, a cluster of old West Indian houses. Very scenic roads lead to Fat Hogs Bay, the site of the island's first Quaker settlement, and to Kingstown, where in 1833 a group of freed slaves built a settlement; today only the ruins of an Anglican church remain. There are some beautiful beaches on the eastern end of the island including Elizabeth Beach and Josiahs Bay, both with powder-white sands and few—if any—footprints.

VIRGIN GORDA

Any resident of Virgin Gorda is likely to tell you, with unimpeachable pride, "I put in an application to be born on Virgin Gorda." Or you may hear the it's-been-said-before-about-Greece story: "When God finished creating the heavens and the earth, he had a fistful of stones left, so he tossed them over his shoulder and made Virgin Gorda."

Virgin Gorda's northern end is dominated by lush green hills; its southern reaches are flat and desertlike, strewn with enormous cacti and whale-size boulders. The origins of these gargantuan boulders have been the topic of much geological speculation. Some say they're the result of a tempestuous storm that hurled them from the sea floor. Others say they're from a volcanic eruption. On the southwestern coast, a massive tumble of these mysterious boulders forms **the Baths**, marvelous little grottoes where the water is as clear as gin. Take time to explore the labyrinthine passageways they form. But if you want to swim, you're better off walking to one of the neighboring beaches to the south; the Baths can get very crowded.

The Spanish Town Area

Spanish Town, also referred to as "The Valley," is Virgin Gorda's largest settlement, spreading over the southern half of the island. Don't bother looking for a real town, because no such thing exists on Virgin Gorda. The only place that comes close is the Yacht Harbour Shopping Center, a group of stores selling island fashions, local crafts and jewelry, tee-shirts, and the like on the edge of a marina, owned by the Little Dix Bay Hotel Corporation.

Among locals, one of Spanish Town's most deservedly popular West Indian restaurants is **Teacher's Pet Ilma's** (Tel: 553-55), a tiny red-and-white building (no sign outside) with plastic flowers on plastic tablecloths and a billiard table dominating the front room. To find the place, just ask any Virgin Gordian—everyone knows Ilma's and can guide you there through the narrow, dusty back roads.

Another local hot spot is **Thelma's** (Tel: 556-46), where you can feast on boiled fish and baked chicken, and—as at Ilma's—dance on weekend nights. One of the island's most highly regarded restaurants, **Chez Michele** (Tel: 555-10), features fresh seafood and homemade pastas; look for it near the Yacht Harbour Shopping Center.

Little Dix Bay, once the indisputable queen of B.V.I. hotels, has changed ownership a couple of times in the last five years along with most of the other Rockresorts, so it no longer has the benefit of Laurance Rockefeller's golden touch. Nor is it any longer *the* hideaway for business-people and celebrities. Now you're more apt to see affluent young couples, many on their honeymoons. Little Dix Bay does, however, preserve Rockefeller's original concept of rough but refined vacationing. There are no phones, TVs, or radios in the rooms, and no outside locks on the doors. What you will find is great food, a lovely private beach, sailing, snorkeling, scuba diving, water-skiing, horseback riding, boat taxis to other beaches, and island sightseeing tours.

The **Olde Yard Inn** is a simple, quiet accommodation most celebrated for its restaurant and library. The dining "room" is a long verandah topped by a roof of banana leaves; the kitchen specializes in local fish dishes and offers a fine selection of wines. The much-talked-about library is a pair of twin octagonal buildings that the original owners put up to house their rare-book collection. Those books have since been replaced by the current owner's collection and by numerous volumes travellers have left behind. There's no pool or beach on the grounds, but **Savannah Beach**—one of the island's best-looking strands—is just a 15-minute walk away. The 14 rooms have been remodeled and are simply but attractively furnished, and all have patios or balconies.

If you're interested in renting a home on Virgin Gorda, contact **Virgin Gorda Villa Rentals** (see Accommodations at the end of the chapter). They provide homes (one to four bedrooms) around the island.

The North End

North Sound Road, connecting Spanish Town with the North Sound Settlement, passes through Virgin Gorda's narrow middle before gradually ascending Gorda Peak. Both the Atlantic and the Caribbean shores are visible from the high road as it meanders along the west side of the mountain, and the vistas are increasingly beautiful the higher you get. You can park and climb any of a number of hiking paths, including the North Sound Trail for an incomparable view and a look at the Nail Bay ruins, a cluster of plantation buildings.

North Sound is a small settlement made up of colorful houses festooned with blossoms and vacation homes that seem to hang off the hillsides. The road dips down like a water slide here and ends at Gun Creek Jetty and aptly named **The Last Stop** bar. Motorboats take off nearby and charge across the bay to two marvelously remote hotels — Biras Creek and the Bitter End Yacht Club.

Elegant **Biras Creek** has a collection of tastefully furnished villas, many right on the beach. Even when there's a full house (a total of 74 guests) you never feel that there are many people around—except at night, maybe, when guests convene in the hilltop bar and restaurant for fine dining and dancing. By day the guests—predominantly couples, many of whom have left the kids at home—tend to bicycle over the resort's dirt roads that pass through semiarid landscapes similar to those of East Africa. Biras Creek also has a pool, tennis courts, sailing, snorkeling, scuba diving, a marina, and boat taxis to nearby beaches.

The **Bitter End Yacht Club** merged with the Tradewinds next door some years back, making it one of Virgin Gorda's largest hotels. This is a place for serious sailors (there's a full-scale sailing school), but it attracts non-nautical types as well, including families with kids. In addition to sailing, the hotel offers snorkeling, scuba diving, a swimming pool, and out-island excursions. Request one of the original Tradewind rooms (in a pyramid-roofed villa) or a Bitter End beachfront room with a wraparound terrace. (The higher it is, the better the view and the more privacy you'll have.)

In the North Sound, on an island of its own (known as Mosquito Island), is **Drake's Anchorage Resort Inn**, a wonderfully secluded accommodation. Its three gingerbread-trimmed wood-frame cottages, which house a total of ten rooms (including two suites), are perched on stilts along the shore. All are tropically decorated with white walls, cool tile floors, and rattan and wicker furniture. Guests convene in the main lodge for exceptionally good meals prepared by Chef Erskine Husbands. The island has several nature trails and beautiful beaches—including one called Honeymoon—from which you can snorkel, swim, and sail, or just loll around in peaceful bliss.

OTHER ISLANDS

At least a half dozen other islands are worth visiting in the B.V.I. However, unless you've given yourself plenty of time, hopscotching among them could defeat the whole purpose of a vacation. If time permits, consider taking the ferry from West End on Tortola to **Jost Van Dyke**, a nice place to spend a day exploring its ruined fort, hiking its good trails, and swimming from its beaches. The ferry makes the trip several times a day. **Anegada** is the only island in this little galaxy that's flat; the highest point is a whopping 28 feet above sea level. It's encircled by dozens of sunken shipwrecks, a boon for serious snorkelers and divers. And because most travellers who come here head for the underwater reefs, the beaches are often pleasantly deserted for serious sun-and-sand lovers. You can only reach Anegada by air (Gorda Aero Service flies from Beef Island; Virgin Air flies from St. Thomas) or by private boat. The **wreck of the Rhone**, which sank in 1867, lies embedded in years of coral growth right off the coast of **Salt Island**. You can reach the wreck by private boat or by taking a guided snorkeling tour from one of the other islands. Most of the hotels offer frequent organized trips leaving from their own docks.

Peter Island Resort and Yacht Harbour, a little oasis of perfection, is sort of a "Bermuda of the B.V.I." It offers a clublike resort with very private (and spectacularly scenic) beaches, a pool, tennis courts, and two restaurants, open to day-trippers as well as hotel guests. Its beach villas are unquestionably the better rooms: noiseless ceiling fans, huge beds piled high with pillows, comfortable bathtubs that open up to window gardens, and terraces from which you can watch the moon rise. The Peter Island ferry shuttles over from Tortola's CSY Dock (east of Road Town) throughout the day, and a launch picks up guests from Tortola's Beef Island Airport.

Norman Island, with caves once said to have contained treasures, is believed to be the original site of Robert Louis Stevenson's *Treasure Island*. There's some fine snorkeling and diving in the caves and at the nearby **"Indians" rock formations** full of submarine canyons, grottoes, and coral.

Guana Island Club is very remote and very private, reachable only by its own private launch (Beef Island Airport pickups are arranged). Guests (no more than 30 at a time) stay in lovely whitewashed cottages, simply decorated and without TVs and radios, and divide their time between swimming, snorkeling, bird-watching, sailing, and basking in the sun on the island's seven beaches. There are also two tennis courts, a croquet course, and hiking trails. The finale of most days is a big seafood dinner on the hotel's terrace.

Necker Island, on its own 75-acre island, is a ten-bedroom villa available for private rentals. The building was originally erected in Bali, then dismantled and rebuilt in the B.V.I. All decor is Balinese, including matching batik bedspreads and bathrobes. Necker Island is surrounded by a coral reef and flanked by three white-sand beaches. There's a fleet of boats, an exercise room, tennis courts, and a Jacuzzi—more than enough diversion to keep a group of friends or a large family content for a week. (Guests are picked up at the Beef Island Airport by private launch or by helicopter.)

USEFUL FACTS

What to Wear

If you'll be staying at Peter Island, Biras Creek, or Little Dix Bay, men will need to pack a jacket. Otherwise, dress on the B.V.I. is very casual; you'll most likely live in bathing suits, shorts, and light tops and shirts. When visiting Road Town, however, it's a good idea to dress a bit more conservatively; swim suits and short shorts are frowned upon. Remember to pack the right shoes for boating, hiking, or horseback riding (you'll find stables in Spanish Town on Virgin Gorda).

Getting In

There are no major airports in the B.V.I., so it is necessary to connect from San Juan, St. Croix, or St. Thomas to either Tortola's Beef Island Airport or to the airport on Virgin Gorda. American Eagle, Virgin Air, and SUNAIRE Express fly from San Juan to Beef Island/Tortola and Virgin Gorda. Virgin Air and SUNAIRE Express fly from St. Thomas to Beef Island/Tortola. SUNAIRE Express also flies between St. Croix and Beef Island/Tortola. From Canada, your best bet is to travel via Miami.

From London you can take British Airways to Antigua and connect to Leeward Islands Air Transport (LIAT). Many of the connections are timed to meet British Airways flights, making an overnight stay on Antigua unnecessary. You can also reach the B.V.I. by taking a ferry from various locations on St. Thomas and St. John in the U.S.V.I. to Tortola, Virgin Gorda, and Jost Van Dyke.

Entry Requirements

U.S. and Canadian travellers need only present a valid driver's license or a voter-registration card. All others must have a current passport. The departure tax is U.S. $10 by air or water.

Local Time

The B.V.I. is on Atlantic standard time year-round, one hour ahead of the U.S. east coast except when the east coast moves its clocks ahead an hour during daylight saving time. Then all keep the same time.

Currency

The U.S. dollar is the official currency. Some hotels and restaurants don't take credit cards, but most accept traveller's checks.

Electrical Current

Same as in the U.S. and Canada—110 volts AC, 60 cycles.

Getting Around

Think twice about renting a car in the B.V.I.: The rollercoaster-like roads are quite treacherous, but the views are spectacular. You can rent a car at Beef Island Airport or in Road Town on Tortola or Spanish Town on Virgin Gorda, or see if your hotel can make the arrangements. You may want to rent a Land Rover or a Jeep so you can forge ahead on roads that might be considered bridle paths back home. You need a valid driver's license and must also buy a temporary B.V.I. license, good for 30 days, for U.S. $10 at the rental agency. Taxis are plentiful and, especially on the smaller islands, should be used instead of a rental. For short distances do as the locals do: Walk.

Business Hours

Shops and museums are generally open from 9:00 A.M. to 5:00 P.M. Monday through Saturday; banks, 9:00 A.M. to 2:00 P.M. Monday through Thursday, 9:00 A.M. to 2:00 P.M. and 4:00 to 6:00 P.M. on Fridays.

Festivals

August is carnival time in Tortola. On the first Sunday through Wednesday of that month everything closes as residents commemorate the 1834 Slave Emancipation with singing, dancing, and parades. Virgin Gorda has a three-day Easter Festival. The islands recognize British bank holidays, Territory Day (July 1), and Saint Ursula's Day (October 21).

For Further Information

British Virgin Islands Tourist Board, P.O. Box 134, Road Town, Tortola, B.V.I., Tel: (809) 494-3134; **in the U.S.,** 370 Lexington Avenue, Suite 511, New York, NY 10017, Tel: (800) 835-8530 or (212) 696-0400; **in Canada,** 801 York Mill Road, Suite 201, Don Mills, Ontario M3B 1X7, Tel: (416) 283-2235; **in the U.K.,** c/o Intermarketing London, 110 St. Martin's Lane, London WC2N 4DY, England, Tel: (71) 935-6726.

ACCOMMODATIONS REFERENCE

The rate ranges given here, in U.S. dollars, are projections for fall 1992 through spring 1993, and span the lowest rates in the low season to the highest in the high season. Unless otherwise indicated, rates are for double rooms, double occupancy. As rates are subject to change, it's al-

ways wise to double-check before booking. The telephone area code (within the U.S. system) for the B.V.I. is 809.

Tortola

▶ **Frenchman's Cay.** P.O. Box 1054, West End, Tortola, B.V.I. Tel: 495-4844; Fax: 495-4056; in U.S., (800) 223-9832 or (212) 599-8280. $100–$180, E.P. (one-bedroom villa).

▶ **Long Bay Beach Resort.** P.O. Box 433, Road Town, Tortola, B.V.I. Tel: 495-4252; Fax: 495-4677; in U.S., (800) 833-9599 or (914) 833-3300. $170–$340, M.A.P.

▶ **Moorings Mariner Inn.** P.O. Box 139, Road Town, Tortola, B.V.I. Tel: 494-2332; Fax: 494-2226; in U.S., (800) 535-7289. $85–$135, E.P.

▶ **Rockview Holiday Homes.** P.O. Box 263, Road Town, Tortola, B.V.I. Tel: 494-2550; Fax: 494-5866; in U.S., Tel: (800) 621-1270; Fax: (708) 699-7583. Weekly: $350–$455 (studio/one-bedroom apartment); $650–$3,500 (two bed-rooms).

▶ **The Sugar Mill.** Box 425, Road Town, Tortola, B.V.I. Tel: 495-4355; Fax: 495-4696; in U.S., (800) 462-8834. $120–$215, E.P.

▶ **Treasure Isle Hotel.** P.O. Box 68, Pasea Estate, Road Town, Tortola, B.V.I. Tel: 494-2501; Fax: 494-2507; in U.S., Tel: (800) 334-2435 or (813) 538-8760; Fax: (813) 530-9747. $90–$155, E.P.

Virgin Gorda

▶ **Biras Creek.** P.O. Box 54, Virgin Gorda, B.V.I. Tel: 494-3555 or 3556; Fax: 494-3557; in U.S., Tel: (800) 223-1108; Fax: (914) 763-5362; in Canada, (416) 485-8724. $350–$475, A.P.

▶ **Bitter End Yacht Club.** Box 46, Virgin Gorda, B.V.I. Tel: 494-2746; Fax: 494-4756; in U.S., (800) 872-2392 or (312) 944-5855. $260–$520, A.P.

▶ **Drake's Anchorage Resort Inn.** P.O. Box 2510, Virgin Gorda, B.V.I. Tel: 494-2254; in U.S., Tel: (800) 624-6651 or (617) 661-4745; Fax: (617) 277-5379. $270–$370, F.A.P.

▶ **Little Dix Bay.** P.O. Box 70, Virgin Gorda, B.V.I. Tel: 495-5555; Fax: 495-5661; in U.S., Tel: (800) 223-7637; Fax: (407) 338-2421. $230–$520, E.P. (meal plans extra).

▶ **Olde Yard Inn.** P.O. Box 26, Virgin Gorda, B.V.I. Tel: 495-5544; Fax: 495-5986; in U.S., (800) 633-7411. $95–$170, E.P. (meal plans available).

▶ **Virgin Gorda Villa Rentals.** P.O. Box 63, Virgin Gorda, B.V.I. Tel: 495-7421; Fax: 495-7367; in U.S., (800) 848-7081. $670–$2,975 for seven nights.

Other Islands

▶ **Guana Island Club.** P.O. Box 32, Road Town, Tortola, B.V.I. Tel: 494-2354; in U.S., Tel: (800) 544-8262 or (914) 967-6050; Fax: (914) 967-8048. A boat meets guests at Beef Island Airport. $385–$530, F.A.P.

▶ **Necker Island.** P.O. Box 315, Road Town, Tortola, B.V.I. Tel: 494-2757; Fax: 494-4396; in U.S., (800) 225-4255 or (212) 696-4566. Low season: $4,950 (1–6 people), $6,950 (7–12 people), $8,950 (13–20 people); high season: $8,250 (1–10 people), $9,900 (11–20 people). Includes three meals, all drinks (open bar, extensive wine cellar), all sports, transfers from Beef Island Airport.

▶ **Peter Island Resort and Yacht Harbour.** P.O. Box 211, Road Town, Tortola, B.V.I. Tel: 494-2561; Fax: 494-2313; in U.S. and Canada, (800) 346-4451; outside U.S., (616) 776-6456. $375–$595, F.A.P.

ST. MAARTEN/ ST. MARTIN

By Julie Wilson

Half Dutch and half French, this 37-square-mile island is the Caribbean's supreme playground. It's cocky, sensual, and exciting; quiet, greedy, and sophisticated; earthy, glamorous, and sleazy—whatever the moment requires. But it's no longer a noticeably two-nation island. The once-distinct personalities of the Dutch and French sides have merged, and the border between the two is more or less ceremonial.

St. Maarten/St. Martin's natural assets include dark green hills, three dozen or so beaches, and the largest inland body of water in the Caribbean (salty, calm Simpson Bay Lagoon). With resources like these, it couldn't miss. It also has two man-made attractions: duty-free status and Princess Juliana Airport. The latter, which processes some 500,000 visitors a year, allows easy access from different parts of the world and provides a base for small planes flying to nearby islands. For a minor dot on the map, the island has a surprisingly impressive traffic pattern.

Among its polyglot residents are transplants from France and the United States who settled here 30 years ago in the wide-eyed frontier days along with Dutch, Italians, Arubans, Chinese, Indians, Scandinavians—and some whose passports change according to circumstances. There are also, of course, the original inhabitants of the island. These are divided between an Old Guard, who remember the sleepy days and wonder where they've gone, and a young generation who came of age during the tourist boom and know nothing else. The real

167

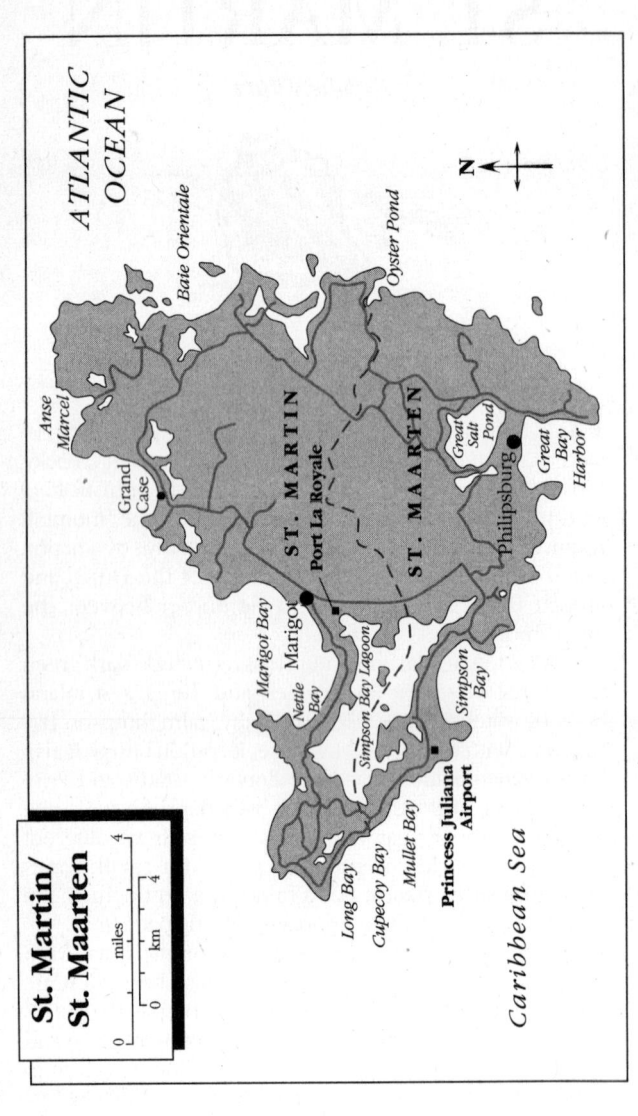

St. Martin/
St. Maarten

ATLANTIC OCEAN

Caribbean Sea

N

miles

km

Baie Orientale

Anse Marcel

Grand Case

Oyster Pond

ST. MARTIN

Port La Royale

Great Salt Pond

ST. MAARTEN

Philipsburg

Great Bay Harbor

Marigot Bay

Marigot

Nettle Bay

Simpson Bay Lagoon

Simpson Bay

Long Bay

Cupecoy Bay

Mullet Bay

Princess Juliana Airport

border on this island is not between Dutch and French but between past and present.

These two harmonious worlds give the hundreds of tourists who pop off planes daily an enviable choice. You can hole up in the quiet island of the past or swing into the constant carnival of the present. Or both. St. Maarten/St. Martin has some of the best sporting facilities anywhere: tennis, golf, great snorkeling, great sailing, good diving, and every manner of water-borne contraption known to man. There's no getting around the fact, however, that dining constitutes the island's major preoccupation. From Creole to "country French," and back through Chinese and *nuova cucina,* the island lays out a fabulous international spread that covers nearly every base but sauerbraten and sauerkraut. Keeping up with what's new is as difficult as it is in a major city, for no sooner does an innovative restaurant appear than a half-dozen imitators sweep in on its coattails.

MAJOR INTEREST

Shopping
Dining
Sailing excursions
Water sports
Casinos (St. Maarten)

No one tours St. Maarten/St. Martin by simply setting out on the road that circles the island. Instead, people decide what they want to do (or where they want to eat) and sightsee along the way. Don't expect many historical sights. On this today-and-tomorrow island, the sights consist mainly of hotels, water-sports centers, duty-free shops, restaurants, and more restaurants.

But just when you've pegged this island as a hotbed of hedonism, St. Maarten/St. Martin comes up with something aesthetic—like an art colony. There have always been a few artists here (Jasper Johns and the late Romare Bearden, for example), but today about two dozen live and work on the island. Some, like Roland Richardson, are homegrown; others, like Gloria Lynn, are transplants. As a group their work is sometimes primitive, sometimes romantic, sometimes glib, sometimes sensual, and always colorful—quite like the island, in fact.

Philipsburg

Though most of Philipsburg's West Indian architecture and historic buildings have been obliterated over two decades of growth and modernization, the Dutch capital still has one historic monument: a nearly 200-year-old colonial-style courthouse smack in the middle of town. Because Philipsburg has so many distractions, some people who have been coming to the island for years have never noticed the courthouse.

In one of the town's few remaining 19th-century cottages, the **Simartn Museum** (Tel: 249-17) makes a dignified effort to preserve and illuminate the island's cultural past through a series of changing exhibits. Near the bottom of Front Street, it's not easy to find (very small sign) but worth the effort. As far as non-mercantile attractions go, that's about it. Unless you consider **Greenwith Galleries,** farther up Front Street, which displays the work of many of the island's fine artists. You're welcome to browse, but you can always buy if the spirit moves you (Tel: 238-42).

Set on a sandbar between a salt pond and Great Bay Harbor (where cruise ships regularly haul themselves over the horizon), Philipsburg is essentially one big duty-free shopping street broken by places to eat, places to sleep, and places to gamble away whatever money you have left. Bring your Christmas list to **Front Street** for French sportswear, tee-shirts, crystal, Italian shoes, perfume, china, cameras, gems, Gucci, gewgaws—whatever the whim demands and the credit card allows. The town recently banned parking on narrow Front Street and widened the walkways, leaving just one traffic lane. On this "walking street," pedestrians are safe from the high-spirited vehicular mayhem found elsewhere.

Old Street represents one of this Caribbean Bloomingdale's latest efforts to provide top-of-the-line merchandise. Looking more like Disney's Magic Kingdom than the old Dutch village it's supposed to resemble, this squeaky-clean, colorfully painted promenade runs between Front and Back streets.

In a town where accommodations range from big hotels to beachfront apartments, **Pasanggrahan Royal Guesthouse** stands out—in a manner of speaking—from the rest. Set off from Front Street on the harbor beach, it can hardly be seen at all. It is, however, the island's original guest house, built back in the days when a tourist boom consisted of the Dutch royal family making a ceremonial visit. (There's still a portrait of Queen Wilhemina in the lobby.) It's a quirky, maybe even slightly seedy, survivor of the old days—and worth staying in if your tastes run to romantic pasts rather than up-to-date luxury.

Picking Philipsburg's best restaurant is really a matter of tuning in to the local grapevine and waiting for a good tip. A couple of establishments, however, are on nearly everyone's short list. The high-priced **Le Bec Fin** (Tel: 229-76), near the bottom of Front Street and behind the museum, consistently delivers top-quality French food. A breadstick away, **Da Livio's** has been justifiably popular for about a decade now. Look for a white stucco façade and a huge mahogany door that would not be out of place on a cathedral. Here you'll find photographs of movie stars who love the place, a backdrop of Great Bay harbor, and a menu starring veal and pasta dishes (with a grand supporting cast of salads and sauces). Prices are surprisingly moderate; Tel: 226-90. For less formal meals, try **Callaloo** (Tel: 235-35) in the Promenade Arcade on Front Street, Chinese **Dragon Phoenix** (Tel: 229-67) on Back Street near a small side street called Emmaplein, or the **Seafood Gallery** (Tel: 232-53) at the top of town by Bobby's Marina.

Philipsburg is also the island's seagoing center, with two neighboring marinas (Bobby's and Great Bay) and the centrally located Little Pier, where cruise-ship tenders tie up. A score of boats leave from the marinas for picnic sails, snorkeling sails, sunset sails, and day trips to St. Barts and other neighboring islands. (These can easily be arranged through any hotel.) The marinas also accommodate private yachts, and their piers swarm with jaunty, sunburned people whose idea of duty-free shopping is having someone else pay for their jeans.

Northeast of Philipsburg

St. Maarten's east coast is the least-developed part of the island, with some least-developed roads to match. At the French-Dutch border though, rapidly mushrooming developments crowd the once-quiet neighborhood. The border itself is typically unmarked, except at **Captain Oliver's** (Tel: 87-30-00), where a wooden "International Bridge" connects the Dutch-side restaurant and the French-side parking lot. (The Captain's accountant must have nightmares.)

The French-accented restaurant looks out on a protected "hurricane hole," where charter yachts herd together, and across to **Oyster Pond Yacht Club**. Seen from this vantage point, Oyster Pond's new units look like beautifully decorated shipping containers backed up on a peninsula looking out toward St. Barts. Ask for one of the original, more atmospheric rooms ringing the center courtyard. Impervious to the French-side construction, Oyster Pond remains secluded, self-contained, and quiet, a place where hotel guests are left to enjoy the beach and each other's company. This isn't the sort of place for a couple whose idea of an evening together is watching the seven o'clock news.

West of Philipsburg

Twisting over the top of Cole Bay Hill and skirting the lagoon, the road from Philipsburg passes the airport and continues to **Mullet Bay Resort and Casino**, the island's only full-scale resort—that is to say, the only one with a golf course. Some people dislike Mullet Bay because it's so big. Others love it because it has shopping plazas, grocery stores, tennis courts, eight restaurants, a beach, water-sports facilities (the best on the island), a disco, a casino, and that 18-hole golf course.

Next to Mullet is the enormous **Maho Beach Hotel & Casino** development. Together, the two resort complexes form what amounts to a new city. At night it is certainly the island's liveliest hot spot. Shops stay open late, Maho's Casino Royale (one of seven, all on St. Maarten) rakes in the chips, and **Cheri's** restaurant/nightclub spills out from under its striped awning, adding tables on surrounding sidewalks to accommodate merrymakers. When the music stops at Cheri's, those still left standing stumble up to **Studio 7** to disco the rest of the night away.

This part of the island has a concentration of hotels, though not all are as big as Mullet or Maho. Back beyond the airport, and reached only by driving through the sprawling Pelican Bay time-share complex, little **La Vista** sits so high on a hill above Simpson Bay that "beachfront" is not one of its claims. It does, however, have a huge pool that seems—when you're in it—to be set in the sky. It also has a small restaurant and 24 big rooms with kitchen facilities. With its wooden decks and stairways, La Vista is beguilingly reminiscent of Nantucket.

A still smaller property, **The Horny Toad**'s inappropriately racy name has occasionally caused revelers looking for a swinging beach bar to seek it out. If they find the place at all, they're disappointed. Located on a dead-end street off a side street, The Horny Toad is a "guest house"—and not for everyone. There are just eight apartments (ask for one in the front) with kitchens in an old West Indian house. There's also a very private beach on Simpson Bay, paths among the gardens, and a quiet, barefoot, Caribbean atmosphere.

Marigot

While the Dutch capital is laid out in straight lines, the French capital is an unruly maze onto which the city fathers have struggled to impose order. Sprawling from the harbor back to Port La Royale on the lagoon, Marigot still speaks with a French accent. The business here is selling: sports clothes (also French accented), meals, baguettes, and baubles. The intense competition drives many small boutiques and cafés out of business, but their replacements are always fresh and hopeful.

From Marigot harbor, high-speed commuter launches make regular runs to Anguilla. Right on the harbor, St. Martin's best outdoor market is at its best on Saturday mornings, when boats from neighboring islands putter in loaded with produce, and local fishermen spill out their colorful cargo. With a whole island behind it for expansion, Marigot has nevertheless chosen to expand into the harbor, dumping in landfill to create a new promenade and parking lot.

Marigot conversations, like those elsewhere on the island, tend to revolve around restaurants. **Poisson d'Or** (Tel: 87-50-33) captures the essence of local dining spots. Its menu is French, its dining porch overhangs the beach, its thick stone walls are decorated with local art, and its prices are high (figure on spending U.S. $150 for two, not including artwork). If Poisson d'Or is booked, head back to the harbor, where a string of long-established restaurants with similar menus and similar prices (and in some cases, the same owners) deliver good value for the money.

Not all Marigot meals cost a bundle. On a deck high above the beach, Claude and Pierre Plessis' **Mini Club** (Tel: 87-50-69) has been serving moderately priced French and Creole dishes since the days of the miniskirt and Sgt. Pepper. Its Wednesday and Saturday night buffets (including lobster, suckling pig, and rivers of wine) are a

U.S. $40 bargain. **Le Bistrot Nu** (Tel: 87-97-09) is another longtime, fair-priced favorite. Down an unglamorous alley, it's got just ten tables, a lengthy list of blackboard specials, and the best mussels this side of a Brussels bistro.

On the harbor's edge, **Le Bar de la Mer** (Tel: 87-52-88) offers light meals at light prices and *pastis* with panache. **Maison sur le Port**'s owner Christian Verdeau has kept his prices in the medium range for excellent lunches and dinners —with no markup for the water views; Tel: 87-56-38. Port La Royale's **Don Camillo** (Tel: 87-52-88) is well known for moderately priced Italian dishes, while coffee and a croissant at **Mastedana** (no phone) costs hardly anything at all.

In-town hotels aren't what you think of in the Caribbean, as there are no beaches or tennis courts in the immediate neighborhood. Consequently, they're less expensive. Right in Marigot's gridlocked center, **La Résidence** makes up in charm what it lacks in sports facilities. Most of its 21 rooms surround a second-floor dining courtyard that is open to the sky and dominated by a dramatic fountain. The rooms won't win any decorating prizes, but they have all the right stuff: TVs, air-conditioners, minibars, and hairdryers.

West of Marigot

Past rows of new condos and instantly forgettable new hotels on Nettle Bay, halfway to the sunset, stands **La Belle Creole**, St. Martin's "historic sight." An impossibly ambitious hotel designed to resemble a Mediterranean fishing village, it nearly opened a couple of decades ago, but cash-flow problems caused the workmen to throw down their tools along with their empty pay envelopes. Conrad International bought it and after a few more false starts La Belle Creole—its grand piazza, poolside café, restaurant, beaches, tennis courts, and croquet lawn—finally opened to guests. After tripping over their own feet for a year or so, the staff caught its stride, and the place is now as civil as it is civilized. "La Belle" will never be what its original creators envisioned some 30 years ago in their Xanadu-like dreams, for the world has changed since then. But, set on its own peninsula far off the main road, it does offer privacy and a rather endearing dignity.

Farther down the road, on Long Bay, lies the legendary **La Samanna**, the last survivor of the glory days when St.

Martin was as exclusive as it is expensive. Celebrities, jet-setters with European accents, and the just plain rich tuck into two-story whitewashed units hidden along a very private beach. Some flaunt their celebrity status, but most appreciate the quiet luxury afforded by this private hotel—so private that La Samanna has all but dug a moat and pulled up the drawbridge. Fortunately, you don't have to swim a moat or even be a hotel guest to dine here. The food is French and the tab is high, but, on an island where good restaurants are the norm rather than the exception, this has consistently been the best for nearly 20 years. La Samanna thinks of everything. Realizing that an overindulgence in sautéed foie gras and grilled red snapper with Creole sauce may cause bathing suits to shrink, they recently built an exercise studio on a garden hillside.

Grand Case

In this case, discovering the "flavor" of the town is easy, for one-street, beachfront Grand Case is devoted to gastronomy. French, Italian, Vietnamese, Creole, and American restaurants elbow each other for a place in the sun. The ever-useful island grapevine keeps tabs on which are this year's best, new find, fairest priced, and rip-off.

There are a number of charming small hotels and guest houses in town, the best of which is the eight-room **Hotel Hévéa**. Owned by Jacqueline and Jean-Claude Dalbéra, it's quiet, romantic, and so immaculate one suspects that the Dalbéras repaint its white trim every other day. As an added bonus, Hévéa's tiny dining room is one of the best restaurants in town. The salad with slices of foie gras and raspberry vinaigrette and the seafood steamed in a morel sauce remain vivid in memory years after lesser meals have been forgotten. This personable couple comes from Nice, where children are *born* knowing how to cook.

The only hotel of any magnitude is the **Grand Case Beach Club**. Anchoring the north end of the bay, it has large, attractively furnished rooms (in a sort of two-story motel layout), most of which look right out over the water. Conversations around GCBC usually center on local restaurants, and the names most likely to be mentioned are **Auberge Gourmande** (Tel: 87-55-45), **Le Tastevin** (same number, same owners), **Rainbow** (Tel: 87-55-80)—and Hévéa.

In their unobtrusive home along Grand Case "Boulevard," Martin and Gloria Lynn (two of the best artists on the island these days) run an informal **gallery**—that is to say, pictures and sculptures by the couple and their two talented sons are strewn around the living room. The Lynns have finally gotten around to putting a sign outside, but if you miss it, anyone in town can tell you where they live.

Northeastern St. Martin

About five minutes from Grand Case, **Le Meridien L'Habitation** has taken root in its very own private cove on Anse Marcel. With the possible disadvantage of being somewhat removed from island action and cut off by a very steep road, Le Meridien L'Habitation has done its best to provide everything right on the premises. Besides a lovely beach, there are three restaurants, a marina, duty-free boutiques, a pool, and—up the hill—a disco and sports center (Le Privilège). Repainted and relandscaped this year, the hotel's 265 rooms have been augmented by the 155 rooms of Le Domaine (same owners and management). You may be removed, but you won't be lonely.

Until recently, **Baie Orientale** (a.k.a., Orient Bay) was so difficult to reach that it was the private province of naturist (i.e., nudist) vacationers. With the French government's current policy of encouraging development in far-flung subprefectures, however, aspiring hotels are replacing the Turk's head cacti that once had the deserted hill slopes all to themselves, and Orient has become a stop on the "island tour" for cruise-ship passengers. The naturists have taken this in stride, mingling with more traditionally clad day-trippers around the hastily rigged tee-shirt kiosks. So far, none of the completed hotels has a distinct enough personality to recommend it.

USEFUL FACTS

What to Wear
Nothing, or anything goes (there are nudist beaches at Baie Orientale, Plum Beach, and Cupecoy). Sports jackets and shorts coexist in even the finest restaurants. Women dress up more than men do.

Getting In
There are direct flights to St. Maarten's Princess Juliana Airport from New York on American and from Newark on Continental; from Raleigh/Durham on American; from Los Angeles and Dallas/Fort Worth on American; from

Boston on Continental; from Miami on BWIA and Air France; and from Paris on Air France. There are also many flights from San Juan and good connections to nearly everywhere in the Caribbean.

Entry Requirements
U.S. and Canadian citizens need only proof of identity—e.g., a birth certificate or voter-registration card; others must have a passport. There is a departure tax of U.S. $10.

Local Time
St. Maarten/St. Martin is on Atlantic standard time year-round, one hour ahead of the U.S. east coast except when the east coast moves its clocks ahead an hour during daylight saving time. Then all keep the same time.

Currency
French francs and Netherlands Antilles guilders are in use, although U.S. dollars are universally accepted. As of this writing the rate of exchange was U.S. $1.00 to 5,FF and NAf 1.77.

Electrical Current
110 volts, 60 cycles on the Dutch side; 220 volts, 60 cycles DC on the French side (U.S.- and Canadian-made appliances require converters, plugs, and transformers).

Getting Around
Rental cars are plentiful and most roads are fine. Driving is on the right. Watch out for traffic jams in the three towns day and night and on access roads during rush hours.

Business Hours
In St. Maarten, 8:00 A.M. to 6:00 P.M., with a one-hour lunch break; in St. Martin, 9:00 A.M. to 6:00 P.M. St. Maarten banks are open Monday through Thursday from 8:30 A.M. to 3:30 P.M., Fridays from 8:30 A.M. to 4:30 P.M. St. Martin banks are open Monday through Friday from 8:30 A.M. to 1:30 P.M.

Festivals
St. Maarten's Carnival is at the end of April; St. Martin's, in February.

For Further Information
St. Maarten Tourist Information, C. Wathey Square, Philipsburg, St. Maarten, N.A., Tel: (599-5) 223-37, Fax: (599-5) 248-84; **in the** U.S., Mallory Factor Sontheimer Group, 275 Seventh Avenue, New York, NY 10001, Tel: (212) 989-0000, Fax: (212) 627-1152; **in Canada**, St. Maarten Tourist Office, 243 Ellerslie Avenue, Willoughdale, Ontario M2N 1Y5, Tel: (416) 223-3501, Fax: (416) 223-6887. **St. Martin Tourist Office**, Port de Marigot, 97150 Marigot, St. Martin, F.W.I., Tel: (590) 87-57-21, Fax: (590) 87-56-43; **in the U.S.**, French West Indies Tourist Board, 610 Fifth Avenue, New York, NY 10020, Tel: (900) 990-0040, Fax: (212) 247-6468.

ACCOMMODATIONS REFERENCE
The rate ranges given here, in U.S. dollars, are projections for fall 1992 through spring 1993, and span the lowest rates in the low season to the highest in the high season. Unless otherwise indicated, prices are for double rooms, double occupancy. As rates are subject to change, it's always wise to double-check before booking. The telephone country code for St. Maarten is 599-5; for St. Martin, 590.

St. Maarten
▶ **The Horny Toad.** Box 3029, Simpson Bay, St. Maarten, N.A. Tel: 543-23; Fax: 533-16; in U.S., (617) 729-3171. $98–$180, E.P.

▶ **Maho Beach Hotel & Casino.** St. Maarten, N.A. Tel: 521-15; Fax: 431-80; in U.S., (800) 223-0757 or (212) 969-9220. $100–$505 (suite), E.P.

▶ **Mullet Bay Resort and Casino.** P.O. Box 309, Philipsburg, St. Maarten, N.A. Tel: 528-01; Fax: 543-98; in U.S., (800) 4-MULLET or (212) 593-8600. $140–$285, E.P.

▶ **Oyster Pond Yacht Club.** P.O. Box 239, St. Maarten, N.A. Tel: 222-06; Fax: 256-95; in U.S., (800) 372-1323 or (212) 696-1323. $120–$310, C.P.

▶ **Pasanggrahan Royal Guesthouse.** P.O. Box 151, Philipsburg, St. Maarten, N.A. Tel: 235-88; Fax: 228-85; in U.S., (800) 365-8484 or (212) 545-8469. $68–$165, E.P.

▶ **La Vista.** P.O. Box 40, Pelican Key Estate, St. Maarten, N.A. Tel: 430-05; Fax: 430-10; in U.S., (800) 365-8484 or (212) 545-8469. $90–$195, E.P.

St. Martin
▶ **La Belle Creole.** B.P. 578, Marigot, 97150, St. Martin, F.W.I. Tel: 87-58-66; Fax: 87-56-66; in U.S., 800-HILTONS; in

Canada, (800) 268-9275; in U.K., (800) 289-303. $165–$365, C.P.

▶ **Grand Case Beach Club.** P.O. Box 339, Philipsburg, St. Maarten, N.A. Tel: 87-51-87; Fax: 87-59-93; in U.S., (800) 223-1588 or (212) 661-4540. $95–$250, C.P.

▶ **Hotel Hévéa.** Grand Case, 97150, St. Martin, F.W.I. Tel: 87-56-85; Fax: 87-83-88; in U.S., (800) 932-3222 or (401) 849-8012. $58–$110, E.P.

▶ **Le Meridien L'Habitation.** P.O. Box 581, Anse Marcel, 97150, St. Martin, F.W.I. Tel: 87-33-33; Fax: 87-30-38; in U.S. and Canada, (800) 543-4300. $177–$456, F.A.B.

▶ **La Résidence.** Rue du Général-de-Gaulle, Marigot, 97150, St. Martin, F.W.I. Tel: 87-70-37; Fax: 87-90-44; in U.S., (800) 932-3222 or (401) 849-8012. $112–$132, C.P.

▶ **La Samanna.** B.P. 159, Baie Longue, 97150, St. Martin, F.W.I. Tel: 87-51-22; Fax: 87-87-86; in U.S., (212) 696-1323. $250–$530, E.P.

ST. BARTS
(ST. BARTHELEMY)

By Julie Wilson

For an eight-square-mile speck of land, St. Barts provokes some mighty strong opinions. No one is ambivalent about this island, which is also known as St. Barths and—officially—St. Barthélemy. Detractors criticize its almost self-conscious chicness and high prices. Admirers adore it passionately, describing the island as they would a lover rather than a vacation destination.

Except for its climate, St. Barts is the least "Caribbean" of the islands. Steep and rocky hillsides tumble down to windswept beaches that are pretty good, but certainly not the best. Its gardens are cultivated, in contrast to the typical Caribbean tangles of wild abandon. There are no golf courses, few tennis courts, and virtually no nightlife. What St. Barts is, is French—so unmistakably French that some call it the Caribbean St. Tropez. It is a place for long lunches by the beach, fine dining (with fine wines) under a starry sky, and long conversations about the romance of food and the mysteries of love. Everyone becomes a little more glamorous just by being here.

MAJOR INTEREST

Small, intimate accommodations
Dining, mostly French
Chic but casual atmosphere
Unabashed commitment to romance and wealth

St. Barts has always been different from the rest of the Caribbean. Because the terrain is unsuitable for growing sugarcane, the island never developed a slave economy,

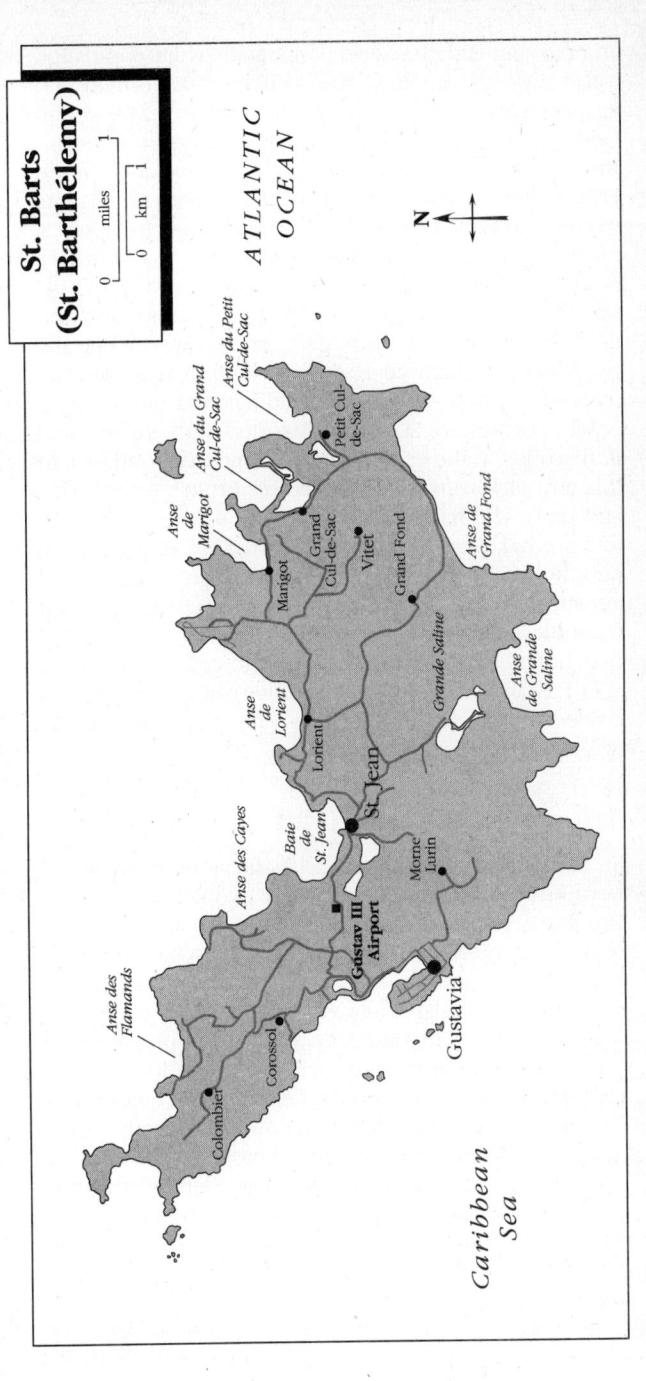

and consequently has a predominantly white population today. Instead, St. Barts was settled by fishermen and farmers from Normandy and Brittany, who over the centuries have remained fishermen and farmers, adhering— more or less—to the culture of their homeland. An old French patois is still spoken in the villages, and some women continue to wear the traditional French *calèche,* a pleated, white, cotton sunbonnet. Today St. Barts is a Sous-Préfecture of Guadeloupe, which itself is an Overseas Department of France, a wonderfully Gallic complication. The truth is, St. Barts goes its own way. While the predominant language is French, English is spoken almost everywhere—though sometimes reluctantly.

Who comes to St. Barts? Assorted Rockefellers and Rothschilds in the early days set a tone that continues to this day. Pick your potentate, power broker, or pop star, and he or she has probably vacationed here. These visitors are balanced by a crowd of attractive, young French people dressed in the latest Côte d'Azur fashions and attractive young North Americans dressed in the latest from Bloomingdale's. Although St. Barts has a number of fine hotels (many with stratospheric prices), renting a villa has always been a popular alternative here. It's become so popular that **Sibarth** (the major real estate agency) has about 250 available.

St. Jean

St. Barts's best swimming beaches lie along its sheltered northern coast. The wide, sandy arc on the bay at St. Jean, roughly in the center, is the island's most famous, backed by a cluster of shops, hotels, and beach restaurants. On an island where fine French restaurants are the norm, the perennially popular **Chez Francine** (Tel: 27-60-49) has made its mark with simplicity. While chefs prepare your lunch (salad, pommes frites, grilled chicken, lobster, tarte au citron), you can nip down the steps for a quick swim. That's simple enough. However, now that the cruise ships have discovered St. Barts, a tide of passengers washes up on St. Jean's beach at lunchtime. To avoid the scene, head uphill behind town to **Le Patio** (Tel: 27-70-67), where you can have a tomato and mozzarella salad on the sunny terrace and look down—so to speak—on the madcap mobs below.

Another detour uphill from St. Jean leads to Eden Rock,

the island's first hotel, built by Rémy de Haenen, a former pilot and Caribbean legend. It's a bit run-down now, but the view, the memories, and the chance to meet the owner are worth the drive. Considerably younger—and far from run-down—**Filao Beach Hotel** sits right on the water's edge in St. Jean. Pathways connecting the 30 units wind their way through lovely gardens. A deck hanging over the beach has a built-in pool and a small bar/restaurant in back. It's a good place to sit with a cool drink while deciding whether you'd like to go down to the beach and rent a windsurfer, swim in the pool, or just sit and enjoy the pleasure of aimless indecision.

If the idea of scuba diving crosses your mind in these idle moments, trot on down the beach to Emeraude Plage, where Daniel Piveteau's **"Dive with Dan"** (Tel: 27-64-78) is considered the best around here. Emphasis is on safety, personal attention, and fun.

Not far from town (but actually in Lorient), a couple of the island's few nightspots bloom vividly after sunset. The excellent food alone of **Club La Banane** (Tel: 27-68-25) makes it worth a trip, but the real excitement starts around dessert time when owner Jean-Marie Riviere's cabaret begins. The show is fun, funny, and a little naughty ("one sees a lot of leg," smiled a prim gentleman), but oh-so-nice.

Just west of St. Jean, arriving planes skim over a saddle in a mountain appropriately named La Tourmente, then do a kamikaze dive to the alarmingly short runway (just 2,626 feet long) at the Gustav III Airport. This runway, suitable only for small planes and specially trained pilots, is one of the reasons St. Barts is so quiet.

Within earshot of this aeronautical oddity, a passel of pastel cottages called **Les Ilets de la Plage** sits among a sea of flowers right next to the sea. There's no restaurant on the premises, but each unit has a shiny new kitchen. Farther up the northwest coast is **Anse des Cayes**. On this secluded cove, **Manapany Cottages** climbs from the beachfront up what is for St. Barts a gentle hill. Small and private, Manapany has just 20 cottages on the hillside and 12 club suites on the beach. Each has a big porch with comfortable chairs facing the water. It also has a tennis court, spa facilities, and two good restaurants. Although the cove is reef-protected, the waters can be a little choppy and the shore underfoot rocky. No matter; Manapany's pool suffices for a whole day. After a morning lounge in the whirlpool, move on to lunch and finish off the afternoon with a game of backgammon beside the big pool, while the affable bartender whips you up a PMC (Perrier, crème de menthe, and citron).

The West End

More than the inhabitants of any other part of the island, residents of the south coast fishing village of **Corossol** retain the character of St. Barts's French settlers. Men tend their colorful—and utilitarian—fishing skiffs, while barefoot, bonneted women sell wide-brimmed Panama hats, purses, and other items woven from dried strips of latania palm fronds.

Inland from Corossol, **François Plantation** perches on a hill at Colombier. The first thing you'll notice about this hotel is the gardens—lush green plants interspersed with the most amazingly beautiful hibiscus, flowering vines trailing over an entry arbor, exotic blossoms like splashes of color on a dark canvas. Talk about first impressions. Set farther up on the hillside, François Plantation's 12 private cottages look "old West Indian" but contain such modern necessities as minibars and satellite TV. Sports activities consist of climbing up to the hilltop pool and casting glances at a view that takes in the coast, the Caribbean Sea, and a few neighboring islands. Best of all are the dinners. Served in a formal, terraced dining room, they are as memorable as dinners can be when one is bewitched by hibiscus.

North of Colombier, **Hotel St-Barth Isle de France** opened on Anse des Flamands to rave notices last winter. Behind a two-story main building on the beach, wooden walkways meander past a pool and cottages to a "heart of the deepest jungle" hillside. Rather than cut down palm trees on the property, the hotel cut holes in the walkways to accommodate them. Suites have Jacuzzis next to mirrored glass windows so you can watch the world go by, splashing and playing unseen. ("It is," giggled a young Parisienne, "so very French.")

The Eastern Route

A succession of sandy coves—Lorient, Marigot, Grand Cul-de-Sac, and Petit Cul-de-Sac—stretches to the east of St. Jean. Behind them the hills climb up (don't they always on St. Barts?) to Vitet, a pastoral region of stone-fenced meadows and tile-roofed farmhouses. Aside from the profusion of tropical flowers (and the weather), this could easily be Brittany.

Except that Brittany probably doesn't have a hotel like Hubert Delamotte's **Hostellerie des Trois Forces**. A gentle, New Age spirit, Mr. Delamotte has named each of the simple rooms for a sign of the zodiac, designing the furnishings and cross-drafts accordingly. The signs of the three forces are painted on the bottom of the swimming pool. The young owner gives yoga classes, reads tarot cards, and casts horoscopes, but only if you wish. If you just want a nice place to stay, he insists, you're free to stay up until 3:00 A.M. drinking Champagne. The restaurant is a big plus. Attractions include grilled fish and meats, fresh herbs, light sauces, freshly baked bread, and fabulous desserts.

Back near the coast, **Comme en Provence** (Tel: 27-76-50) at Blue Marlin Hotel is new and delightful. On a poolside dining terrace, Patrick and Patricia Quenet serve sparkling renditions of garlicky lamb rib chops, ratatouille encased in red snapper filets, crème brûlée, and all sorts of Provençal dishes. The busy Quenets, who moved here from Paris because it's a nice place to bring up their four children, also own **Marius & Fanny** (Tel: 27-66-19) in Gustavia.

Guanahani, the largest (62 rooms) of St. Barts's luxury hotels, is out at Grand Cul-de-Sac, on the banks of a bay so shallow that even diminutive swimmers can wade out hundreds of yards before submerging completely. Some rooms have private pools and all have decks or patios with a view of the sea. Guanahani has two restaurants: a poolside café/bar by the beach and the highly respected **Bartolomeo**, with dining deck and piano bar, for more formal evenings. There are two tennis courts, one at the top of the hill and one at the bottom.

Nearby, **Club Lafayette** (Tel: 27-62-51)— open for lunch only—is uniquely St. Barts. The guest book is signed by Raquel Welch, Steve Martin, and their starry ilk, and gorgeous young models parade around in fashions from the restaurant's boutique on weekends. Those who care about such things know enough to reserve a table on the terrace. A table in the sand is like . . . well, my dears, it's like being in Siberia. Prices start at about U.S. $15 for a green salad and go way, way up from there. A little easier on the pocketbook, **Marigot Bay Club** (Tel: 27-75-45) is a moderately priced charmer at this end of the island. Its attractions include a deck dining room on the water's edge, *acras morue* (cod fritters), christophine stuffed with lobster—and a refreshing lack of pretension. Albert Balayn's **Le Flamboyant** (Tel: 27-75-65), way up a hill overlooking Grand Cul-de-Sac, isn't flamboyant in the slightest. It's small and friendly. Neither the menu nor the prices change very often, and the lobster cassoulet (with zucchini, potatoes, cream, and all manner of wonderful surprises) is as dependably delicious as things get in this world.

Gustavia

The capital of this very French island sounds remarkably Swedish for a good reason: It was named for King Gustav III of Sweden back in 1784 when the French traded it off in one of those misguided "outfielder for two pitchers and a player to be named later" deals. By the time the French got St. Barts back, the Swedes had already established its duty-free status, a valuable bonus when the tourist trade began.

Gustavia today is three blocks deep and runs along a sheltered, yacht-filled harbor. It is dollhouse pretty, a mix of island gingerbread and a Swedish clock tower. Chic boutiques stock French and Italian designer fashions, and duty-free shops sell the usual range of perfume, jewelry, watches, china, and crystal.

Down by the old anchor at the public dock, local fishermen used to bring in their catch about ten in the morning. Though the fishermen have moved on, visitors accustomed to this mid-morning ritual still show up and mill about for a while. Then they repair to the **Bar de l'Oubli** for a late-morning omelet, or amble over to **Le Select** for a beer before heading out to its garden restaurant, **Cheeseburger in Paradise**. On Sunday mornings, old men play dominoes in the garden. As a spectator sport, this is considerably more exciting than watching for nonexistent fishermen.

For such a little town, Gustavia has an amazing number of good restaurants. One of the best (and surely the most romantic), **Le Sapotillier** (Tel: 27-60-28) has a half-dozen tables in an old *case* (house), and a few more on the patio under a giant sapodilla tree. This year **Citronelle** (Tel: 27-80-78), the new kid in town, has attracted most of the attention. Part-owned by Jean-Georges Vongerichten (of New York's JoJo), it dazzles with such gems as salmon in rice paper with citrus vinaigrette and extracts a pretty penny in return. Closed from April to November.

Though a few have claimed they had to remortgage the family homestead in order to afford a meal on St. Barts, Gustavia meals can be reasonable. A soup-and-salad lunch (ah, but such a fine, fresh soup, such a perfect salad) at Hotel Hisbiscus's **Le Vieux Clocher** (Tel: 27-64-82) is a bargain. No charge for views of town and harbor. Despite a number of good Creole dishes on the menu, **La Langouste** (Tel: 27-69-47) obviously specializes in langouste—and doesn't charge an arm and an antenna for it. On Thursdays and Saturdays the ultracasual **La Marine** (Tel: 27-70-13) flies in mussels from France and serves them *à la marinière*. Finally, wedged between a cemetery and the sea not far from town, **Maya's** (Tel: 27-73-61) offers relatively inexpensive open-air dining at its most enchanting. Maya's is what St. Barts was like before it realized it was St. Barts.

For a truly bargain-priced meal on the hoof, stop in one of Gustavia's boulangeries. A croissant for a few coins, or a baguette for a mere bagatelle.

Though hotels in the Caribbean are seldom built in town, the highly touted **Carl Gustaf** is an exception. On Gustavia's steep outskirts, its 14 suites have decks, "plunge pools," VCRs, direct-dial telephones, fax machines—all the things you need for a relaxing vacation. It opened with an atmosphere as chilly as a meat locker, but maybe things have improved. (Or maybe Carl Gustaf was the player to be named later.)

Outside Gustavia

Halfway up the steep switchbacks of Morne Lurin (a *morne* is a "mountain peak") you may begin to wonder where in the world you are going. You are going to **Sapore di Mare**, formerly known as Castelets. Last year this regally private, aerie-like hotel was purchased by Pino Luongo (of New York's Le Madri), Cesare Dell'Aguzzo (of Southampton's Sapore di Mare), and other lesser-known bankrollers. The hotel is as distinguished as ever. Its ten rooms, all furnished with antiques or Old World imitations, have porches overlooking hills and bays. From the deck outside the dining room, the views encompass the Baie de St. Jean, a pilot's-eye perspective of the airport runway, and all of the world that really matters at the moment. What has changed is what's on the plate and in the kitchen. The talented and charming Dell'Aguzzo is the mastermind of such creations as warm seafood salads, local fish alla Livornese, steak seared with olive oil and herbs—and an array of perfect pasta dishes.

USEFUL FACTS

What to Wear

Dress is casual chic, but what you wear is important. By day, bikinis, tight jeans, status tee-shirts, *pareos* (cotton sarongs), and loose cotton shirts are de rigueur. By night, island cottons, dressy pants, or caftans for women, and sports shirts for men are the uniform. Ties and jackets are not required.

Getting In

The best connections are from St. Maarten via Windward Islands Airways (WINAIR). Flights from there to Gustav III Airport take 10 minutes. Sailing and motor catamarans run between Philipsburg (on St. Maarten) and Gustavia; the trip takes 1½ hours, depending on the weather. Seas can be rough. Both air and boat fares run about U.S. $50 round trip. There is also air service to St. Barts from St. Martin, San Juan, St. Thomas, Antigua, and Guadeloupe. You must pay a 10-franc departure tax when leaving St. Barts for St. Martin and Guadeloupe; the tax is 15 francs for other destinations.

Entry Requirements

A passport or other proof of citizenship, such as a notarized birth certificate with a raised seal or a voter-registration card accompanied by a government-authorized identification with photo, is required.

Local Time

St. Barts is on Atlantic standard time year-round, one hour ahead of the U.S. east coast except when the east coast moves its clocks ahead an hour during daylight saving time. Then the two keep the same time.

Currency

The legal tender is the French franc. U.S. dollars are accepted nearly everywhere, but you'll get change in francs. As of this writing the rate of exchange was U.S. $1.00 to 5,3FF.

Electrical Current
220 volts, 50 cycles. U.S.- and Canadian-made appliances require converters, plugs, and transformers.

Getting Around
Small cars such as Suzuki Jeeps are most practical for navigating the narrow, hilly island roads, but it helps if you are comfortable using a stick shift. Even with an automatic, you'll find yourself downshifting on the hills. Motor bikes may also be rented (driver's license required), and there is ample taxi service—during the day at least.

Business Hours
Shops are open from 8:00 A.M. to noon and 2:00 to 6:00 P.M. and are closed on Sundays. Banks are open Monday through Friday from 8:00 A.M. to noon and 2:00 to 3:30 P.M.

Festivals
The Festival of St. Barthélemy, the feast day of the island's patron saint, is celebrated on the weekends preceding and following August 24. The Pre-Lenten Carnival ends with a Mardi Gras. Carnival's highlight is the Regatta, drawing about 100 boats bent on pleasure from all over the Caribbean.

For Further information
L'Office du Tourisme, Quai du Général-de-Gaulle, Gustavia, 97113, St. Barthélemy, F.W.I., Tel: (590) 27-87-27; Fax: (590) 27-74-47; **in the U.S.**, French West Indies Tourist Board, 610 Fifth Avenue, New York, NY 10020, Tel: (900) 990-0040; Fax: (212) 247-6468.

ACCOMMODATIONS REFERENCE
The rate ranges given here, in U.S. dollars, are projections for fall 1992 through spring 1993, and span the lowest rates in the low season to the highest in the high season. Unless otherwise indicated, prices are for double rooms, double occupancy. As rates are subject to change, it's always wise to double-check before booking. The telephone country code for St. Barts is 590.

▶ **Carl Gustaf**. P.O. Box 700, Gustavia, 97133, St. Barthélemy, F.W.I. Tel: 27-82-83; Fax: 27-82-37; in U.S., (800) 932-3222 or (401) 849-8012. $510–$760, C.P.

▶ **Filao Beach Hotel**. St. Jean, 97133, St. Barthélemy,

F.W.I. Tel: 27-64-84; Fax: 27-62-24; in U.S., (800) 932-3222 or (401) 849-8012. $140–$580, A.P.

▶ **François Plantation.** Colombier, 97133, St. Barthélemy, F.W.I. Tel: 27-78-82; Fax: 27-61-26; in U.S., (800) 932-3222 or (401) 849-8012. $200–$380, F.A.B.

▶ **Guanahani.** Marigot, Anse du Grand Cul-de-Sac, 97133, St. Barthélemy, F.W.I. Tel: 27-66-60; Fax: 27-70-70; in U.S., (800) 223-6800 or (212) 838-3110. $220–$450, C.P.; suites, $400–$690, C.P.

▶ **Hostellerie des Trois Forces.** Vitet, 97133, St. Barthélemy, F.W.I. Tel: 27-61-25; Fax: 27-81-38; in U.S., (800) 932-3222 or (401) 849-8012. $90–$170, E.P.

▶ **Les Ilets de la Plage.** P.O. Box 203, 97133, St. Barthélemy, F.W.I. Tel: 27-88-57; Fax: 27-88-58; in U.S., Tel: (800) 932-3222 or (401) 849-8012. $160–$380; $1,120–$2,450 per week (bungalow).

▶ **Manapany Cottages.** P.O. Box 114, Anse des Cayes, 97133, St. Barthélemy, F.W.I. Tel: 27-66-55; Fax: 27-75-28; in U.S., (800) 847-4249 or (212) 719-5750. $190–$525, C.P.; suites, $240–$1,045, C.P.

▶ **Sapore di Mare.** P.O. Box 60, 97133, St. Barthélemy, F.W.I. Tel: 27-61-73; Fax: 27-85-27; in U.S., (212) 319-7488. $95–$325, C.P.

▶ **Hotel St-Barth Isle de France.** Baie des Flamands, 97133, St. Barthélemy, F.W.I. Tel: 27-61-81; Fax: 27-86-83; in U.S., Tel: (800) 932-3222 or (401) 849-8012. $210–$490, C.P.

▶ **Sibarth.** For villa rentals contact WIMCO, Tel: (800) 932-3222 or (401) 849-8012. $505–$2,800 per week for one-bedroom accommodation.

ANGUILLA

By Julie Wilson

Just 17 miles long and three miles across at its widest point, sinuous Anguilla (an-GWIL-a) is so slender that Columbus gave it the Spanish name for "eel." It was one of the few islands he didn't name after a saint. Then everyone pretty much forgot about the island for a few centuries until 1967, when Anguilla refused to accept independence from England and gained lighthearted notoriety as "the eel that squealed."

Point made, and permanently secure as a Crown Colony, the island settled back into amiable somnolence—until recently. Anguilla is now the scene of considerable development, spearheaded by an ambitious collection of luxury hotels.

What attracted the hotels were Anguilla's 33 white-sand beaches, generally acknowledged to be the best in the Caribbean. A ring of offshore reefs ensures calm waters and snorkeling that is as good as snorkeling can get. The island itself isn't particularly lush; what even-handed Nature lavished on the beaches, she stinted on the flora.

With a lifestyle that is a mixture of island traditions and gilt-edged sophistication, Anguilla can be divided unofficially between the West End (development) and the East End (still traditional).

MAJOR INTEREST

White-sand beaches
Offshore reefs for snorkeling
New luxury hotels

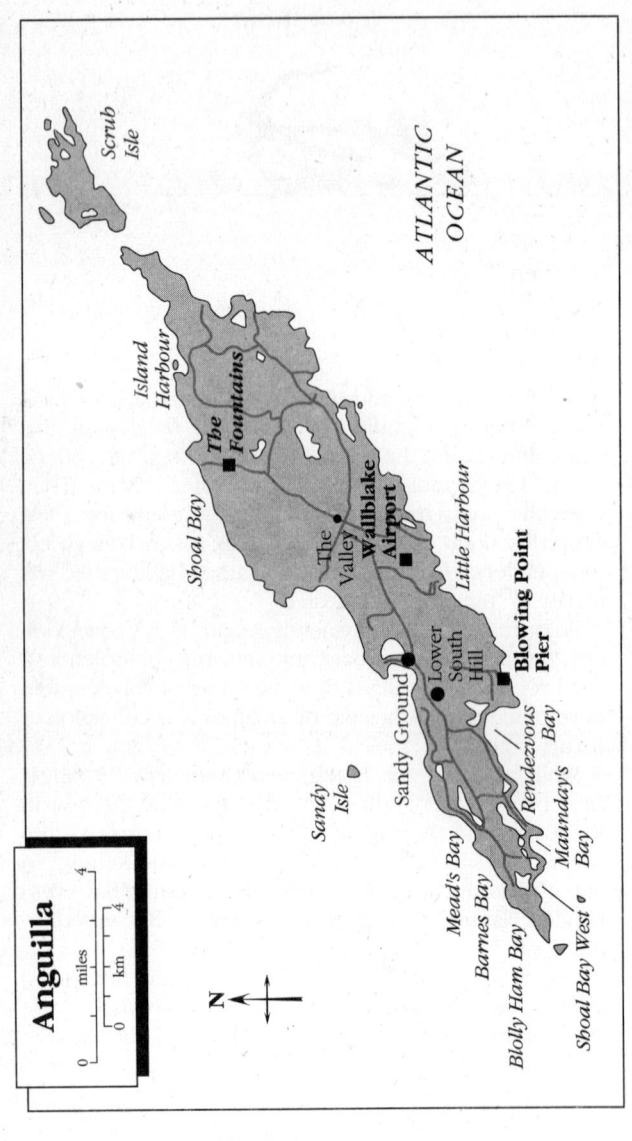

Anguilla

West End

The main road runs straight from the roundabout above Sandy Ground to Blolly Ham Bay, with a few spurs leading to the shoreline hotels. **Malliouhana**, on splendid Mead's Bay, started the boom just eight years ago. Jet-setters and the otherwise well-heeled (this is the sort of place where there's always a lot of Louis Vuitton in the lobby) lounge around its pools and watch the waterfalls, play a little tennis, take out a Sunfish, or just walk the long beach. The kitchen is directed by Michel Rostang, who has taken up where his father, the late, Michelin-starred chef Jo Rostang, left off, and the "French-Caribbean" food is superb. From plant-filled lobby right down to beautiful beach, Malliouhana (the Arawak name for the island) sparkles like a rare gem.

Coccoloba Plantation is the new name given to the hotel that was once called La Santé, whose original owners, for unknown reasons, designed an A-frame main building that looked like a ski lodge gone south. Over the past few years, after several face-lifts, they finally got it right, dividing the stadium-size lobby into separate areas, adding bright new fabrics, knocking down an outside kitchen that clumsily blocked the view, and replacing it with a dining terrace—views intact. Face-lifts being terribly expensive, the hotel ran out of money last year and was sold to an English company. The new owners promise only minimal changes. With two beaches (on Mead's Bay and Barnes Bay), the hotel draws a well-bred crowd who appreciate the private cottages (modern with a West Indian gingerbread overlay), the fabulous food (don't miss the conch cake), and one of the nicest staffs in the Caribbean. Coccoloba is designed for unwinding: While it has all manner of sports and gym facilities, it's more conducive to floating over to the swim-up bar in the pool, watching lobsters in the moat, or sitting on the beach observing the dive tactics of pelicans.

Cap Juluca (Juluca is an Arawak rainbow god) opened five years ago. This Moorish fantasy is located on the dazzling, near-deserted beach at Maunday's Bay, and includes the 179 acres behind the hotel, ensuring an enviable kind of privacy. It was built by Robin and Sue Ricketts, the attractive couple who codeveloped Malliouhana. The Ricketts left the hotel after a falling out with the major shareholder, but it still bears their imprint. Visionary in concept, Cap Juluca represents the future of top-class resorts—unbridled luxury tinged with subliminal hedonism. Huge bedrooms have enormous beds set on raised platforms, and marble bathrooms the size of Rhode Island open onto private walled gardens for sunbathing or any other activity that comes to mind. Breakfast is served on your terrace, and, if you wish, a maid will come in to cook dinner in the kitchenette. That's nice, but it means you'll miss dinner at **Pimms**, the hotel restaurant. Pimms is decidedly romantic: open-sided on the water's edge, white canopies like puffy clouds overhead, and spotlights on the water luring a crowd of curious manta rays and sea turtles.

Despite its futuristic *Star Wars* architecture, **Covecastles** on Shoal Bay typifies today's Anguilla—luxurious villas lining a perfect beach, hammocks on the porches, fully equipped kitchens, tableware straight from a bridal registry. Aside from the sound of the sea, it's quiet here; for nightlife excitement, you look across the water to the twinkling lights of St. Martin.

Less ambitious, but utterly charming, the new **Anguilla Great House** is Anguillian owned and built. Besides its nine unspoiled acres along equally unspoiled Rendezvous Bay, it offers small rooms in cottage units (set back, as they say, "so as not to intimidate the beach"), turn-of-the-century Anguillian furnishings, a big pool, a cheery poolside bar/restaurant... and archaeological sites on the lawn. The great house itself is still in the planning stages.

Swiss-run **La Sirena** is a crisply clean small hotel with rooms surrounding a pool, and Mead's Bay is just a few sandy steps away through the gardens. Americans Peter and Frieda Holleran recently took over the dining room and quickly gained a reputation for their chicken quesadillas, light quiches, and great wines. Every Thursday night the **Mayoumba Folkloric Troupe** performs here. A select group culled from the ranks of the Anguilla Choral Circle, they are the island's most endearing attraction, singing West Indian folk songs and playing and dancing up a storm.

Not surprisingly, aspiring restaurants have swept ashore in the wake of the grand hotels. Just down the beach from Coccoloba, **Mango's** is the recent venture of Bob and Melinda Blanchard (they developed, then sold, the Blanchard & Blanchard sauce line). Creative sauces sparkle here, along with such captivating desserts as tropical fruit fondue and Key lime pie. Dinners only; Tel: 6479 (reservations necessary). **Arlo's Place** (Tel: 6810) in Lower South Hill is known for Italian food—the take-out pizza especially beloved by locals.

At the east end of the West End, ferries arrive at Blowing Point Pier carrying commuters, day-trippers, and suitcase-toting vacationers. Close by, the **Ferryboat Inn** is a good place to begin or end a trip to Anguilla. Chef/owner John McClean offers a full lunch and dinner menu including the best black bean soup in the Caribbean. And if you don't want to budge, the McCleans have a number of reasonably priced housekeeping apartments set just back from their private beach. (For information about other apartments, contact the tourist offices; see the Accommodations Reference at the end of the chapter.)

Sandy Ground

Anguilla's deep-water port, Sandy Ground is lined by a beach behind which is one of those salt ponds that were so important in the days before refrigeration. The town is nearly as sleepy as it is sandy. There are a couple of watersports centers here, and small restaurants/watering holes line Sandy Ground's beachfront. Town cuisine is pretty basic—simple West Indian fare with the occasional stab at *nouvelle* something. Restaurant staples include fresh fish, conch, and langoustes, along with stews made of less elegant animals and their less elegant parts. The major hangout down here is **Jonno's** (Tel: 2728), where locals catch up on the latest news near the bar and beery-eyed youths on vacation stumble around having fun.

The **Mariners**, built in old West Indian style, occupies one end of the beach. It's a less expensive hotel than the West End blockbusters and a favorite among old Anguilla hands who swap the latest gossip in the bar or over dinner on the verandah. And if you tire of gossip, you can thrash around the tennis courts, take a swim off the beach, or wander down to see what's going on in town.

From Sandy Ground, boats speed out to **Sandy Isle**, a tiny coral island covered with palm trees. Snorkelers snorkel off Sandy Isle, and the lazy lounge on the sand, enjoying the delicious isolation. There are several islands farther out, as well as a number of good dive sites, including seven wrecks. Try **Enchanted Island Cruises**, a.k.a. Wildcat Cruises (Tel: 3111) for the former, **Tamariain Watersports** (Tel: 2020) for the latter.

The Valley

Driving east from Sandy Ground, you will soon come to Anguilla's capital, The Valley. While there really isn't much reason to linger in The Valley, do stop in at the Department of Tourism (in the Secretariat) and say hello. Across from The Valley Secondary School, the **Anguilla Arts and Crafts Center** displays local embroidery, woodwork, and shellwork—along with a peculiar collection of mismatched sandals (not locally made). In Old Factory Plaza the **Devonish-Cotton Gin Art Gallery** (Tel: 2949) exhibits the works of internationally known sculptor/potter Courtney Devonish, along with works by other artists. Pieces of the cotton gin machinery once used here are not for sale.

There are a number of fun and funky places to eat in The Valley, but for a rather special meal try **Koal Keel** (Tel: 2930), on a new deck attached to an 18th-century plantation great house formerly known as The Warden's Place. Fried snapper on couscous with fresh mint or rack of lamb and ratatouille share the menu with local dishes. Though they'll sell you a rum punch, they'd rather you enjoyed something from their excellent wine list. The decor was done by Suzanne Seitz, late of Haiti's Grand Hotel Oloffson and St. Maarten's Oyster Pond Yacht Club. She's also opened **Caribbean Styles** on the property, the best place in these parts for West Indian (especially Haitian) art and antiques.

Outside town across from the airport, the casual and relatively inexpensive **Old House** (Tel: 2228) assumes a somewhat formal air in the evening, with flowers and linens on the tables and a wine list in evidence. "Potfish," a local fish stew served over rice, and coconut ice cream are highly recommended. The nearby **Aquarium** (Tel: 2720) serves down-home Anguillian cooking—curried conch, stewed turtle, pigeon peas and rice—in a leisurely Anguillian manner. If you're timid about turtle, they'll proffer a splendid grilled red snapper.

Down another one of those spur roads, **Cinnamon Reef Beach Club** on the little beach at Little Harbour has been perking along happily for about a decade now. In many ways as glamorous as its West End competition—vast rooms, sunken showers, knockout dining room overlooking the water, Olympic-size pool, tennis courts—Cinnamon Reef remains determinedly low-key and lazy. "Lazy," it should be said, refers to the mood, not the service.

East End

Driving along the eastern half of the island, you'll see the more traditional side of Anguilla: cement-block houses with fretwork overlays, chickens in the road, old stone ovens in side yards, banana trees, undernourished flamboyants, and other trees no taller than a man.

Island Harbour, up on the north shore, is a small settlement with an expensive roadside restaurant (the French-Creole Fish Trap, serving bouillabaisse and stuffed crab backs; Tel: 4488), a couple of cheap beachfront restaurants (Smitty's has a steel band on Sundays; Tel: 4300), and a pier. If you stand on the pier and wave, a small launch will scoot over from **Scilly Cay** and take you out to this private island. Owner Eudoxie Wallace grills lobsters, crayfish, and chicken for lunch, while you swim, snorkle, or lap up a rum punch in the shade of a Tiki hut. Not far out of town, a half-French/half-Irish couple have opened **Hibernia** (Tel: 4290), a charming restaurant in a small house overlooking coastline and sea. The food is outstanding—especially the local fish smoked over wood shavings.

Giving Sandy Ground competition as the "fun center" of Anguilla, Island Harbour is still, basically, what it's always been—the fishing center. Scores of colorful fishing skiffs are pulled up on the beach by mid-morning. Their design is unique to the island. Long before they started building hotels, the Anguillians were great boat builders.

Shoal Bay, just down the coast, ranks first among Anguilla's beaches. Long the favorite spot for secluded picnics and snorkeling, it has recently become more civilized, with villa/hotel complexes and a clutch of simple restaurants. Of the new hotels, the most promising is **Fountain Beach,** on the western end of the beach. Beautifully designed (with decorative accents by Suzanne Seitz), it is distinctly Mediterranean in feeling, with a fine Italian restaurant, **La Fontana,** occupying a slice of the beachfront. The Costa Smeralda has come to Anguilla.

Heading back inland, you will come to The Fountains, underground springs where the ancient Indians painted petroglyphs on the cave walls. The Anguillian government is constructing an entrance tunnel to replace the rickety ladder that now provides the only access and is mapping out a four-acre park around The Fountains. Due to inadequate funding, progress merely sputters along, but the project itself is typical of Anguilla, where preservation of history and nature is still as important as new hotels and tourist dollars.

USEFUL FACTS

What to Wear
The dress code is conservatively casual, and no nude bathing is allowed. "Elegantly casual" is standard during the evening at the fancy resorts.

Getting In
There are several daily flights to Wallblake Airport from San Juan (American Eagle), St. Maarten (Windward Islands Airways), and St. Thomas, and several flights weekly from Antigua and St. Kitts. Ferries from St. Martin's Marigot to Anguilla's Blowing Point Pier run every 40 minutes. A one-way ticket costs U.S. $9 (U.S. $12 at night). The journey takes 20 minutes at most.

Entry Requirements
A passport is required, but U.S. and Canadian citizens may use another form of official identification that has a photograph, such as a driver's license or voter-registration card. A departure tax of U.S. $6 is levied at the airport, U.S. $1.15 at Blowing Point Pier.

Local Time
Anguilla is on Atlantic standard time year-round, one hour ahead of the U.S. east coast except when the east coast moves its clocks ahead an hour during daylight saving time. Then the two keep the same time.

Currency
Eastern Caribbean dollar; U.S. dollars are accepted nearly everywhere. As of this writing the rate of exchange was U.S. $1.00 to E.C. $2.67.

Electrical Current
Same as in the U.S. and Canada—110 volts AC, 60 cycles.

Getting Around
To rent a car, you must have a valid license and obtain a three-month permit (U.S. $6). Driving is on the left.

Business Hours
Businesses are open from 8:00 A.M. to 5:00 P.M.; some close between noon and 1:00. Banks are open Monday through Thursday from 8:30 A.M. to 3:00 P.M., Fridays from 8:00 A.M. to 5:00 P.M.

Festivals
Carnival is the first week in August; boat racing is the highlight.

For Further Information
Anguilla Department of Tourism, The Valley, Anguilla, B.W.I., Tel: (809) 497-2759, Fax: (809) 497-2751; **in the U.S.**, c/o Medhurst & Associates, Inc., 2171 Main Street, Northport, NY 11768, Tel: (800) 553-4939, Fax: (516) 261-9606; **in the U.K.**, WINDOTEL, No. 3 Epirus Road, Kensington, London SW6 7UJ, England, Tel: (71) 937-7725, Fax: (71) 938-4793.

ACCOMMODATIONS REFERENCE
The rate ranges given here, in U.S. dollars, are projections *for fall 1992 through spring 1993, and span the lowest rates in the low season to the highest in the high season. Unless otherwise indicated, prices are for double rooms, double occupancy. As rates are subject to change, it's always wise to double-check before booking. The telephone area code (within the U.S. system) for Anguilla is 809.*

▶ **Anguilla Great House.** Rendezvous Bay, Anguilla, B.W.I. Tel: 497-6061; Fax: 497-6019; in U.S., (800) 553-4939 or (516) 261-1234; in Canada, (800) 225-3393 or (501) 921-4237. $115–$200, E.P.

▶ **Cap Juluca.** P.O. Box 240, Maunday's Bay, Anguilla, B.W.I. Tel: 497-6779; Fax: 497-6617; in U.S., (800) 323-0139. $268–$910, C.P.

▶ **Cinnamon Reef Beach Club.** P.O. Box 141, Little Harbour, Anguilla, B.W.I. Tel: 497-2727; Fax: 497-3727; in U.S., (800) 223-1108; in Canada, (416) 485-8724; in U.K., (453) 83-58-01. $150–$325, E.P.

▶ **Coccoloba Plantation.** P.O. Box 332, Barnes Bay, Anguilla, B.W.I. Tel: 497-6871; Fax: 497-6332; in U.S. and Canada, (800) 833-3559; in New York, (212) 545-8469; in Connecticut, (203) 230-0011; in U.K., (71) 730-7144. $225–$460, F.A.B.

▶ **Covecastles.** P.O. Box 248, Shoal Bay West, Anguilla,

B.W.I. Tel: 497-6801; Fax: 497-6051; in U.S., (800) 348-4716. $320–$490, E.P. (only two- and three-bedroom suites).

▶ **Ferryboat Inn**. P.O. Box 189, Blowing Point, Anguilla, B.W.I. Tel: 497-6613; in U.S., Tel: (800) 553-4939; Fax: (516) 261-9606; in U.K., Tel: (71) 937-7725; Fax: (71) 938-4793. $75–$150.

▶ **Fountain Beach**. Shoal Bay, Anguilla, B.W.I. Tel and Fax: 497-3491; in U.S., (800) 633-7411. $160–$260, E.P.

▶ **Malliouhana**. P.O. Box 173, Mead's Bay, Anguilla, B.W.I. Tel: 497-6111; Fax: 497-6011; in U.S., (800) 835-0796 or (212) 696-1323. $240–$720, E.P.

▶ **Mariners**. P.O. Box 139, Sandy Ground, Anguilla, B.W.I. Tel: 497-2671; Fax: 497-2901; in U.S. and Canada, (800) 848-7938. $125–$225, E.P.; $300–$460, per person all inclusive.

▶ **La Sirena**. P.O. Box 200, Mead's Bay, Anguilla, B.W.I. Tel: 497-6827; Fax: 497-6829; in U.S. and Canada, (800) 331-9358 or (212) 545-8435; in U.K., Tel: (71) 937-7725; Fax: (71) 938-4793. $115–$235, E.P. (villa, $340).

SABA

By Julie Wilson

Twenty-eight miles southwest of St. Maarten, the five-square-mile rock that is Saba (SAY-ba) rises improbably from the sea. Because of the rain cloud that is hooked permanently on the top of its highest peak, Saba is a very green, flower-bedecked rock. With its tiny, red-roofed cottages, built beside tropical gardens in which the residents' ancestors are buried, Saba elicits such adjectives as "storybook," "quaint," and "picturesque." Visitors frequently dub it Shangri-la. Sabans call it the Unspoiled Queen.

A darker side rescues Saba from cloying sweetness. Seen close up from the water, Saba is jagged, forbidding, brooding. The bare rock of its cliff-rimmed shoreline, gouged by deep gulleys, disappears into the sea. There's no place to get a handhold here, no place to go but away. Seen from this angle, Saba is so inhospitable it seems to repel even the rain. This sweet/savage contrast makes for a very interesting island.

MAJOR INTEREST

Scuba diving
Small-town peace and quiet

Scuba divers have long known about Saba's dramatic underwater pinnacles and caves, its fathoms-deep undersea mountain valleys. Experienced divers cannot help but bring along an underwater camera to record their "you won't believe this" dives. Saba is one of a handful of the best diving sites in the Caribbean, its natural attractions now protected by the Saba Marine Park, which maintains

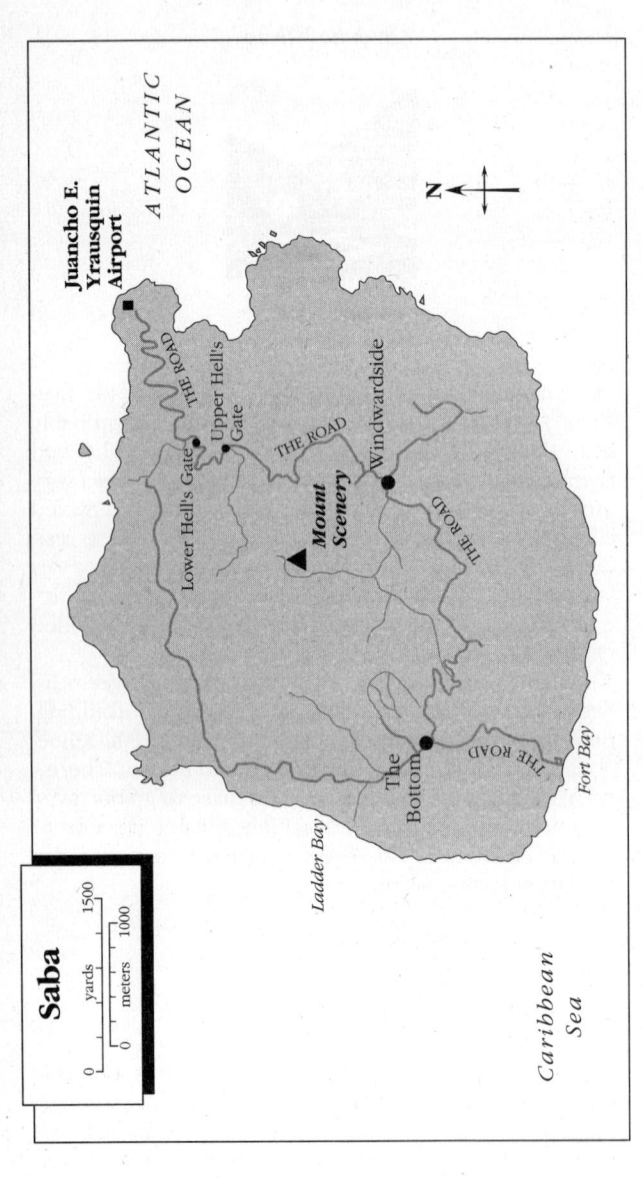

SABA

permanent moorings and safeguards fragile dive sites. There are no beaches and precious few protecting reefs, so, aside from divers, the vacationers who come to Saba are those who like quiet and more quiet.

Though Saba is a self-governing part of the Netherlands Antilles, most of its 1,100 inhabitants have Irish-Scottish backgrounds (going back to Elizabethan days). And most of them, white and black, are named Hassell or Johnson — except for those who are named Simmons. Rumor has it that Saba consumes more Heineken beer per capita than any other nation on earth. Sabans don't confirm the rumor, nor do they deny it.

Saba begins and ends with The Road, a well-maintained two-lane highway built by hand in the 1940s when the Sabans discovered Detroit. Hugging the mountainsides, The Road climbs steeply, drops alarmingly, snakes wildly, looks like the Great Wall of China, and offers views that are both beautiful and terrifying—that ever-present Saban dichotomy. Walls on one side keep The Road clear of falling rocks; walls on the other side keep it from sliding into the ravines (presumably). The Road begins at Fort Bay and ends at the runway of Juancho E. Yrausquin Airport, or the other way around.

Fort Bay

For most people, Fort Bay is just a place to arrive or leave by boat, though local residents use the concrete ramp as a beach. Divers regard Fort Bay as a launch pad, because Lou and Joan Bourque's **Sea Saba** (Tel: 6-2246; headquarters in Windwardside) and Mike Myer's **Saba Deep** (Tel: 6-3347) keep their boats and equipment here. Though these waters are heaven for serious divers, both operations offer courses for beginners. If you just want to watch the launchings, Saba Deep has added a restaurant and sun deck on top of its dive shop. Otherwise, it's off to The Road, past tangles of flowers the Sabans call "love weed" and the rest of the world calls coralita.

The Bottom

Plopped down in a hollow spot among the hills, Saba's capital gets its name from the Dutch *de botte,* which means "the bowl" but which Saba has chosen to translate as "the bottom." Along lanes hemmed in by knee-high, waist-high, and shoulder-high walls, the few government buildings are of little interest to anyone outside the government. One of The Bottom's attractions is the **Saba Artisan's Foundation**, a local industry producing some very attractive fabrics, resort wear, and tee-shirts at moderate prices. At the crossroads where the heliconia bloom (Saban sights are always similarly signposted), **Heleen's Art Gallery** (Tel: 6-3348) displays works by artists who live or vacation on the island (Sea Saba's Joan Bourque among them).

Although Saban meals tend toward home cooking on the simple side, **Queenie Simmons's Serving Spoon** (ask a local for directions) is an exception. Queenie has no menu, offering instead a "plate of food" for those who care to make a reservation (Tel: 6-3325). Some plate. Onion chicken or curried goat, flanked by rice and beans, french fries, fritters, vegetables, and salads add up to more food than the average mortal could eat in a week. There's no service charge, but if you care to leave a tip, "God will surely bless you."

One of The Bottom's progressively narrow roads—ask directions—culminates in the old "step road" to Ladder Bay. The strong of limb can climb down and up, gaining with each step increased respect for the Sabans who once carried up every imported essential, from flour to cement, on their backs.

Windwardside

From The Bottom, The Road climbs upward, and at an altitude of about 1,500 feet it reaches Windwardside, a town that slides up and down a few steep alleys, against which the tourist office, Sea Saba's Dive Shop, and other relevant buildings gather. Before you get there you'll come across **Lollipop's** (Tel: 6-3330), the recently realized lifelong dream of part-time cab driver Carmen "Lollipop" Hassell. Spotless, sweet, and unsophisticated, the restaurant offers a "Lollipop Special" (scrambled eggs, bacon, and pancakes) in the morning and, for lunch and dinner, fish soup, grilled grouper, and "the best fish cakes on the island."

In Windwardside the **Saba Museum** occupies a sea captain's cottage built around the time of the American Revolution and displays old (no one knows how old) family (but everyone knows which family) heirlooms. At Sunday afternoon croquet matches on the lawn, anyone who wants to play wears white and drinks mimosas.

Penalty fees for profanity or other unsportsmanlike conduct benefit the museum.

A few shops in town sell postcards and souvenirs, as well as Saba's major products: Saba Lace and Saba Spice. Intricately hand-drawn threadwork, the lace is embroidered onto shirts, aprons, napkins, and other items. Saba Spice, home brewed and rum based, has a fragrant bouquet and a mule-like kick.

From Windwardside 1,064 slippery steps, overhung by vines and crowded in by jungle and dark imaginings, climb another 1,500 feet to the top of Mount Scenery. The moderately able can manage the climb, though even if the greenery doesn't swallow you up, the cloud at the top may carry you off. (The Saba Conservation Foundation has opened up six other hiking trails on the island, all easier than this one; ask at the tourist office.)

Windwardside has most of Saba's hotels. Scout's Place and Captain's Quarters (with a couple of dozen rooms between them) are the hangouts for divers, day-trippers, locals, and retired North Americans who live on the island—in short, everyone. Simple but well-prepared lunches and dinners have the air of a family gathering, and much Heineken is consumed in the course of a day. **Captain's Quarters** was—no surprise—once the home of a Saban sea captain. But that was some 160 years ago. It's now an antiques-furnished, gingerbread-trimmed, small inn with a big cliffside pool and a dining pavilion enveloped by tropical foliage. Up the hill a few steps, **Scout's Place** was created many years ago by an expatriate from Ohio as an escapist's hideaway. Though it has recently added a few more rooms, a pool, and a small café, it maintains its nonchalant, slightly raffish charm. Low-flying clouds occasionally roll like fog across the dining terrace, a peculiar experience that leaves you with damp clothing.

Midway between the two, **Juliana's Apartments** are balconied, comfortable, and brightened with fabrics from the Saba Artisan's Foundation. The gardens along the pathways are filled with flaming spears of ginger plants, orange hibiscus as big as pie plates, and turtles the size of army helmets gobbling up any fallen blossoms. Juliana's **Tropics Café** (breakfast and lunch only) is a fresh addition to the boomlet of Windwardside restaurants. At **Brigadoon** (Tel: 6-2380), Greg and Penny Johnson serve Creole specialties, grilled fish, and fresh vegetables from this bountiful island. And at **Guido's Disco** (Tel: 6-2230), Guido (whose real name is Rob) makes a terrific pizza.

Though it really is a disco, the young Saban crowd—all dressed in the latest Benetton fashions—seems as interested in the pool table and the dart board as the dance floor.

Road's End

From Windwardside, the remarkable Road slashes through Hell's Gate, a town where neighborhood women sell more Saba Lace and Saba Spice in the Community Center behind the Holy Rosary Church. The Road drops through Lower Hell's Gate, then down a series of switchbacks to the airport—a Band-Aid slapped down on a flat part of a cliff. WINAIR's crack pilots negotiate the short runway as though it were three miles long, but for a newcomer to Saba, takeoffs and landings are, again, both beautiful and terrifying.

USEFUL FACTS

What to Wear
Casual sports clothes of a conservative nature (i.e., no tank tops). Bring a sweater; cool winds blow across Windwardside in the evening.

Getting In
Windward Islands Airways (WINAIR) makes the 15-minute flight from St. Maarten's Juliana Airport five times a day. The *Style,* a high-speed boat, makes the run from Philipsburg in St. Maarten to Fort Bay several times a week; a round trip costs U.S. $60 (Tel: 426-40 on St. Maarten.)

Entry Requirements
Passports are required, but U.S. and Canadian citizens may substitute other proof of citizenship, such as a birth certificate or a voter-registration card. There is a U.S. $1 departure tax if you are returning to St. Maarten or Statia; for other destinations, the tax is U.S. $4.

Local Time
Saba is on Atlantic standard time year-round, one hour ahead of the U.S. east coast except when the east coast moves its clocks ahead an hour during daylight saving time. Then the two keep the same time.

Currency
The Netherlands Antilles guilder; U.S. dollars are accepted everywhere. At press time the current rate of exchange was U.S. $1.00 to NAf 1.77.

Electrical Current
Same as in the U.S. and Canada—110 volts AC, 60 cycles.

Getting Around
Depend on taxi drivers. The Road is picturesque but no fun to drive.

Business Hours
Businesses are open from 8:00 A.M. to noon and 1:00 to 5:00 P.M. The bank is open Monday through Friday from 8:30 A.M. to 12:30 P.M.

Festivals
Carnival, known as the Saba Summer Festival, is in late July.

For Further Information
Saba Tourist Bureau, Windwardside, Saba, N.A., Tel: (599-4) 6-2231; Fax: (599-4) 6-2350; **in the** U.S., c/o Medhurst & Assoc., Inc., 271 Main Street, Northport, NY 11768, Tel: (800) 344-4606 or (516) 261-7474, Fax: (516) 261-9606.

ACCOMMODATIONS REFERENCE
The rate ranges given here, in U.S. dollars, are projections for fall 1992 through spring 1993, and span the lowest rates in the low season to the highest in the high season. Unless otherwise indicated, rates are for double rooms, double occupancy. As rates are subject to change, it's always wise to double-check before booking. The telephone country code for Saba is 599-4.

► **Captain's Quarters.** Windwardside, Saba, N.A. Tel: 6-2201; Fax: 6-2377; in U.S. and Canada, Tel: (800) 344-4606; Fax: (516) 261-9606. $95–$125, E.P.

► **Juliana's Apartments.** Windwardside, Saba, N.A. Tel: 6-2269; Fax: 6-2389; in U.S. and Canada, Tel: (800) 344-4606; Fax: (516) 261-9606. $75–$100, E.P.

► **Scout's Place.** Windwardside, Saba, N.A. Tel: 6-2205; Fax: 6-2388; in U.S. and Canada, Tel: (800) 344-4606; Fax: (516) 261-9606. $100, with full breakfast in the newer rooms; $65, with full breakfast in the older rooms.

STATIA
(ST. EUSTATIUS)

By Robert Grodé

Robert Grodé, a journalist, reviewer, and longtime resident of the Caribbean now based in New York City, has written articles on travel and culture for magazines in the United States and abroad. He is the author of a book on the gravestones of St. Eustatius.

Exactly what St. Eustatius is, is hard to say. "An eight-square-mile island in the Netherlands Antilles Windwards," while accurate, hardly describes the special charms of this relatively undiscovered dot of green.

Friendliness may be what distinguishes Statia (STAY-sha) from its more developed neighbors. Statians seem genuinely delighted to welcome visitors (whom they prefer to call guests). In this, Statia is the perfect choice for self-sufficient travellers seeking the Caribbean as it once was.

MAJOR INTEREST

The feeling of a friendly small town
Peace and quiet
No mass tourism
History

A 20-minute flight from St. Maarten will deposit you at St. Eustatius's recently expanded Franklin Delano Roosevelt Airport, whose runway is now capable of accommodating small jets. So far, however, the 19-passenger STOL's that have been dragonflying in and out for years

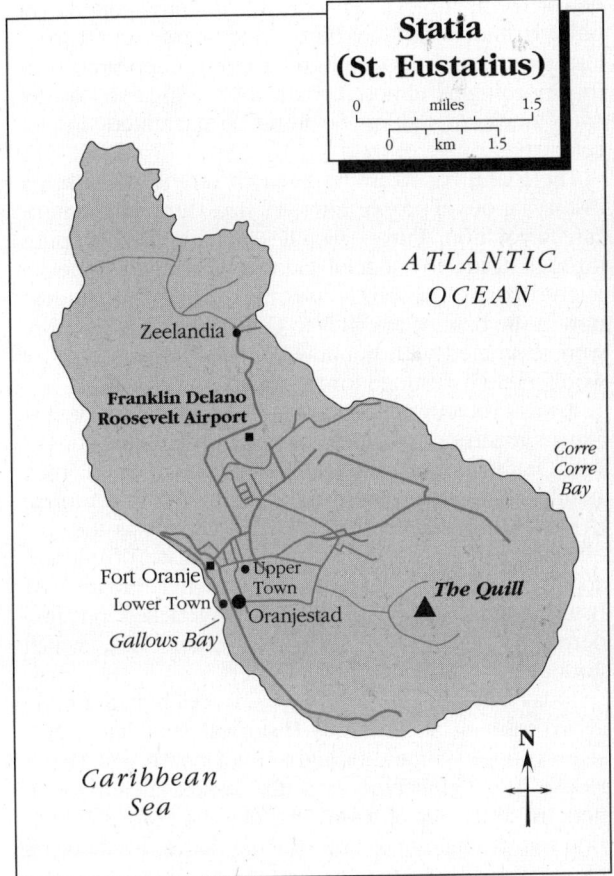

Statia
(St. Eustatius)

0   miles   1.5

0   km   1.5

ATLANTIC
OCEAN

Zeelandia

Franklin Delano
Roosevelt Airport

Corre
Corre
Bay

Fort Oranje
Upper
Town
Lower Town
Oranjestad
Gallows Bay

The Quill

Caribbean
Sea

N

continue to provide the main service. From here it's only a mile or two by taxi to Oranjestad, the island's capital and, it must be admitted, its only town. **Oranjestad** is a gallimaufry of yellow-brick buildings dating from the island's heyday in the 18th century, when it was the mercantile center of the Caribbean; shingled "zinc"-roofed 19th-century town houses; and a smattering of newer cement-block structures, vibrantly painted in pink, lavender, and sky blue. "Good-days" sound from just about every doorway, and a visitor's appearance in the morning is almost certain to be discussed avidly over lunch. Arrival on St. Eustatius guarantees instant celebrity.

The island hasn't always been so serene. Statia has a history far out of proportion to its size. During the American Revolution, European allies transshipped supplies through Statia to General George Washington's beleaguered troops. The warehouses, the ruins of which huddle now at the base of the cliffs in Oranjestad's Lower Town, were crammed with gunpowder, muskets, and bolts of woollen cloth destined for the American colonies.

It was probably with an eye on this lucrative trade that Statia's governor, Johannes de Graaff, ordered the guns of Fort Oranje to salute the colors of the newly proclaimed republic flying from the mast of the brig-of-war *Andrew Doria* on November 16, 1776. His salute was the first official foreign recognition of the United States of America, and it proved to be disastrous for Statia. In February 1781 British Admiral George Bridges Rodney attacked and plundered the island, long called "the Golden Rock," which Rodney now dubbed "a nest of vipers."

Today Statia's colorful history is celebrated in the award-winning **St. Eustatius Historical Foundation Museum** (no telephone), located in the Doncker–De Graaff House. The 18th-century structure stands, tall and dignified, in the center of town. Two elegantly furnished period rooms suggest just how well the "haves" lived during the island's brief "golden age." Coins minted on the island, glistening examples of delftware and Chinese export porcelain, and other artifacts also attest to Statia's wealth two centuries ago. The island's pre-Columbian history is encapsulated in displays that include a 1,500-year-old skeleton of an Arawak Indian and examples of astonishingly elegant Indian pottery.

Statia's Caribbean beaches, tucked away among the ruins, are hardly the stuff of travel posters; they're small and volcanic (read "gray"). The surf is gentle, however, and the water invitingly warm. The wheat-colored sands along the Atlantic shore, on the other hand, are excellent for sunning and beachcombing, though a treacherous undertow makes swimming here inadvisable.

Statia's other diversions are generally of the very low-keyed, do-it-yourself variety: exploring the graveyard of the 18th-century Dutch Reformed Church; visiting the ruins of Honen Dalim, the second-oldest synagogue in the New World; prowling the ramparts of Fort Oranje; or descending to the rain forest that flourishes in the crater of The Quill, the extinct volcano whose symmetrical silhouette dominates the island.

Divers can investigate the wreck of a man-of-war that capsized in the 1700s or snorkel over the walls of buildings that sank beneath Gallows Bay at about the same time. **Dive Statia**, Tel: 8-2435, located next door to the Old Gin House (see below), offers complete rental gear, trips, and instruction (PADI-certified). For tennis buffs there's a night-lighted cement court at the Community Center off Rosemarielaan. (Bring your own racquet and balls.)

While duty-free shopping on Statia is fairly limited—cigarettes and liquor are good buys—Jana Morrison and her partner, Marianne Fitzsimmons, offer their own hand-painted resortwear at the tiny, aptly named **Hole in the Wall**, Tel: 8-2265. And at **Park Place**, just in front of the museum, Barbara Lane features her own ceramics, plus a selection of paintings and woven sculptures by local artists. For more "run of the molen" items—magazines, postcards, swimsuits, sunscreen, an impressive selection of wines—stop at **Mazinga Gift Shop** on Fort Oranjestraat; Tel: 8-2245.

Accommodations are moderately priced and yet surprisingly sophisticated for an island where annual tourism is measured in four-digit figures. The 20-room **Old Gin House** in Oranjestad is an imaginatively restored 18th-century cotton mill, popular with writers, theater people, and other creative types. A rare Bristol clock ticks away the lazy hours in the rosy-brick taproom, candles flicker in tin wall sconces, and a Vivaldi suite plays softly on the stereo. A small freshwater pool reflects the vine-covered galleries on the inland side of the inn. (There are several seaside rooms overlooking the most appealing of the island's pewter-colored beaches and the tranquil Caribbean.) Four-course dinner menus change daily and often include such unusual offerings as Dutch Gouda cheese soup, red snapper with almonds and yogurt, and a fresh peach crepe laced with Cointreau.

A few yards down the shore, the **Golden Era Hotel** offers accommodations that make up for their somewhat motel-ish appearance—chenille bedspreads, plastic flower arrangements—by being priced with recession-riddled pocketbooks in mind. The rooms are spacious and each boasts a balcony. One word of caution here, however: Specify a water-view when reserving space; otherwise, you may find yourself contemplating the tropical sunsets as reflected on the Gin House's rooftop ventilation ducts next door. The large pool, located on the bay's edge, is a winner. Though the cuisine runs more to "hearty" than to "haute," the chef's infatuation with fresh fish seems ongoing, a love affair that's fortunate in an area where "frozen" is too often the fashion.

Relaxed and inexpensive restaurants featuring many West Indian dishes include **L'Etoile** on Heillegerweg and **The Stone Oven** in town. It's a good idea to call ahead to discuss what will be available on the menu that evening; Tel: 8-2299 (L'Etoile) and 8-2543 (Stone Oven). For the latest news about island events, stop by the recently expanded **Cool Corner** on Van Tonningenweg for a Heineken (called "a greenie"). Close to the government offices in Fort Oranje and at the crossroads of town, this friendly rum shop seems to be, at one time or another, the gathering spot for just about everyone on the island.

"Lord Gene" Schmidt's Killi-Killi Band, with its blend of tinkling steel "pans" and its slightly raffish calypso lyrics, generally livens up the after-sunset scene several evenings a week. You might want to give "Lord Gene" a call at Tel: 8-2264 to find out where and when the band will be appearing during your stay.

USEFUL FACTS

Getting In
There are several flights daily to Franklin Delano Roosevelt Airport on Windward Islands Airways (WINAIR) from St. Maarten.

Entry Requirements
U.S. and Canadian citizens arriving for stays of up to three months must have a valid passport or one that has expired only within the past five years; a notarized birth

certificate; or a voter-registration card. Others require a valid passport or Alien Registration Card. A return or ongoing ticket is also necessary for all visitors. There is a departure tax of U.S. $1 if you are returning to St. Maarten or Saba. For other destinations, the tax is U.S. $4.

Local Time
Statia is on Atlantic standard time year-round, one hour ahead of the U.S. east coast except when the east coast moves its clocks ahead an hour during daylight saving time. Then the two keep the same time.

Currency
The legal tender is the Netherlands Antilles guilder. U.S. and Canadian dollars are accepted everywhere. At press time the current rate of exchange was U.S. $1.00 to NAf 1.77.

Electrical Current
Same as in the U.S. and Canada—110 volts AC, 60 cycles.

Getting Around
Several local car-rental agencies operate on the island. A valid driver's license is required.

Business Hours
Banking and business hours: Monday through Thursday, 8:30 A.M. to 1:00 P.M.; Fridays, 8:30 A.M. to 1:00 P.M. and 4:00 to 5:00 P.M.

For Further Information
St. Eustatius Tourist Bureau, Oranjestad, St. Eustatius, Netherlands Antilles, Tel and Fax: (599-3) 8-2433; **in the** U.S., c/o Medhurst & Assoc., Inc., 271 Main Street, Northport, NY 11768, Tel: (800) 344-4606 or (516) 261-7474; Fax: (516) 261-9606.

ACCOMMODATIONS REFERENCE
The rate ranges given here, in U.S. dollars, are projections for fall 1992 through spring 1993, and span the lowest rates in the low season to the highest in the high season. Unless otherwise indicated, rates are for double rooms, double occupancy. As rates are subject to change, it's always wise to double-check before booking. The telephone country code for St. Eustatius is 599-3.

▶ **Golden Era Hotel**. P.O. Box 109, St. Eustatius, N.A. Tel: 8-2345; Fax: 8-2445. $75, E.P.

▶ **The Old Gin House**. Lower Town, St. Eustatius, N.A. Tel: 8-2319; Fax: 8-2555; in U.S., Tel: (800) 223-9832 or (212) 599-8280; Fax: (212) 599-1755. $100–150.

ST. KITTS AND NEVIS

By Jennifer Quale

If only life could be so simple: to be obliged to make the bittersweet choice between a pair of idyllic islands for your holiday. But then, you needn't choose. Unless the risk of breaking the spell seems too great, your stay could well be split equally between St. Kitts and Nevis, with half the heart left on each. To find Caribbean islands where colonial buildings outnumber the new, where the endearing inns make you feel at home, and where the islanders never run out of ways to "take care of you" is rare indeed.

Not that St. Kitts (a.k.a. St. Christopher, after guess-who-discovered-it) and Nevis are twins. A sometimes treacherous two-mile strait called The Narrows divides the two-island federation of little (36 square miles) Nevis and big (65 square miles) St. Kitts. An even bigger gulf separates them temperamentally. Petite, sophisticated Nevis (NEE-vis) long ago turned its plantation great houses into inns and capitalized on its romantic history. Like an awkward big brother, St. Kitts, doggedly growing sugarcane long after anyone wanted to pay much for it, let most of its great houses crumble into ruins, playgrounds for marauding goats and sheep. Still hunkering in the rain forests deeper in the island, the vervet monkeys wait for dry weather before swinging down to civilization in search of water—of which there was plenty in the wake of Hurricane Hugo, now a faded memory.

A few years ago, St. Kitts built a new airport and deep-water port, and waited—and the tourists are finally coming. (But at least the hordes are confining themselves to

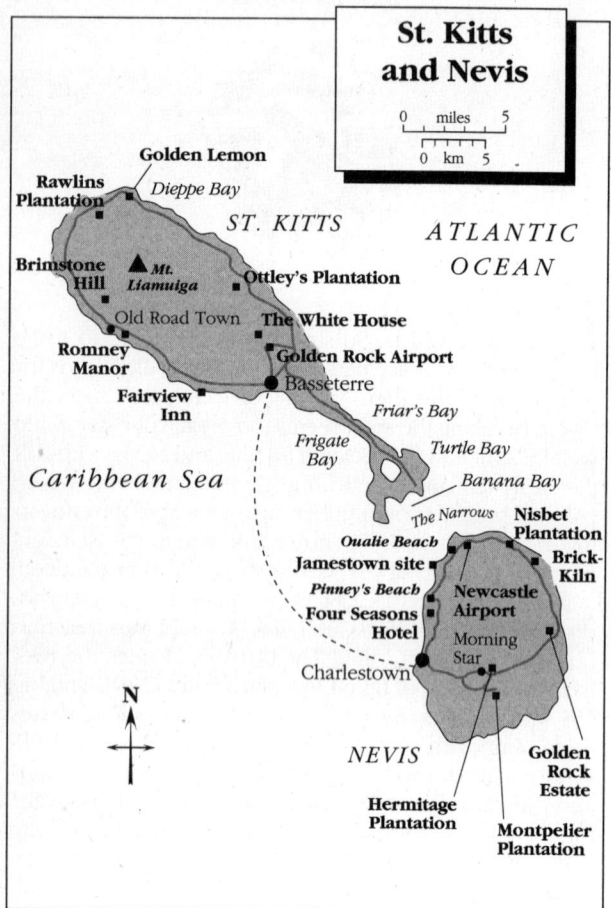

St. Kitts and Nevis

0 miles 5

0 km 5

Golden Lemon

Rawlins
Plantation

Dieppe Bay

ST. KITTS

ATLANTIC
OCEAN

Brimstone
Hill

▲ *Mt.
Liamuiga*

Ottley's Plantation

Old Road Town

The White House

Romney
Manor

Golden Rock Airport

Basseterre

Fairview
Inn

Friar's Bay

*Frigate
Bay*

Turtle Bay

Caribbean Sea

Banana Bay

The Narrows

Nisbet
Plantation

Oualie Beach

Jamestown site

Brick-
Kiln

Pinney's Beach

Newcastle
Airport

Four Seasons
Hotel

*Morning
Star*

Charlestown

N

NEVIS

Golden
Rock
Estate

Hermitage
Plantation

Montpelier
Plantation

the newly developed area on the peninsular end.) This pleases the Kittitians enormously but worries those visitors who love the island for its otherwise quaint air. Nonetheless, those stupefyingly beautiful cane fields are finally paying off: In 1989 Baron Edmond de Rothschild sailed by the island, spotted the fields, and started producing his toney "C.S.R." (Cane Spirit Rothschild)—making the "Spirit of St. Kitts" a potable memory.

MAJOR INTEREST

Exquisite inns
Peace and quiet
Excellent West Indian cuisine
Colonial architecture
Hospitable, gracious people
Beaches (particularly on Nevis)

ST. KITTS

Shaped like a violin, St. Kitts has a fat end that is dominated by rain forests, mountain ranges, and sugarcane fields. Towering above it all, the nearly 4,000-foot-high peak of Mount Liamuiga never seems to take off its bowler-like hat of gray clouds. (*Liamuiga* is a Carib word meaning "fertile isle"; until recently, the mountain was called Misery, but that didn't square with the new tourist image.) The other end, the skinny southeast peninsula, is scrubbier and somewhat flatter. The best beaches are where the two ends meet, at Friars Bay, and at Banana Bay (temporarily closed to the public) on the far end of the southeast peninsula.

Basseterre

The capital's French name and British face are a tip-off to just who fought over St. Kitts in colonial days. In case anyone should mistake its allegiance, Basseterre's terribly British treasury building on the waterfront, its statue of Queen Victoria, and its tidy, formally laid out Independence Square make things perfectly clear. The British-style Circus includes a four-sided clock tower that few pedestrians bother to look at (although it now works), preoccupied as they are with dodging Kittitian taxis. At the same time, two-story, pastel-colored Basseterre, located near Golden Rock Airport, is unmistakably Caribbean. Christmas lights decorate the Circus's palm-lined perimeter year-round, chickens share pathways with pedestrians, and on occasional Saturday nights the entire town turns out for wingding block parties, a must for anyone with a taste for gay abandon. Visitors afflicted with shopper's mania will want to call on **Palm Crafts** and duty-free **Slice of the Lemon** in the gingerbread-y arcade just off the Circus. Palm Crafts now carries the fetching line of St. Kitts's new resident designer John Warden, creator of Ivana Trump's wedding gown.

While there are relatively few restaurants on this West Indian island, those in Basseterre run the gamut from the somewhat formal, stone-walled **Georgian House** on Independence Square, for trumped-up pasta (Tel: 465-4049) to the second-floor balcony of bustling **Ballahoo** (Tel: 465-4197), in its new and bigger location overlooking the Circus (try toasted lobster sandwiches for lunch, blue parrot fish or shrimp in chilli butter for dinner, and the fabulous pumpkin tart for any time at all). The **Spencer Cameron Fabrics** boutique, with attractive island-made clothing, occupies a tiny niche of the balcony; its branch, the **Spencer Cameron Gallery**, in an old colonial building next to the Georgian House, showcases serious art.

The multilevel **Ocean Terrace Inn** spills down a hillside on the edge of town, encompassing condos, pools, bars, and gardens; it leads to the more appealing "Fishermen's Village," a casual annex of OTI with rustic efficiency bungalows overlooking the water's edge, next to an intriguing boutique/restaurant/marina complex (check out local artist Paula Fiori's painted bowls in the boutique). Admirers compare the place to Singapore's Raffle's; detractors complain about OTI's Florida-condo feeling, but at least the food has improved a bit. In any case, sooner or later everyone shows up here for a meal, a drink, a boat trip, or just to meet someone else.

The Road

St. Kitts's main road follows the shoreline around the island, running parallel to and sometimes crossing a narrow-gauge sugarcane railroad with tooting engines that haul their cargo to the refinery near the airport. The Atlantic (windward) side of the island is still in the thrall of cane and is notable mainly for its small hamlets, which vie annually for the Best-Kept Village Award. With its clipped hedges and stone embankment (the old and colorful outdoor mural washed away with Hugo), the originally French settlement of Cayon has taken top honors the last few years. No doubt the hopping Friday-evening hangout **Henry's Nightspot**, (a.k.a. the 18-Hour Bar, which serves as the daytime Lunch-Special Restaurant for schoolchildren) had some influence on the judges' decision.

Running up the leeward coast you'll come across the **Fairview Inn**. One of the island's pioneer hotels, built by and for West Indians, this is where Prince Charles sought refuge as a young naval officer and where the Rotary meets regularly for lunch. Budget-minded travellers overlook the motel-type rooms in low season for host Freddie Lam's gregarious welcome and genuine (though heavy) West Indian cooking—especially the angel pie.

The coastal road continues through Old Road Town, where Sir Thomas Warner established Britain's first New World settlement and supposedly where Columbus landed. The oldest (1623) house on St. Kitts is Sir Thomas's former residence. It still stands, in ruins, on Road Town's waterfront, the subject of many a painter's canvas.

Romney Manor

Caribelle Batiks set up shop and showroom in the 1970s at Romney Manor, an old estate house surrounded by rain forest and formal gardens. An enormous 350-year-old saman tree looms over the entrance. Unfazed by onlookers, local girls with steady hands use old hot-wax techniques to batik cotton destined to become sports shirts, skirts, and sundresses in rather dated styles. The tropical designs incorporate local flora and copies of Arawak Indian petroglyphs that have been discovered on the island. You can see some of these ancient markings down by the main road near the manor, inscribed on a pile of otherwise undistinguished lava rocks. One of the images looks like the symbolic monkey of St. Kitts but in fact represents a pregnant woman praying to the sun god to save her baby.

Brimstone Hill

A couple of miles beyond Romney Manor looms one of the Caribbean's most startling sights: Brimstone Hill, 32 acres of a no-nonsense British fort capable of defending a small continent. Wedged between mountains and sea and looking toward half a dozen neighboring islands, the "Gibraltar of the Caribbean" took a century to build and changed hands twice—once by battle, once by treaty. In both cases ceremony took precedence over bloodshed.

The contrast of massive black walls made of lava rock (also known as brimstone) and the peaceful green landscape surrounding them exaggerates the enormity of Brimstone Hill. Carefully maintained, the fort is not yet completely restored, but you may climb the extremely steep steps to the topmost part of the citadel, which contains a few interesting rooms devoted to English, French, North American, and pre-Columbian influences.

The Inns

Two exceptionally fine inns coexist harmoniously up where the road swings over the northern tip of St. Kitts. **Rawlins Plantation**, reached by narrow tracks through cane fields less than a mile inland, has been home to the Walwyn family for just over 200 years. Philip Walwyn and his wife, Frances, turned the estate into an uncommon hotel several years ago. In 1990 they sold the inn (but kept the ancestral house) to friends Claire and Paul Rawson. Rawlins regulars may rest assured that little, except refurbishing, has changed: It's still isolated amid 25 rolling acres of orchards, pastures, and gardens, its ten rooms divided among enchanting cottages and a restored sugar mill, the most-photographed site on St. Kitts. With a spring-fed pool big enough for laps, a grass tennis court, and a croquet lawn, the inn offers just enough to do for guests (such as the baron Edmond de Rothschild) who appreciate the privacy, the sweet staff, and the better-than-ever meals (the lobster salad with homegrown greens and herbs can't be beat). Rawlins is the sort of dreamy place where you're likely to make friends for life—with the owners as well as the other guests.

Rawlins's guests share the black-sand beach of Dieppe Bay with Arthur Leaman's **Golden Lemon Hotel**. (They also share the well-informed services of Oliver Spencer, who gives custom tours of the rain forest.) Long recognized as a Caribbean legend among those who don't bestow legend status lightly, the Lemon is reason enough to come to St. Kitts. Whether you stay in the 17th-century great house or the contemporary seaside villas, you'll find a very personal combination of Colonial antiques, sumptuous beds, Caribbean colors, unobtrusive service, and island food that falls in the "comfort" range (e.g., the breakfast porridge brings back memories of grand-mother's and the hand-cranked ice creams are never forgotten). After dinner, the natty bar—with Arthur's part-ner at the keyboard—is the closest you'll get to Broadway in the Caribbean. So harmonious are the guests (no children) that you would almost think King Arthur hand-picks them for his ongoing, but never rowdy, house party. The Golden Lemon is quiet and clubby, except for those days when knowledgeable passengers from cruise ships head up the coast for lunch here.

As if it weren't dilemma enough to choose between Rawlins and the Lemon, two newer inns, resurrected from abandoned great houses, opened two years ago. High on a hill off the east coast, **Ottley's Plantation Inn** dates from 1706; by nightfall, with lights ablaze, the exist-ing great house (c. 1832) could pass for a 19th-century Mississippi showboat. The emphasis here is on food, which the Massachusetts-born chef describes as "creative island cuisine," with the Sunday Champagne brunch the showstopper of the week. Ottley's private rain forest, enormous lap pool, and exuberant owners are all icing on the cake.

Take away the copious Laura Ashley fittings and **The White House** could be just as it was in the early 1700s, so precise is its restoration. Although outbuildings (e.g., erst-while stables and coach house) serve as guest quarters, the feeling here is intimate, as if you're at home with the young English couple who brought the place back to life. Many of the guests come from the hosts' home turf (the others from North America), armed with books, croquet expertise, and curiosity about St. Kitts's oldest existing great house. All is quiet—despite its proximity to the airport—behind the old brimstone and iron gates, from tea and cocktails on the gallery to sotto voce dinners beautifully presented on the tiny covered terrace or in one of the two more formal dining rooms inside. Only an occasional splash from the pool on the slope should jar you back into the 20th century.

Frigate Bay

The government has earmarked the Frigate Bay Develop-ment area, near Basseterre on the "handle" side of the island, for tourist facilities. So far there is the island's 18-

hole golf course, a casual casino, a good beach with bar/restaurant/water-sports operations, and an ever-increasing number of hotel/condos. Frigate Bay is also the site of the hard-to-overlook Jack Tar Village. A prepaid, all-inclusive resort, massive Jack Tar supplies just about any sport imaginable, along with all the booze its pack-'em-in clientele can drink. Jack Tar guests can be recognized by the required photo I.D. they wear around their necks.

The only reason to go to Frigate Bay is to dine at **The Patio**, which serves in a caring atmosphere (the chef's home) what many gourmands consider some of the best food on St. Kitts. (By reservation only; Tel: 465-8666.)

Southeast Peninsula

St. Kitts has now extended the paved road some six miles down the nearly uninhabited peninsula that forms the southeastern part of the island—a multimillion dollar project that has been the major topic of conversation here for the last several years. Long ago, two small inns entrenched themselves at the far end of the peninsula, just two miles across from Nevis and accessible only by boat. What was once the idyllic haven known as Banana Bay now has been sold to the developers of Sandals Resorts, and will eventually reopen as yet another all-inclusive, prepackaged, 250-room resort. With the road finished, people can now drive up to the back door feeling as if they've just passed through the Antillian version of Big Sur; it's doubtful, however, that this land's end will remain a sublime escape, a place of quiet and beauty. For now, you can dine and dive at **Turtle Beach Bar & Grill** (Tel: 469-9086), where the road stops, just above Banana Bay.

NEVIS

Imagine the island in the shape of the big, bulbous green lemon that grows there. Then picture young Alexander Hamilton, sad-eyed Fanny Nisbet, the evil, slave-flogging planter Edward Huggins.... On Nevis these historic figures are as much a part of the present-day scene as the fellow travellers at the next dinner table. On a clear day it is entirely possible to believe that a speck on the horizon is the H.M.S. *Boreas,* bringing Horatio Nelson back again. But what brings visitors back with amazing regularity today, beyond the time warp, is the sense of intimacy with nature and a civility seldom encountered on other islands. The fact that the cuisine and beaches are great doesn't hurt either. It's almost hush-hush here, as if Nevis habitués don't want anyone else to know about their perfect little hideaway.

Charlestown

The ferry from Basseterre on St. Kitts docks on Nevis at Charlestown, the island's capital, which dates from 1660 and is the only town on Nevis of any consequence. Quite conveniently, all the action (which isn't much) in Charlestown centers around the town square, with a lackadaisical tourist office next to a musty shop that sells local handicrafts, homemade chutneys, and hot sauce. Boutique addicts should venture just beyond the square to the **Sand Box Tree** at Evelyn's Villa. Eating options here include **Caribbean Confections** deli (try the pumpkin bread) and the arbored **Courtyard Café** behind it; there's also **Eddie's Restaurant** (Tel: 469-5958), a new, humming spot just off Main Street for light lunches and weekend dinners. A few steps off the square sits the very bureaucratic philatelic bureau, adjacent to the open concrete structure housing Nevis's produce market.

The waterfront birthplace of Alexander Hamilton, not far from the pier, was restored as a small museum with Hamilton mementos and Amerindian artifacts. A new **museum**, honoring Nevis's other local hero, Horatio Nelson, opened last year next to Government House with an expanded, extraordinary collection from its former repository at Morning Star Plantation.

Out on the Island

From Charlestown the road runs parallel to the island's beaches. Starting at palm-backed, four-mile-long **Pinney's**, it follows the coast to the **Oualie** (in Carib, "land of the beautiful water") **Beach Club**—home of Nevis Watersports, a wee cluster of boxy, clean guest bungalows and a casual restaurant known for delectable daily specials (e.g., shrimp de jonge). Two years ago the once-tranquil Pinney's was forever changed with the new 196-room **Four Seasons Resort** and its Robert Trent Jones II 18-hole golf course (where a one-hole course used to satisfy Nevis devotees). Not merely a hotel but a whopping chunk of international grandeur on one of the Caribbean's best beaches, the Four Seasons brings CNN, foodie cuisine, and amazing amenities to this erstwhile dozy island. The head-spinning roster of daily activities guarantees nary a dull moment, while the level of service could win any hotel war. And so what if the guests don't know they're on Nevis? The locals love it—it's their bread and butter, their Taj Mahal.

Continuing north you come to the site where, some 200 years ago, young Captain Nelson was watering his boats at the freshwater springs ("Nelson's Spring") near Jamestown when he first saw Fanny Nisbet. Or so one story goes; another has them meeting at a dinner party on the other side of the island. An earthquake and tidal wave wiped out Jamestown, Nevis's first capital, in 1680, and a few cannons along a wall are all that remains. Only a jailed convict survived the disaster. He may have wondered if answering his prayers for freedom with total destruction was a bit excessive.

Just a mile or so north of the Jamestown site on Jones Bay, the alfresco seaside bar and restaurant **Prinderella's** (Tel: 469-9291) was recently rebuilt, once again to draw cognoscenti with its eclectic but leaning-toward-Mediterranean menu and the bubbly cheer of English owners Ian and Charlotte Mintrim. Prinderella's claims they stay open even later than Dick's Bar, the Saturday night hangout of choice just around the island's tip in the village of Brick-Kiln.

At the top of the island, not far from Newcastle Airport's short runway, history of a different sort surfaces. At **Newcastle Pottery**, Almena Cornelius and her acolytes use Amerindian techniques, passed down generation after generation, to produce primitive red-clay pottery, firing the finished works in open fires fueled by coconut husks. For a good, authentic West Indian lunch head about a mile inland from the village of Newcastle, on Shaw's Road, to family-run **Cla-Cha-Del Restaurant** (Tel: 469-9640), famed for its killer cocktails. Never mind the plastic-covered tablecloths: The blue parrot fish, tannia fritters, and turtle stew (in season), at bargain prices, amply compensate.

Nisbet Plantation Beach Club, across the road from the pottery center, has become a well-known inn, with a stately path running between coconut palms a quarter of a mile down to the splendid beach—once one of the Caribbean's most photographed sights (Hugo thinned out the palms). Here, contemporary cottages are set among the trees on lawns suitable for the game of bowls, while the great house retains 18th-century charm with its mahogany bar and fine dining room. Nisbet's current, Bermudian owner has refurbished the whole place (except for the tennis court), homogenizing it with a new tea terrace behind the great house, a lap pool and children's pool alongside a Tahitian-style beach restaurant, and a dozen additional duplex guest units. Hail to the new German chef.

A tale worthy of the Brontë sisters surrounds Eden Brown Estate, now in romantic ruin farther down the east coast. After a pre-wedding party here the groom and his best man killed each other in an ill-timed duel. The bride, it is said, screamed until she died, and her ghost can still be heard moaning in the moonlight.

A pocket of historic-homes-turned-inns nestles up in the hills above the east coast. Beaches are a ways below, but these places all have pools, and each has its champions who claim it serves the best food on the island. And those hospitable little inns do serve good food—imaginative without being terribly fancy, with lots of fresh fish, vegetables, and fruits. Golden-haired Pam Barry owns **Golden Rock Estate**, which occupies an erstwhile sugar plantation that has been in her family (she is a Huggins, one of Nevis's oldest colonial clans) for generations. In a casual, modern-day rendition of noblesse oblige, gracious Pam brings together earnest locals and guests who share common interests such as bird-watching, painting, and environmental concerns. (Now called the Nevis Academy, Pam's cultural-vacation enterprise offers a new course in "Caribbean Style.") The inn's pleasantly cool public rooms, with their thick walls of hand-carved lava stone, are in an old estate building, and the bedroom units are scattered across the hillside. Honeymooners—and families—favor the suite called the "Sugar Mill," with the oldest mahogany four-poster bed on Nevis. "Paradise" comes in a close second, with bamboo four-poster beds and a private porch screened by plantings. In addition to the newly cut nature trail (leading up to the rain forest), a spring-fed pool, and a tennis court on the grounds, Golden Rock has its own patch of sand at Pinney's Beach—Carousel, for grilled burgers and seafood lunches, drinks, and water sports. (Though Pinney's Beach is across the island, nothing is far away on Nevis, and the hotels in the hills customarily offer free transportation to the beach.) Golden Rock also has

David Freeman, its head gardener who moonlights as leader of The Honey Bees, a Nevisian string band of considerable charm and enthusiasm. The band plays at most of the island's inns.

Croney's Old Manor Estate rambles around yet another plantation, this one from the 17th century. A warren of cut-stone buildings that could serve as a film set for some Gothic tale set in the tropics, the place isn't completely restored, but its **Cooperage Restaurant** (Tel: 469-3445) gets rave reviews and sizable queues for its Friday night musical barbecue.

Hermitage Plantation's great house, complete with original wood shingles, is the oldest occupied house in the Antilles. Since the 1970s it has been the family home of the Philadelphia-fled Lupinaccis, who parlayed it into a charming inn several years ago. Seen from the front, it appears to be a strong wind away from oblivion, but don't be deceived; those planters usually built things to last forever. Cottages climb up the hill (so do monkeys), and most of them offer a hammock on a porch facing the sea. Come sunset everyone gathers in Nevis's tiniest but most fun bar (they don't call this place "Camp Loupi" for nothing). Wonderful if expensive meals, including roast duck with mango sauce, Lovey's carrot cake, or pumpkin pancakes for breakfast, are served on the terrace at the antiques-filled main house, and Hermitage is so easygoing that more than one guest has gone into the kitchen to ask for a recipe. Recent additions: another fretworked cottage with great flair, a large villa, and a riding stable with seven steeds and English tack—just up the hill from the swimming pool. In true camp style, the Lupinaccis are now sending "happy campers" off on horse-drawn carriage rides on an old circular road to Charlestown and back.

A few miles farther south, Fanny Nisbet and Horatio Nelson were married under a breadfruit tree at **Montpelier Plantation**, home of Fanny's uncle. (The marriage certificate is recorded nearby in the sturdy stone **Fig Tree Church**.) Neither the original house nor the marriage survived the test of time, but the stone inn built in the 1960s on the slopes of Mount Nevis looks as though it's been there for centuries—and more than compensates in charm for the odd, motel-style guest bungalows. Breadfruit trees abound on the 100-acre estate, along with fruit orchards, a brilliant garden containing hybrid hibiscus, wood roses, and bougainvillaea, and a huge *Ficus benjamina* tree that nearly swallows the entrance of the great house. Montpelier boasts Nevis's best lap pool, framed by a stone wall with an enchanting mural depicting the island terrain; a tennis court; and a slice of Pinney's with a new barbecue grill and beach bar for lunch, changing cabanas, and a speed boat at the ready for snorkeling, water-skiing, or fishing. Owners James and Celia Milnes-Gaskell are delightfully English, as are many of the guests—who come, again and again, mostly for the superb food (much of it from the Gaskells' own garden) and personal pampering.

As you near Charlestown on your way back along the shore road you'll come to the 18th-century **Bath Hotel**, a relic from the days when Nevis was Queen of the Caribees and the fashionable of the known world sailed here to take the waters. Long deserted, this place by all rights should have crumbled years ago had it not been built well enough to withstand earthquakes, floods, and every force nature could throw at it. The floors have been shored up, so you can walk through the old rooms and listen for echoes of long-forgotten waltzes and flirtatious whispers. Hot-spring streams still flow below the hotel's balconied façade, affording curative baths to those who have a desire to plunge into the past (get the key from the gas station on the corner).

USEFUL FACTS

What to Wear
Attire is casual, sometimes elegantly so. A sweater or jacket is advisable for cool evenings in the hills.

Getting In
American Airlines flies daily from New York to Golden Rock Airport on St. Kitts and from other major cities with a brief connection in San Juan. BWIA has direct flights to Golden Rock Airport from New York on Sundays and Thursdays and from Toronto on Saturdays; Air Canada operates connecting flights from Montreal and Toronto. There are connecting flights from San Juan, St. Maarten, Antigua, St. Thomas, St. Croix, and Guadeloupe. Connections to Nevis's Newcastle Airport can be made via Antigua and St. Croix as well as St. Kitts.

Entry Requirements
Passports are required; U.S. and Canadian nationals may, however, substitute another proof of identity, such as a

birth certificate or voter-registration card. The departure tax is U.S. $8.

Local Time

St. Kitts and Nevis are on Atlantic standard time year-round, one hour ahead of the U.S. east coast except when the east coast moves its clocks ahead an hour during daylight saving time. Then all keep the same time.

Currency

The Eastern Caribbean dollar; U.S. dollars are universally accepted. As of this writing the rate of exchange was U.S. $1.00 to E.C. $2.67.

Electrical Current

220 volts AC, 60 cycles. Some hotels have converted to 110 volts AC, but U.S.- and Canadian-made appliances still may require converters and three-square-pronged adaptors.

Getting Around

Driving is on the left. Roads are good on both islands but are narrow on Nevis. A temporary local license costs U.S. $13. On Nevis, where a car is more desirable, TDC Car Rental offers a full range of vehicles at good rates (Tel: 809/469-5430; on St. Kitts, Tel: 809/465-2991). Taxis are plentiful, the rates government-fixed, but make certain to establish the price (and in which currency) before setting off.

Excursions

Tours of St. Kitts's volcano and primate research center and both islands' rain forests, as well as day sails to Nevis on the Caona catamaran (Tel: 465-7474) with a wonderful picnic on a deserted stretch of Pinney's beach, are worthy diversions and can be arranged through local hotels.

Getting Across

A government-operated ferry runs between Basseterre and Charlestown two or three times a day (depending on the day; no crossings on Thursdays and Sundays). The crossing takes 40 to 45 minutes and costs U.S. $4 each way. A newer, daily (except Wednesdays) alternative is the *Spirit of Mt. Nevis* boat, which costs U.S. $6. Speedboat charters, although expensive, are easily arranged through hotels. The Caona catamaran (see above), by arrangement, will book one-way crossings. Leeward Islands Air

Transport (Tel: 809/465-2286 or 469-5238) and Carib Aviation (Tel: 809/465-3055) operate daily, 10-minute flights between the islands; LIAT charges U.S. $30, Carib Aviation, U.S. $20.

Business Hours

Mondays through Saturdays, 8:00 A.M. to noon and 1:00 to 4:00 P.M. Some businesses close Thursday afternoons. Banks are open from 8:00 A.M. to 1:00 P.M. weekdays; on Fridays they reopen from 3:00 to 5:00 P.M. On Saturdays the St. Kitts and Nevis National Bank is open from 8:30 to 11:00 A.M.

Festivals

Carnival is in late December. Whit Monday Race Meet is held at the Nevis Turf and Jockey Club.

For Further Information

St. Kitts & Nevis Department of Tourism, Pelican Mall, Bay Road, Basseterre, St. Kitts, W.I., Tel: (809) 465-9727; Fax: (809) 465-8794; **in the U.S.**, 414 East 75th Street, New York, NY 10021, Tel: (800) 582-6208 or (212) 535-1234, Fax: (212) 734-6511; **in Canada**, 11 Yorkville Avenue, Suite 508, Toronto, Ontario M4W IL3, Tel: (416) 921-7717, Fax: (416) 921-7997.

ACCOMMODATIONS REFERENCE

The rate ranges given here, in U.S. dollars, are projections for fall 1992 through spring 1993, and span the lowest rates in the low season to the highest in the high season. Unless otherwise indicated, rates are for double rooms, double occupancy. As rates are subject to change, it's always wise to double-check before booking. The telephone area code (within the U.S. system) for St. Kitts and Nevis is 809.

St. Kitts

▶ **Fairview Inn.** Box 212, St. Kitts, W.I. Tel: 465-2472; Fax: 465-1056; in U.S. and Canada, Tel: (800) 223-9815 or (212) 251-1800; Fax: (212) 545-8467. $70–$140. Various meal plans available.

▶ **Golden Lemon Hotel.** Dieppe Bay, St. Kitts, W.I. Tel: 465-7260; Fax: 465-4019; in U.S., (800) 633-7411 or (803) 785-7411. $260–$350 for great-house rooms, $310–$475 for seaside villas (some with plunge pools), M.A.P., including tennis, afternoon tea, and laundry; ask about E.P. option.

▶ **Ocean Terrace Inn.** P.O. Box 65, Basseterre, St. Kitts, W.I. Tel: 465-4121 or 2754; Fax: 465-1057; in U.S. and Canada, (800) 223-5695; in U.K., (81) 367-5175. $125–$204, E.P.

▶ **Ottley's Plantation Inn.** P.O. Box 345, Basseterre, St. Kitts, W.I. Tel: 465-7234; Fax: 465-4760; in U.S., (800) 772-3039 or (609) 921-1259. $110–$275, includes full breakfast, dinner, and beach shuttle; ask about special packages and weekly rates.

▶ **Rawlins Plantation.** P.O. Box 340, St. Kitts, W.I. Tel: 465-6221; Fax: 465-4954; in U.S., (800) 745-3490 or (617) 367-8959. $150–$375, M.A.P., including afternoon tea and laundry. No credit cards.

▶ **The White House.** P.O. Box 436, St. Peter's, St. Kitts, W.I. Tel: 465-8162; Fax: 465-8275; in U.S., (800) 223-1108. $275–$350, M.A.P., including afternoon tea and laundry, airport transfers, and beach transportation.

Nevis

▶ **Four Seasons Resort.** P.O. Box 565, Nevis, W.I. Tel: 469-1111; Fax: 469-1040; in U.S., (800) 332-3442; in Canada, (800) 268-6282; in U.K., (71) 834-4422. $225–$550 (suites higher); $75 per person per day, M.A.P.; ask about golf, tennis, and other packages.

▶ **Golden Rock Estate.** P.O. Box 493, Nevis, W.I. Tel: 469-3346; Fax: 469-2113; in U.S. and Canada, Tel: (800) 223-9815 or (212) 251-1800; Fax: (212) 545-8467. $100–$200, E.P.; $160–$235, M.A.P., including wine with dinner; Sugar Mill Tower suite $25 extra.

▶ **Hermitage Plantation.** St. John Fig Tree Parish, Nevis, W.I. Tel: 469-3477; Fax: 469-2481; in U.S. and Canada, Tel: (800) 223-9815 or (212) 251-1800; Fax: (212) 545-8467. $100–$295; $45 per person per day, M.A.P.

▶ **Montpelier Plantation Inn.** P.O. Box 474, Nevis, W.I. Tel: 469-3462; Fax: 469-2932; in U.S., (800) 243-9420 or (804) 460-2343; in Canada, (800) 268-0424; in U.K., (81) 367-5175. $175–$350, M.A.P. (E.P. available in low season.) Closed September.

▶ **Nisbet Plantation Beach Club.** Nevis, W.I. Tel: 469-9325; Fax: 469-9864; in U.S. and Canada, Tel: (800) 344-2049 or, in Maryland, (410) 321-1231; $190–$398, M.A.P.

▶ **Oualie Beach Club.** Nevis, W.I. Tel: 469-9735; Fax: 469-9176; in U.S., (800) 328-2288. $100–$115; ask about diving packages.

ANTIGUA

By Julie Wilson

It is odd that Antigua (an-TEE-gah), rich in British naval history and a place where (supposedly) prehistoric megaliths keep their secrets up in inaccessible hills, somehow seems to have sprung from the sea around 1960. That year marked the beginning of Antigua's ascent as a serious sailing center, the beginning of big-time tourism on the island, and the opening of the first beachfront luxury hotels. Nevertheless, whether it is the British influence on this former colony or the influence of the wealthy professionals from the U.S. Northeast, who were among Antigua's first regulars, the island still has a conservative air to it. At times Antigua seems as much a club as it does a vacation spot; people seem to return loyally to the same hotel year after year. And that is a great part of the island's charm. You have the feeling that no matter how much mass tourism touches it, it will remain—like Bermuda—essentially unchanged.

MAJOR INTEREST

365 fine beaches
St. John's for its cathedral, museum, and Redcliffe
 Quay
Darkwood Beach for shelling
Nelson's Dockyard complex at English Harbour
Interesting variety of accommodations
Day trip to tranquil Barbuda

Both volcanic and coral, sometimes painfully dry, Antigua claims some 365 beaches—though no one is quite sure who counted them. The beaches are as different as the days of the year and all are beautiful, but getting from one

231

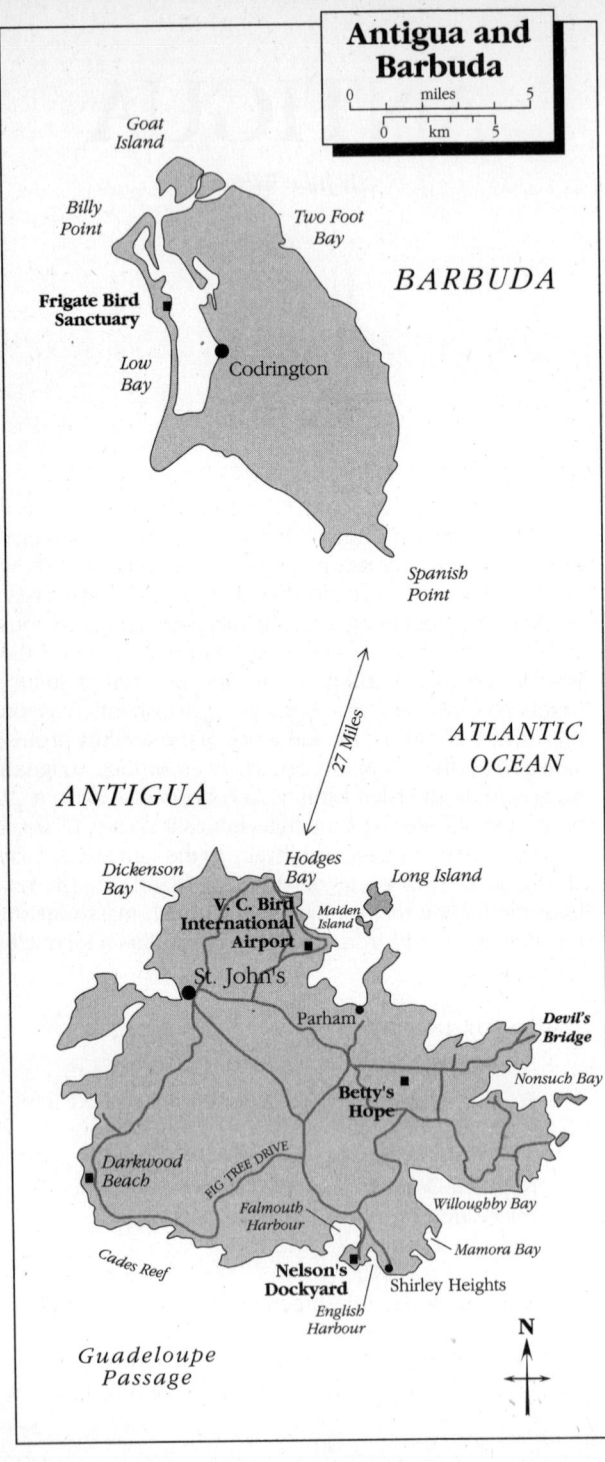

to another can be difficult, for this is a big island (108 square miles), and the roads that cross its central plains are in the market for road engineers. For this reason vacationers tend to stay on one coast or another, venturing cross-country during the day and sticking pretty close to their own beaches at night.

Getting around delightful little Barbuda, another member of this three-island nation, is also difficult, due to a paucity of roads. Getting around tiny Redonda, the third island, is pointless because it's deserted.

North Shore

Heading west from Antigua's V. C. Bird International Airport, the main road hugs the shore through prosperous residential neighborhoods, then twists around to **Dickenson Bay**. Here is one of the best of the 365 beaches, the "action beach," often as populated with vendors as it is with bathers. This part of the north shore has a concentration of small hotels, restaurants, and beach bars—or off-the-beach bars, as in **Warri Pier**, which is built on stilts; Tel: 462-0256. One of the best known of the restaurants is **Coconut Grove** (Tel: 462-1538). Only a few steps from the water, under a quasi lean-to roof, it always has a jolly crowd around the bar. Dinners are quite romantic, and worth a pricey splurge on wine and local lobster.

Mostly, Antiguan restaurants are expensive, due in part to the government's punishingly high taxes on imported foodstuffs. Until recently they have also been so uninspired as to make baked beans on toast sound good. A happy culinary turnaround can be witnessed at such restaurants as **L'Auberge de Paris** (what this name has to do with the island is open to question) on a hilltop overlooking Dickenson Bay. Try chef Peter Becker's lobster with orange curry sauce or sautéed beef tenderloin strips and you'll see what we mean; Tel: 462-1223. One old-timer that always managed to buck the trend toward blandness is **Le Bistro** (Tel: 462-3881). Situated in the middle of a scrubby field, Le Bistro never counted waterfront location among its attractions. The food (French, with a few Italian accents) and service are what matter here.

Not far from Le Bistro, long-established **Blue Waters** attracts what the hotel calls a "traditional West Indian clientele" (which means about 75 percent British). The waterfront hotel is discreet and lovely, with plumbago around the pool, hammocks on the lawn, and an air of well-practiced gentility.

St. John's and the North Shore

The streets of the capital, hilly and traffic-jammed, call for stout walking shoes. St. John's does have a few attractions, but it is not a town in which you'll want to spend much time—especially when there are all those beaches out there. You will, however, want to take a look at the enormous **Cathedral of St. John the Divine**, atop one of the town's highest hills. The history of Christian Antigua is etched on the church's polished brass plaques and carved in the stones of its graveyard—where you may have to push aside a snoozing goat to read who lies beneath a marker. In any city the cathedral would be impressive; in St. John's it is astounding.

The **Museum of Antigua and Barbuda** is housed in the 240-year-old Neoclassical Old Court House, halfway between the cathedral and the harbor. It is remarkable for the coherent and thoughtful manner in which the displays of Amerindian culture and the island's later history are presented, and it is one of the Caribbean's best sources of information about Arawak and Carib cultures. No dusty, fusty museum, it also displays a cricket bat used by Antigua's Viv Richards. Tel: 462-3946.

Down on the waterfront the shops and restaurants of **Redcliffe Quay** occupy the buildings that once housed slaves awaiting auction. Among the discos and pizza parlors you'll find an old island tradition, Antiguan pottery. Rough, primitive, and functional, much of the pottery is made in the backyards of homes in Seaview Farms, an inland village where mothers have handed down pottery techniques to their daughters for generations.

The new, exceedingly modern **Heritage Quay** represents Antigua's attempt to tap the duty-free mine. Here are the usual roundup of duty-free shops (Little Switzerland, Colombian Emeralds, Benetton). You'll also find the newest of Antigua's three casinos; this one opens at 10:00 A.M.

For lunch or dinner in town try **18 Karat** (a.k.a. 18K; Tel: 462-0016). An open-air porch in a back alley, it's all done up in white lattice-work, a plethora of plants, and hot-pink tablecloths. The food is good and "introductory Antiguan": steamed cockles, pan-fried snapper, broiled lobster—nothing wildly exotic. Government ministers

and local politicians are much in evidence at lunch. Who-
ever isn't at 18K is probably at the **Lemon Tree** (Tel: 462-
1969), next to the museum; at **Hemingway's** (Tel: 462-
2763) on St. Mary's Street; down at Redcliffe Quay's **Big
Banana Holding Company** (a.k.a. Pizza's on the Quay; Tel:
462-2621), or at **Ginger House** (Tel: 462-2317). They're all
pretty casual: Power-lunching has yet to come to town.
The top choice for dinner is **Chez Pascal** (Tel: 462-3232),
a delightful bistro on Tanner Street.

Just out of town (heading back toward Dickenson Bay),
Le Gourmet is the favorite secret of in-the-know
islanders—including other restaurant owners. Chef/
owner Jochen Mathé mixes classic European dishes with
his own creations, utilizing local seafood and produce.
Prices are surprisingly moderate; Tel: 462-2977.

Parham, Antigua's original capital— east of St. John's
on the north shore—has no restaurant scene, just a lot of
memories. Aged stone foundations still support wooden
second floors, unless the last inhabitants were termites, in
which case the foundations support vines. Back from the
harbor, St. Peter's Anglican Church stands in a windswept
field suggesting the setting for a Sir Walter Scott wedding
scene. The church is totally out of proportion to the little
town; massive and six-sided, with coral walls and an
inverted ship's hull for a ceiling, it is also said to be the
prettiest church in the West Indies. Like all of Parham, it
combines past and present with a refreshing lack of senti-
mentality.

Jumby Bay Resort owns the 300-acre Long Island, off the
northeast shore. This, the newest of Antigua's conservative,
expensive resorts, reached only by a private launch arranged by the hotel from a mainland dock, has a style of its
own. Dinners are served in a pavilion behind a 200-year-
old plantation great house. There is a resident horticulturist and a resident naturalist—the latter a marine biologist
who acts as mother hen to the hatchlings of hawksbill
turtles who lay their eggs on one of the island's beaches.
Jumby's wealthy, high-powered clientele find three tennis
courts and all manner of water sports to help them un-
wind. Rooms range from the original two-unit rondavels to
newer accommodations in the Pond Bay House, where
bathrooms open out onto private gardens. Privacy is what
Jumby Bay is all about. And luxury, of course.

East Coast

The least developed, least accessible shore of Antigua, this coast has such special attractions as **Devil's Bridge**—a wild and windy point where the Atlantic surf has cut blowholes in the jagged coral outcropping. There are a few hotels in the neighborhood, the most interesting of which is **Long Bay**. Run by the Lafaurie family since the early 1960s, it's a small (20 rooms, six cottages) hotel, awash with "expat" charm. A tennis court, water sports, a beach where the sand is as fine as talcum powder, hammocks strung between shade trees, a beach bar, weekly barbecues, a library stacked with books, and the occasional steel band—that's Long Bay. Don't look for fancy amenities or air-conditioning; the simple rooms are cleverly placed to catch the tradewinds. That's the way they did things in the 1960s. The way of the 1990s, increasingly, is to include everything (room, food, drinks, sports) in a flat rate. At least that's what **Pineapple Beach Club** does. A short stroll down that marvelous beach from Long Bay, it fairly bubbles over with the high spirits of a young, active crowd with its smattering of budget-minded Europeans.

Back inland from the coast, you may—if you watch carefully—see a small sign for **Betty's Hope**. Follow a rutted track up the hill to a clearing where a couple of windmill towers and the rubble of some long-fallen buildings are all that remains of Antigua's largest sugar plantation. A brief sketch of the plantation and its history is tacked to a tree, along with the suggestion to contact the Museum of Antigua and Barbuda in town for more information. Plantation restoration is not a governmental priority, so the monumental task of rebuilding it as a museum rests on volunteers. Talk about hope.

Down on the southeast tip of the island, **Halfmoon Bay Hotel** is an old resort known for its tennis, water sports, big pool, and nine-hole golf course. Locals claim Halfmoon Bay makes far and away the best chef's salad on the island. They also ruefully admit that this venerable landmark seems a little dowdy these days.

Because this part of Antigua is pretty far from the rest of the island, many people stop for a swim at Halfmoon Beach on their way to **Harmony Hall** art and craft gallery (Tel: 460-4120) on Nonsuch Bay. This sister gallery to Harmony Hall in Jamaica's Ocho Rios also displays the work of well-known Caribbean artists, including the puckish Jonathon Routh, and is worth the trip. After browsing through the displays, have a drink in the sugar mill bar, a splash in the pool, and a quiet lunch on the shaded terrace.

West Coast

Darkwood Beach is Antigua's best shelling beach. The early bird catches the keyhole limpet here, and by the time the casual beach bar opens for breakfast, the prize shells may be in someone else's sandy pocket. Never mind; stay around for a beach-bar lunch of hamburgers, chicken and chips, or fresh fish right off one of the boats pulling up on the beach.

Not all west coast beaches are so tranquil. Up the coast the **Ramada Renaissance Royal Antiguan** is the island's first high-rise (nine stories) hotel. It's basically a 282-room convention hotel and, as such, has lots of facilities — tennis courts, color TVs, pool, water sports, shops, restaurants, a casino . . . and a beauty salon.

Not far away in miles, but worlds away in style, **Galley Bay** is another of Antigua's fine, old-style hotels. "Gauguin" cottages — thatched-roof huts with whitewashed walls and ceiling fans — face a lagoon that teems with bird life. Guests with more traditional tastes favor the beachfront rooms that open onto a half mile of cove beach, all of it Galley Bay's. Swimming, sunning, snorkeling, windsurfing, bicycling or walking around the 40 acres, and waiting for the next delicious meal constitute the highlights.

A well-landscaped resort hotel, **Hawksbill** is named for the rock sticking up in its bay that looks —sure enough— like a hawksbill turtle's head. It's got all the expected water-sports facilities, plus a boutique in an old sugar mill and a nude beach, the latter tastefully secluded. Hawksbill has always attracted a lot of Europeans —so many that menus are printed in both English and German.

South Shore

In the days of the Royal Georges, **Nelson's Dockyard** at **English Harbour** was the headquarters of the British Fleet— one of whose captains was the eager 26-year-old Horatio Nelson. These days Nelson's Dockyard crosses a maritime museum with a yachting center, hotels, restaurants, and other facilities of modern commerce. Plan on spending the better part of a day here, breaking for a salad, omelette, or grilled fish on the tree-shaded terrace at **Admiral's Inn,** then going back to watch the activity on the charter yachts. In fact, plan on spending a night in one of the charming, old (and small) rooms. Best bet is number 1, the "bridal suite," with a four-poster bed and harbor views.

Nearby, the 200-year-old **Copper and Lumber Store** (now a hotel) has larger rooms, and prices to match. Each room is named after a ship that fought in the battle of Trafalgar, and some of the rooms are furnished with Georgian antiques. The hotel boasts a pub as well as a more serious restaurant with "international cuisine." The whole renovation has been done quite well, but, given the setting and the crowds of daytime tourists, staying here is a little like getting a room in Disney World's Magic Kingdom.

The current dining choice in these parts is **La Perruche** (Tel: 460-3040), located in a miraculously renovated old "rum shop." Another of Antigua's bright new restaurants, La Perruche serves wildly imaginative dishes—a honeyed duck confit with green cabbage, conch salad with sweet peppers and grapefruit—with panache at no extra charge.

Always a busy place, English Harbour really swings in the spring during Sailing Week, a time for some serious racing and some serious partying. Desmond Nicholson (archaeologist, director of the museum, and a member of the family whose yacht-broker/charter-service business is headquartered at English Harbour) and Howard Hulford (the dashing owner of the Curtain Bluff hotel; see below) originated the event some 24 years ago with the vague intention of extending the winter season a bit. They succeeded.

The road on the other side of the harbor leads up to Shirley Heights, the site of the ruins of an old fort, which is remarkable mainly for its photographic possibilities. Part way up is **Clarence House**, built in 1787 as a home away from home for the 23-year-old duke of Clarence (later King William IV) when he was stationed here. It is now the governor general's official country residence and is open to the public for short tours. There is no fee, but you should tip the caretaker—and the caretaker will politely indicate so.

Farther uphill, the **Shirley Heights Lookout Restaurant** (Tel: 460-1785) throws the best Sunday party on the island. Start in the afternoon with a steel band and barbecue; move on to reggae in the evening; throw in a spectacular sunset for free—and you can see why everyone wants to come to the party.

East of English Harbour, **St. James's Club** resembles a small village rising behind Mamora Bay. The original rooms, restaurants, pool, seven tennis courts, and casino have been joined by a whole hillside of villas, another restaurant, another pool, and a small shopping center. Liza Minnelli, Joan Collins, and other celebrities stay here occasionally, but you're more likely to rub shoulders with a young, athletic, international, fashionably dressed crowd of unknowns. Martina Navratilova is the official tennis pro, but she doesn't give lessons on any of the seven tennis courts. If tennis and water sports don't interest you, St. James's Club offers horseback riding. The Club also has the advantage of being fairly close to **Alberto's** (Tel: 460-3007) on Willoughby Bay. Despite its somewhat remote location, this "gazebo-shaped" restaurant is consistently one of the island's most popular dinner spots. For good reason: Alberto is a charming host and his wife, Vanessa, a superb cook. Late arrivals may find such winning dishes as osso buco, homemade cannelloni, grilled tuna steaks, or breadfruit with garlic butter erased off the blackboard menu. No matter, whatever's left will be delicious.

West of English Harbour, Fig Tree Drive twists and dips its way through a lush rain forest full of mango, avocado, breadfruit, and guava trees. At the end of the drive is Howard Hulford's **Curtain Bluff**, a hotel that has made the "Ten Best" list of knowledgeable travellers for over 30 years now. Nicely situated between breezes and two beaches, Curtain Bluff is as nearly perfect as a Caribbean hotel can be—perfect enough for gentlemen to comply gracefully with the jacket-and-tie dress code at dinner. Genuine hospitality, beautiful rooms, superb meals, and an improbably fine wine cellar are a small price to pay for a tight collar. There's nothing uptight about Curtain Bluff, however. Relaxed moods prevail on the tennis and squash courts, at the exercise studio, on the snorkeling trips to Cades Reef, the croquet lawn, the putting green, at the weekly beach buffet—and around the new "beach club." For real relaxation you can just sit and watch the giant hybrid hibiscus blossoming. Not surprisingly, each bloom is as nearly perfect as a flower can be.

BARBUDA

Sixty-four square miles of scrub and pink sand, Barbuda (bar-BEW-dah) gives new meaning to the word "flat." Its one hill would be dwarfed by a four-story building, and Martello Tower, from which defenders could scan the horizon, isn't much bigger than a fire hydrant. But this matzo on the waters possesses an inordinate amount of charm. Just 15 minutes by small plane from Antigua's airport, it is the quietest place imaginable, where time has no relevance and simplicity comes stripped down. In **Codrington**—the village in which most of Barbuda's 1,200 residents live—a petrol-filled drum and siphon constitute the gas station, and the very rumor of paving a street causes much excitement. Visitors to Barbuda find themselves doing such long-forgotten things as noticing the sound of the wind and watching clouds form pictures in the sky.

The **Frigate Bird Sanctuary**, just two miles by boat from Codrington's pier, is reason enough to go to Barbuda. From a small skiff puttering in and out among the mangrove bushes, you will see male frigate birds—their scarlet neck pouches puffed up like bright balloons—swoop, soar, and court possibly amorous females. What with thousands of birds flying just overhead, the scene has a certain Hitchcockian menace.

Though Barbuda is basically a day trip from Antigua, it does claim two strangely spectacular—and rivalrous—resorts. Built in the 1960s, **Coco Point Lodge** seems to some to make a fetish out of its remoteness. It's got its own airstrip, its own private beach, and no telephones in the rooms. But the food is good, the service professional, the mood convivial. For those who really want to get away from it all—and can afford the steep rates—this has traditionally been the place to be.

Built at the end of the 1980s, the much-discussed **K-Club**—charging even steeper rates—promised to be "the better place to be." Located down the beach from Coco Point, this ambitious resort planned by the Italian owners of the fashion house of Krizia postponed its inaugural a number of times before opening for the 1991 season. (These ambitious resorts take time to get themselves together. It takes time, for example, to build a nine-hole golf course on Barbuda if you want anything more than sand traps.) K-Club's architecture, decor, pool, and beach were nearly as stunning as its prices. The service was straight from "Fawlty Towers." A new management company promises to set that right and *really* give Coco Point a run for its money. Stay tuned; this is better than a soap opera. Overhead, the frigate birds watch it all with cool aplomb.

USEFUL FACTS

What to Wear
Dress is casual but conservative; some restaurants require a jacket at dinner.

Getting In
From New York, American Airlines and BWIA have daily flights; from Newark, Continental has daily flights; from Miami, BWIA has daily flights; from Toronto, BWIA and Air Canada have several flights a week; from London, British Air has several flights a week; from Frankfurt, Lufthansa has two flights a week. There are easy connections from San Juan, St. Maarten, and other Caribbean airports.

Entry Requirements
A passport is required, but U.S., Canadian, and U.K. citizens may substitute another proof of citizenship, such as a birth certificate. There is a U.S. $10 departure tax.

Local Time
Antigua is on Atlantic standard time year-round, one hour ahead of the U.S. east coast except when the east coast moves its clocks ahead an hour during daylight saving time. Then the two keep the same time.

Currency
Eastern Caribbean dollar; U.S. dollars are accepted widely. As of this writing the rate of exchange was U.S. $1.00 to E.C. $2.67.

Electrical Current
220 volts, but most hotels have 110 volts, 60 cycles.

Getting Around
A local driving permit costs U.S. $12 and isn't worth it: Roads are unmarked and pocked with craters; other hazards include goats, sheep, cows, and maniacal drivers.

Car-rental companies charge as though buying into these hazards is a privilege. Driving is on the left, as are most steering wheels. Taxis are also expensive. Although rates are government-fixed, few drivers know what they are. Best bet: Find a driver who seems to be attached to your hotel; use him exclusively and negotiate.

Business Hours
Monday through Saturday, 8:00 A.M. to 1:00 P.M. and 2:00 to 4:00 P.M. Most stores close at 1:00 P.M. on Saturdays; some close at noon on Thursdays. Banking hours are Monday through Thursday from 8:00 A.M. to 1:00 P.M., Fridays from 8:00 A.M. to 1:00 P.M. and 3:00 to 5:00 P.M.

Festivals
Carnival begins in late July; Sailing Week begins in late April.

For Further Information
Antigua Department of Tourism, Thames Street, P.O. Box 363, St. John's Antigua, W.I., Tel: (809) 462-0480; **in the** U.S., Antigua and Barbuda Department of Tourism, 610 Fifth Avenue, Suite 311, New York, NY 10020, Tel: (212) 541-4117; **in Canada,** 60 St. Clair Avenue East, Suite 205, Toronto, Ontario, M4T IN5, Tel: (416) 961-3085; **in the** U.K., Antigua House, 15 Thayer Street, London W1M 5DL, England, Tel: (71) 486-7073.

ACCOMMODATIONS REFERENCE
The rate ranges given here, in U.S. dollars, are projections for fall 1992 through spring 1993, and span the lowest rates in the low season to the highest in the high season. Unless otherwise indicated, rates are for double rooms, double occupancy. As rates are subject to change, it's always wise to double-check before booking. The telephone area code (within the U.S. system) for Antigua and Barbuda is 809.

▶ **Admiral's Inn.** P.O. Box 713, St. John's, Antigua, W.I. Tel: 460-1027; Fax: 460-1534; in U.S., (914) 833-3303 or (800) 223-5695; in Canada, (416) 447-2335 or (800) 387-8031; in U.K., (628) 477-088. $68–$116, E.P.

▶ **Blue Waters.** P.O. Box 256, St. John's, Antigua, W.I. Tel: 462-0290; Fax: 462-0293; in U.S., (800) 372-1323; in U.K., (81) 367-5175. $135, E.P.–$355, M.A.P.

▶ **Coco Point Lodge.** P.O. Box 90, St. John's, Antigua,

W.I. Tel: 462-3816; in U.S., (212) 986-1416. $450–$950 (includes all meals, drinks, and sports). Closed through the summer.

▶ **Copper and Lumber Store.** Nelson's Dockyard, English Harbour, Antigua, W.I. Tel: 460-1058; Fax: 460-1529; in U.S., (800) 633-7411; in Canada, (416) 961-3085; in U.K., (45) 383-5801. $80–$280, E.P.

▶ **Curtain Bluff.** P.O. Box 288, St. John's, Antigua, W.I. Tel: 462-8400 through 8402; Fax: 462-8409; in U.S., (212) 289-8888. $425–$825 (includes all meals, bar drinks, afternoon tea, and sports).

▶ **Galley Bay.** P.O. Box 305, St. John's, Antigua, W.I. Tel: 462-0302; Fax: 462-1187; in U.S., Tel: (800) 223-6510 or (402) 398-3217; Fax: (402) 398-5484; in Canada, (800) 424-5500; in U.K., (306) 740-888. $255–$415, all inclusive.

▶ **Halfmoon Bay Hotel.** P.O. Box 144, St. John's, Antigua, W.I. Tel: 460-4300; Fax: 460-4306; in U.S., Tel: (800) 223-6510 or (402) 398-3217; Fax: (402) 398-5484; in Canada, (800) 424-5500; in U.K., (306) 740-888. $190–$475, A.P.

▶ **Hawksbill Hotel.** P.O. Box 108, St. John's, Antigua, W.I. Tel: 462-1515 or 0301; Fax: 462-1515; in U.S., Tel: (800) 223-6510 or (402) 398-3217; Fax: (402) 398-5484; in Canada, (800) 424-5500; in U.K., (306) 740-888. $160–$370 (full breakfast).

▶ **Jumby Bay Resort.** P.O. Box 243, St. John's, Antigua, W.I. Tel: 462-6000; Fax: 462-6020; in U.S., (800) 421-9016; in U.K., (71) 730-7144. $575–$895 (includes meals, drinks, most water sports).

▶ **K-Club,** Barbuda, W.I. Tel: 460-0304; Fax: 460-0305; in U.S., (800) 648-4097. $700–$2,500, M.A.P. Closed May through October.

▶ **Long Bay Hotel.** P.O. Box 442, St. John's, Antigua, W.I. Tel: 463-2005; Fax: 463-2439; in U.S., Tel: (800) 225-4255, (800) 448-8355, or (212) 696-4566; Fax: (212) 689-1598; in U.K., (71) 581-0851. $250–$350, M.A.P. Cottages, $200–$360, E.P.

▶ **Pineapple Beach Club.** P.O. Box 54, St. John's, Antigua, W.I. Tel: 463-2006; Fax: 463-2452; in U.S., (800) 223-9815 or (212) 545-8469. $250–$420, A.P.

▶ **Ramada Renaissance Royal Antiguan.** P.O. Box 1322, St. John's, Antigua, W.I. Tel: 462-3733; Fax: 462-3732; in U.S., (800) 228-9898. $110–$250, E.P.

▶ **St. James's Club.** P.O. Box 63, St. John's, Antigua, W.I. Tel: 460-5000; Fax: 460-3015; in U.S., (800) 274-0008 or (212) 486-2575; in Canada, (800) 268-9051 or (416) 598-2693; in U.K., (71) 495-1799. $300–$850, M.A.P.

MONTSERRAT

By Julie Wilson

From various points on the British Crown Colony of Montserrat, the neighboring islands of Guadeloupe, Antigua, Nevis, and St. Kitts can be seen on the horizon. This is a nice neighborhood. Few people come to Montserrat (mon-sur-RAHT) on business. Nobody comes looking for jet-skis or jet sets. Rather, people come to enjoy the neighborhood and to be neighborly.

"Neighborly" defines Montserrat. Because there are only a handful of small hotels on the 39-square-mile island, most visitors rent villas or apartments. So, no artificial barriers (lobbies, room service, valet parking) separate visitors from the locals. Everyone shares the same street, the same market aisle.

For a number of years this out-of-the-way island was the improbable site of a major recording studio to which the nobility of rockdom flocked. Hurricane Hugo destroyed the studio in 1989, but the memories are still fresh. Every Montserratian has tales of conversations or encounters with Paul McCartney, Eric Clapton, Elton John, or Sting. Wistfully, they admit they're going to miss those exotic visitors.

MAJOR INTEREST

Getting away in a quiet way
Galway's Soufrière

Blessed with a lushness that makes most other Caribbean islands look like sand traps, mountainous Montserrat is as green as the Irish shamrock on its passport stamp. Islanders have even been known to call their home the "Emer-

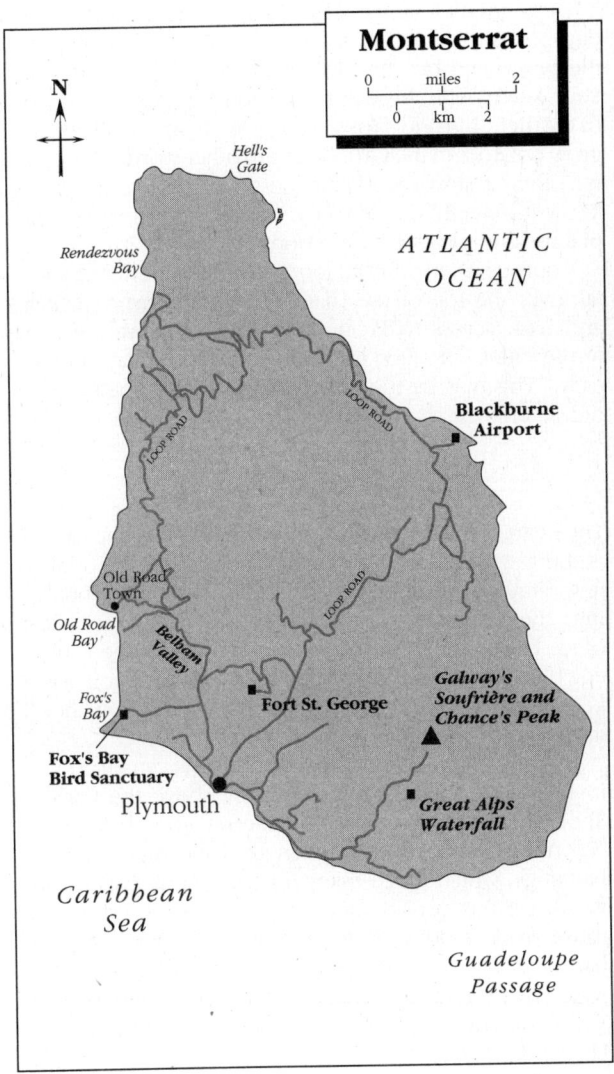

Montserrat

| 0 | miles | 2 |
| 0 | km | 2 |

N

Hell's
Gate

*ATLANTIC
OCEAN*

*Rendezvous
Bay*

LOOP ROAD

LOOP ROAD

**Blackburne
Airport**

Old Road
Town

*Old Road
Bay*

*Belham
Valley*

LOOP ROAD

*Fox's
Bay*

Fort St. George

*Galway's
Soufrière and
Chance's Peak*

**Fox's Bay
Bird Sanctuary**

Plymouth

*Great Alps
Waterfall*

*Caribbean
Sea*

*Guadeloupe
Passage*

ald Isle." This bit of whimsy, and the shamrock, go back to 1632, when Irish settlers from English St. Kitts came to Montserrat. Even today the phone book reads as though it could have been lifted straight from County Cork.

There aren't too many brogues left on Montserrat today, nor is there much sailing, fishing, or snorkeling off the black-sand beaches. However, farmers do lead donkeys laden with produce—including potatoes—down from their hillside farms. (Only an Irish island would grow potatoes in the Caribbean.) In other words, Montserrat offers a slow-paced lifestyle and a chance to get to know the neighbors. If you're looking for an easygoing, picturesque vacation place, Montserrat is it.

Montserrat's main road loops from Plymouth, the capital, over the top of the island, past Blackburne Airport, and back across to Plymouth through a vibrant green, fertile valley that often inspires taxi drivers to say immodestly, "This may be the only paradise you see before you die, so enjoy it."

Plymouth

The heart of this engagingly unsophisticated island capital is the town square and its clock-faced War Memorial. A few cannons—taxi drivers stuff empty soft-drink bottles into the barrels—point listlessly toward the sea. Post office boxes are stuck into the outer walls of the robin's egg blue Treasury Building. Just about everybody in town knows everybody else. And if they don't know you, they'll greet you as cheerfully as if they did.

Whatever is worth buying on Montserrat can be bought in Plymouth. In the center of town, above the Carlisle Shoe Store, **Tapestries of Montserrat** (Tel: 2520) sells colorful, hand-hooked wall hangings and rugs. The wall hangings, which grace many a home on the island, are worth serious consideration for possible purchase. Because work is done on the premises, you can meet the hand that hooks, so to speak. At **The Island House** (Tel: 3938) Chris and Barbara Crowe (who created Belham Valley Restaurant, described below) specialize in fine Haitian paintings—and know all there is to know about them. If you're not interested in paintings, you'll be smitten while wandering through the two-story house by the pottery, the faux parrots on swings, and a raft of colorful knickknacks. There are usually a number of well-dressed ladies in **Jus' Looking** (Tel: 4076) chatting with the attractive owner Jadine Glitzenhirn, browsing among Caribelle batiks and locally designed frocks, picking up some Sunny Caribee jam for their morning scones. If you're not in the market for jam, head over to the public market for fresh produce or perhaps a freshly made batch of bull-foot souse.

Island nightlife, such as it is, centers around a few bar/discos, which are usually open only on weekends. (**Le Cave** at Evergreen Circle is the Saturday night "scene.") And it's on weekends that restaurants rustle up batches of goatwater (an earthy, clove-scented stew) and curried mutton. The island's best-known dish is mountain chicken, which is not chicken at all, but leg of frog. Mountain chicken comes dear because, well, there just aren't that many good-size frogs to go around.

One restaurant where mountain chicken often appears on the menu is **Emerald Café** (Tel: 3821). Enclosed gardens behind a pair of adjoining, streetside houses are decorated with a veritable jungle of potted plants and lit, partially, by colored lights hanging from tin roofs. Besides mountain chicken, chef/owner Alvin Greenaway is known for his hearty seafood crepes, braised beef, and rosemary chicken (the real chicken). At lunch time hamburgers are a big seller in this popular restaurant. Across the street **The Iguana** (Tel: 3637) was opened by a young couple from the States as a rather serious restaurant. Almost as an after-thought, they included pizza on the menu. Guess what sold best. These days the lively bar and backyard dining deck are crowded with pie-romaniacs gobbling up pizzas with all kinds of toppings—including pineapple.

The current hot spot is **Ziggy's** (Tel: 6582), in Oriole Plaza, with its "9 to 9" blackboard menu (try the chicken fried rice) and big outside terrace. For a real down-home West Indian meal, find **The Golden Apple** (Tel: 2187) just outside Plymouth at Cork Hill. Doreen Williams makes a mean goatwater as well as savory pulaus, curried conch, grilled fish, and chicken—"fried, boiled, roasted, every-one loves chicken."

Galway's Soufrière and Plantation

From Plymouth a spur road leads down the southwest coast, then cuts inland to Galway's Soufrière, a 3,000-foot-high "inactive" volcano. From a recently constructed look-out point you can peer down at the hot sulphur springs that bubble up from its restless innards. If you're moderately fit and quite careful, it's far more rewarding to walk to the springs yourself. The trail shifts frequently because of washouts and periodic collapses, but it's worth persevering on the 15-minute scrabble through a bleak, merciless, foul-smelling landscape to get to the source, from which boiling water trickles over bare lava and rock. Galway's Soufrière was named after David Galway, whose nearby 18th-century sugar plantation is being restored by a team of archaeologists and the Montserrat National Trust. Because Galway's Plantation remained untouched from the time it was abandoned, it is one of the "purest" examples of a sugar plantation left in the West Indies. Work is proceeding in a slow, very scholarly fashion, so don't expect to find docents in period costume on the grounds. Instead, bring a picnic lunch, sit among the ruins, and use your imagination.

Or if you're really stout of limb, climb the 3,000-foot **Chance's Peak**. Supposedly there's a singing mermaid (early rock star) in a pool near the top. Ask at the tourist office in Plymouth for a guide.

South of the volcanic scar, on the way back toward the coast, **Great Alps Waterfall** pushes through a narrow spot in the rocks and gushes down some 70 feet. To see it requires a stiff hike from car park to falls—not to be attempted wearing sandals.

Around Plymouth

From Plymouth the main road goes north to **Fort St. George,** built in 1782 as a defense against the French and now a popular place for church picnics beneath the tamarind trees and a spreading flamboyant. Looking at the little that remains of the never-used fort, including its cannons, you can see just what a strategic view it affords of Plymouth's harbor, a good two and a half miles away.

Egrets, herons, kingfishers, coots, and their feathered relatives live down the hill from the fort at **Fox's Bay Bird Sanctuary.** Unfortunately, Hurricane Hugo removed a number of trees from the sanctuary, leaving the birds to consider temporary relocation elsewhere. (Hummingbirds seem to have decamped permanently—few are seen on the island anymore.) Even so, you can have a good walk over dim, damp trails that meander among sweet lime and manchineel trees and are laced with crab holes so big a Honda could disappear in one. As you step over fallen cherry trees thick with termite nests, you'll see why Montserratians build their houses of stone.

Belham Valley

Up by Old Road Town, Belham Valley is known locally as Beverly Heights. Wealthy foreigners have built some impressive villas here, and the well-manicured gardens are a testament to the skills of the gardeners who beat back an ever-encroaching jungle. The 11-hole **Montserrat Golf Club** (where one of the hazards is likely to be a flock of sheep moving briskly down the edge of the fairway) is in the neighborhood, as is the excellent **Belham Valley Restaurant**, the island's only "dress up/special occasion" restaurant. Co-owner Eileen Fenton is a gracious hostess and a fine cook who knows her way around a Continental menu, skillfully avoiding the pitfalls of clichéd dishes. Pepper steak, for example, receives such fresh treatment here that it seems like a brand-new idea. Understandably, it's one of the restaurant's bestsellers. Tel: 5553.

The island's best hotel—**Vue Pointe**—is up here, too. Right next to the golf course, Vue Pointe has a couple of tennis courts (lighted for night play), two small beaches on Old Road Bay, a nice pool, and kippers on the breakfast menu. Dotted across the hillside, each with a porch facing the bay, individual rondavels provide delightful privacy (along with such thoughtful touches as hair dryers). Vue Pointe has so many repeat guests that it's almost like a club—an easygoing club whose members will loan you a book if you've run out of things to read, and warmly welcome you into full membership. And with all those gorgeous villas in the neighborhood, many of whose owners are attracted to the ambience at Vue Pointe, it makes for an interesting social mixing of an evening. That's *so* Montserratian. (For **rentals** of homes or apartments see the Accommodations Reference at the end of this chapter for details.)

Not far away, **The Village Place** (Tel: 5202) in Salem was the hangout for rock stars. Bet they miss the "Emerald Fry Chicken," the rice and peas, the coconut cream pie. Don't bother to dress formally—this fun place is little more than a tin-roofed shed open to the sunset.

From Belham Valley the road loops up into fairly deserted territory—over bridges crossing deep *ghauts* (gorges), and past high, windy plains where goats graze—then back to the airport. The island's only white-sand beach, **Rendezvous Bay**, is up here. It's about an hour's hike from the road, and likely to be pretty quiet.

USEFUL FACTS

What to Wear
Conservatively casual clothes are in order. Bring sturdy shoes for climbing.

Getting In
Leeward Islands Air Transport (LIAT) flies from Antigua to Blackburne Airpoint several times a day; Montserrat Airways (Tel: 809/491-5342) has charter flights.

Entry Requirements
U.S., Canadian, and U.K. citizens need only a driver's license, voter-registration card, or birth certificate. Others must have passports. There is a departure tax of U.S. $6.

Local Time
Montserrat is on Atlantic standard time year-round, one hour ahead of the U.S. east coast except when the east coast moves its clocks ahead an hour during daylight saving time. Then the two keep the same time.

Currency
Eastern Caribbean dollar. The U.S. dollar is widely accepted. As of this writing the rate of exchange was U.S. $1.00 to E.C. $2.67.

Electrical Current
220 volts; U.S.- and Canadian-made appliances require converters.

Getting Around
For an extended stay, you will probably want to rent a car (about U.S. $30–$35 a day). Driving is on the left, and roads are good. A permit that is valid for six months costs U.S. $12. The tourist office in Plymouth has a list of taxi drivers and government-fixed prices.

Business Hours
Businesses are open from 8:00 A.M. to noon and 1:00 to 4:00 P.M., some with half days Wednesdays and Saturdays. Bank hours are Monday through Thursday from 8:00 A.M. to 1:00 P.M., Fridays 8:00 A.M. to 4:00 or 5:00 P.M.

Holidays
St. Patrick's Day, rather than Carnival, is the big celebration on Montserrat. It's a day of picnics, impromptu concerts, and general merriment.

For Further Information
Montserrat Tourist Board, P.O. Box 7, Plymouth, Montserrat, W.I., Tel: (809) 491-2230; **in the U.S.**, c/o Pace Public Relations, 485 Fifth Avenue, New York, NY 10017, Tel: (212) 818-0100, Fax: (212) 818-0120; **in Canada**, Melaine Communications Group, Inc., 33 Niagara Street, Toronto, Ontario M5V 1C2, Tel: (416) 362-3900, Fax: (416) 362-9481; **in the U.K.**, Caribbean Tourism Organization, Commonwealth House, 18 Northumberland Avenue, London WC2N 5RA, England, Tel: (71) 839-8480, Fax: (71) 976-1541.

ACCOMMODATIONS REFERENCE
The rate ranges given here, in U.S. dollars, are projections for fall 1992 through spring 1993, and span the lowest rates in the low season to the highest in the high season. Unless otherwise indicated, rates are for double rooms, double occupancy. As rates are subject to change, it's always wise to double-check before booking. The telephone area code (within the U.S. system) for Montserrat is 809.

▶ **Vue Pointe Hotel**. P.O. Box 65, Plymouth, Montserrat, W.I. Tel: 491-5210; in U.S., Tel: (800) 223-6510, (508) 533-4426, or (201) 902-7878; Fax: (809) 491-4813. $70–$166, E.P. (add $35 per day per person for M.A.P.).

▶ For **rentals** of homes or apartments, contact the Montserrat Tourist Board, P.O. Box 7, Plymouth, Montserrat, W.I. Tel: 491-2230. They have a list of the half-dozen rental agencies. In the U.S., contact Carol Banner at Caribbean Connection, P.O. Box 261, Trumbull, CT 06611; Tel: (203) 261-8603; Fax: (203) 888-4167.

GUADELOUPE

By Robert Grodé

Halfway down the archipelago that stretches from the Florida Keys to the coast of South America is an island spread out on the sea like a butterfly. Guadeloupe, the *papillon* of the French West Indies, is in fact a pair of islands joined with airy grace by a thin isthmus of land. Grande-Terre, the eastern "wing," is a rolling, beach-ringed coral atoll; its western counterpart, Basse-Terre, is volcanic, mountainous, and lushly beautiful. Together they form an island that offers a blend of French, East Indian, and African cultures. Such surprising pleasures as curry-scented stew served on a Sevres china plate and music with Creole patois lyrics and a pulse-quickening beat testify to the island's mixed heritage and make Guadeloupe an intoxicating place to visit.

MAJOR INTEREST

Exploring Pointe-à-Pitre (markets, restaurants)
French and Creole dining
The Parc National
Offshore islands

GRANDE-TERRE

Much of the resort activity takes place in Grande-Terre. **Gosier,** 10 km (6 miles) from the international Raizet Airport and 6½ km (4 miles) from Guadeloupe's capital, Pointe-à-Pitre, is the location of what might somewhat overstatedly be called the hotel strip. The shoreline, scal-

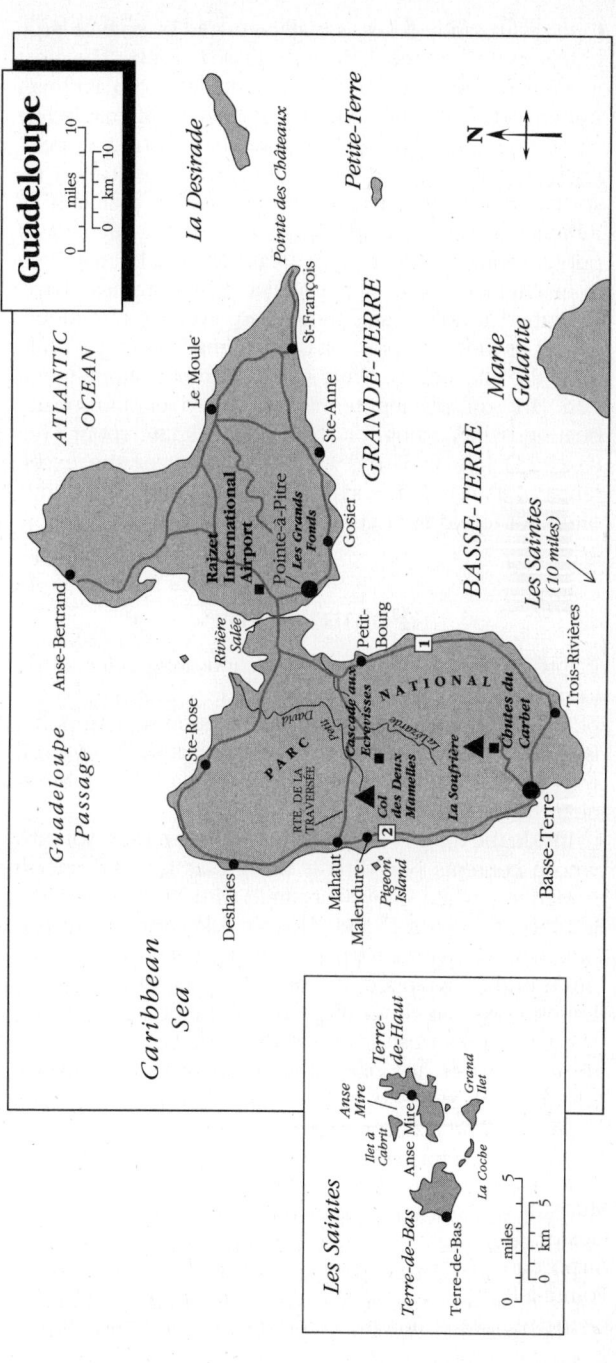

loped with sandy coves, actually *is* edged by several large hotels, as well as one of the island's two casinos. The most inviting of the hotels is the moderately priced **Pullman Auberge de la Vieille Tour**, which, after being mauled by Hurricane Hugo, has been restored to its former appealing self. The 80-room Vieille Tour, while offering a resortlike roster of activities, has managed to maintain an intimate atmosphere thanks to a friendly staff and to public rooms and recreation areas that have been kept to a manageable size. It's popular with families; bare-bottomed toddlers and their sharp-eyed grandmothers gather around the pool or on the small beach to while away the afternoons, while more energetic family members are off playing tennis or volleyball and pedal-boating, windsurfing, or sailing. The dining room (Tel: 83-23-23) has an island-wide reputation for the excellence of its classic French cuisine, an unexpected bonus often not found in larger hostelries.

Pointe-à-Pitre

Pointe-à-Pitre is one of the most captivating cities in the Caribbean, and you should set aside a morning to explore it. The bustling marketplace, a good starting point, is liveliest in the early hours. The market stalls, covered with a vast cast-iron shed, spread over a full city block near the center of town.

Inside the market *aerosols de benedicion* (aerosol cans whose contents purportedly bring blessings—financial, romantic—when sprayed around!) with names like "High John the Conqueror" and "Double Fast Luck" are spread out on broad marble-topped counters, along with mysterious bundles wrapped in banana leaves and tied with lemon grass. On closer inspection these prove to contain live land crabs fresh from the rain forests and ready for the pot. Aisles are piled with straw mats, palm-frond brooms, and stacks of broad-brimmed fishermen's hats, called *salakos*. Half sombrero and half coolie hat, salakos make perfect sunshades for the beach.

Coffee bars dot the neighborhood around the market, and you might want to take a break at one. Inside, elderly gentlemen, each sipping a morning *decollage* (literally, "takeoff") tot of rum, study their copies of *Le Figaro* or *Le Monde*. Order a café au lait and join in that time-hallowed Gallic pastime: watching passersby. On Guadeloupe they're likely to be even more animated than their Parisian cousins on the boulevard St-Germain.

The **Musée St-John Perse** is just a few blocks south of the outdoor market at the corner of rue de Nozieres and rue Achille René-Boisneuf. The 19th-century *folie,* with pale yellow walls and turquoise-painted cast-iron galleries, contains a splendid upstairs collection of memorabilia of the poet, diplomat, and Nobel Prize winner, who was born in Guadeloupe in 1887. On the main floor of the magnificently restored colonial town house, furnishings, costumes, and artifacts recapture the atmosphere of a late-19th-century Guadeloupean home. Tel: 90-01-92; closed Sundays.

A few blocks north on rue Peynier, the **Musée Schoelcher** celebrates the memory of the creator of the 1848 decree that freed 87,500 slaves in Guadeloupe and 72,000 in Martinique. Well-mounted displays of such items as medals awarded Victor Schoelcher, leg irons, slave-trading beads, and abolitionist tracts tell the story of the humanitarian's life and trace the history of slavery and the emancipation. The exhibits are labeled only in French. Tel: 82-08-04; closed Sundays.

Guadeloupe is regarded by many as the culinary capital of the Caribbean. More than 200 restaurants — from elegant hotel dining rooms to "front porch" establishments where a few tables are set up on the cook's breezy verandah — serve the island. Pointe-à-Pitre itself is chockablock with restaurants. One of the most popular for lunch and dinner is **La Canne à Sucre**, located a few steps from the water on the quay of the Centre St-John Perse. The elegant upstairs dining room is open only for dinner; on the lower level a less formal brasserie provides both lunch and dinner. La Canne à Sucre serves what owner/chef Gérard Virginius describes as nouvelle Creole cuisine; his grilled lamb chops with chicken livers and ginger are excellent. Tel: 82-10-19.

Another lunch or dinner possibility is **La Plantation** (Tel: 90-84-83), a short distance out of town at the Marina Bas-du-Fort. The restaurant's banal exterior is deceptive; just through the front door is a pair of small, coralita-pink dining rooms. The lamps hanging over each table are draped in *broderie anglaise,* the china is sprigged with flowers, and the crystal sparkles as brightly as the mirrored walls. In charge of the kitchen is Francis Delage, whose *Encyclopedia of Creole Cuisine* is regarded hereabouts as a culinary classic. Delage also oversees the kitchen at his l'Habitation, the inviting restaurant at the Canella Beach residence in Gosier (Tel: 90-44-00).

Also at the Marina Bas-du-Fort is another splendid restaurant, **Le Barbazar,** a crisply contemporary dining room with white stucco walls and pale oak furnishings. Meticulously prepared Creole dishes add all the spice and color needed to accent Le Barbazar's coolly understated interior. The service at lunch and dinner is attentive without being intrusive.

Diners at La Plantation or Le Barbazar might want to explore **A la Recherche du Passé,** a tiny shop a few steps away from the restaurants. Here, owner Laurent Chassaniol and his wife have assembled a collection of delightful bibelots. Children find the brightly painted whirligigs downright lovable. There are also handsome, old, hand-colored maps and antique volumes of Antillean lore, many illustrated with fine engravings. Tel: 90-84-15 or 90-92-44.

Another collection to explore at the Marina Bas-du-Fort is the **Guadeloupe Aquarium**—*A la Recherche des Poissons?* The largest in the Antilles and the fourth largest in all of France, the aquarium is home to hundreds of species of marine creatures. Angelfish and devilfish, hammerheads and needlenoses dither, dart, and dawdle through the well-lighted tanks. Many of the tropical varieties are so bespangled and beruffled they might have been designed by Christian Lacroix. The aquarium is open daily from 9:00 A.M. to 7:00 P.M.; Tel: 90-92-38.

Out on Grande-Terre

For a pleasant morning excursion head across Grande-Terre to its easternmost tip at Pointe des Châteaux. Driving on Guadeloupe can provide its own pleasures—and distractions. "*Attention!*" is the byword along the highways, and almost every crossroads is dominated by an ex-voto shrine, where rusting tin cans brimming with sunflowers and oleander huddle at the foot of a cross or the hem of the Virgin's mantle.

About halfway between Pointe-à-Pitre and Pointe des Châteaux, the village of Sainte-Anne, site of **Caravelle,** Guadeloupe's Club Med complex, curves along the island's most inviting beach. The Caravelle is popular with Europeans and North Americans, with both younger and more mature vacationers, and the mix creates a lively and sophisticated atmosphere. Looking down on the reef-bracketed bay is a cozy, decently priced caravanserai called

Hotel La Toubana. Its housekeeping cottages crown a landscaped hillside, clustering about a gaily painted dining area presided over by an immense fabric fish. A swimming pool just outside seems to be suspended in space above the shimmering sea. A narrow path winds down the hillside to the beach below.

Shortly before Pointe des Châteaux the road passes through another seaside village, **Saint-François.** A large East Indian population, descendants of workers brought here from India in the mid-1800s, lends colorful touches to Saint-François, particularly during the Fête Annuelle each October. For one long weekend the waterfront is transformed into a lively street fair. Booths are draped in cotton printed with traditional red-and-white Indian designs; the air fills with the sounds of sitars and steel "pans"; and the scent of sandalwood incense mingles with that of curry. Any time of year, however, Saint-François offers travellers on their way to Pointe des Châteaux a chance to sample one of Guadeloupe's innumerable *ti-lolos.* These tiny rum shops are especially inviting in Saint-François because many have a view of the busy waterfront. Life seems to center about the ti-lolo. Everyone from the local fishermen to the gendarmes in their *kepis,* it seems, stops by for a bit of gossip over a "ti-punch," the potent mix of rum, lime juice, and sugar syrup that is something of a national drink.

Outside Saint-François is one of Guadeloupe's most comfortable and highly praised hotels, **Le Hamak.** This cluster of bungalows is set amid manicured gardens at the edge of a tranquil 800-acre lagoon. Le Hamak has three small, private beaches and offers golf at the nearby Robert Trent Jones–designed 18-hole course (the only one on Guadeloupe), gambling at a nearby casino, and windsurfing, water-skiing, and sailing. Adjoining Le Hamak is **Le Méridien,** with 267 rooms. Popular with families and groups, Le Méridien is set on an excellent beach with its own water-sports facilities, and, like Le Hamak, it provides easy access to the Robert Trent Jones course and the casino.

Right on the beach next to Le Méridien, the new **La Cocoteraie**'s 52 sybaritic suites blend European elegance with West Indian informality into a *ne plus ultra* resort. Pricey, true, but paradisaical.

La Cocoteraie is not Saint-François's only recent addition—far from it. Since being savagely mauled by Hurricane Hugo back in 1989, Saint-François has undergone an astonishing apotheosis. The island's largest hostelry, the **Anse des Rochers**, now rises to the west of the village. The 356-room family-oriented resort deals in multiples—two beaches, three restaurants, and seemingly numberless activities. Another newcomer to the Saint-François scene is the **Plantation Ste-Marthe**, built to resemble a sprawling manor house and with a pool so large you almost expect the *Ile de France* to come steaming into view. The four-star restaurant at the Ste-Marthe is presided over by chef Pascal Jacek, whose tartar of tuna and beef medallions in puff pastry turn even the most demanding gourmand rhapsodic.

Pointe des Châteaux itself provides a dramatic view of foaming breakers and stunted windswept trees. The limestone cliffs and sea-sculpted rocks reminded early settlers of the ruined walls of some great country house and gave the place its name. A tall cross crowns the heights; visitors who climb the winding path to it are treated to a sweeping view of sea and sky, with the islands of La Desirade and Petite-Terre floating in between. The climb is more demanding than it seems from below and should be undertaken only by the strong of wind and stout of heart. Nor is swimming recommended for the faint-hearted, as the surf can be rough along this Atlantic shoreline.

A winning luncheon spot a few minutes down the road from Pointe des Châteaux is **Chez Honoré**, an airy, rustic pavilion with a view of breaking surf. *Christophine au gratin* (a mélange of tropical squash, onions, herbs, and cheese baked in a scallop shell) and crispy *accras* (the traditional deep-fried codfish fritters of the Antilles), as well as snapper, langouste, and *colombo de cabri* (a curried stew), are on the Creole-accented bill of fare. Tel: 88-52-19.

From Saint-François the road veers north through rolling countryside to the village of **Le Moule**. Here, the Atlantic breakers roll in, dotted with surfers drawn to the village by what is possibly the finest surfing in the Caribbean. Just north of Le Moule the road swings inland again through a region of hilly farmland known as Les Grands Fonds. The settlers here were originally Bretons, and their descendants, a self-sufficient lot, have retained many of the traditions of their forebears. Long-skirted women in flaring sunbonnets stride along the roads, and families eye passersby from shadowed front porches with a reserve not found elsewhere on the island.

Scattered along the coast and in the countryside

throughout the island you'll find intimate, frequently family-run guest houses known as **Gîtes Ruraux de Guadeloupe**. They are unpretentious and perfect for getting to know your Guadeloupean hosts and their friends. (A passing familiarity with French will prove helpful.)

BASSE-TERRE

Another five- or six-hour excursion takes you through one of the Caribbean's most impressive nature reserves. A few years ago, in what must have been one of the ecological breakthroughs of the century, the government of Guadeloupe set aside nearly one-fifth of its entire area as a natural park, located in the mountainous interior of Basse-Terre. Today it's possible to explore this vast area by car, hike its well-marked trails, picnic in its sun-dappled glades, and inspect its several small *maisons* with their exhibits about volcanoes, the forest, coffee, sugarcane, and rum.

Parc National

To get to the Parc National take Route 1 west from Pointe-à-Pitre across the Rivière Salée and then south to Petit-Bourg, the site of the delightful **Auberge de la Distillerie**, which might have been the setting for an early film by Jean Renoir. Wrapped around with grape arbors and decorated in a style best described as eclectic—antimacassars, a jaunty plastic parrot, and framed samplers—the inn offers such simple pleasures as picnicking in meadows, boating, and bathing in La Lézarde river. There is also a freshwater pool a few steps from the shady dining verandah. Tel: 94-25-91.

From Petit-Bourg go west again, following the route de la Traversée through the mountains to the village of Mahaut. You should stop at the Cascade aux Ecrevisses, named for the freshwater crayfish that are a staple of Guadeloupean cuisine. The waterfall is an easy ten-minute walk along the banks of the Corossol river. A mile or two farther, at Bras David, nature trails of various distances and difficulties have been created. Next to the parking lot a small exhibition hall, La Maison de la Forêt, displays the various flora and fauna you may encounter during your hike. (Hours are 10:00 A.M. to 5:00 P.M.) There is also a new Parc Zoologique nearby. The Col des Deux

Mamelles is about halfway along the Traversée; the view back to Pointe-à-Pitre 2,000 feet below is spectacular, and a rustic restaurant here, the **Gîte des Deux Mamelles** (no phone), offers light lunches.

More ambitious nature lovers may prefer to explore the southern portion of the Parc National, dominated by La Soufrière. This nearly 5,000-foot-high volcano still spews forth sulphurous fumes and jets of steam from its fumeroles, though its vents and fissures have lost a great deal of their drama since a minor eruption in 1976. Instead, you may wish to sign up for a guided nature hike to the Chutes du Carbet, a series of three spectacular waterfalls, each plunging hundreds of feet down the mountainside. Arrangements can be made on the island by telephoning Monsieur Berry of the Organisation des Guides de Montagne de la Caraibe; Tel: 81-45-79.

At the west coast of Basse-Terre the Traversée joins Route 2. Turn south for a few miles to the village of Malendure. Here you can board a glass-bottom boat for an hour-long excursion to **Pigeon Island**, described by Jacques Cousteau as "one of the world's ten best diving sites." Having explored the watery depths, retrace your route to the town of Mahaut, then continue north to the village of Deshaies, where you'll be rewarded with a dip in the calm sea and lunch at the edge of a beach the color of raw sugar. At **Restaurant Karacoli** (Tel: 28-41-17) owner Madame Lucienne Salcede greets her guests at the door and seats them either indoors or in the palm-shaded garden. The hum of conversation around the oilcloth-covered tables mingles with the sound of the surf a few feet away. Creole dishes, as well as Continental entrées, are splendidly prepared and served by a smiling staff who seem genuinely eager to make lunch at this out-of-the-way spot memorable.

From Deshaies, Route 2 continues across the northern coast of Basse-Terre, through pineapple plantations and banana groves, to the hamlets of Sainte-Rose and the aptly named Monplaisir, finally winding its way back to Pointe-à-Pitre.

OFFSHORE ISLANDS

Les Saintes has been described as "St. Tropez before Bardot." It remains to be seen if this quiet octet of islets off Guadeloupe's southern coast will eventually take on the cachet that transformed the Riviera resort into a favorite dateline for gossip columnists around the world. Today Les Saintes remains blissfully "undiscovered." On **Terre-de-Haut**, the largest of the islands and the only one with tourist accommodations, the pace is turtle-ish, the air sparkling, and the local residents always ready with a bright *"bonjour."* Of the seven hotels on the island, **Auberge des Anacardiers**, within an easy walk of the beach, is the most appealing, with a breathtaking view, a swimming pool, and the atmosphere of a relaxed weekend house party. Terre-de-Haut hasn't a single car-rental agency, so taxis, bikes, and motor scooters are the wheels of choice—though many visitors are happy to rely on shank's mare. Diving enthusiasts will want to stop by the **Club Nautique des Saintes**, where Michel Ané rents tanks and gear, gives lessons, and puts together excursions to Les Saintes' superb dive spots. Tel: 99-54-25.

Daylong excursions to the tranquil, unspoiled island of **La Desirade** aboard the motor launches *La Kikalie* and *La Fregate* leave from Saint-François's Marina de la Grande Saline. The service also offers island-bound excursions from Pointe-à-Pitre to **Marie Galante** and from Trois-Rivières in Basse-Terre to Les Saintes. For those who feel uncomfortable on the water, there is regular air service to all the islands. Contact the Guadeloupe tourist office in Pointe-à-Pitre for schedules and rates; Tel: (590) 82-09-30.

USEFUL FACTS
See Martinique. For *Getting In:* Air Guadeloupe serves the Guadeloupe archipelago—St. Martin, St. Barts, La Desirade, Les Saintes, and Marie Galante—daily.

For Further Information
Office Départmental du Tourisme de la Guadeloupe, Square de la Banque, P.B. 1099, Pointe-à-Pitre 97181, Guadeloupe, F.W.I., Tel: (590) 82-09-30, Fax: (590) 83-89-22. For tourist offices in the U.S., Canada, and the U.K., see Martinique.

ACCOMMODATIONS REFERENCE
The rate ranges given here, in U.S. dollars, are projections for fall 1992 through spring 1993, and span the lowest rates in the low season to the highest in the high season. Prices are for double rooms, double occupancy, unless otherwise noted. As rates are subject to change, it's always

*wise to double-check before booking. The telephone coun-
try code for Guadeloupe is 590.*

▶ **Anse des Rochers.** Saint-François 97118, Guadeloupe, F.W.I. Tel: 82-51-57; Fax: 82-52-61. $80–$90, E.P.

▶ **Auberge des Anacardiers.** La Savane 97137, Terre-de-
Haut, Iles des Saintes, Guadeloupe, F.W.I. Tel: 99-50-99;
Fax: 99-54-51. $81–$120, M.A.P.

▶ **Auberge de la Distillerie.** Tabanon 97170, Petit-
Bourg, Guadeloupe, F.W.I. Tel: 94-25-91; Fax: 94-11-91.
$90–$130, E.P.

▶ **Caravelle/Club Med.** Sainte-Anne 97180, Guadeloupe, F.W.I. Tel: 88-21-00; Fax: 88-06-06; in U.S., (800)
CLUB MED. $1,099–$1,499 per week including airfare,
depending on gateway. Excluding airfare: $130 daily,
$830 per week, all meals and most activities included.

▶ **La Cocoteraie.** Saint-François 97118, Guadeloupe,
F.W.I. Tel: 88-79-81; Fax: 88-78-33; in U.S., (800) 543-4300.
$510 (suites only).

▶ **Gîtes Ruraux de Guadeloupe.** Contact Office Depart-
mental du Tourisme, 5 Square de la Banque, 97110
Pointe-à-Pitre, Guadeloupe, F.W.I. Tel: 82-09-30.

▶ **Le Hamak.** Saint-François 97118, Guadeloupe, F.W.I.
Tel: 88-59-99; Fax: 88-41-92; in U.S., (800) 633-7411,
(800) 372-1323, or (803) 785-7411. $200–$400, E.P.

▶ **Le Méridien.** B.P. 37, Saint-François 97118, Guadeloupe, F.W.I. Tel: 88-51-00; Fax: 88-40-71; in U.S., (800)
543-4300 or (212) 265-4494. $224–$380, E.P.

▶ **Plantation Ste-Marthe.** Saint-François 97118, Guadeloupe, F.W.I. Tel: 88-72-46; Fax: 88-72-47. $166, F.A.B.

▶ **Pullman Auberge de la Vieille Tour.** Gosier 97190,
Guadeloupe, F.W.I. Tel: 84-23-23; in U.S., (800) 223-9862.
$116–$345, E.P.

▶ **Hotel La Toubana.** B.P. 63, Sainte-Anne 97180, Guadeloupe, F.W.I. Tel: 88-25-78; Fax: 88-38-90; in U.S., Tel: (800)
223-9815, (800) 366-1510, or (212) 477-1600; Fax: (212)
995-0286. $120–$237, C.P.

DOMINICA

By Robert Grodé

The Dominican landscape is a constantly shifting kaleidoscope of emeralds, viridians, celadons, and jade greens, splashed here and there with chartreuse and absinthe. Traveller's palms spread their fronds like peacock tails; pale pink cedar blossoms drift across terracotta hillsides. Perhaps nowhere else in the Caribbean is nature so unstinting in its bounty. The highlands in the center of the island receive approximately 300 inches of rain each year. Vegetation runs riot, and streams and rivulets, cascades and waterfalls streak the landscape. Almost every afternoon the horizon blurs as fog sweeps across the placid sea, accented here and there with the dark hulls of tiny fishing boats returning to port.

MAJOR INTEREST

Lush vegetation and natural beauty
Freshwater swimming
Nature hiking
Creole dining
Unspoiled and tranquil atmosphere

However, on Sunday, November 3, 1493, Christopher Columbus was apparently not inspired by all this beauty. Rather than naming the mountainous, mist-shrouded island that loomed before him after a saint or a religious shrine, he decided to call his latest discovery "Sunday"—*"Dominica"* in 15th-century Spanish (pronounced "do-mi-NEE-kah"). Of course, his lack of inspiration might have been due to his brief acquaintance with the island: Threatened by spear-wielding Carib Indians, Columbus stopped only long enough to put a few goats ashore in

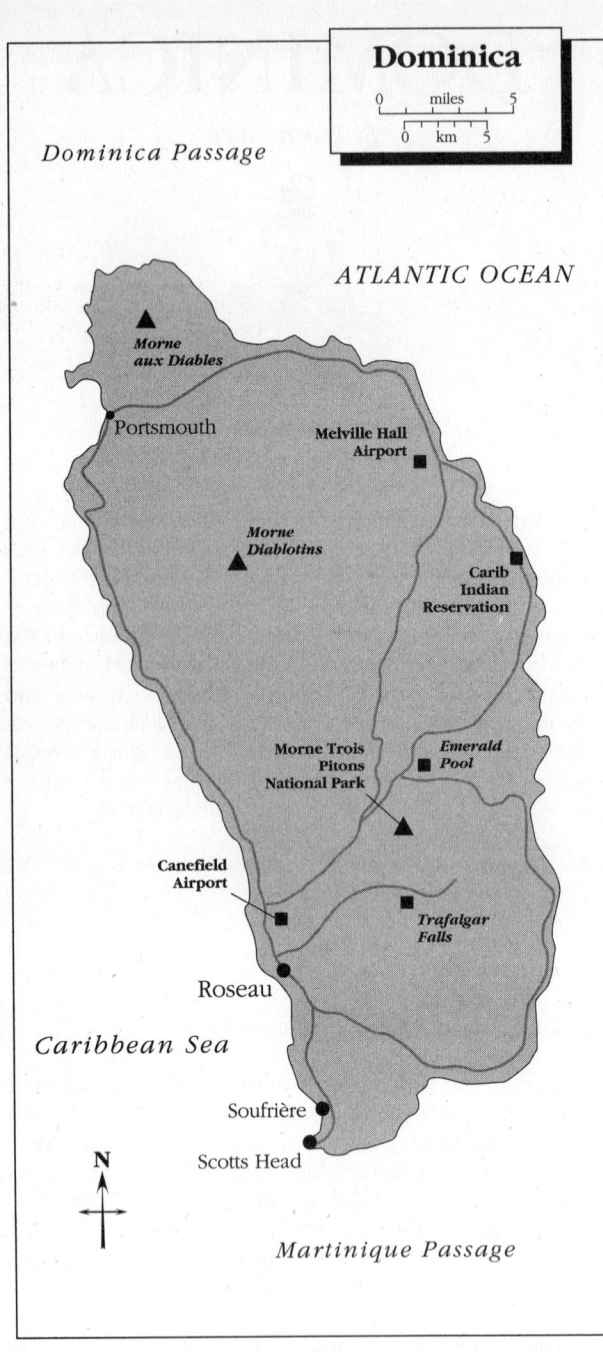

hopes of establishing a herd that would provision future expeditions, then sailed north in search of more hospitable lands.

The Caribs' unwelcoming ways discouraged European settlement of the 290-square-mile island for more than two centuries. Even as late as 1748, when the French and British were slicing up the West Indian pie at the Treaty of Aix-la-Chapelle, they agreed to leave Dominica alone; the Indians were just too difficult to subdue. Naturally, this arrangement didn't last. The Europeans, armed with greed, guile, and guns, soon established footholds on the island, and bloody battles between the two major Old World rivals began to break out with disconcerting frequency.

Finally, in 1795, after the French had torched the island capital of Roseau, the exhausted British paid what they termed "a ransom" of 12,000 pounds to the French and, in 1805, took sole possession of the island. It remained a British Crown Colony until it gained independence in 1978. As a result of this mixed heritage Dominicans speak both English and a French-Creole patois.

Now, after several years of national unrest, Dominica is serene. Its approximately 75,000 people seem eager to welcome visitors. Dominicans, who ordinarily are among the most dedicated individualists in the Caribbean, are joining together these days in dozens of projects — from producing prefabricated houses to restoring a massive fortification in Portsmouth that dates from the heyday of British power. At Canefield Airport a terminal building with a soaring gull's-wing roof has replaced the hot, dusty wooden shed that used to make arrivals and departures something of a trial. Happily, the immigration officials in their crisply starched white jackets are just as accommodating in these spiffy surroundings as they were before. Roseau's **Fort Young Hotel** (opposite the botanical gardens on the edge of town), long popular for its "Sadie Thompson" atmosphere but destroyed by pounding seas a decade ago, has been rebuilt—33 rooms, a disco, and a swimming pool—and is accepting reservations. Dominica, it seems, is on the move.

Is the island, then, on its way to becoming another of the Caribbean's mini-Miamis? Far from it. Dominica's very real pleasures are of the simpler sort: freshwater swimming in lakes and rivers (Dominica's beaches, while swimmable, fall somewhat short of dazzling), bird-watching, hiking, sampling such local dishes as *ti-ti-ri* (tiny freshwater fish) and *crapaud* (immense island frogs), and, best of all, getting to know the Dominicans themselves.

Roseau

Most of these delights are to be discovered outside of Roseau. During his 1859 visit Anthony Trollope felt that everything in Roseau seemed "to speak of desolation," and today's visitors usually agree. Though the explanation most commonly given for Roseau's general air of dilapidation is David, the devastating hurricane that ravaged the island in 1979, neglect, not nature, must take a large share of the blame. The reason for the neglect is not hard to discover. With an annual per capita income only slightly higher than that of Haiti, Dominica is one of the poorest of the West Indian nations.

The best of the little shopping available in Roseau is at the restored **Old Market** at the southern edge of town on a cobblestone square bright with oleanders and hibiscus. Here, tiny crafts shops offer exquisite baskets made by the Carib Indians, whose reservation, the only one in the world, is on the Atlantic side of the island (see below). The market also offers dolls, dressed in the madras skirts and bandannas that are the Dominican national costume, and a selection of locally crafted jewelry and hand-carved figurines.

Another Roseau establishment worth visiting is **Tropicrafts**, the island's largest producer of the straw rugs that, over the years, have decorated nearly every inn and private home in the West Indies. In a factory tucked away on Turkey Lane, a staff of about eight chattering, nimble-fingered women, hunkered down on the cement floor, plait dried palm fronds into rugs, handbags, valises, and hats. Tropicrafts offers a behind-the-scenes glimpse of a continuing island tradition. Tel: 8-2747.

The Roman Catholic cathedral is located, appropriately enough, on Virgin Lane, on a hill overlooking the roadstead. If nothing else, you'll enjoy the chance to catch the cool breezes that seem to constantly sweep through the church's open windows. There is also a charmingly naïve mural adorning the Mary altar. In depicting the flight into Egypt, the artist has filled the sky with cherubs strewing roses in the path of a Holy Family whose members seem to be suffering from a bad case of "donkey lag."

Local well-heeled diners regard the air-conditioned **La**

Robe Creole near the Old Market as Roseau's best restaurant. Attractively done up in madras cloths and slowly revolving ceiling fans, it features a well-thought-out, subtly seasoned Creole/Continental menu. Unfortunately, its charm is a sometime thing. At some meals the radio blares and the service gives new meaning to the term "lackadaisical." On other occasions, however, everything seems shipshape. Tel: 8-2896.

A more informal in-town dining possibility, popular with the Roseau business set, is the **Guiyave Restaurant** (Tel: 8-2930) on Cork Street. The atmosphere is "down home" Dominica style and the Creole dishes on the menu are prepared from the freshest of island-grown produce—avocado, squash, breadfruit, snapper, crab.

Dining reservations aren't usually necessary on this easygoing isle, except perhaps if you are planning to sample the fare at an inn or hotel other than your own. The chef may prepare only enough for the registered guests unless notified that you will be joining them. Even when the occasional cruise ship disgorges its passengers in town, restaurants are not ordinarily crowded with these (literally) "galloping" gourmets.

Dive sites stretch along the western shoreline from Roseau to Scott's Head, the spit of land that extends into the Caribbean like a beckoning finger. The visibility is good, the coral formations impressive. **Dive Dominica** (Tel: 8-2188) can make all arrangements.

Around Roseau

Outside the capital the mood of desolation sensed by Trollope vanishes and all is well, from places to stay to places to see. Accommodations on the island are, as might be expected, small and unpretentious. The 17-room **Reigate Hall**, two miles outside Roseau, is a restored estate house, all whitewashed walls and mahogany planter's chairs. It also has a swimming pool, tennis court, sauna, gym, and the slightly formal air of a British colonial club.

The **Evergreen Hotel**, about 1½ km (1 mile) from town, is a bit more relaxed. This reasonably priced guest house has spotless rooms and a staff as smiling and helpful as can be found anywhere. Dining is family style, and such superbly prepared Dominican specialties as mountain chicken (frogs' legs) and stuffed crab back are often on the menu. Another plus: an atmosphere that encourages an easygoing camaraderie among the guests. Most are Americans and Europeans assigned to one or another of the development programs that are transforming Dominica, and after-dinner talk on the broad, breezy, second-story verandah generally concerns one project or another. A new guest with a sharp ear can become an instant authority on the latest happenings around the island.

Three smaller properties, each with its personal charms, are scattered across the island. **Springfield Plantation** recalls the days when lime juice and bay rum produced on the island's sprawling estates were important exports. Furnished with West Indian antiques, Springfield enjoys a mountaintop location that is an easy ten-minute drive from Roseau. **Layou Valley Inn** lies in the shadow of Morne Trois Pitons. The inn's kitchen reflects Dominica's Gallic heritage with a menu that emphasizes *la cuisine française*. **Floral Gardens** near Castle Bruce on the Atlantic side of the island is set, as you might suspect, on grounds as bright and perfumed as a tropical Eden. The dining room here is noted for its imaginative Creole offerings and makes a relaxing spot for lunch during island tours.

Undoubtedly the most unusual accommodations on the island are at **Papillote Wilderness Retreat**, straight out of Edgar Rice Burroughs and nestled near the foot of the stunningly beautiful Trafalgar Falls. Former New Yorker Anne Baptiste and her island-born husband have put together a bird-watcher/hiker/nature lover's Eden: a half-dozen cozy, comfortable rooms, decked out with handmade quilts (nights can be chilly here in the foothills) and colorful wall paintings. A rustic, covered dining terrace looks out over a tangle of breadfruit and mahogany trees, lobster claw ginger, and trailing lianas. In one corner a hot tub, bubbling with water from a natural hot spring, invites diners to take a pre- (or post-) prandial dip. The tranquillity is occasionally shattered by the raucous cry of the Baptistes' pet peacock, but this merely adds to the jungle atmosphere.

Touring the Island

A network of excellent roads links almost all parts of the island, thanks largely to aid provided by several foreign governments. The roads make a circuit of the northern

half of the island a pleasant and varied four- to five-hour
excursion. Visitors who are a bit nervous about left-hand
driving may want to hire a car and driver, which should
present no problem; putting together personalized island
tours seems to be a growth industry here. (There are
currently 14 local tour operators on the island.) Your
hotel will almost certainly be happy to contact one of
them for you.

An early morning start is best; beginning your circuit
on the western (Caribbean) coastline is also a good idea,
because the western coast tends to be warmer than the
eastern side in midday. The highway threads through
several fishing villages — each with a dazzling view of the
sea and, on clear days, a vista that stretches as far as
Guadeloupe — to **Portsmouth**, Dominica's second-largest
town.

This village, set along the edge of a curving, palm-
fringed harbor, was slated to be the island capital in the
18th century. Unfortunately, frequent outbreaks of ma-
laria and yellow fever in this then-swampy area soon put
an end to these plans. The diseases have long since been
eradicated, but Portsmouth remains a sleepy spot, now
favored by visiting yachtsmen because it offers the most
protected anchorage in these parts.

Cabrits is the 18th-century fort that crowns the heights
at the mouth of the harbor. Restoration is far from complete, and the climb up the rock-strewn path can be
tricky. The fort's battlements are impressive, however,
and a few small gun emplacements have been outfitted
with historical displays.

From Portsmouth the highway swings east into country
that would have sent Le Douanier Rousseau scurrying for
his paintbox: Banana plantations glow in the tenderest of
blue-greens on terraced hillsides, and African tulip trees
tilt their scarlet blooms toward the sky. At the Atlantic
coast the road sweeps past Melville Hall, the island's
"second" airport.

About midway down the Atlantic flank of the island is
the **Carib Indian Reservation**. Visitors expecting exotic
ethnicity are bound to be disappointed—no quaint
thatched-roof longhouses or colorfully costumed villagers here. The Caribs have adopted the West Indian style,
and their homes, yards ablaze with canna blossoms, are
all but indistinguishable from those of their neighbors.
Several small shops line the road, and prices for the

Carib crafts—fine basketwork, irresistible model boats, carved calabash bowls, straw cassava strainers—are temptingly low.

Morne Trois Pitons National Park is reputedly the oldest in the English-speaking Caribbean, and the park's **Emerald Pool**, about a 20-minute hike from the highway, one of its loveliest sights. Wear rubber-soled shoes for the excursion because the sun-dappled path, though not difficult, can be slippery. It descends in a series of doglegs, with benches at convenient intervals, to Emerald Pool itself, a swirling body of water at the base of a 50-foot cascade that tumbles over fern-hung grottoes. Only those with the stamina of a buffalo and the surefootedness of a Sherpa should consider a trek through "The Valley of Desolation" to simmering, sulphur-scented **Boiling Lake**. The terrain is often steep, the tracks unmarked and rutted. Stout walking boots, canteens of water, and a guide are absolute musts, but for the dedicated hiker, Boiling Lake probably will be worth the effort.

Trafalgar Falls cascades down the hills just above Roseau. This billowing veil of water plunging 100 feet down a sheer cliff captures, in one heart-stopping image, just what it is that has made Dominica a favorite for travellers in search of the unspoiled beauty of the tropics.

USEFUL FACTS

Getting In
Leeward Islands Air Transport (LIAT) has daily flights to Canefield or Melville Hall airports from Antigua, St. Lucia, Guadeloupe, Martinique, Barbados, St. Maarten, and Puerto Rico. From Guadeloupe there are flights daily except Sundays on Air Guadeloupe.

Entry Requirements
U.S. and Canadian citizens arriving for stays of up to three months must have a valid passport, a notarized birth certificate with raised seal, or a voter-registration card, as well as a return or ongoing ticket. There is a departure tax of U.S. $10.

Local Time
Dominica is on Atlantic standard time year-round, one hour ahead of the U.S. east coast except when the east coast moves its clocks ahead an hour during daylight saving time. Then the two keep the same time.

Currency

The legal tender is the Eastern Caribbean dollar, but U.S. and Canadian dollars are accepted almost everywhere. As of this writing the rate of exchange was U.S. $1.00 to E.C. $2.67.

Electrical Current

Voltage is 220 AC, 50 cycles. U.S.- and Canadian-made appliances require converters.

Getting Around

The island has several local car-rental agencies. A valid driver's license is required, as is a visitor's driver permit (about U.S. $8), obtainable at airports and at the Police Traffic Department in Roseau.

Business Hours

Banks are open Monday through Thursday, 8:00 A.M. to 3:00 P.M. and Fridays, 8:00 A.M. to 1:00 P.M. and 3:00 to 5:00 P.M.

Festivals

The island celebrates Korné Korn-La (which means "blow the conch shell") on the second Saturday of every month at Soufrière or Scotts Head. There's usually a lot of other music, too, and delicious food sold from stalls on the beach.

For Further Information

Division of Tourism, National Development Corp., P.O. Box 293, Roseau, Commonwealth of Dominica, W.I., Tel: (809-44) 8-2351 or 2186, Fax: (809-44) 8-5840; **in the U.S.,** Caribbean Tourism Organization, 20 East 49th Street, New York, NY 10017-2417, Tel: (212) 682-0435, Fax: (212) 697-4258; **in the U.K.,** 1 Collingham Gardens, London SW5 OHW, England, Tel: (71) 835-1937, Fax: (71) 373-8743.

ACCOMMODATIONS REFERENCE

The rate ranges given here, in U.S. dollars, are projections for fall 1992 through spring 1993, and span the lowest rates in the low season to the highest in the high season. Unless otherwise indicated, rates are for double rooms, double occupancy. As rates are subject to change, it's always wise to double-check before booking. The tele-

phone area code (within the U.S. system) for Dominica is 809-44.

▶ **Evergreen Hotel**. Castle Comfort, Box 309, Commonwealth of Dominica, W.I. Tel: 8-3288 or 8-3276; Fax: 8-6800. $100; M.A.P.

▶ **Floral Gardens**. P.O. Box 192, Roseau, Commonwealth of Dominica, W.I. Tel and Fax: 5-7636. $50.

▶ **Fort Young Hotel**. P.O. Box 519, Roseau, Commonwealth of Dominica, W.I. Tel: 8-5000; Fax: 8-5006. $100, E.P.

▶ **Layou Valley Inn**. Layou & Werner roads, P.O. Box 196, Roseau, Commonwealth of Dominica, W.I. Tel: 9-6203; Fax: 8-5212. $66, M.A.P.

▶ **Papillote Wilderness Retreat**. Trafalgar, Box 67, Roseau, Commonwealth of Dominica, W.I. Tel: 8-2287; Fax: 8-2285. $50–$60, E.P. (for M.A.P., add $30 per person).

▶ **Reigate Hall**. Reigate, Commonwealth of Dominica, W.I. Tel: 8-4031; Fax: 8-4034. $95, E.P.

▶ **Springfield Plantation**. P.O. Box 456, Roseau, Commonwealth of Dominica, W.I. Tel: 9-1401 or 1402; Fax: 9-2160. $105–$130, M.A.P.

MARTINIQUE

By Robert Grodé

Martinique is the scent of frangipani mixed with a trace of Gauloise smoke; the strains of "Island in the Sun" sung *en français;* an haute couture gown accented with a hibiscus blossom. Arriving on the island, there is no mistaking you are in the tropics, but these are tropics that have been refined and enlivened by a French sensibility. There is a flirtatiousness, subtle as perfume, in the glances of women and a Gallic insouciance in men's strides as they swing along the streets of Fort-de-France.

Martinique has always inspired superlatives. Long before the arrival of the French in 1635, Christopher Columbus called the island the "best, richest, sweetest, most charming country in the world." In 1859 Anthony Trollope, taking a break from his duties as a postal inspector on the English islands, cast aside his British reserve and praised Martinique's "rich green... beauties." A few years later Paul Gauguin confessed he "could live here as happy as could be." Today's visitors will almost certainly agree with all of the above. From the mountainous north, with its towering green peaks and dew-spangled banana plantations, to the shimmering coral beaches and rustling cane fields of the south; from the sophistication of Fort-de-France to the simple appeal of such villages as Sainte-Luce and Trinité, Martinique offers a variety and charm equaled on few, if any, West Indian islands.

MAJOR INTEREST

The blend of French and West Indian influences
Shopping and dining in Fort-de-France
Excellent small museums
Tropical beauty

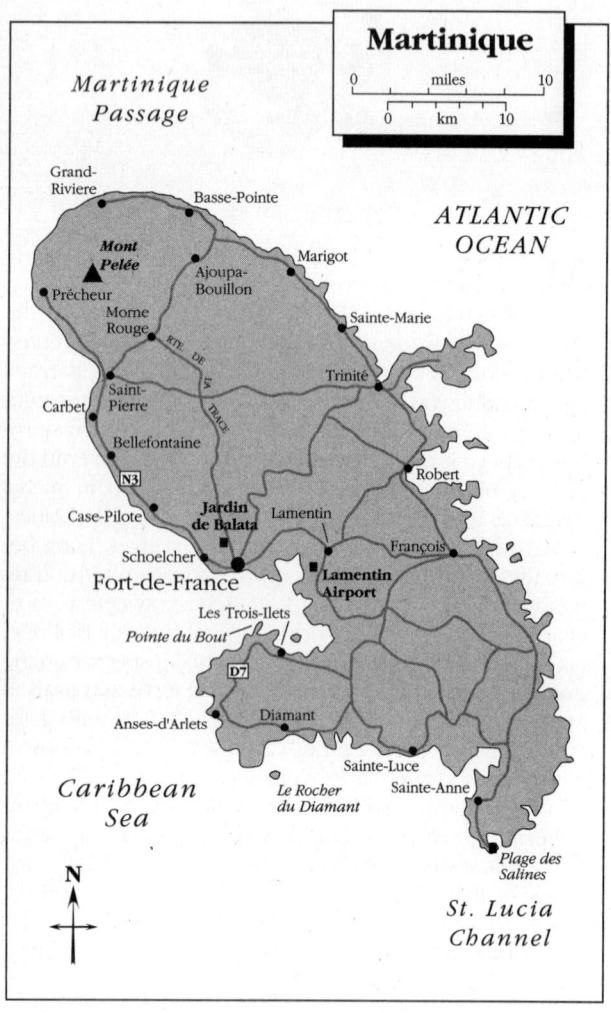

Martinique

0 ___ miles ___ 10
0 ___ km ___ 10

Martinique Passage

Grand-Riviere
Basse-Pointe
Mont Pelée
Ajoupa-Bouillon
Marigot
Prêcheur
Morne Rouge
Sainte-Marie
RTE. DE LA TRACE
Trinité
Carbet
Saint-Pierre
Bellefontaine
N3
Robert
Case-Pilote
Jardin de Balata
Lamentin
Schoelcher
François
Fort-de-France
Lamentin Airport
Les Trois-Ilets
Pointe du Bout
D7
Diamant
Anses-d'Arlets
Sainte-Luce
Sainte-Anne
Le Rocher du Diamant
Plage des Salines

ATLANTIC OCEAN

Caribbean Sea

N

St. Lucia Channel

Fort-de-France Area

Martinique's capital and major city is Fort-de-France. Set in the middle of the Caribbean Sea side of the island between rolling hills and the island's most protected harbor, the city glows with the vibrant pinks, greens, and blues of the tropics—in its building façades, the madras headdresses of its market women, and the sky and sea that provide its background. Drivers maneuver their vehicles along the narrow streets with the élan of Grand Prix contenders, and the air is often raucous with the blare of horns and the shouts of motorists. It's all part of the liveliness that characterizes Fort-de-France.

La Savane Park, with its verdant lawns and arching palms, provides a momentary respite from the clamor of the city. Stretching away from the busy waterfront, it is dotted with fountains and statues, notably one of the empress Josephine, who was born just across the bay at Les Trois-Ilets. She stands atop a pedestal, holding a medallion of her husband in her left hand. It's been observed that she looks more like a housewife who has been interrupted while drying the dinner dishes than the wife of Napoléon.

Just across rue de la Liberté from the Josephine statue is the **Bibliothèque Schoelcher**, a cast-iron and tile quasi-Byzantine structure transported here from Paris after the Exposition of 1889. This soaring example of Belle Epoque exoticism houses exhibits of French and Martiniquais culture. Tel: 72-45-55 for schedule information.

Tiny boutiques line the streets of Fort-de-France, offering Paris couture and Riviera resort wear at real savings, and exploring them will provide a pleasant few hours. **Mounia**, on rue Perrinon, carries such labels as Claude Montana, Dorothée Bis, and Yves Saint-Laurent; in fact, it is owned by a Martiniquaise who began her phenomenal fashion career as a top Saint-Laurent model. Many larger shops deal in luxury items such as Baccarat and Lalique crystal and Hermès bags and scarves. At 72 rue Antoine Siger, **Cadet-Daniel**, established in 1840, is a favorite of shoppers in search of Christofle silver and Sevres china. The counters of **Roger Albert**, on rue Victor Hugo, glitter with bottles of French perfumes, often sold at one-half the U.S. and European prices. (Many stores give a 20 percent discount on luxury items purchased with traveller's checks or certain credit cards; be sure to ask.) Traditional Creole bracelets and necklaces, made on the island in 18-karat gold, are particularly evocative of Martinique, especially the *colliers choux* (darlings' necklaces), which for centuries have been treasured heirlooms for the island's women. **Montaclair** and **L'Or et L'Argent** on rue Victor Hugo and **Thomas de Rogatis**, on rue Antoine Sigere, are three shops that have outstanding collections of Creole jewelry.

An equally traditional island product is fine rum, first produced here in the 17th century by French friars. It's both light and dark, reasonably priced, and will prove to be, as Ernest Hemingway said, the "perfect antidote to a rainy day."

The Gallic emphasis on fine dining is evident in the many superb restaurants in Fort-de-France. Martiniquais take their gourmandizing seriously, and the island chefs are constantly coming up with imaginative (and delicious) adaptations of classic dishes. The Chef at **La Biguine**, for example, has a real genius for working subtle variations on such Creole staples as *crabes farcis* (land crab mixed with herbs, spices, and bread crumbs and baked in the shell) and *blaff* (the West Indian version of bouillabaisse). Located in a time-mellowed Creole house on the route de la Folie, La Biguine offers a choice of the Provençal dining room upstairs or the more informal grill downstairs.

There are many other excellent restaurants in Fort-de-France. A good choice for lunch, both because of its menu—including an unusual sea-urchin quiche—and its sweeping view of La Savane and the busy harbor, is **Le d'Esnambuc**. On the third floor of a building at the foot of the rue de la Liberté, the light-filled dining room provides a view of the statue of its namesake, Belain d'Esnambuc, the first settler of the island. Next door, on the second floor of the **Lafayette Hotel**, Dominique Laval and Jean-Pierre Lemoine-Busserolles offer classic French-Creole dishes in a sophisticated setting bright with tropical flowers, sparkling crystal, and gleaming china; Tel: 63-24-09. And just out of town in Lamentin, **Le Verger** (Tel: 51-43-02), set on a breeze-cooled covered terrace, combines French-Creole specialties with the regional dishes of Perigord.

Fort-de-France offers a few compelling reasons to stray from your hotel after dark: A number of clubs feature local groups such as Kassav and Malavoi. Two of the most popular night spots are **Elysses Matignon** (Tel: 63-17-06), at 109 rue Ernest de Proge, and the **New Hippo** (Tel: 60-20-22), at 24 boulevard Alegre. Most clubs feature the hot new *zouk* (a kind of West Indian jazz).

Jazz has found a home in Martinique, the land of the beguine. During the first two weeks of December in odd-numbered years (like 1993), Fort-de-France welcomes an array of European, North American, and Antillean jazz soloists and sidemen to the city's International Jazz Festival. During even-numbered years the spotlight shifts to the guitar with a fortnight of concerts, seminars, and classes in both the classical and avant-garde modes.

Just on the outskirts of Fort-de-France the hotel **La Batelière** sits amid poinciana-shaded gardens on low cliffs with stairs leading to a small, sandy cove. Smaller than Le Méridien at Pointe du Bout (see the South, below), it has comfortable, air-conditioned rooms, a pool, a discotheque, and indoor and outdoor restaurants that offer everything from pizza to filet mignon. A piano bar overlooks the sea, and guests eager to improve their French arithmetic might do well to take part in the bingo games — "B–sept," "O–soixante-huit"— that take place here every evening except Sunday, at six. If bingo is too tame for your tastes, La Batelière also has a casino, where the action is also in French.

Grands Ballets de la Martinique, a folkloric group that performs such traditional island dances as the calenda, the beguine (yes, Cole Porter heard it first on Martinique), and the ting bang, appears at various hotels on different evenings during the week. Performances are generally preceded by eye-popping and belt-stretching buffets. (Check with the Martinique tourist office in Fort-de-France or at your hotel for schedules.) Grands Ballets makes up in charm and enthusiasm for any slight lack of sophistication and polish.

Jardin de Balata

It is outside Fort-de-France that many of Martinique's special charms become apparent. Because the island is relatively small (just 50 miles long and 22 miles wide), excursions into the countryside are easy and may range from a morning's tour to a day-long exploration. One of the best destinations is the Jardin de Balata, just north of Fort-de-France on the route de la Trace. Here, Jean-Philippe Thoze and his wife, Marie-Claude, have created a picture-perfect tropical Eden that even those who don't know a bougain-villaea from a breadfruit will find enchanting.

Only an acre in area, the gardens are so superbly laid out that they seem much larger. Gently graded gravel paths ramble beneath arbors festooned with orchids, through groves of palms, and past trees hung with salmon-pink bromeliads.

The tour of the garden begins and ends at a charmingly restored West Indian cottage, the former country home of Monsieur Thoze's family. The sparkling white house, laced with gingerbread-trimmed verandahs, is furnished with antiques and reproductions of Martinique armoires and side chairs, crystal lamps, and sepia photographs. The louvered windows look out onto a vista of mist-shrouded peaks. Tel: 64-48-73; open 9:00 A.M. to 6:00 P.M. daily.

On the half-hour journey to the gardens, you will pass the **Sacré Coeur de Balata**, a scaled-down version of the church in the Montmartre section of Paris. Pilgrims, seeking favors or acknowledging an answered prayer, light candles in the amber glow of stained-glass windows that capture in Matisse-like forms Martinique's lush tropical foliage—croton and breadfruit leaves—a fitting prelude to a visit to the Balata gardens.

The Island's North

Martinique's 12 small museums rank as some of the Caribbean's most delightful surprises. Commemorating everyone and everything, from Empress Josephine to the cataclysmic volcanic eruptions of Mont Pelée in 1902, and celebrating dolls, dugout canoes, and the "demon rum," these intriguing collections offer insights into Martinique's history and culture. (A museum credit card, available at all museums for approximately U.S. $6, enables users to visit all the museums without further admission fees.)

Four of the most fascinating museums can be seen during one day-long excursion around the northern section of the island. Set off from Fort-de-France on route N 3, then head north along the Caribbean coast through a series of drowsy seaside villages. At Case-Pilote is the island's oldest church, a specimen of colonial Baroque exuberance that's all bonbon-colored garlands and dimpled cherubs. On a hillside in Bellefontaine rises a house shaped like a ship, the creation of a retired sea captain.

At the village of Carbet, its stone walls draped with golden-trumpet vines, keep an eye peeled for the sign on the right announcing the **Centre d'Art Paul Gauguin**. This museum commemorates the four months that this Post-impressionist artist spent on Martinique in 1887. Family photographs and copies of letters the painter wrote during his island stay are on display, as are reproductions of the 12 paintings Gauguin completed in a nearby hut. Downstairs, a display of antique Creole costumes evokes the days when the ever-susceptible Gauguin praised the beauty of the island women and found them "gay and affable." Open 10:00 A.M. to 5:00 P.M. daily.

The next stop is the village of **Saint-Pierre**. At the turn of the century a visitor described the then-thriving city as having "a population of the Arabian Nights." On May 8, 1902, the fairy tale ended. A massive cloud of white-hot dust and gas burst from the side of nearby Mont Pelée, wiping out in a single blinding flash the town and all but one of its 30,000 inhabitants. Today a small museum tells the story of the catastrophe in haunting displays. Some potent reminders of the disaster still stand in the town: the sweeping double staircase of the opera house, the shattered façade of the cathedral, and the underground cell in which the only survivor, a prisoner named Cyparis, was protected from the destruction.

From Saint-Pierre head inland into the lush mountains, passing through Morne Rouge and the village of Ajoupa-Bouillon, where a floral *bienvenue* planted at the roadside marks the city limits. Continue north a short distance along the Atlantic coast to Basse-Pointe. A mile or so out of town (and from the beach) is **Plantation Leyritz** (Tel: 78-53-92). At the superbly restored 18th-century estate, now a nearly irresistible resort, visitors can eat lunch in the excellent dining room located in what was formerly the plantation granary, then examine the delightful creations of Will Fenton. This talented young artist has fashioned a gallery of what he calls *poupées vegetales,* sophisticated doll-size mannequins that he makes from more than 600 kinds of fronds, leaves, and other plant parts.

Leyritz also offers accommodations that recall gentler days. Of its 50 rooms, the most gracious are the four guest chambers on the second floor of the main house, furnished with four-poster canopy beds, cane rocking chairs, and toile hangings. Other rooms are located in the former guard house, the family cookhouse, workers' cottages, and a six-room annex. The fountain-fed swimming pool is set in a formal garden, trimmed and trained to 18th-century perfection.

Return to Basse-Pointe, then swing south along the coast through Marigot, where **Habitation LaGrange**, a restored 18th-century mansion in seven and a half acres of tropical gardens, pampers guests with antique four-poster beds and a dining salon brightened with a hand-painted mural in the classical style. Air-conditioning, plus ceiling fans, phones, TVs, pool, and lighted tennis court add the contemporary touches. From Marigot it's on to Sainte-Marie. In Sainte-Marie the **Musée de Rhum**, operated by the St. James Distillery, is set in still another restored estate house. Its displays outline the long, colorful history of rum production in Martinique with implements and rare old prints. Information about the exhibits is available in English. Tel: 75-30-02.

The road winds on to Trinité and Robert, a pair of villages overlooking the island-studded sea. The **Saint Aubin**, atop a low hill outside Trinité, is a splendidly reconstructed colonial manor house ringed with broad galleries. Now a small hotel, it has 15 rooms. The graceful exterior and the manicured grounds promise more than the slightly Spartan accommodations inside, but the rooms are clean, comfortable, and air-conditioned. Just pulling up under the soaring porte cochère or lolling beside the pool in the immaculately tended gardens inspires reveries of a more gracious age. Turn west again and drive through cane fields to Lamentin, the site of Martinique's international airport, then back to Fort-de-France.

The Island's South

Southern Martinique was the birthplace of the empress Josephine, and **La Pagerie**, just outside the village of Les Trois-Ilets, was her childhood home (Tel: 68-34-55). Set among verdant hills, it now houses a tiny museum in what was once the kitchen of the estate. Perhaps the most unusual item on display is a passionate letter from the emperor enclosing "*mille baisers amoureux, partout, partout*" for the woman he called "incomparable, completely divine." Nearby is the island golf course, which was designed by Robert Trent Jones.

After Trois-Ilets the **Pointe du Bout** curves protectively about the entrance to the harbor at Fort-de-France. A 20-minute ferry ride carries Pointe du Bout vacationers to the city for shopping, dining, or sightseeing. The service is frequent, the boats immaculate, and the views spectacular. Several fine hotels, including Le Bakoua and the Carayou-PLM Azur, stretch along the shore. **Le Bakoua**, recently enlarged, is a well-run commercial-style hotel with many balcony rooms. From the pool area the view of Fort-de-France across the harbor is dazzling. Le Bakoua's restaurant is noted for its Continental and Creole cuisine. The **Carayou-PLM Azur**'s 200 air-conditioned rooms are set around a tropical courtyard; the hotel also has three restaurants, a discotheque, a pool, tennis courts, and a private beach.

Perched like a seabird at the farther tip of the point is the 295-room **Le Méridien–Trois-Ilets**, Martinique's premier hotel. With its spacious, airy lobby—glittering with mirrors and brightly decorated with island-inspired murals—well-appointed rooms, a pool and a beach, two restaurants, shops, a casino, lounge, nightclub, and water-sports marina, Le Méridien has been designed for those seeking an everything-within-easy-reach vacation.

From Trois-Ilets or Pointe du Bout, drive south along route D7 to **Anses d'Arlets**, a village that might have been inspired by a Van Gogh seascape. Fishing boats painted in reds and yellows are beached under spreading sea grapes hung with bright blue nets. Le Rocher du Diamant is a vast rock two-and-a-half miles offshore that was defended by English tars for 18 months during the French and British skirmishes of the Napoleonic Wars. Later designated a man-of-war by the Royal Navy, it is still known in English naval records as H.M.S. *Diamond Rock* and given a 12-gun salute by every passing British warship. At the village of Diamant **Le Plein Sud** hotel offers 52 apartments ranging from studios to two-bedroom suites. A Martiniquais couple-in-residence assists guests with settling in and with suggestions for things to see and do around the island. No restaurant, but the bar serves light meals.

One of the island's most spectacular (and most popular) beaches, the **Plage des Salines**, is flung like a silk scarf along the coast south of **Sainte-Anne**. Palms cast flickering shadows along the edge of the coral sand and across topless torsos. Weekdays are the best time to visit Sainte-Anne; on weekends it seems that the entire population of Fort-de-France has converged in campers, on mopeds, and on racing bikes to bask on the two-mile strand.

From Sainte-Anne winding country roads lead north to the town of François. Outside François the recently opened **La Frégate Bleue** offers seven large studio apartments, superbly furnished with antique mahogany beds, Oriental carpets, and comfortable armchairs. Each unit includes a luxurious bath, kitchenette, and private verandah. A turquoise-and-white garden house overlooks the pool, and the beach is a short distance away. Another newcomer to the François hotel scene is the 14-room **La Riviera**, an airy Caribbean-style caravanserai created by owners Anne-Marie and Erick Priam. Delights include private terraces with breathtaking ocean views and a gourmet restaurant with a *carte* that lists some of the most delectable entrées on the island. In the center of the village a massive Corbusier-style church, all soaring concrete walls and abstract stained glass, contrasts with a fretwork-trimmed Victorian city hall in a silent confrontation between past and present. Between the two a memorial to the dead of World War I is strung incongruously with Christmas tree lights. From François it's a short drive back to Fort-de-France.

For visitors seeking a holiday *chez une famille creole,* there are a number of small, often family-operated guest houses—**Relais Creoles**—throughout the island; these are good places to meet local people and sample island life. Some knowledge of French will increase the pleasures of these friendly, personal hostelries.

USEFUL FACTS

Getting In
There are regular flights to Lamentin Airport on Martinique (or to Raizet Airport on Guadeloupe) on American Airlines from New York, and from other U.S. cities via San Juan; on Air France from Miami and San Juan; on Leeward Islands Air Transport (LIAT) from neighboring islands; and on Air Martinique to and from St. Maarten, Dominica, Barbados, St. Lucia, St. Vincent, Mustique, Union Island, and Trinidad.

Entry Requirements
For stays up to three months, U.S. and Canadian citizens must have a valid passport or one that has expired within the past five years. A notarized birth certificate with raised seal or a voter-registration card is also accepted if accompanied by another authorized government I.D. with photo. The above documents qualify a visitor for a tempo-

rary visa issued upon arrival at no charge. Citizens of most other countries must have a passport, as well as a return or ongoing ticket.

Local Time
Martinique is on Atlantic standard time year-round, one hour ahead of the U.S. east coast except when the east coast moves its clocks ahead an hour during daylight saving time. Then the two keep the same time.

Currency
The legal tender is the French franc, but U.S. and Canadian dollars are accepted almost everywhere. As of this writing the rate of exchange was U.S. $1.00 to 5, 3FF.

Electrical Current
Voltage is 220 AC, 50 cycles. U.S.- and Canadian-made appliances require converters.

Getting Around
Major U.S. car-rental companies, including Avis, Budget, Hertz, and National, have offices on Martinique and Guadeloupe, as do several local agencies. A valid driver's license is required to rent a vehicle for up to 20 days; for longer periods an international driver's permit is required.

Banking Hours
Banks are open Monday through Friday, 7:30 to noon and 2:30 to 4:00 P.M., and closed on the afternoons preceding public holidays.

Festivals
Martinique's Vaval, as carnival is called on the island, erupts every weekend between New Year's and the beginning of Lent.

For Further Information
Office Départemental du Tourisme de la Martinique, Boulevard Alfassa, P.B. 520, Fort-de-France, Martinique 97206, F.W.I., Tel: (596) 63-79-60, Fax: (596) 73-66-93; **in the U.S.,** French West Indies Tourist Board, 610 Fifth Avenue, New York, NY 10020, "France on Call" Tel: (900) 990-0040; **in Canada,** 30 St. Patrick Street, Suite 700, Toronto, Ontario, M5T 3A3, Tel: (416) 593-4723; **in the U.K.,** 178 Piccadilly, London W1V OAL, England, Tel: (71) 499-6911.

ACCOMMODATIONS REFERENCE

The rate ranges given here, in U.S. dollars, are projections for fall 1992 through spring 1993, and span the lowest rates in the low season to the highest in the high season. Unless otherwise indicated, prices are for double rooms, double occupancy. As rates are subject to change, it's always wise to double-check before booking. The telephone country code for Martinique is 596.

▶ **Le Bakoua.** Pointe du Bout, Martinique 97229, F.W.I. Tel: 66-02-02; Fax: 66-00-41; in U.S., (800) 221-4542. $140–$308, C.P.

▶ **La Batelière.** Schoelcher, Fort-de-France, Martinique 97233, F.W.I. Tel: 61-49-49; Fax: 61-70-57; in U.S., (800) 223-6510. $170–$267, E.P.

▶ **Carayou-PLM Azur.** Pointe du Bout, Martinique 97229, F.W.I. Tel: 66-04-04; Fax: 66-00-57; in U.S., (800) 221-4542 or (800) 223-9862. $82–$174, E.P.

▶ **La Frégate Bleue.** François, Martinique 97240, F.W.I. Tel: 54-54-66; Fax: 54-78-48; in U.S., (800) 633-7411. $120–$225 (full breakfast).

▶ **Habitation LaGrange.** Marigot, Martinique 97225, F.W.I. Tel: 53-60-60; Fax: 53-50-58; in U.S., (800) 633-7411 or (803) 785-7411. $250–$300, C.P.

▶ **Le Méridien–Trois-Ilets.** Pointe du Bout, Martinique 97229, F.W.I. Tel: 66-00-00; Fax: 66-00-74; in U.S., (800) 543-4300. $230–$280, C.P.

▶ **Plantation Leyritz.** Basse-Pointe, Martinique 97218, F.W.I. Tel: 78-53-92; Fax: 78-92-44; in U.S., (800) 366-9815, (800) 366-1510, or (212) 477-1600. $102–$147, E.P.

▶ **Le Plein Sud.** Quartier Dizac, Diamant, Martinique 97223, F.W.I. Tel: 76-26-06; Fax: 76-26-07. $75–$132, E.P.

▶ **Relais Creoles.** Contact Office Départemental du Tourisme de la Martinique, Boulevard Alfassa, P.B. 520, Fort-de-France 97206, Martinique, F.W.I. Tel: 63-79-60; Fax: 73-66-93.

▶ **La Riviera.** Route du Club Nautique, François, Martinique 97240, F.W.I. Tel: 54-68-54; Fax: 54-30-43. $72–$110, C.P.

▶ **Saint Aubin.** Trinité, Martinique 97220, F.W.I. Tel: 58-34-77. $65–$78, E.P.

ST. LUCIA

By Jennifer Quale

It's said that St. Lucia has always been on the verge of being discovered (even Columbus passed it by). Although it's now in the throes of commercial development, this lush, mountainous island in the Windward chain still retains the elsewhere-vanishing vestiges of West Indian culture: It's just that they're getting harder to find than when Somerset Maugham and Alec Waugh discovered St. Lucia's charms a generation or so ago.

After being tossed back and forth like a tennis ball between the British and the French for two centuries, St. Lucia finally landed on the English side of the court during King George III's reign, in 1803. Although political independence within the Commonwealth was achieved in 1979, the island still exudes both a Gallic flair and English comities; while English is the official language, patois is the native tongue.

Mostly, though, St. Lucia exists for and of itself. Bananas, not tourists, bring in the bulk of its foreign income, which is to say the St. Lucians are just now sorting out what to do with the other assets they've got and sometimes they're going over the top with hasty solutions. For instance, on a lofty helicopter tour you can now buzz the Pitons, the most magnificent pair of mountains in the Caribbean, which rise half a mile above the sea like woolly green pyramids. (They're better seen from the ground.) The island's rugged interior rain forest conjures visions of *Green Mansions,* and its drive-in volcano and sulphur springs could save Hollywood a fortune in special effects. St. Lucia's plucky capital of Castries and its environs teem with hotels and restaurants, marinas and shopping malls, while the soporific town of Soufrière in

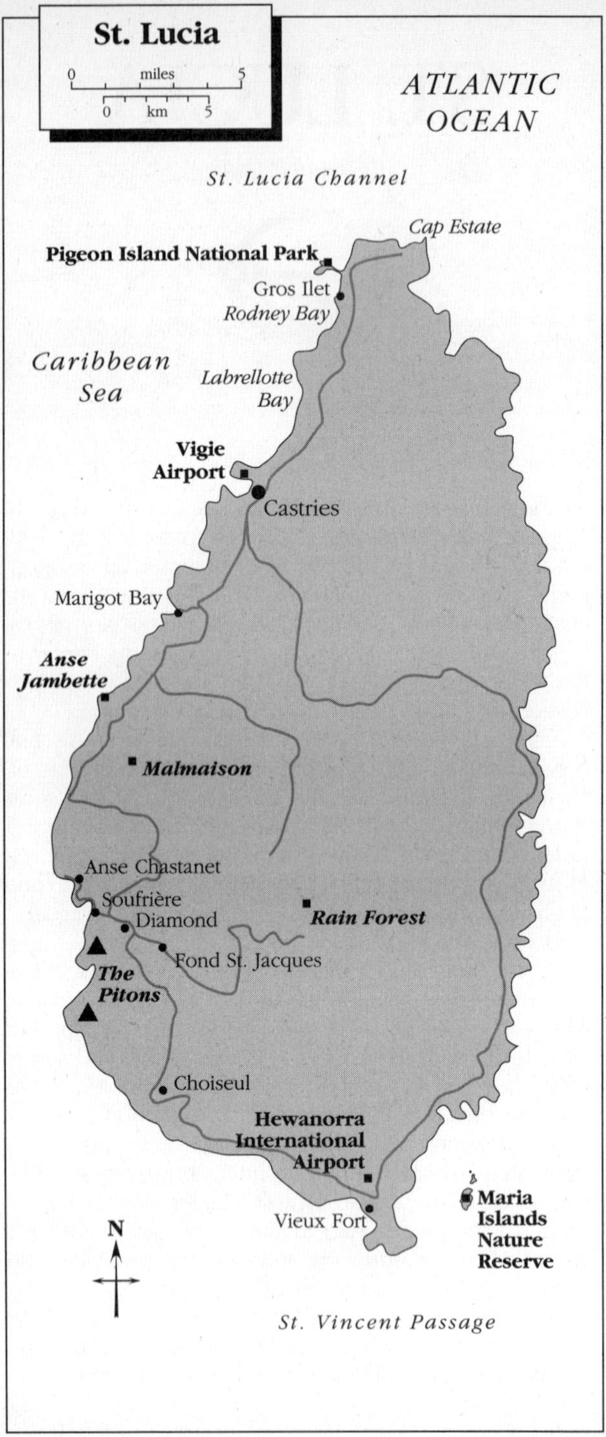

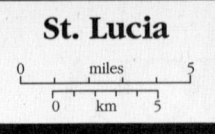

St. Lucia
0
miles
5
0
km
5
ATLANTIC
OCEAN
St. Lucia Channel
Cap Estate
Pigeon Island National Park
Gros Ilet
Rodney Bay
Caribbean
Sea
Labrellotte
Bay
Vigie
Airport
Castries
Marigot Bay
Anse
Jambette
Malmaison
Anse Chastanet
Soufrière
Diamond
Rain Forest
Fond St. Jacques
The
Pitons
Choiseul
Hewanorra
International
Airport
Maria
Islands
Nature
Reserve
Vieux Fort
N
St. Vincent Passage

the south has barely budged from the 19th century. And the beaches are sufficiently inviting to make you want to forget about all the things to see and do. Luckily, the island is relatively small (14 miles wide, 27 miles long), so the compulsive visitor who wants to do it all can manage comfortably in a week's stay.

Overall, St. Lucia offers a sense of discovery in its remote reaches, natural wonders, especially the Pitons, and a rich West Indian culture.

MAJOR INTEREST

Castries
The Pitons' natural beauty
A "drive-in" volcano and the Sulphur Springs
Diamond baths
The rain forest

Picture St. Lucia in the shape of your right hand signaling "stop." At the tip of the index finger is Cap Estate, primarily a villa community of 1,500 manicured but arid acres, complete with golf course and riding stables, squash courts and beaches. Castries lies between the forefinger and thumb on the Caribbean side (almost everything of interest is on the Caribbean, or leeward, side—which is fortunate, because the roads on the windward side of the island make the lunar surface look smooth). Soufrière, home of the Pitons and the volcano, sits on the base of the thumb. Hewanorra Airport, which serves international carriers, is at the bottom of the hand, at St. Lucia's southern tip. (Vigie Airport, wedged between a beach and a cemetery outside Castries, now with its extended landing strip, accommodates an increasing number of overseas aircraft as well as interisland flights.) Most first-time visitors, lured by the (relatively) more aggressive marketing of the northwest, make the mistake of spending their entire vacation in and around Castries. But a day trip to Soufrière just isn't long enough. You will be much happier if you spend a few days in the north and the same—or more—in the south.

Castries

The town of Castries, laid out in grid style along its huge, almost landlocked harbor, looks neither old nor quaint, having burned to the ground several times. Despite the 1950s replacement architecture, Castries carries on by the spunk of its people—and to the stop-and-go beat of befuddling traffic lights just installed two years ago. With its bustle and patois and *je ne sais quoi,* it's more French than English, more frenzied than languid.

For the savvy traveller Castries is **Rain**. This winsome bar and restaurant on Columbus Square, set like a stage for the Maugham short story with its paddle fans, ferns, and gingerbread trim, occupies one of the few colonial buildings that survived the last fire. When New Yorker Al Haman, Rain's creator and master of nostalgic ceremonies, came to St. Lucia some 20 years ago, he revived a certain style that had long lain dormant (19th-century Castries was quite a cultural scene, with its fancy dress balls and performances of the latest Paris comedies). Every night Haman re-creates—with poetic license— the historic Champagne banquet of 1885 as served to members of the Castries Philharmonic Society. Indeed, Rain is a sort of salon for local and visiting intelligentsia; if native son Derek Walcott were in town, you would expect to find him lunching on the balcony, perhaps with resident poet Robert Lee. Although no one goes to Rain for the food, it's really quite good (especially the stuffed crab backs and hand-cranked ice creams); be sure to book a table on the balcony so you can watch the town go by on the square below. Tel: 452-3022.

In the heart of town **Columbus Square** contains a sprawling, ancient saman tree. From here you can walk about in search of the town's nooks and crannies, such as the iron market, stamp shop, the Sunshine Bookstore, and West Indian Sea Island Cotton shop. On the square the massive **Cathedral of the Immaculate Conception** is worth seeing for its painted interior, particularly the unusual flying buttresses; on the occasion of the Pope's visit in 1986, the island's leading artist, Dunstan St. Omer (who recently opened his own gallery), got carried away with his colors and patterns upon patterns—but somehow it all works. New on the scene: St. Omer and sons' mural on the walls of Castries' central bus depot—a somewhat off-the-wall view of the island's culture and history.

Because of its spectacular landscapes, St. Lucia has always attracted foreign artists. Recently, however, expatriates and local artists have joined together to stimulate and recognize local talent, which is prodigious considering the island's small population. **Artsibit**, as au courant as the gallery's name implies, exhibits a wide range of works (including Derek Walcott watercolors) in its corner space at Brazil and Mongiraud streets. About 15 minutes south of town at **Eudovic's** studio, you sometimes can watch the master carver working on a huge tree stump, absently tweaking two long gray strands of hair from his beard. The highly polished, fluid forms of Eudovic's sculpture and furniture all start with the right root or tree, which he finds on foraging trips in the forest. Not long ago he opened a tiny pub at his compound, with a limited menu featuring curried goat and Creole fish fingers.

Back toward Castries, just over the hill (St. Lucia seems entirely hilly, even the beaches) lies **Bagshaw's**, the renowned shop that turns silk-screening and batiking into a local art form. (Forget the dowdy clothing and go for the table linens.) Bagshaw's draws most of its free-spending customers from the neighboring **Cunard Hotel La Toc** and its swish sister property, **Cunard La Toc Suites**. Until recently the main hotel and the villa suites strung along the ridge behind it were operated as one large complex. To stay at the Cunard resort was like being on the QE2, with the suites comparable to first class and the hotel rooms akin to below decks.

Recognizing the difference, Cunard officially split the properties, thus making the suites the best place to stay in the Castries area (although with continuing improvements the hotel units are agreeable). Where else can you leap from your bedroom into a private plunge pool (feet first, and forget about laps: The pool's about six by ten), turn on a VCR in your living room when it rains, and call for room service from the island's finest restaurant? In general, service here is exceptional, owing to the tight-ship training of the genial St. Lucian staff. On the 110 acres of Cunard grounds, guests have free access to the better of the island's two nine-hole golf courses, a professionally managed tennis club, and a superb beach with the usual array of water sports and instructors. If the red flag goes up, precluding swimming in a sometimes dangerous undertow, head for the unusual pool, with its own palm tree–studded island. During the day the top local steel band may play such incongruous tunes as "In the Mood" for visiting Cunard cruise-ship passengers on the hotel terrace, but come nightfall all is quiet on the blissful suite-side beachfront. Suite guests (an eye surgeon there, a money broker here) mingle at the natty Les Pitons piano lounge, which, like most St. Lucian bars, offers a wildly inspired "cocktail of the day," along with the most addictive homemade plantain chips in the Windwards.

Next door, or actually outdoors, the surf almost rolls in to the elegant **Les Pitons Restaurant**, where the lobster comes fresh from the hotel's own traps (unfortunately many local restaurants serve lobster that has been frozen), and the Dutch chef's passion for presentation and quality rarely misses a beat (try the scallops and baby vegetables in saffron sauce). Non-hotel guests may eat here as well, but reservations are essential; Tel: 452-3081.

Most of the restaurants within easy reach of Castries are on the water, along the harbors, or in Rodney Bay—which makes sense considering St. Lucia is quite a yachting center. Creole cuisine reigns supreme, with a few aberrations (such as the worthy Italian menu at **Capone's**, a tropical Art Deco–styled entry from Al Haman). You would have to stay in Castries a month to try all its funky spots, but among the more intriguing are **Jimmy's**, **Eagles Inn** (Tel: 452-0650), the **Charthouse** (Tel: 452-8115), and **Key Largo** for brick-oven pizza. At Jimmy's (Tel: 452-5142), for instance, you'll find this local character presiding over his hopping harborside eatery, where visitors from the U.K. go potty over the Ploughman's Lunch, while casual regulars clamor for seafood risotto, *bouyon* (Creole beef stew), and a selection from the dessert menu, which consists entirely of desserts made from bananas.

Best new bets include **Le Bistro** (Tel: 452-9494), run by the former owners of San Antoine and housed in the old A-Frame Pub at Rodney Bay, and **D's Restaurant and Bar** (Tel: 453-7931) in Vide Bouteille, just beyond the airport. Never mind the plastic furniture at D's; instead, savor the alfresco setting on the deserted beach, the chicken in coconut cream, or the lime-garlic shrimp. Prices are reasonable. And for a recession-proof holiday, the surrounding **Edgewater Beach Club** offers a handful of tidy self-catering cottages, newly renovated.

San Antoine, the highly touted restaurant on the historic Morne (Hill), makes you yearn for the days of its colonial splendor, when Maugham and Waugh stayed here—and for the more recent past, when the food was worthy of its surroundings. Once a private great house, San Antoine was converted into St. Lucia's first hotel in the 1920s and became the domain of English portrait painter Aubrey Davidson-Houston. Although San Antoine burned in 1970, an expatriate couple from the States parlayed the stone shell and archways that were left into one of the most romantic spots in the Caribbean. Although the current owners, a young British couple, carry on with attentive service, it's better to skip the food and go for drinks on the clifftop terrace banked by whispering trees and a vista of the sparkling lights of the harbor below.

Forget about the touristy Green Parrot Restaurant and head instead to the close by, family-run **Bon Appetite** (Tel: 452-2757). This small house with a big view is just what the Morne needs: great home cooking in a whimsically elegant setting—and a few rooms to let for the self-sufficient traveller.

Beyond Castries

Nightlife in Castries consists of predictable live entertainment and discos, but on Friday nights everyone seems to turn out north of Castries at **Gros Ilet** (by day a small, picturesque fishing village) for its street festival. With a Creole-cum-Latin beat, it's a little like Mardi Gras in New Orleans: By ten the streets are so packed you can hardly squeeze past the impromptu jam sessions, coalpot cook stands and rum carts, and "roll and tumble" gambling tables. For a bird's-eye view head to **Scott's Café**, where everyone hangs off the balcony in a merry stupor. For midnight chicken it's off to **Hector's**.

Although much ado is made of Morne Fortune (Hill of Good Luck—whose, nobody knows) as the stronghold of the ever-changing colonial powers, the more significant outpost was **Pigeon Island**, a few miles north of Castries past Gros Ilet. It was from here that Admiral Rodney sailed in pursuit of Count de Grasse, routing the French in the crucial battle of the Saints and giving the British the final edge in the West Indies. Legend has it that the island was named for the carrier pigeons Rodney bred. Now a national park, with the old naval barracks housing a rather dusty museum, it's connected by a causeway to the mainland. There is a splendid view of St. Lucia—and Martinique 20 miles to the north—from the fort ruins atop the hill.

A couple of miles south of Pigeon Island, the **Eastwinds Inn** on Labrellotte Bay, with its secluded beach and pool, draws Europeans and laid-back North Americans for its anachronistic nature. The inn has been here for ages, but a change in owners and refurbishments now make the small complex of hexagonal bungalows much more appealing.

The newer **Windjammer Landing Villa Beach Resort**, just around the bend in Labrellotte Bay, could easily swallow up little Eastwinds in its seaside sprawl. Although locals compare Windjammer to a rudderless ship, they nonetheless recommend it to visiting friends who appreciate a modicum of charm, good value, and a nod to the family. Its sun-kissed architecture, incorporating a motley blend of styles from Mykonos to Morocco and Mexico, sometimes feels claustrophobic. But most guests happily rise above Windjammer's flaws (even the tiny beach that looks like St-Tropez in August and the main pool that precludes serious swimming) for the complimentary facilities such as nightlit tennis courts and nearby golf course, water sports, and a supervised children's program—plus a microwave and cable TV in every villa.

What used to be the German-run Cariblue Hotel on the island's northern tip was recast as **Le Sport**, the ultimate all-inclusive spa resort. Not long ago they did away with both the erotic logo of Michelangelo's *David* and Botticelli's *Venus,* and also scrapped the health-farm emphasis in order to appeal to a more rounded clientele. Still, this massive place done up in brilliant Caribbean colors promises every seawater treatment imaginable, along with light French cuisine (designed by the master himself, Michel Guerard) and not-so-light for those bodies on holiday from diets, plus nearly round-the-clock entertainments. Devotees of Le Sport overlook the erratic service and uninspired guest rooms for the value-priced spa package. As well, the views from this beachside setting and the wild winds of the Atlantic here make you feel much farther away from the bustle of Castries than the scant nine-mile distance.

Martinique likes to claim Josephine Tascher de la Pagerie as its native daughter, but St. Lucia insists Napoléon's empress was born on her family's plantation at Morne Paix Bouche northeast of Castries. Although the house overlooking Marquis Valley has fallen into ruin, a visit to the working **Marquis Plantation** affords a cool and peaceful look into the past. Plans are afoot to establish a museum honoring Josephine in Soufrière, where the Taschers kept their second estate, Malmaison.

Soufrière

Getting to Soufrière can be either a sublime experience or a tribulation, depending on how you go. Avoid the tortuous roads and spend the extra money on boat passage from Castries harbor (one hour by speedboat, three by sail), which your hotel can arrange. Time and captain's flexibility permitting, stop mid-way at **Anse Jambette** (Tel: 452-3399) for lunch and a swim (closed Mondays, Thursdays, and Fridays). For a cheaper—but less serene—alternative to a private boat charter, book a one-way trip on the tall ship *Brig Unicorn,* as Prince Charles did in 1989 during his visit to commemorate St. Lucia's tenth anniversary of independence. The old wooden schooner makes a day out of cruising the coast, sightseeing in Soufrière, and lunch and punch on board, complete with steel band.

Seen from the sea, St. Lucia's immense natural beauty is almost overwhelming. When the producers of *Doctor Dolittle* were scouting Caribbean locations for Everyman's vision of a tropical paradise (but one that few had seen) they chose **Marigot Bay**, about 10 miles (16 km) south of Castries. The film crew left behind their commissary, now a popular restaurant called Dolittle's, along with memories of the late Rex Harrison's 1967 star vehicle. Long a favored anchorage among discerning yachtsmen, Marigot harbor once provided safe haven for a British fleet hiding from the French; by lashing coconut fronds to their masts, the British fooled the French into thinking their ships were just another thicket of palm trees. Skip their nondescript hotel, but if you want to charter a boat—for a day or a week—**The Moorings** operation here is the place to do it; P.O. Box 101, Castries, St. Lucia; Tel: (809) 451-4357; Fax: (809) 451-4353.

The farther south you sail, the more exotic the coast becomes, with empty, tempting beaches giving way to tiny fishing villages where children play in the surf right off the town's doorstep. Then, suddenly, the boat rounds the headland off Anse Chastanet Hotel and you realize what you came for: **the Pitons**. These volcanic spires are the most compelling sight in the Caribbean. In fact, travellers have been known to sit and stare at them for hours, so entrancing is their stark beauty.

One of the best vantage points is the hillside cluster of open-to-the-view bungalows at **Anse Chastanet Hotel**, a wonderful place for those who revel in seclusion and unpretentious but seductive surroundings. After years of mediocre food the hotel acquired some European expertise and finally hit its stride with a much-improved Creole menu and wine cellar. Except for the beach-level suites, most of the bungalows cling—along with bougainvillaea—to the hillside. The 125-step climb is a killer, but the view makes it worthwhile. Add another 75 steps to make it to the top, where new and bigger bungalow suites were built, some with startling touches such as a gommier tree soaring through the ceiling of a shower stall. This year a swimming pool is slated for the hillside. There are no phones, TVs, or room service (except breakfast), but that's the way the hotel's guests want it (indeed, many repeat customers would prefer that the road to Anse Chastanet remain in a state of disrepair to keep it that much more remote). Here you bow to nature, especially on the hotel's half-mile-long beach of fine gray sand, although daily guided hikes in the surrounding bush are now available. With plenty at hand—*bobios* (tables with sturdy thatched, wooden umbrellas for shade), a superb diving operation (with Californian instructors for beginners and experts, ample reefs and wrecks in the adjacent marine reserve, and underwater camera equipment) among other watersports facilities, an open-air bar and restaurant, and one of the best shops on St. Lucia—some guests never leave the beach until sunset (except possibly for a game on the nearby tennis courts). The more adventurous hop a boat or walk down the beach and over the rocks to the neighboring coconut plantation, where the stone buildings lie in ruins but the old overseer commands as if it were still the thriving place it was in the 19th century. (To relive the bygone era, book a stay at the old estate house, **St. Remy Villa**, on the south side of the Pitons, with its English-style gardens, rockers on the verandah, and polite staff.)

This anachronistic mode of life spills over from **Soufrière**, two miles distant and the oldest settlement on St. Lucia. A guillotine once dominated the central square on the wharf, which now serves as a gathering spot for Rastafarians, suitcase vendors, and aggressive youngsters who greet incoming yachts. The fishermen who give the town its raison d'être live in squalor just beyond the wharf, in the shadow of the Pitons, but if the town fathers have their way, the waterfront will soon complete its ongoing face-lift—with care not to sacrifice its aura. The wooden colonial buildings, some painted in vibrant colors that only could be concocted in the Caribbean, contribute to that aura, along with the courtly ways of the older townspeople, who know their big attraction is the volcano. The new jetty, tourist center, and covered crafts market with its naïve muraled façade make the cruise ships happy, but you shouldn't miss the little things here—like the church, the rum bars, and the hole-in-the-wall crafts shops. Check out **Fergie's Art Gallery**, next to the market (he did one of its murals), and keep an eye peeled for canvases of rising young painter Carmilus Calixte. Some of his work hangs in the NCB Bank and at the **Soufrière Sailing Club**—perhaps the world's only sailing club *not* on the water—in its new location at the Villa des Pitons (see below). It's really more of a bistro with rooms to let upstairs and a boat to charter down to the Grenadines. The blond German manager, once an art dealer, would set Somerset Maugham running for his pen.

If you don't mind eating lunch above the local gas station, the Sunset Restaurant serves chicken and chips and a good roti (meat and potatoes rolled West Indian style in a pancake). However, the roti war may be won by the **Sulphur Club**, the bubblegum-pink, second-story restaurant on Bridge Street. If you can stand the seediness, head for **Captain Hook's Hideaway** just off the road to Anse Chastanet for fresh tuna sandwiches made by one of Soufrière's most respected cooks (there aren't many). About half a mile up the road from here, the **Villa des Pitons**, despite its French name, offers good local cooking and a splendid view of guess what.

The "**drive-in**" volcano, over the ridge behind town, is actually a seven-acre, smoking crater: You drive up to the rim and proceed on foot with a guide (ask for Pontion, Peter, or Sly). Negotiating the sulphur beds and springs, bubbling like so many pots of pea soup, requires not only a nimble foot but a sturdy snout to withstand the rotten-egg odor. Occasionally one of the guides will bring along an egg or potato to demonstrate the volcano's cooking capacity.

The **Sulphur Springs** feed the mineral baths on the adjacent site of the **Diamond Waterfall and Botanical Garden** (part of the domain of the **Soufrière Estate**, which, with its old great house and grounds, is now open to the public). St. Lucians make an annual ritual of soaking in the hot tubs, claiming the waters take off ten years and ten pounds. This rejuvenating experience was discovered in 1784 when the French found that the water contained the same medicinal minerals as those at Aix-les-Bains. Forthwith, Louis XVI ordered construction of the baths to keep his troops fit. Although largely destroyed after the French Revolution, the baths were resurrected in 1966 and now, for a small fee, anyone may use them (bring a towel). This is definitely the place to go if you've stayed up half the night at the Hummingbird or the **Sulphur Club**—Soufrière's night spot of choice when the music is live.

On the waterfront, just off the road to Anse Chastanet, the **Hummingbird Restaurant and Beach Resort** feels like a cozy cave with its stone walls. It opens onto a fish-eye view of the Pitons and a pool set in a garden, but few come here to swim; rather they come for the rum-inspired cama-raderie, along with ceviche, curry, and Joyce's incompara-ble chocolate rum cake, not to mention shopping at the nifty adjacent boutique. Proprietress Joyce Alexander re-cently added ten guest bungalows on stilts to her enclave, overlooking a patch of gray-sand beach: Numbers three and four are favorites and a fair value if the nighttime noise level doesn't intrude. For those who prefer to look *down* on the Pitons, the once-beloved, intimate Dasheene Hotel has reopened after years of jungle taking over what the owners had left. Reconstructed, refurbished, and re-named, **Ladera** feels like a tree house perched on a leafy ridge 1,000 feet above the sea. Overlooking the pool, the not-always-open restaurant (Tel: 459-7850)—still called **Dasheene**—serves excellent fish and desserts in a friendly fashion befitting its legacy.

You can get to **Jalousie Plantation**, the new 110-acre resort nestled on a coconut-studded strip between the Pitons, most dramatically by boat (hire an ersatz water taxi in town or at Anse Chastanet). Such a glorious en-trance is just what lord of the plantation Colin Tennant intended (although a road to the site from Soufrière was completed not long ago). Known primarily as the British magus of Mustique in the nearby Grenadines, Tennant (a.k.a. Lord Glenconner) has initiated here another facet of his fantasies: a great-house hotel with clusters of cot-tages and pools smack between the Pitons, and, on the drawing board, villas à la Mustique eventually to grace the lushly quilted slopes.

For now, big spenders keep busy stalking the extraordinary array of "everything included," from daily massages and Champagne to scuba diving and midnight snacks. Here you can hop from the tennis or squash courts to the aerobics studio, the swimming pool (big as a lake), saunas and Jacuzzis, and onto the beach (chock-full of water-sports facilities), and still have room on your dance card. Which is good—because you won't want to spend much time around your cottage (unless you need TV, stereo, and radio): Generic urban-hotel decor, along with skimpy views and "get-wet" pools (more like vertical bathtubs), render the public areas that much more inviting in comparison. Tennant himself designed the Great Room, a lavish card-and-game area replete with aristocratic accoutrements and an endless verandah for sunset gazing. From there it's all downhill; the closer you get to the beach, the less formal become the restaurants and bars. Take the shuttle.

Nonetheless, with Tennant's touch (and Persian financing), the resort is sure to bring mainstream pizzazz as well as toney travellers to Soufrière (Princess Margaret heads the roster of early guests). On Jalousie's beach, Bupa—Tennant's smiling pet elephant—occasionally emerges from the bush to take a swim or to eat your camera if you didn't bring her a banana.

Special-Interest Excursions

The road to the **rain forest**, from Soufrière toward Fond St. Jacques in the interior, is often impassable due to rain. In dry weather the half-day trip stuns the senses with a riot of tree ferns and orchids cloaking the sounds of the rare St. Lucia parrot (*Amazona versicolor*)—but don't expect to see one. Your best bet is to go in late afternoon with a guide, such as Marshall Simon, who doubles as an antiques dealer at Serville's Unique Boutique off the quay in Soufrière (Tel: 459-7390). Wear sturdy shoes for this muddy, aerobic workout and bring a swimsuit. If the parrots prove elusive, you might take in a cockfight at Fond St. Jacques.

The **Maria Islands Nature Reserve**, off the southern tip of St. Lucia on the Atlantic side, has an abundant variety of nesting sea birds and endemic species of reptiles. Before you go, check with your hotel to make certain the reserve is open. (The caretaker at the reserve's office near the airport often seems to be out for lunch.) Anse Chastanet, for example, will arrange the trip, which involves an adventurous passage on an inflatable boat from Pointe Sables (at the eastern end of the runway in Vieux Fort).

Newly developed by the St. Lucia National Trust (Tel: 452-5005), the tour to the **Fregate Island Nature Reserve** on the Atlantic coast appeals to the ardent nature lover. Summer is the best time to see frigate birds (when they nest), but other birds make their homes here year-round, as does the shy boa constrictor.

A visit to **Choiseul**, the charming hamlet on the lee-ward side south of Anse Chastanet that always wins the Best-Kept Village Award, is well worth the detour off the main road. Plan to stop at the **Choiseul Art and Craft Center**, now aided by a Peace Corps volunteer, for gifts you forgot to buy elsewhere. The goods, especially those of sisal, are beautifully and earnestly made.

USEFUL FACTS

What to Wear
This is one island where ties look silly; even jackets at Les Pitons Restaurant seem out of place. Cottons are most comfortable, but shorts are frowned upon in town.

Getting In
With a swift change of planes in San Juan, American Airlines makes the trip to Hewanorra and to Vigie Airport (just outside Castries) from New York a breeze. Other carriers serving the island include BWIA (now from European as well as North American gateways), Air Canada, Balair, and British Airways. If you're island-hopping, say from Barbados or Mustique, interisland planes put down at Vigie Airport. Save about U.S. $10 for departure tax.

Entry Requirements
British, Canadian, and U.S. citizens must present a passport, voter-registration card, or other valid form of identification, as well as a return or ongoing ticket. Citizens of other countries must present a passport.

Local Time
St. Lucia is on Atlantic standard time year-round, one hour ahead of the U.S. east coast except when the east coast moves its clocks ahead an hour during daylight saving time. Then the two keep the same time.

Currency
Legal tender is the Eastern Caribbean dollar. U.S. currency is also accepted. As of this writing the rate of exchange was U.S. $1.00 to E.C. $2.67.

Electrical Current
220–230 volts, 50 cycles. U.S.- and Canadian-made appliances require converters and three-pronged (squared) adapters.

Business Hours
Shops are normally open from 8:00 A.M. to 4:30 P.M. weekdays, 8:00 A.M. to noon on Saturdays. Bank hours are 8:00 A.M. to 1:00 P.M. Monday through Thursday (some stay open until 3:00 P.M.); 8:00 A.M. to 1:00 P.M. and 3:00 to 5:00 P.M. Fridays.

Festivals
Aqua Action, a three-day event now of international stature, takes place annually in mid- to late May with competitions in all water-related sports from yachting to snorkeling. For more information contact any St. Lucia Tourist Board (see below).

Getting Around
The dilemma of whether or not to rent a car is best solved by hiring a taxi at the airport (unless your hotel arranges the transfer) and deciding after your first bout with the local roads whether or not you want to tackle them yourself. Despite recent improvements in the main road from Hewanorra Airport to Castries, it's a standard joke that while driving is on the left, there is usually no left or right, and barely a middle. The taxi drivers, among the Caribbean's most knowledgeable and polite, not only know every pothole in the road but even apologize for each one. Most drivers double as guides, but despite government-set rates taxis don't come cheap. In Soufrière ask for Alfred Augustus (Tel: 459-7577); in Castries call Alfred Anderson (Tel: 452-0527). If you rent a car (get a Jeep), plan to buy a local driver's license (about U.S. $13) and let your hotel assist in the arrangements.

For Further Information
St. Lucia Tourist Board, P.O. Box 221, Castries, St. Lucia, W.I., Tel: (809) 452-4094, Fax: (809) 453-1121; **in the U.S.**, 820 Second Avenue, 9th Floor, New York, NY 10017, Tel:

(800) 456-3984 or (212) 867-2950, Fax: (212) 370-7867; **in Canada**, 151 Bloor Street, Suite 425, Toronto, Ontario M5S 1S4, Tel: (416) 961-5606, Fax: (416) 961-4317; **in the U.K.**, 10 Kensington Court, London W8 5DL, England, Tel: (71) 937-1969, Fax: (71) 937-3611.

ACCOMMODATIONS REFERENCE

The rate ranges given here, in U.S. dollars, are projections for fall 1992 through spring 1993 and span the lowest rates in the low season to the highest in the high season. Unless otherwise indicated, rates are for double rooms, double occupancy. As rates are subject to change, it's always wise to double-check before booking. The telephone area code (within the U.S. system) for St. Lucia is 809.

▶ **Anse Chastanet Hotel.** P.O. Box 7000, Soufrière, St. Lucia, W.I. Tel: 459-7000; Fax: 459-7700; in U.S. and Canada, (800) 223-1108 or (914) 763-5526. $120–$400, E.P. In winter, M.A.P. is obligatory; at other times it's optional at $40 extra per person. Ask about their dive and "escape" packages. (They also manage some villas in the area.)

▶ **Cunard Hotel La Toc.** P.O. Box 399, Castries, St. Lucia, W.I. Tel: 452-3081; Fax: 452-1012; in U.S., Tel: (800) 222-0939; Fax: (718) 361-4176; in Canada, (800) 468-7745; in U.K., (71) 493-8181; in Australia, (02) 264-9966. $100–$299, E.P.

▶ **Cunard La Toc Suites.** See Cunard Hotel La Toc for address and telephone numbers. $190–$790 (ask about M.A.P. and all-inclusive plans). The suites on the Point are worth the higher rate for the greater privacy and dramatic setting.

▶ **Eastwinds Inn.** P.O. Box 1477, Castries, St. Lucia, W.I. Tel: 452-8212; Fax: 452-5434. $300–$340, all inclusive.

▶ **Edgewater Beach Club.** P.O. Box 962, Castries, St. Lucia, W.I. Tel: 452-4872; Fax: 452 3125. $45–$65.

▶ **Hummingbird Restaurant and Beach Resort.** Soufrière, St. Lucia, W.I. Tel: 459-7232; Fax: 459-7033. $55–$180, negotiable.

▶ **Jalousie Plantation.** Soufrière, St. Lucia, W.I. Tel: 459-7667; Fax: 459-7666; in U.S., Tel: (800) 877-3643 or, in Florida, (305) 856-5405; Fax: (305) 858-4677. $400–$600, all inclusive.

▶ **Ladera** (formerly Dasheene Hotel). Soufrière, St. Lucia, W.I. Tel and Fax: 459-7323; in U.S., Tel: (800) 633-3284; Fax: (201) 767-5510. $110–$150, including Continental breakfast, afternoon rum punches, and airport transfers (three-bedroom villas with pools also available).

▶ **Soufrière Sailing Club.** Villa des Pitons, Soufrière, St. Lucia, W.I. Tel: 459-7797; Fax: 459-7070. $75 per person, including breakfast; add $15 per person for dinner.

▶ **Le Sport.** Cariblue Beach, P.O. Box 437, St. Lucia, W.I. Tel: 450-8551; Fax: 450-0368; in U.S., (800) 544-2883. $185–$400, per person per day, includes everything (also airfare credit if you stay seven nights).

▶ **St. Remy Villa and other villa rentals.** Tropical Villas, Box 189, Castries, St. Lucia, W.I. Tel: 452-8240, Fax: 452-8089; in U.S., (800) 433-3020 or (212) 759-1025. Rates for St. Remy Villa: $1,680–$2,275 per week.

▶ **Windjammer Landing Villa Beach Resort.** Labrellotte Bay, P.O. Box 1504, Castries, St. Lucia, W.I. Tel: 452-0913; Fax: 452-9454; in U.S., (800) 243-1166. From $180 per day (one-bedroom suite) to $330 per day (two-bedroom villa with private plunge pool). M.A.P. optional; ask about weekly packages and three-bedroom villas.

BARBADOS

By Susan Farewell

Rarely does a visitor return from Barbados without mentioning the people. More than the beaches, more than the scenery, more than anything else, the Bajans— short for native-born Barbadians—are what you remember most. Very simply, they're "people people." So much so that they choose to build their houses facing the road rather than the sea, so they can watch passersby. They don't look at you, they look into you. Unlike on some islands, you're not whisked away from the airport to a walled-in tourist fortress (though you can be, if that's what you want). The Bajans are a wonderfully welcoming people and by their very nature invite visitors to join their society for a while.

Britain was considered the mother country for almost 350 years until 1966, when the umbilical cord was cut and independence declared. Today Barbados is an independent state within the Commonwealth, structured with an elected representative assembly. There are signs of England everywhere: place names like Windsor, Yorkshire, and Trafalgar Square; afternoon tea at many hotels; and cricket, the national sport. But the island's West Indian culture is—without question—dominant.

Barbados has all of the Caribbean island requisites, among them seemingly endless stretches of sloping white-sand beaches, all sorts of water sports, and tepid breezes off the sea. There are small, classic hotels hidden under clusters of palm trees and a handful of reliably good restaurants that serve spicy island dishes, fish just minutes out of the water, and frosty rum punches. And, yes, there's duty-free shopping. Added to all this there's a wonderful carnival-like spirit in Barbados. It's not uncom-

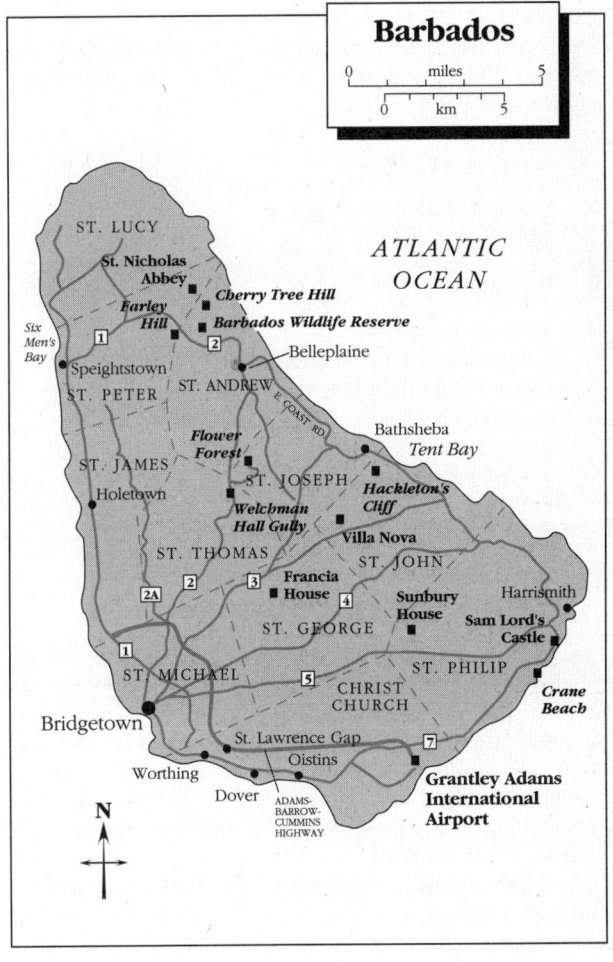

mon to see a Bajan dancing at a bus stop or, for that matter, a tourist (whether it's a sun-worshipping teenager or a middle-aged housewife). Everyone seems to join in the island's ongoing party.

What may come as an unwelcome surprise for those wanting to plop down on a beach for a week is the multitude of attractions on Barbados. You could easily fill seven days touring its old gardens and nature preserves, cave dwellings, gracious plantation houses, and other sights in between.

MAJOR INTEREST

British colonial atmosphere
West Indian culture

Bridgetown

Around the Island
The Scotland District and East Coast scenery
Barbados Wildlife Reserve
St. Nicholas Abbey
Andromeda Gardens
Sunbury House
Flower Forest
Francia House

Bridgetown

The greatest appeal of Bridgetown, the island's capital, is what isn't there. Though much-visited by tourists, it doesn't have a generic any-port-in-the-Caribbean feel about it. Streets aren't filled with duty-free shops (though there are enough); you are not constantly bothered by hawkers pushing their wares. Rather, Bridgetown is a thriving little metropolis where life goes on as usual and tourists aren't everything.

You can see all of the town in about an hour. Start in the general area of the Careenage on the harbor-side promenade, where a reincarnated warehouse now houses a couple of restaurants and shops that are popular among locals and tourists alike. For lunch try the second-floor **Fisherman's Wharf** (Tel: 436-7778). On Fridays and Sundays they spread out an exceptionally good Bajan buffet. ("Bajan" is used interchangeably with "Barbadian.") With its huddle of sidewalk tables, the **Waterfront Café** downstairs has become a magnet for passersby (Tel: 427-0093). The place provides a fine perch for watching the activity in the busy harbor while sipping a cold Banks beer or a glass of iced tea; the service, though, can be lamentable. (Most of Barbados's finer restaurants—and hotels—are outside town, along the west and south coasts.)

Trafalgar Square, across the bridge, is all the more British for its bronze statue of Lord Nelson, which, unveiled in 1815, predates London's by several decades. (Nelson was a local of sorts, as he was stationed for many years in the West Indies.) The square is surrounded by Victorian Gothic government buildings, including the House of Assembly, with its stained glass windows representing English monarchs from James I to Victoria. A block or so south is **St. Michael's Cathedral**, noted for its arched roof, which used to be the widest in the world. Amen Alley, to its side, was so named because slaves—forbidden entry into the church—listened outside, exclaiming "Amen" at the end of services. On Synagogue Lane, about a five-minute walk away, the restored **Bridgetown Synagogue**, one of the Western Hemisphere's oldest, is surrounded by graves of the island's early Jewish settlers.

Though Barbados is not known for its exceptional shopping, you will find duty-free stores (including large department stores that sell everything from plastic sandals to Hilda of Iceland sweaters) crowding around Broad Street. At the **Best of Barbados** shop, tucked away in Mall 34, you can pick up fine-quality island crafts and silk-screen prints. If you have a strong interest in local crafts, poke around the **Temple Yard District**, where a group of Rastafarians have set up shop. Steps away stands the geared-for-tourists complex called **Pelican Village**. Its shops are worth a look, especially Karl Broodhagen's painting and sculpture gallery.

Just on the edge of town, in historic Belleville (the island's most posh district, distinguished by its columnar royal palms), is the **Barbados National Trust**, modeled after the National Trusts of England and Wales. The Trust is a Victorian Barbadian house, the Ronald Tree House, furnished to look as it would have in 1893. It also has a riveting photographic display of old Barbados and churches around the island. Tel: 436-9033.

The Garrison Savannah, farther out of town, was the training ground for British soldiers stationed in Barbados during the 1600s, and is now the site of major sporting and ceremonial events. It is also the home of the **Barbados**

Museum (Tel: 427-0201), which occupies what was a British military prison back in the early 1800s and displays Arawak Indian artifacts, plantation furnishings, and an impressive collection of old maps. To one side stands the Savannah Club, a historical regimental building overwhelmed by a four-faced clock. The coat of arms of King William IV on its façade is the only one outside the United Kingdom.

After dark Bridgetown lights up like a Christmas tree, and all-night revelers emerge from their daytime slumbers. Tanned beachgoers also show up, clad in crisp whites. There are a couple of discos and clubs worth a visit, including **The Warehouse** (Tel: 436-2897) in town, **After Dark** (Tel: 435-6547) in St. Lawrence Gap, and **Harbour Lights** (Tel: 436-7225) in St. Michael, where dancers can sway under the stars to the rhythm of local bands or a top deejay (who reportedly has the best record collection on the island). Even if you're not up for the loud, pulsating sounds and strobe lights, you can't help but find yourself mesmerized watching the Barbadians dance. Try to catch a performance by Spice, the island's—and much of the Caribbean's—most popular band. Their music is a blend of calypso, soca, and reggae, and can be heard at the island's top night spots (including Harbour Lights and After Dark). For performance information, Tel: 428-2074.

Perhaps the most fascinating nighttime attraction in town is **Baxter's Road**, a little strip of inextinguishable vitality. Sometime after midnight and before dawn, all strata of society make their way to this row of rum shacks. At the northern end a quartet of feisty women vie for your attention as they prepare the catch of the day, usually dolphinfish, over wood fires.

The West Coast

The **St. James Coast**—also known as the Platinum Coast—is lined with one hotel after another, all set within feet of the water. This is the playground of the island, with every kind of water sport and bathing suit imaginable.

The **Treasure Beach Hotel**, right on the beach a couple of miles south of Holetown, is one of the island's smallest and most personally run hostelries. Owners Tony and Elaine Bowen, who took over in 1989, have indeed inherited a little treasure. A collection of suites surrounds a central courtyard verdant with lush greens and tropical blossoms. Almost all of the suites have cathedral ceilings, kitchenettes, and living rooms that open onto enormous balconies. It's necessary to reserve rooms well in advance because there are many repeat guests (mostly couples from Europe and families with older children).

Nearby **Sandy Lane Hotel** has recently undergone a major face-lift. Since opening about 30 years ago, Sandy Lane has been one of the most highly regarded hotels in Barbados. Its guest rooms are located in two- and three-story wings amid enormous mahogany and tamarind trees and meticulously maintained flower beds. All are well equipped with balconies or lanais, wet bars, cable TV, and other amenities. There's a pool, a tennis club (five courts; lighted at night), an 18-hole golf course, and a slice of the west coast beach from which guests can snorkel, water-ski, windsurf, sail, or boat.

Holetown, where the British landed in 1627 on the *Olive Blossom,* is just about halfway up the coast. An obelisk commemorates the event, but its plaque says the landing was in 1605. No matter; it's not uncommon to hear conflicting dates and facts about the history of the island. Settlers built the island's first church in Holetown. Unfortunately, both the original and, later, its replacement were washed away in hurricanes. The **St. James Church** that now stands on the site dates to 1875 and houses a bell from 1696, predating the U.S. Liberty Bell by 54 years.

Just north of Holetown is the **Sandpiper Inn,** with a marvelous South Seas atmosphere. Guests stay in one- or two-story cottages on the beach or by the pool or gardens. Several new rooms can be interconnected to make two-bedroom suites. All have kitchenettes, jalousie doors, and patios overlooking the gardens. It's a quiet spot that attracts couples of all ages.

A little farther up the coast is the **Coral Reef Club,** comprised of a former private house and cottagelike buildings that spill over 12½ acres fronting the water. All rooms are air-conditioned and have private patios or terraces. Guests here are mostly couples who want peace and quiet and the impeccable service provided by the owners—the O'Hara family—who tend to all the details. There are tennis courts and a pool on the grounds, and a restaurant that is especially delightful for breakfast, with tables right next to the water and hundreds of chirping birds.

The nearby **Colony Club** is a classic Barbados hotel with a wonderful low-key elegance and a British air. It also has the required island amenities: beach, pool, patios. Guests stay in the main house (an old planter's beach house) or in the more modern, low-lying buildings just off the beach. Its loyal guests come back year after year.

The resort at **Glitter Bay**, an old great house a bit farther north that has a series of three- and four-story buildings on 22 acres of lawns and gardens, was originally conceived as a condominium complex, so most of the accommodations are suites with kitchenettes. The coveted rooms (only five suites) are those in the Beach House, a coral-stone villa literally inches from the water. Glitter Bay is a very lively place with a split-level pool, a huge sweep of beach (and water sports galore), and two tennis courts.

Next door stands the **Royal Pavilion**, one of the island's newest hotels (it opened its doors in December 1987). All but three of its 75 rooms face the sea and all are very elegant, with pastel fabrics, light pickled-wood furniture, and exquisite marble bathrooms. There are plenty of sports (both water and terrestrial) and a satiating selection of restaurants. Cartier and Valenti boutiques, as well as other haute couture shops, surround the hotel's open-air lobby.

Cobblers Cove, the northernmost of the west coast hotels (near Speightstown), is one of the most exclusive properties on the island. Its main building, a beach house that once belonged to a planter, is now encircled by buildings housing suites with living rooms, bedrooms, baths, and kitchens that are well stocked with British teas and Bajan rums. Dining in the open-air, gable-roofed restaurant on the water's edge is first rate. During the winter months the clientele is predominantly English; the rest of the year it's mixed, with many repeat guests. Ask for a room with a sea view.

The island's second-largest town is **Speightstown**, a fishing port of old two-story wood buildings, many in the process of being renovated. Just to the north is **Six Men's Bay**, one of the last places on the island where wooden fishing boats are still made. Boat building is one of the oldest livelihoods on Barbados, and painting these boats—in crayon-bright colors—is an island art.

Whether you settle on the west coast or not, you'll undoubtedly head here for a meal in one of its restaurants. There are several commendable ones, all on the expensive side. Top of the list these days is **Raffles**, in Holetown, where the menu includes such island dishes as blackened fish, curried shrimp, and baked chicken with mango chutney (Tel: 432-1280). The nearby **La Cage aux Folles** (Tel: 424-2424) is a close second, with Creole fish soup and orange-flavored chicken. It's owned by chef Nick Hudson, who formerly ran Nick's Diner in London. The **Bagatelle Great House** (Tel: 421-6767) is a longtime favorite on Highway 2A in St. Thomas, with elegant five-course meals served amid antique furnishings. **Reid's**, on Highway 1 south of Holetown, specializes in fresh fish and lobster (make reservations at least a week in advance; Tel: 809-432-7623). Poised on a cliff over the sea also on Highway 1, north of Bridgetown is the **Carambola**, not only one of the most beautiful restaurants on the island but is one of the most highly regarded among local gourmands. Tel: 432-0832. If you just want a simple but good pub lunch or dinner, try **Nico's Champagne and Wine Bar** (Tel: 432-6386), on the beach at Holetown; it's one of two places on the island that sells wine and Champagne by the glass. The other is **The 39 Steps**, a wine bar serving snacks and light fare just south of Bridgetown. The latter really comes to life late in the evening; Tel: 427-0715.

The Scotland District

One look at the view from **Farley Hill** and you'll know why the northeastern part of Barbados is known as the Scotland District. Rugged green hills spread out before you, and the thrashing Atlantic crashes against jagged shores.

Farley Hill is the shell of an old mansion whose late-19th-century gentleman owner, Thomas Graham Briggs, entertained royalty and neighboring gentry in lavish style. You'll see the house's exquisite furnishings in buildings all over the island, including the Ronald Tree House and the Barbados Museum; they were auctioned off after a devastating fire. The government now owns and maintains the grounds and what remains of the structure.

Directly across the road the **Barbados Wildlife Reserve**, lovingly cared for by Canadian primatologist and environmentalist Jean Baulu and his wife, Suzanne. Here, all sorts of wild birds and creatures—from cockatoos and parakeets to the Barbados green monkey and South American alligators—roam freely in their natural habitat. An impressive education center, with displays of Arawak artifacts, houses an animal nursery, breeding area, and laboratory

(Tel: 422-8826). Also at the reserve, a new reforestation nature trail passes through a grotto (with wild orchid and tree ferns) in the neighboring Grenade Hall Forest.

The next stop is **St. Nicholas Abbey**, one of the two 17th-century Jacobean-style plantation houses on the island, furnished with a fine collection of 18th- and 19th-century antiques. But the real attraction here is the film that tells the story of a honeymoon trip that the owner's grandfather made on a ship from Dover to Barbados in 1934. If you continue east, you'll pass through a canopy of mahogany trees approaching Cherry Tree Hill, the customary pull-over-for-a-picture stop.

The East Coast Road follows the path of the old railroad that ran between Bridgetown and Belleplaine from 1881 to 1938, slicing through some of the island's most beautiful scenery. The surf rushes in on one side, and black-bellied sheep crowd over soft green hills on the other. Though you may pull over for a rest along the seemingly endless wide beach here, don't try to swim; the undertow is extremely dangerous.

About midway down the coast is the small fishing village of **Bathsheba**, where gigantic waves draw expert surfers from around the world. The attraction for landlubbers is the cliff-clinging **Andromeda Gardens** (Tel: 433-9261), named after the Greek maiden who was chained to a rock. The gardens are filled with exotic orchids maintained by a resident horticulturist.

The noonday buffet at the **Atlantis Hotel** (Tel: 433-9445) always attracts a knowing local crowd as well as a handful of tourist buses. Here (overlooking Tent Bay near Bathsheba) you can watch the waves roll in while you sample all sorts of Bajan specialties—pumpkin fritters, fried eggplant and plantains, eddoes, breadfruit, flying fish, dolphinfish, and turtle steak. Be careful with the seemingly innocent yellow sauce in small jars on the tables: Bajan hot sauces are wondrously flavorful but hot as lava.

The South

The parish of St. John is richly cultivated country covered with banana and sugar plantations. Its church stands at the southern edge of Hackleton's Cliff, which offers more beautiful views of the Scotland District. The crowded little churchyard has an intriguing gravestone proclaiming "here lyeth ye body of Ferdinando Paleologus, lyne of the last Christian Emperors of Greece, Churchwarden of this parish, died Oct. 1678." Nearby **Villa Nova** (Tel: 433-1524) is a magnificently preserved house that sugar baron Edmund Haynes built in 1834. In the garden are two portlandias that Queen Elizabeth II and Prince Philip planted in 1966, when they were luncheon guests of the earl and countess of Avon. Codrington Theological College, at the end of a long drive lined with royal palms, is a seminary of the Anglican community that was opened in 1745.

The coastline of St. Philip's parish has some of the island's most beautiful and least discovered beaches. The one at **Harrismith**, at the end of a long, bumpy dirt road, is carved out of the base of limestone cliffs and bookended by large boulders, sheltering it from ferocious waves and winds.

Perhaps the best-known (but somewhat overrated) attraction on the island is **Sam Lord's Castle**, an opulent, mahogany-furnished mansion in the center of what are now the grounds of a Marriott resort on the southeastern tip of the island. (The castle, a customary stop on all Barbados island tours, is worth seeing if you find yourself in the area—don't make a special trip to see it.) Sam Lord was a despicable character known for luring ships onto the nearby reefs and looting them. He was also said to have locked his wife in the cellar to collect an inheritance meant for her.

If you stay any place other than the west coast, consider **Crane Beach** in the parish of St. Philip, a simple, yet elegant hotel overlooking an astoundingly beautiful pink-sand beach. It was originally built in the 18th century as a retreat for travellers seeking the medicinal effects of the Barbadian air. Rooms have high ceilings, canopy beds, antiques, and fabulous views. The view is also magnificent from the restaurant; the food, however, is unremarkable. The hotel's out-of-the-way location is ideal if you really want to get away and relax, though there are tennis courts for the energetic.

If you are going to visit just one great house on Barbados, make it **Sunbury**, a bit inland in the parish of St. Philip. Well-versed docents lead you through every room, not just two or three that have been roped off for visitors. The original part of the house is a stately Georgian box built in 1660. Owners Sally and Nick Thomas have added a delightful restaurant in the back courtyard for coffee, a light lunch, or afternoon tea, and also added a formal restaurant where they serve plantation dinners twice a week.

Christ Church Cemetery stands on a ridge overlooking Oistins, the island's fishing center. This is the scene of the Great Coffin Mystery of 1820, in which coffins in a crypt began to rearrange themselves. Some Barbadians brush off the strange events as earthquakes, but most believe it was a divine act. If the churchyard attendant is about, ask him to take you into the Chase Vault, now empty since the coffins were ordered removed.

In St. Lawrence Gap, a little village between Worthing and Dover, you'll find three of the island's best restaurants. **Josef's** (Tel: 435-6541) is the one you hear the most about. Though it's no longer owned by its founder, Austrian chef Josef Schwaiger, who almost single-handedly introduced the island to a very sophisticated international cuisine, its new owners — Charlene and John Peterson — along with Nils Ryman, their Swedish chef, are intent on maintaining Josef's fine cuisine and reputation. By and large the menu is the same (the dolphinfish meunière continues to astound gourmands who complain about the food in the Caribbean); however, Chef Nils periodically adds new specialties, often of the seafood variety. **Witch Doctor** (Tel: 435-6581) is known for its spicy Bajan specialties and ice cream smothered with homemade rum-raisin topping. **Pisces** (Tel: 435-6564) serves unfailingly good seafood, though service can be slow.

Inland Barbados

One of the island's greatest treasures hangs above the altar of St. George Parish Church—*The Resurrection,* a painting by U.S. artist Benjamin West. (Take Highway 4 from Bridgetown.) Two other masterpieces, the work of nature, are nearby: the **Flower Forest** (Tel: 433-8152), 50 acres of well-nurtured blossoms in the parish of St. Joseph, and **Welchman Hall Gully** (Tel: 438-6671), a botanical garden filled with indigenous plants and trees on Highway 2 in St. Thomas.

The island's newest attraction, **Francia House** at Signal Station in St. George, is a traditional plantation house that is now open to the public. Inside, in addition to antique furnishings, is an impressive collection of historical West Indian and South American maps. This working plantation still harvests sugarcane and other agricultural crops. Tel: 429-0474.

USEFUL FACTS

What to Wear

Barbados dress leans toward the conservative, a result of the island's lingering Britishness. For touring, shorts or slacks for men and shorts or skirts for women are appropriate. Bathing suits are appropriate only on the beaches; there's no topless—let alone nude—sunbathing. A few hotels require jackets on Saturday nights and during the winter holiday season. It's a good idea to take along a sweater or windbreaker for cool evenings and boat rides.

Getting In

BWIA flies nonstop from New York. American Airlines flies from New York and Miami with stopovers in San Juan. Air Canada flies from Toronto. The Trump Shuttle flies from New York, with a stop in Miami. Leeward Islands Air Transport (LIAT) connects Barbados with other Caribbean islands. British Airways flies in every day (except Thursdays) from London (five days a week in summer).

Barbados's Grantley Adams International Airport is modern by Caribbean standards. The terminal was built by the Canadians and supposedly can stand five feet of snow. The only inconvenience you should anticipate is long lines for immigration when the big planes arrive. Airport taxis are abundant, right outside the door once you pass through customs. A dispatcher usually will set you up with a driver.

Entry Requirements

U.S. and Canadian citizens must have either a valid passport or birth certificate with a photo I.D. British, Australian, and New Zealand citizens need passports. All visitors must have a return or ongoing ticket. There is a departure tax of U.S. $12.50.

Local Time

Barbados is on Atlantic standard time year-round, one hour ahead of the U.S. east coast except when the east coast moves its clocks ahead an hour during daylight saving time. Then the two keep the same time.

Currency

The Barbadian dollar—the official currency—is pegged to the U.S. dollar. Most shops, hotels, and restaurants accept U.S. and Canadian bills as well as traveller's checks. As of this writing the rate of exchange was U.S. $1.00 to Bds$1.98.

Electrical Current
Same as in the U.S. and Canada—110 volts AC, 50 cycles.

Getting Around
By car. Driving is on the left side of the road. Though the roads are well kept and reasonably well marked, driving can be a bit nightmarish at times; many roads are narrow and windy and frequently clogged. Roundabouts can make the most careful driver a victim of hopeless confusion.

You can rent a MiniMoke from one of the major hotels or at rental agencies in Bridgetown. These open-air vehicles are easy to drive (all standard) and are one of the island's most economical buys. Drivers' permits, which cost U.S. $5, are arranged through rental agencies.

By taxi. Though all are unmetered, prices are uniform, so your best bet is to confirm the fare before settling in. There are some good fares for island tours. Keep in mind that some drivers have great imaginations; they love to make up stories about island characters, past and present. Those displaying the Barbados Board of Tourism (B.B.O.T.) badge have attended a two-week-long tourism seminar. (See Special Tours, below.)

By bus. There are two types of buses on Barbados, state-owned (big and blue) and privately run (yellow with a blue stripe). You can pick up either at any of the red-and-white bus stop markers along roads all around the island. Avoid the buses on Saturdays, when everyone piles in with their week's worth of groceries from the market.

Special Tours
Custom Tours conducts tours of the island customized to your liking, with elegant picnic lunches in some of the island's most beautiful settings. Cost is U.S. $25 per hour for up to four people; lunch and admission fees are extra. Contact Margaret Leacock; Tel: 425-0099. The **Barbados National Trust** leads free walking tours in various areas around the island on Sunday mornings; Tel: 426-2421 or 436-9033.

Bajan Helicopters offers panoramic tours of the island. Pilot Carroll George Morris can take up to five passengers at a time in his Bell Jet Ranger. The 20-minute Island Tour flies east from Bridgetown to Bathsheba, follows the coast north over the beaches, then heads west and south again over Farley Hill, the resorts, and cruise ships back to Bridgetown; the Island Experience Tour lasts 30 minutes and includes the whole coastline, except the far northern and southern tips. Private tours can be arranged. Prices range from U.S. $60 to $90. Call (809) 431-0069 for reservations and information.

Business Hours

Shops normally open from 8:00 A.M. to 4:00 P.M. weekdays, 8:00 A.M. to noon Saturdays. Bank hours are 8:00 A.M. to 1:00 P.M. Monday through Thursday; 8:00 A.M. to 1:00 P.M. and 3:00 to 5:30 P.M. Fridays. Museum hours are 9:00 A.M. to 6:00 P.M., Monday through Saturday.

For Further Information

Barbados Board of Tourism, P.O. Box 242, Harbour Road, St. Michael, Bridgetown, W.I., Tel: (809) 427-2623; Fax: (809) 426-4080; **in the** U.S., 800 Second Avenue, New York, NY 10017, Tel: (212) 986-6516, Fax: (212) 573-9850.

ACCOMMODATIONS REFERENCE

The rate ranges given here, in U.S. dollars, are projections for fall 1992 through spring 1993, and span the lowest rates in the low season to the highest in the high season. Unless otherwise indicated, rates are for double rooms, double occupancy. As rates are subject to change, it's always wise to double-check before booking. The telephone area code (within the U.S. system) for Barbados is 809.

▶ **Cobblers Cove.** St. Peter, Barbados, W.I. Tel: 422-2291; Fax: 422-1460; in U.S., (800) 223-6510; in Canada, (800) 424-5500; in U.K., (81) 995-8211. $180, E.P.–$795, M.A.P.

▶ **Colony Club.** St. James, Barbados, W.I. Tel: 422-2335; Fax: 422-1726; in U.S., Tel: (800) 422-1323; Fax: (203) 656-3475; in Canada, (800) 268-0424. $190–$450, M.A.P.

▶ **Coral Reef Club.** St. James Beach, Barbados, W.I. Tel: 422-2372; Fax: 422-1776; in U.S. and Canada, (800) 223-1108. $200–$575, M.A.P.

▶ **Crane Beach.** St. Philip, Barbados, W.I. Tel: 423-6220; Fax: 423-5343. $116–$380, C.P.

▶ **Glitter Bay.** St. James, Barbados, W.I. Tel: 422-5555; Fax: 422-3940; in U.S., Tel: (800) 223-9815 or (212) 545-8469; Fax: (212) 545-8467. Member Pemberton Resorts. $185–$500, E.P.

▶ **Royal Pavilion.** St. James, Barbados, W.I. Tel: 422-5555; Fax: 422-3940; in U.S. and Canada, Tel: (800) 223-9815 or (212) 545-8469; Fax: (212) 545-8467; in U.K., (81) 367-5175. Member Pemberton Resorts. $215–$515, E.P.

▶ **Sandpiper Inn.** Holetown, St. James, Barbados, W.I. Tel: 422-2372; Fax: 422-1776; in U.S. and Canada, (800) 223-1108. $133–$515, E.P.

▶ **Sandy Lane Hotel.** St. James, Barbados, W.I. Tel: 432-1311; Fax: 432-2954; in U.S., (800) 223-6800 or (212) 838-3110. $230, E.P.–$900, M.A.P.

▶ **Treasure Beach Hotel.** Payne's Bay, St. James, Barbados, W.I. Tel: 432-1346; Fax: 432-1094; in U.S., (800) 223-6510; in Canada, (800) 424-5500; in U.K., (81) 995-8211. $143–$466 (full breakfast).

ST. VINCENT AND THE GRENADINES

By Jennifer Quale

If Gauguin's search for the unfamiliar hadn't taken him to Tahiti, he might have been equally content in the Grenadines, easily the most exotic cluster of islands in the Caribbean. That they are also the least accessible, as the southernmost of the Windward Island chain, protects them from the incursion of high-rise tourism. These are islands mostly without cars, where even the dogs have character and the human characters are the stuff of Conrad novels.

Here you can do nothing at all and not feel guilty about it. While there are a few compelling "sights," the history of this archipelago can be grasped in a wink and its culture absorbed by merely adapting to the uncomplicated way of life. In the Grenadines, Mother Nature provides the luxuries—such as incomparable waters for sailing and diving, some truly deserted beaches, and sunsets that weaken the knees.

Getting to these secluded, spectacular islands, however, is rarely a fraction of the fun. The journey normally involves changing planes in Barbados (100 miles to the east) or St. Lucia for St. Vincent, which is the gateway and government seat of the Grenadines, or Union Island (see Getting In, below), depending on your final destination. You might choose to charter a sailing vessel, perhaps the best way to see all the Grenadines. Although it's possible to island-hop, spending a few days each at different re-

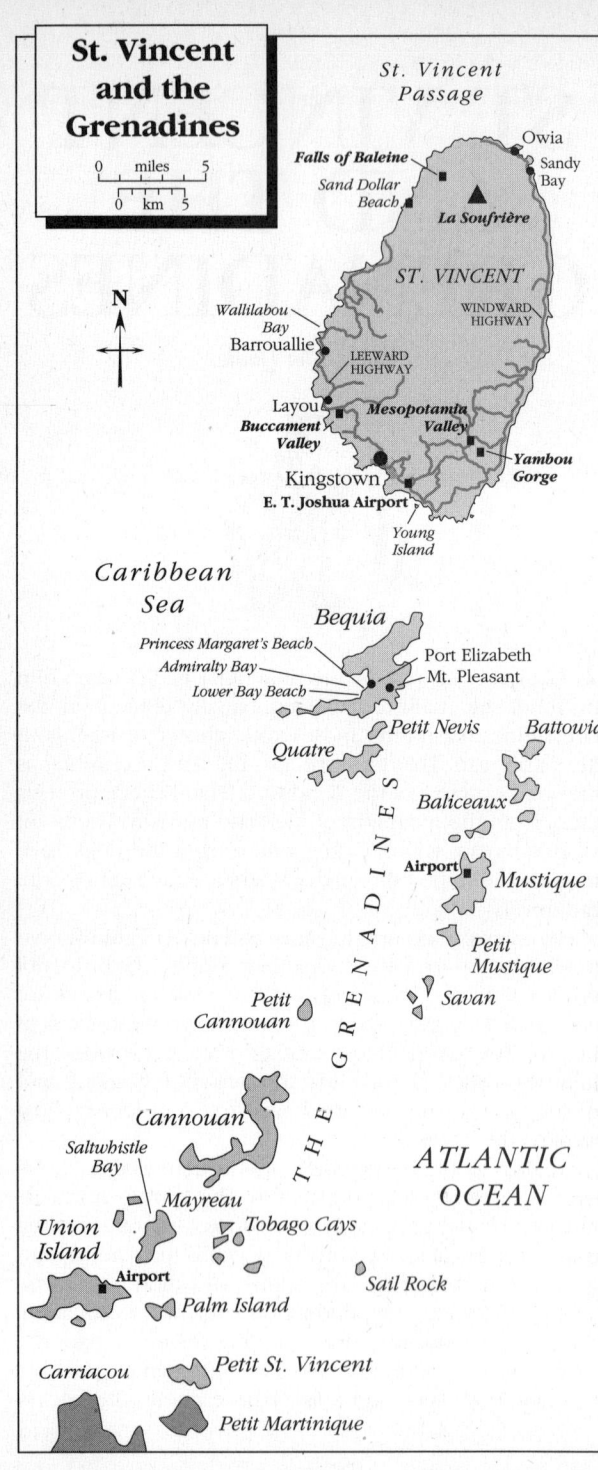

St. Vincent and the Grenadines

miles 5
km 5

N

St. Vincent Passage

Owia
Sandy Bay

Falls of Baleine
Sand Dollar Beach
▲ *La Soufrière*

ST. VINCENT

WINDWARD HIGHWAY

Wallilabou Bay
Barrouallie
LEEWARD HIGHWAY

Layou
Buccament Valley
Mesopotamia Valley

Yambou Gorge

Kingstown
E. T. Joshua Airport

Young Island

Caribbean Sea

Bequia
Princess Margaret's Beach
Admiralty Bay
Lower Bay Beach
Port Elizabeth
Mt. Pleasant

Petit Nevis
Battowia
Quatre

Baliceaux

Airport
Mustique

Petit Mustique
Savan

Petit Cannouan

Cannouan
Saltwhistle Bay
Mayreau

Tobago Cays

T H E   G R E N A D I N E S

ATLANTIC OCEAN

Union Island
Airport

Sail Rock

Palm Island

Carriacou
Petit St. Vincent

Petit Martinique

sorts, most visitors usually stay in one place and make day trips to nearby islands.

MAJOR INTEREST

St. Vincent
Little North American–style development
Kingstown
Botanic Gardens
The coastal drives
Diving
Young Island

The Grenadines
(in order south from St. Vincent)
Bequia
Mustique
Mayreau
Tobago Cays
Palm (Prune) Island
Petit St. Vincent

Imagine these 40-odd tiny islands as a stream of teardrops falling from the eye of St. Vincent—known locally as The Mainland—with Grenada as the puddle 50 miles to the south.

The 133 square miles of St. Vincent, a volcanic cone with volatile Mount Soufrière dominating its northern reaches, make few demands on visitors, except those with a botanical bent. You would not go to St. Vincent for its beaches, which on the windward side are rough and rocky and on the leeward side are mostly integral parts of the coastal villages. (The beaches of the Grenadines more than compensate.) The handful of historical venues is concentrated in the south, around the capital of Kingstown. In spite of its lush, mountainous, and often mysterious terrain, most first-time visitors bypass St. Vincent unless they are obliged to overnight en route to the Grenadines. This is unfortunate, because St. Vincent could well be the last sizable island in the Caribbean untouched, as yet, by North American–style development, reminiscent of Tahiti 25 years ago.

About a dozen of the Grenadines are inhabited. A few are privately owned, some comprising a single resort. Each hotel reflects the personality of its creator, an effect perhaps more profoundly felt in such isolated milieus. Despite significant variations in atmosphere, the resorts have much in common: They are small, with 30 units at most; informal and friendly (the first order of arrival is always a ruthless rum punch); and well equipped with tennis and water-sports facilities (diving instructors abound as well as untainted walls, wrecks, and reefs for the diver who has seen it all). The architecture is most often an extension of the environment, and cottages are built in native stone and wood. Simple furnishings combine paddle fans, rattan chairs, and rush mats—with a blessed lack of TV and telephone. Here you can throw away the room key (if they even give you one).

Most resorts can arrange a day's sailing trip to the **Tobago Cays**, the uninhabited, once-pristine group of five tiny islands protected by a horseshoe reef—and, somewhat, by the government. Almost a shrine for sailors and snorkelers, the cays have suffered in the last few years from too many cruise ships, vendors, and local fishermen's camps; with the recent removal of the last, the tiny archipelago has been declared a national park. At the moment the only cay not yet spoiled is Petit Tabac on the windward edge of the group—but you need a boat with a shallow draft to reach it. (These cays are part of the Grenadines and not, despite their name, Trinidad and Tobago.)

ST. VINCENT

The best reason to go to St. Vincent is to see the Caribbean the way it used to be, something that can be accomplished in a couple of days. There are no resorts on St. Vincent (unless you count Young Island, only 200 yards off its shore), just a handful of small West Indian hotels and guest houses.

The most sprightly of these—and a great bargain—is the **Umbrella Beach Hotel**, about ten minutes from Kingstown, on "the Strip" across from Young Island. Trimmed with a white picket fence on the shoreline, the Umbrella consists of ten units with separate dollhouse-size kitchens and porches overlooking the bay. Adventurous North Americans and Europeans love the place for its gentle nature plus the hardwood floors, ceiling fans, and armoires that recall old-style Caribbean inns. There's no restaurant in-house, although breakfast comes to your porch and the inn's proprietor also owns **The French Restaurant** next door, which serves the finest food on the island. Indeed, many locals, along with savvy visitors, usually end their day at "The French." The open-air seaside setting, combined with genial service, a Parisian chef, and the best *pommes frites* south of St. Barts, make this the most endearing restaurant in St. Vincent and the Grenadines. Tel: 458-4972. For up-to-date Antillean fare (how about smoked sailfish pizza?) walk down the strip to the **Lime 'N' Pub** (Tel: 458-4227), a green and white latticed café on the waterfront. To dance the night away, head to **Basil's Too** in the heart of the strip. Tel: 458-4205.

Kingstown

The concept of zoning, much less tourism, seems to have eluded Kingstown, but that's part of its charm. Grace and civility run neck and neck with the naïveté of the Vincentians: Even at the market—the town's heartbeat—vendors approach visitors with a Tiffany's aplomb, switching from patois to the King's English in a flash of deference. But Kingstown is changing: The Japanese, who covet the rich tuna breeding grounds off the island, are wooing St. Vincent with yen-funded buildings on the waterfront—a fish market, bus terminal, phalanx of shops. It's no coincidence that most of the cars here come from Japan.

Capturing the town's old flavor is best done by ambling along Bay Street, ducking into the Cobblestone Inn arcade for lunch at **Basil's Bar and Restaurant** (where the West Indian cuisine gives buffets a good name) or upstairs to the **Rooftop Restaurant** (Tel: 457-2713), a more reasonably priced choice among discerning locals. Shopping forays include the **St. Vincent Philatelic Society**, which produces some of the world's most impressive stamps, and the government-sponsored **Craftsmen's Centre**, housed in the old Sea Island Cotton ginnery, with finely made straw goods that they will ship. Other worthy stops, under the old Heron Hotel on Bay Street, include the **Made in de Shade** and **96° Degrees** boutiques, and the **Wayfarer Bookstore**. Scholars who want to study several architectural styles—from Moorish to Georgian—in a single building can visit **St. Mary's Catholic Cathedral**, across the street from the Anglican church.

About a mile (½ km) west of town, the **Botanic Gardens** are the oldest in the Western Hemisphere, having been established in 1765 as a quarantine for medicinal plants bound for England's Kew Gardens. The variety of tropical species here is stunning, as is the recently installed aviary sheltering precious St. Vincent parrots. Be sure to hire one of the guides, who will point out such oddities as the mimosa plant (light a match near its leaves and they fold up like an army closing ranks), as well as the gardens' most renowned tree, a spur of Captain Bligh's original breadfruit plant. The story goes that when Bligh first tried to bring breadfruit to the Caribbean on board the *Bounty*, he gave more water to the plants than he did to his crew, thus instigating the mutiny. His second voyage was more successful and, ever since, the starchy stuff has been a delicious staple in the West Indian diet. (Combined with jackfish it supplies the national Grenadine dish.)

Set among these 20 parklike acres is the last curator's home, which now houses the small, rather informal, but remarkable **Archaeological Museum**. The museum's artifacts are the legacy of Dr. Earle Kirby, St. Vincent's most respected historian and a great raconteur who leaves no stone unturned. Among his prize specimens is a bat effigy stand carved out of stone, an early Indian icon dating from the seventh century found in a fossil swamp near the airport some 15 years ago. Since the museum opens only on Saturday afternoons and Wednesday mornings, an appointment with Dr. Kirby is well worth arranging (through your hotel) if you have a serious interest.

The Black Caribs

Like most of the Caribbean, these islands were originally settled by the Arawaks, or Amerindians, who came from South America in their dugout canoes—the likes of which still ply the Grenadine waters. A few centuries later the stronger Caribs followed. What differentiated St. Vincent and the Grenadines was the evolution of the Black Carib tribe, so fiercely independent that the British (who ultimately added the islands to their empire) could never organize a sugar industry here. In 1675, when a slave vessel sank off Bequia, the Africans who swam ashore joined forces with the Caribs. For the next 200 years the Black Caribs fought the French and English to maintain possession of St. Vincent with a determination unparalleled in the Caribbean. A series of paintings poignantly depicts their struggle. Ironically, these paintings, the Lindsay Prescott collection, hang in the erstwhile officer's quarters of Fort Charlotte, the last British stronghold, on a ridge above Kingstown. Today descendants of the Black Caribs live quietly in the villages of Owia and Sandy Bay at the northern tip of the island.

Out on the Island

The coastal drives along the leeward and windward sides of St. Vincent yield stunning and often unexpected scenery. The Leeward Highway hugs steep cliffs that dip down into tiny fishing villages on the shore, among them Barrouallie, where whalers still go out in search of blackfish and small pilot whales. Near the quaint town of Layou, a huge pre-Columbian petroglyph on a riverbank attracts intrepid visitors; you would expect such a significant rock carving to be treated as a national monument, but here it's private property and the owner can be less than hospitable. Calling ahead, through your hotel or directly (Tel: 458-7243), puts Mr. Hendrickson in a receptive mood.

The wide-open windswept expanse of the windward side brings to mind the wilder reaches of Scotland's Argyle, for which part of this area is named. Indeed, the village of Escape, where cattle graze by the sea beneath the old stone church on a grassy knoll, makes for a perfect Turner landscape.

Turning inland along the Yambou Gorge brings another surprise: the **Mesopotamia Valley**, a great, fertile bowl with a froth of mist. The valley is cool enough to grow grapes along with bananas, cocoa, nutmeg, and the like.

Special-Interest Excursions

At **Buccament Valley**, 5 miles (8 km) northwest of Kingstown, the marked **Vermont Nature Trails** lead through a tropical rain forest, providing an opportunity to see in their natural habitat the protected St. Vincent parrot (*Amazona guildingii*) and whistling warbler, both endemic to the island. Chances of seeing the birds in the recently designated Parrot Reserve improve between 4:00 P.M. and dusk. Plan to spend the day, with a picnic and a swim in the Coco River at Table Rock (a spot known primarily by locals).

The **Falls of Baleine**, on the leeward side almost at the northern tip of the island, make for another day's splendid outing, especially if you hire red-bearded Texan Bill

Tewes as boat captain, dive expert, and guide. However, the falls are accessible only by boat (easily arranged through your hotel) and well-shod foot. **Sand Dollar Beach**, where the boat anchors for drinks and a swim, proves a happy exception to St. Vincent's generally uninviting beaches. Tewes's boat stops at the **Wallilabou** anchorage beach bar and restaurant for an authentic West Indian lunch.

If you really want to get away from it all (including running water, electricity, and private baths), head to the new retreat at **Petit Byahaut**, a couple of miles south of Wallilabou. For all its emphasis on oneness with nature, veggie lasagna, and queen-size bedded tents, this place puts "California Dreamin' " smack in the bush (its owners come from San Francisco). Prices seem steep considering the lack of amenities, albeit everything comes in by boat—even the guests. Try it for lunch and a dive, or a swim; they'll pick you up in town ($20 per person; Tel: 457-7008).

Because of the sudorific climate, the three-plus-mile hike up to the crater of **La Soufrière** should only be tackled by the fit. Start early in the morning.

Young Island

Although Young Island is just a few minutes' boat ride from St. Vincent (boarded across from The French Restaurant on the Strip), it's in a 35-acre world by itself. The feeling here is playful, as if the staff and guests were all suiting up for some TV sitcom about life on a resort-contained island. Even the peacocks strutting about seem preened for the dramatic setting. (But mind you, Young is environmentally correct, having just been deemed a wildlife preserve—mostly for the sake of the small population of agouti, a Caribbean cousin of the guinea pig.) You'll enter the world of Young Island with the chug-chug ride on a diesel-powered vessel reminiscent of the *African Queen*. Greetings at the dock include the customary welcome drink, proper fortification for hiking up to one of the 29 fetching, Tahitian-style cottages (beachside accommodations suit the weary, but the extra privacy and better views of the hilltop aeries are worth the hike). While every water sport imaginable is available here—as well as a rather seductive swimming pool tucked in a jungly garden and fine tennis courts (if you need a partner, try the owner)—most guests seem content to loll in a hammock on the beach or wade out to the Coconut Bar, a thatched bamboo hut secured to a raft offshore.

By twilight entertainment starts in the Captain Bligh bar, a most convivial place where patrons occasionally initiate their own jump-ups, those movable musical feasts that are so contagious in the Grenadines. Creole and Continental feasts continue in the grotto-like restaurant, where the Argentine chef garners mixed reviews (although breakfast is a consistent winner). On Thursday nights all the stops are pulled out when Vidal Browne, Young Island's sleek owner/manager, ferries his guests over to the nearby islet of Fort Duvernette for a torchlit cocktail party, complete with the Bamboo Melodians band rocking out on the rocks.

THE GRENADINES
Bequia

With its amusing cafés and boutiques, and a harbor full of foreign sailboats, Bequia (BEK-wee) casts a certain spell over its visitors, some of whom have never left. Until last spring, when the much-debated airport finally opened, the only way to get here was by boat, either on the cargo (e.g., goats) schooner that makes a round trip daily from St. Vincent or on the supply boat that services the islands (both leave from the main harbor in Kingstown); the nine-mile trip, an adventure in itself, takes about an hour and a half. If you come on your own yacht (or charter), **Admiralty Bay** makes a lovely, if sometimes crowded, anchorage. Many sailors will never forget their first night here, enchanted by Bequians who used to row out to the yachts to serenade them with songs of the islands. Now they motor out in water taxis to bring "yachties" ashore and to sell ice, coral trinkets, or whatever. Try to avoid Bequia on Thursdays, when the cruise ships anchor.

Of all the Grenadines Bequia has the most local color—there's even a boutique by that name. In fact its plethora of boutiques (and the new Bayshore Mall) has now earned Bequia the nickname "Boutique." But its history is nautical, with Yankee whalers setting its course from the 1870s. They came to hunt the humpback whale, and the generations of local fishermen that followed now include the world's last hand-harpooners, sailing out in open wooden boats as they did a century ago. The annual catch of one or two whales keeps the island's economy—as well as its spirit—going. Even when the whales aren't running you can take a cruise aboard the *Fredag,* a 50-foot wooden sailing ship that makes a day of touring and snorkeling around the whaling station on nearby Petit Nevis.

Boat building, too, is part of the Bequian tradition, from little fishing boats to major schooners, such as Bob Dylan's 68-foot *Water Pearl* (which sank in 1989 off the Panama coast). When a new boat is launched, the town of Port Elizabeth, true to its jolly nature, turns out at water's edge with sufficient rum to celebrate. In the hands of Lawson Sargeant, model-boat building has become the Grenadines' most notable art form; his replicas of some of the world's finest yachts, built from blueprints to scale, include H.M.Y. *Brittania,* commissioned for Queen Elizabeth on the occasion of her visit in 1986. Sargeant's workshop, with models in progress as well as for sale, ranks as a museum in itself.

The shoreline of **Port Elizabeth** is almost wall-to-wall cafés and boutiques—the most gratifying in the Grenadines, even though you have to walk along the beach to get to many of them, often through the water and up and down jetty walls. A few years ago a cement path was laid, making the trek more predictable but less precarious. Among the better shops are the **Crab Hole** and the **Garden Boutique**, both specializing in brilliant batiks and silkscreens, the **Wearable Art Shop**, **Noah's Arcade**, and the **Bequia Bookshop**, with its outstanding selection of books about the Caribbean, scrimshaw, and old island prints. Unfortunately, most of the best shops close for the weekend. But the good cafés stay open, such as **The Green Boley**, the **Port Hole**, and **The Old Fig Tree**. **Maryann's** draws Bequian devotees anytime for fruit-infused ice creams and sorbets, while those in the know often head over for dinner to award-winning **Daphne Cooks It** near the police station. The idea is to call ahead with your request and Daphne will cook it—or you can entrust the Creole menu to her own ample imagination. Tel: 458-3271. Long-term visitors dine frequently at **Le Petit Jardin** (Tel: 458-3318), with its New York–trained Bequian chef, tucked behind the waterfront strip. Prices may seem high for these parts and service erratic, but the food, along with its presentation, rates among the best in the Grenadines. It's just down the street from **Julie's Guest House**, a "cheap and cheerful" spot where the amenities consist mainly of mosquito nets and good home cooking.

Nobody goes to Bequia without stopping at **Mac's Pizzeria**, lauded for its lobster pizza and home-baked goods. Next door the venerable **Frangipani Hotel** serves as the island's social hub, where visiting literati and other creative types mingle with local characters and the yachting crowd. Memorable moments come from sipping drinks on the Frangi's terrace while gazing at the sea of boats in Admiralty Bay and chatting with knowledgeable strangers and kindred spirits. Politics often dominate the conversation, particularly since Bequian James "Son" Mitchell came into power as the country's prime minister and Queen Elizabeth's only privy councillor in the Caribbean. The Frangi was formerly the Mitchell family home and was operated by Son and his former wife, Pat, as a hotel for 23 years. (Longtime manager Marie Kingston carries on in the absence of Pat, who has since created the nearby **Gingerbread** complex, with a trendy, jam-packed restaurant, bar, and café, plus a few self-catering apartments and the inevitable boutique.) Despitè a lack of creature comforts (i.e., some rooms in the main house share a bath down the hall), the Frangi has always been the place to stay or eat on Bequia (unless you're on a boat), and it's a bargain to boot. The newer rooms, with private baths and sundecks, in the garden behind the main house are quieter and well worth the higher tab. The resorts on the island's other side may offer more space and tranquillity, but staying there would be missing the point of Bequia, which is to be part of a beguiling island scene. Even the most reluctant visitor can't resist joining in the jump-ups. One of the best is at **The Plantation House** (Tel: 458-3425), formerly the Sunny Caribee Hotel (Bequia's first), and once again, a geniàl place to stay. Thanks to the presence of the Italian owner, *la dolce vita* now prevails at this rebuilt inn—the only one in town with a beach, a scrap though it may be. What brings guests back: the spacious grounds, tennis and diving facilities, a fondness for families, and the superb homemade fettucini with lobster sauce.

The exception to the stay-in-town rule is the relatively new **Old Fort**, a tropical auberge flung out on Mount Pleasant, with a spectacular view of Mustique ten miles to the south. Otmar and Sonja Schaedle, German expatriates, literally unearthed the 18th-century French fort, creating a rare retreat for travellers bent on solitude and excellent food. At night the Old Fort takes on a magical air when the fireplace lights up the stone-walled den, hung with Afghanistan rugs, and makes you think you're in Morocco.

To see the rest of Bequia hire a taxi (ask for Noel, Gideon, or Curtis); a tour of the island, complete with folklore and visits to the whaling village of Paget Farms and deserted beaches, takes a couple of hours, depending on how long you linger. If you want to swim off Princess Margaret's Beach—Bequia's best—it's a short walk over the hill back into town. "Expats," as the foreign homeowners are known, usually plop on Lower Bay beach at De Reef, with facilities and a fun restaurant—or they head to **Theresa's** (Tel: 458-3802) for serious pubbing and varied ethnic cooking. If you are sailing out of Bequia to the south, keep an eye peeled for Moonhole, an extraordinary group of homes carved out of a rocky headland.

Mustique

The mystique of Mustique can be explained rather simply: It's the only privately owned island in the world where royalty and rock stars gather regularly, hiding out from the press and entertaining one another with parties that nonetheless ooze their way into the more enviable social columns. Ah, the bliss of finding a place where one's bodyguard can take the day off! Along with peace and privacy, such are the lures that bond Mustique's imposing band of homeowners.

Thirty years ago Mustique was nothing but a barren spit of 1,350 acres. Then along came Colin Tennant, the Scottish aristocrat (now Lord Glenconner), who could afford to parlay his eccentric fantasies into a utopian verity. He planted the rolling hills with a lush green carpet, brought in set designer Oliver Messel to fashion some exquisite villas, and turned the old **Cotton House** into one of the Caribbean's prettiest hotels. Its main salon, with verandahs that go on forever, was initially done up with treasures from Tennant's ancestral castle in Scotland, while each of the original 22 guest rooms is a cozy mix of English country style and West Indian touches. (The newer "presidential" suites overlooking the beach, however, seem overpriced and underdone.) The beach, recently spiffed up with shingled umbrellas, a dive shop, and gratis Windsurfers, is just a short walk away. Still, many guests prefer the pool, which is framed in Romanesque columns like some operatic stage set. The shaded poolside verandah makes a fine venue for sumptuous daily buffet lunches featuring grilled local fish, French cheeses, and water by Erté. Occasionally the feast moves to Macaroni Beach (Mustique's finest).

As a wedding present Tennant gave Princess Margaret a piece of Mustique (on which her uncle Oliver built a Neo-Georgian villa), thus setting the precedent for membership in his unofficial club. There's no roster per se, just a natty six-page telephone book with listings like "Jagger, Mick," and "Lichfield, Lord."

Things have changed since the 1980s: Tennant sold his interest in the Mustique Company to Venezuelan capitalists, and anyone can stay, for a price, at Princess Margaret's Les Jolies Eaux, one of 40 privately owned rentable villas. Billy Mitchell, one of Mustique's first landowners, opened up "Firefly" (**Firefly House**), her four-bedroom hilltop home, to guests seeking lovely but low-key and low-cost accommodations. Thus Billy's motto: "You don't have to be rich and famous to enjoy Mustique." Still, although references are no longer required, the unheralded visitor might feel a bit on the outs in season.

To remedy such holiday insecurities, head for the rendezvous of choice in the Grenadines—**Basil's Bar and Raft Restaurant**. Basil Charles, the flamboyant Vincentian, brings Mustique's regulars and the uninitiated together under his thatched roof for barracuda sandwiches, barbecued whatever, and inimitable jump-ups on Wednesday nights. Ever the entrepreneur, Basil also offers all manner of water sports, island tours, and even a Balinese boutique that (along with the new glow-in-the-dark pink and purple boutiques, **Muskito** and **Treasure II**, just opposite Basil's Plaza) makes shopping on Mustique a pleasant, if pricey, diversion.

Mayreau

At first blush Mayreau appears to be a humble island with a church on its goat-nibbled hilltop, a ho-hum village on one side, and a magnificent horseshoe beach on the other. Then you discover the **Saltwhistle Bay Club**, a magical enclave set in a sea-grape and palm grove fringing the beach. Like extra-virgin olive oil, this tiny inn captures that first pure essence of the Grenadines, enhancing nature's stage with its deceptively simple aura. (For instance, the absence of tennis is by the Canadian

owner's design, because the pong-whap of balls would
disturb the ineffable peace.) What may prove too rustic
for some yields a Robinson Crusoe dream for others—
it's the sort of place where you wonder why you brought
any luggage, where the nearest telephone, until recently,
was an island away. With Mayreau's new phone system
and jacks to be hooked up in the bungalows, communica-
tion with the outside world soon should be there for the
asking. (For now, a boat phone suffices.) The dream
begins from the moment the skipper fetches guests from
the airstrip on nearby Union Island and sails literally into
the sunset to Mayreau. Chances are they never leave,
unless to explore the **Tobago Cays**, a half-hour's sail or
cruise from Saltwhistle. Even the mere 20-minute hike
over the hill to **Dennis's Hideaway** for lunch seems tantamount to a major expedition. At night most of the
guests—from James Taylor to burned-out executives and
royal who-hahs—thank the stars there's nothing to do
but make their way through the wooded, sandy garden to
the beachside bar and the intimate dining tables, made of
stone and roofed with thatch, that could serve in a tropical Camelot.

Palm Island (Prune Island)

A dozen years ago Palm Island had a barefoot, carefree
atmosphere much like that of Mayreau. And then came
the mammoth cruise ships, making Palm a regular port of
call. Since then **Palm Island Beach Club**, the island resort
that the legendary "Coconut Johnny" built from scratch,
has changed, its once homey feeling giving way to a
camplike bustle. The chief attraction is John Caldwell
himself, who (if you haven't read his book, *Desperate
Voyage*) will recount how he sailed around the world
until he landed here a quarter of a century ago, planting
thousands of palms and leasing the island for 99 years. He
then set about building a dozen duplex bungalows with
patios along the dazzling but now eroding white beach,
as well as tennis courts, an open-air bar, and restaurant
pavilions. As John puts it, guests (who run the gamut from
cornrow-braided tourists to Ringo Starr) come here to
"hang loose." In 1989 John started a quasi-health club,
added TV and video to the game room, and camouflaged
a satellite dish among a clump of palms. To encourage
exercise he laid out "Highway 90," named for longevity

and cutting a one-and-a-half-mile path around the island. He also got rid of his short-term partner and brought home his sons to help take Palm Island out of the mainstream: That is, he's promised to prune Palm of its cruise-ship day-trippers. But it's a painstaking process, with the Windjammer *Mandalay, Yankee Clipper,* and the *Sea Cloud* still coming to shore. To accommodate the day-trippers (including those on private boats), John has built a holding pen dubbed The Yacht Club near the main dock. With its own boutique, bar, and restaurant, the enclave should help ensure the privacy of the hotel guests on the palmier side of Palm. What's next? Maybe a spa. Stay tuned.

Petit St. Vincent

PSV, as this private island is known, ranks among the Caribbean's top resorts (with prices to match) because its owner, Haze Richardson, keeps an eye on every detail. Even getting here is relatively worry-free, since the Stateside reservationist also books connecting flights and alerts PSV's cruiser to pick up guests at Union Island, 30 minutes away. Run with the efficiency of a big-city hotel and the grace of West Indian hospitality, **Petit St. Vincent Resort** puts Herman Wouk's *Don't Stop the Carnival* to shame: Indeed, where else in the tropics can you order, at the hoist of a room-service flag, an egg boiled to the minute of choice, and see it delivered to your suite as fast as the MiniMoke can ferry it? Perfection such as this rarely prevails in such remote ends of the earth—which is what PSV feels like, except for all the improbable amenities (for instance, Julia Child's Cambridge, Massachusetts, butcher provides the meat for PSV's bountiful table). The older, repeat clientele like to think of PSV as their country club in the sun, while the younger, cosmopolitan set mostly work on their tans and bar bills. A few strike out for the day on one of the house yachts—to Grenada, Carriacou, Mustique, or the Cays; some give the tennis courts a shot, the jogging trail a run, or dabble in water sports. Serious anglers venture out with Captain Chester on the powerful *Jahash;* whatever they catch, Slick the chef will gladly cook.

What they all have in common is a desire to get away from everything but pampering. PSV is so private that a guest could easily pass the day without seeing anyone in the seclusion of a hilltop or beachside cottage or at one

of the hammock-studded beaches for two that rim the
island—or on Petit St. Richardson, a whimsically named
islet in the middle of nowhere, a saucer of sand with
nothing but a beckoning shade of thatch. Those who
prefer rubbing elbows with their 40-odd fellow guests
can take in the weekly buffet luncheon on the beach or
match wits with their host at a drinks party in Haze's
hilltop home. Come early evening most of the guests,
along with a few chic yachtsmen, gather at the cliffside
main pavilion, perhaps to the tune of fishermen by day,
musicians by night. Garbo-types who nab cottage number 18—among the most romantic retreats *anywhere*—
and succumb to room service may never even see the
dining pavilions.

USEFUL FACTS

What to Wear
Bug repellent. Unless you're Princess Margaret's Mus-
tique houseguest, leave the major jewels at home; ditto,
ties for men. At Saltwhistle Bay even shoes are optional.
White pants make the ideal base for evening attire in the
Grenadines.

Getting In
International airlines that serve Barbados and St. Lucia
include American, BWIA, British Airways, and Air Canada.
The most reliable, hassle-free way to get to St. Vincent,
Mustique, or Union from Barbados is on Mustique Air-
ways, which operates daily flights in and out of Barbados
and is available for charter at surprisingly modest fares.
Tel: (809) 458-4380; in the U.S., c/o Anchor Reservations,
Tel: (800) 526-4789; in New Jersey, Tel: (201) 569-5464.
Some hotels will arrange the air charter and meet their
guests at one of these airports. Martinique is now an
alternative gateway to the Grenadines. Air Martinique and
LIAT also offer interisland service.

As a way station **Union Island** is sort of fun—full of
Europeans in eternal transit, boats, a café pungent with
Gauloise cigarettes and espresso. But you wouldn't want
to stay there, especially now that the airstrip and terminal
are undergoing expansion. If you get stuck on Union at
lunchtime, head to the **Sunny Grenadines** restaurant (try
the callaloo soup with aioli).

Entry Requirements
Valid passports required for all except nationals of Canada, the U.K., and the U.S. who hold proof of identity and whose stay will not exceed 6 months.

Local Time
St. Vincent and the Grenadines are on Atlantic standard time year-round, one hour ahead of the U.S. east coast except when the east coast moves its clocks ahead an hour during daylight saving time. Then all keep the same time.

Currency
Eastern Caribbean, or E.C., dollars depict a windsurfer in one corner. U.S. dollars are generally accepted, although usually you'll get a slightly better rate if you pay in E.C. currency. As of this writing the rate of exchange was U.S. $1.00 to E.C. $2.67.

Electrical Current
Mostly 220 volts; U.S.- and Canadian-made appliances may require converters. Bring a three-pronged (squared) adaptor plug.

Getting Around
Except for St. Vincent and Bequia (the latter has a few taxis), and the Jeeps on Mustique, there are no cars. Renting one on St. Vincent, along with buying a local driver's license, is hardly worth the trouble for a short period; taxis, with government-set rates, are plentiful and the drivers are courteous (they open doors and wish you "all the best"). A 10-percent tip is customary.

To island-hop, contact Mustique Airways (see Getting In, above) or Grenadine Tours (see Sailing the Islands, below). For one-way passage from Bequia to Mustique (U.S. $80), contact "The Kingfisher" Donovan Ollivierre, taxi driver with speedboat; Tel: (809) 458-3462.

Sailing the Islands
In some Caribbean waters sailing has become so popular that it's more like playing bumper boats; not so here, where you can occasionally find an anchorage all to yourself. The most reliable charter company in St. Vincent is Barefoot Yacht Charter, Box 39, St. Vincent, W.I.; Tel: (809) 456-9526; in the U.S., Tel: (800) 677-3195. Or you may prefer to charter out of St. Lucia, 22 miles north (a day's sail) of St. Vincent, in which case, contact The Moorings,

USA, Inc., 19345 U.S. 19 North, Suite 402, Clearwater, FL
34624; Tel: (800) 535-7289; in Florida, Tel: (813) 535-1446.
For a fee The Moorings will pick up the boat in the Grenadines (to avoid your having to sail it back to St. Lucia). Day
trips to the Tobago Cays or other islands can be easily
arranged through your hotel or through Grenadine Tours;
Tel: (809) 458-4818; in the U.S., c/o Anchor Reservations
(see Getting In, above).

Diving
Bill Tewes, father of diving in these parts, operates Dive
St. Vincent across from Young Island; Tel: (809) 457-4714.
Dive packages are available through Anchor Reservations
(see Getting In, above).

Business Hours
Lunch is strictly observed between noon and 1:00 P.M.
Everything shuts down at 4:00 P.M. Monday through Friday
and at noon on Saturdays (except for some hotel boutiques). Banks close at noon, except on Fridays when they
reopen from 3:00 to 5:00 P.M.

Festivals
Carnival, a.k.a. Vincy Mas (for "Masquerade"), lasts for 10
days in late June and early July, a change from the traditional winter Mardi Gras date. Also, Bequia Easter Regatta.

For Further Information
St. Vincent and the Grenadines Department of Tourism,
Administrative Centre, P.O. Box 834, Kingstown, St. Vincent and the Grenadines, W.I., Tel: (809) 457-1502, Fax:
(809) 456-2610; **in the U.S.,** 801 Second Avenue, 21st
Floor, New York, NY 10017, Tel: (800) 729-1726 or (212)
687-4981, Fax: (212) 949-5946; **in Canada,** Suite 504, 100
University Avenue, Toronto, Ontario M5J 1V6, Tel: (416)
971-9666, Fax: (416) 971-9667; **in the U.K.,** 10 Kensington
Court, London W8 5DL, England, Tel: (71) 937-6570, Fax:
(71) 937-3611.

ACCOMMODATIONS REFERENCE
*The rate ranges given here, in U.S. dollars, are projections
for fall 1992 through spring 1993, and span the lowest
rates in the low season to the highest in the high season.
Unless otherwise indicated, rates are for double rooms,
double occupancy. As rates are subject to change, it's
always wise to double-check before booking. The tele-*

phone area code (within the U.S. system) for St. Vincent and the Grenadines is 809.

▶ **Cotton House.** Box 349, Mustique, St. Vincent and the Grenadines, W.I. Tel and Fax: 456-4777; in U.S. and Canada, (800) 223-1108 or, in New York, (914) 763-5526; in U.K., (45) 383-5801. $260–$730, A.P.; ask about special weekly packages.

▶ **Firefly House.** P.O. Box 349, Mustique, St. Vincent and the Grenadines, W.I. Tel: 458-4621. $70–$85 with breakfast.

▶ **Frangipani Hotel.** Bequia, St. Vincent, W.I. Tel: 458-3255; Fax: 458-3824. $40–$120.

▶ **Julie's Guest House.** P.O. Box 12, Port Elizabeth, Bequia, St. Vincent and the Grenadines, W.I. Tel: 458-3304; Fax: 458-3812. $52 (no kidding), M.A.P.

▶ **Old Fort.** Mt. Pleasant, Bequia, St. Vincent and the Grenadines, W.I. Tel: 458-3440; Fax: 458-3824. $100–$130, (M.A.P. optional, $70 per couple extra).

▶ **Palm Island Beach Club.** St. Vincent and the Grenadines, W.I. Tel: 458-8824; Fax: 458-8804; in U.S., (800) 776-PALM; in Canada, (301) 309-1698. $210–$320, A.P.

▶ **Petit St. Vincent Resort.** The Grenadines, St. Vincent, W.I. Tel: 458-8801; Fax: 458-8428; in U.S., (800) 654-9326 or, in Ohio, (513) 242-1333 (collect); in U.K., (800) 181-123. Closed September and October. $430–$680, A.P. No credit cards.

▶ **The Plantation House Hotel.** P.O. Box 16, Admiralty Bay, Bequia, St. Vincent and the Grenadines, W.I. Tel: 458-3425; Fax: 458-3612; in U.S. and Canada, (800) 223-9832, or, in New York, (212) 599-8280. $180–$325, M.A.P.; ask about special packages.

▶ **Saltwhistle Bay Club.** Mayreau, St. Vincent and the Grenadines, W.I. Tel: 493-9609; in U.S., (800) 263-2780; in Canada, (613) 634-1963 (collect); Fax: (613) 384-6300. Closed September and October. $270–$420, M.A.P.

▶ **Umbrella Beach Hotel.** P.O. Box 530, St. Vincent, W.I. Tel: 458-4651. $48.

▶ **Young Island.** P.O. Box 211, St. Vincent, W.I. Tel: 458-4826; Fax: 457-4567; in U.S. and Canada, (800) 223-1108 or, in New York, (914) 763-5526; in U.K., (45) 383-5801. $240–$550, M.A.P.; ask about "Stay and Sail" programs.

▶ For staffed **villa rentals** on Mustique (each comes with a vehicle) contact The Mustique Co., Ltd. Tel: 458-4621; Fax: 456-4565; in U.S., Tel: (800) 225-4255 or (212) 696-4566; Fax: (212) 689-1598. Weekly rates for two- to six-bedroom villas range from $2,500 to $15,000.

GRENADA

By Julie Wilson

Grenada, just 100 miles off the Venezuelan coast, is one of the lushest of the Caribbean islands. It is the "Isle of Spice," and of fruits, vegetables, flowers—anything that grows. Throw a seed on the ground, say the Grenadians, and it sprouts. Instantly, it seems. The mountains are covered with a tropical green so intense it can almost be felt. The scent of spice rides on the merest breeze and clings to the skin like perfume.

In addition to this fecundity Grenada (greh-NAY-dah) has the allure of a dramatic past that was once a painful present. In this case it's the "past" of October 1983, when the U.S. 82nd Airborne swarmed onto the 120-square-mile island after the assassination of Prime Minister Maurice Bishop. Whatever the rest of the world thinks about "the Intervention," the Grenadians consider it a blessing, pointing out rusting remains of Cuban trucks and planes with a combination of pride and reflection.

Despite its past troubles and the gradual rebuilding of its economy, Grenada is neither dispirited nor depressing. The Grenadians are optimistic, gutsy, polite, warm, and generous. They are also independent. Don't expect big resorts with international staffs or branches of duty-free department stores. Nearly all hotels and businesses are locally owned, small, and personal—in an unmistakably Grenadian way.

The combination of sensibility, sensuality, and history makes Grenada a pleasantly unsettling island—conducive to sudden romance or a previously unsuspected interest in poetry. Or maybe it's just all that spice in the air.

Grenada is actually a three-island nation. The other members are Carriacou and Petit Martinique. The major

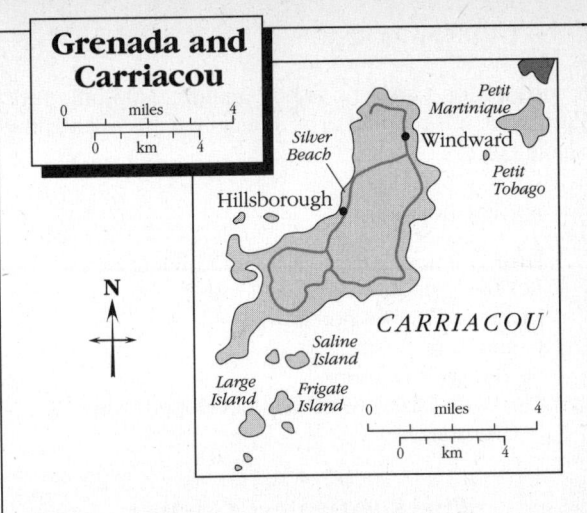

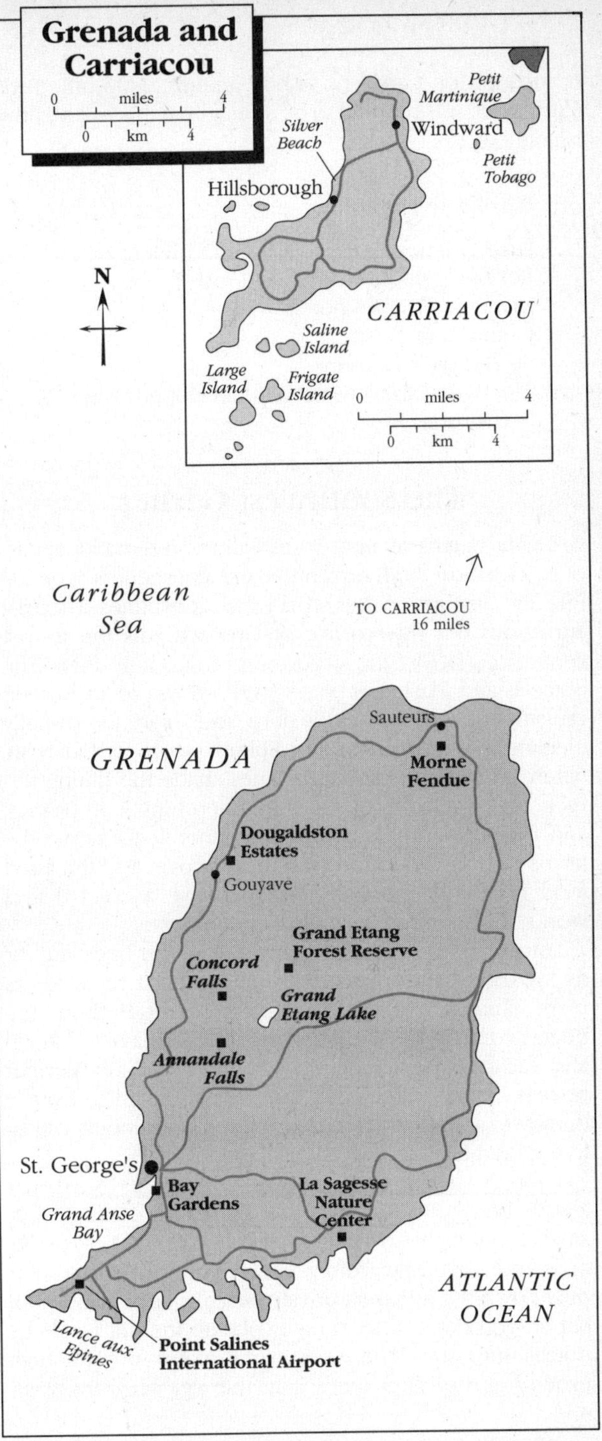

Grenada and Carriacou

0 — miles — 4

0 — km — 4

N

Silver Beach

Petit Martinique

Windward

Petit Tobago

Hillsborough

CARRIACOU

Saline Island

Large Island

Frigate Island

0 — miles — 4

0 — km — 4

Caribbean Sea

TO CARRIACOU
16 miles

GRENADA

Sauteurs

Morne Fendue

Dougaldston Estates

Gouyave

Grand Etang Forest Reserve

Concord Falls

Grand Etang Lake

Annandale Falls

St. George's

Bay Gardens

La Sagesse Nature Center

Grand Anse Bay

ATLANTIC OCEAN

Lance aux Epines

Point Salines International Airport

occupation on Carriacou is boat building. On little Petit Martinique it is reputed to be smuggling; this is a wealthy island.

MAJOR INTEREST

Lush greenery—especially Grand Etang Forest
Relatively undeveloped for tourism
Lance aux Epines hotels
Grand Anse Beach
St. George's Harbour
Carriacou Island (even less developed than
    Grenada)

The Southwest Corner

Grenada begins at new Point Salines International Airport, a focus of the Intervention and, consequently, one of the few airports in the world that constitutes a tourist attraction. But this corner of Grenada was the tourist center long before the airport was built, and it still is. The Spice Island Marine Services (well known to yachtsmen cruising the Grenadines) is here, and so are the casually elegant hotels of **Lance aux Epines**—such as **Calabash**, where flowering thunbergia vines shade the dining terrace, high-walled pool suites are the ultimate in privacy, and the scent of ylang-ylang blossoms floats across the lawns right down to the quiet beach cove. Add the good food here into the mix, and you have a hotel that is wonderfully, quintessentially Grenadian.

Long known for its mahogany four-poster beds and for its sybaritic bathrooms (tiled tubs set next to windows overlooking Mount Hartman Bay), **Secret Harbour** has been acquired by The Moorings, a Florida-based hotel and yacht charter company, as one of its Club Mariner resorts. Eager sailors can take off in anything from a dinghy to a 43-foot yacht; determined landlubbers can sit in the tiled tubs and watch other people sail.

Though it's not even a hotel, **12 Degrees North** has always been one of Lance aux Epines's treasures. Very small (only eight apartments), it's one of the best places on earth to get away from whatever you wish. Just a short hike down the hill are a private beach, a pool, and a pool bar so you don't have to hike back up the hill for some nourishing rum. There's a tennis court on the high ground as well, but that's it in the way of distractions.

Each apartment has its own deck and its own maid who slips in to prepare your breakfast in the morning. If you like, she'll even make dinner.

On a deserted beach not far from the airport, **La Source** is scheduled to open this season. The first major hotel to be built in nearly 20 years, it has 102 rooms, excellent spa facilities (one of the owners is also involved in St. Lucia's spa resort, Le Sport) and a nine-hole mashie course.

Also down in the southwest corner is the blinding-white two-mile **Grand Anse Beach**. Students from the St. George's School of Medicine jog daily along the beach, in front of the excellent hotels that seem to have been dropped like coconuts behind the strand. On the breezy dining terrace at **Spice Island Inn** an international clutch of guests watch the joggers over cups of breakfast coffee, then walk a few steps from their cottage to the beach or retire to the seclusion of a pool suite. The 56-room hotel presents whirlpool baths in all rooms, a lighted tennis court, and a spectacular Wednesday-night buffet starring suckling pig. Across the road **Blue Horizons** consists of comfortable cottages dotted around a hillside, together with one of Grenada's best restaurants, **La Belle Creole**. Co-owner Arnold Hopkin oversees the kitchen, serving such memorable dishes as callaloo and chicken mousse or sautéed lobster in a Creole sauce—Grenadian cooking with a sophisticated edge. Guests of Blue Horizons have use of Spice's water sports and (for a small fee) tennis court.

Not far from "Blue," the casual Green Flash Restaurant (Tel: 444-4646) at Siesta Hotel is a good "light meal" restaurant. (Not an elfin exhibitionist, the "green flash" is a meteorological phenomenon that streaks across the horizon at sunset.) The blackboard menu includes such simple offerings as guacamole and just-fried taco chips, curried chicken, and—thanks to the Syrian owners— some Eastern Mediterranean dishes. Up the hill tiny (13 tables) **Canboulay** has been Grenada's most exciting restaurant since it opened its door in January 1991. Owners Erik and Gina-Lee Johnson flavor traditional Caribbean dishes with a touch of Thailand, a dash of Africa, a pinch of Paris. Save room for desserts—coconut crème brûlée, chocolate and orange mousse with whipped cream and nutmeg, or "Grenadian Frivolities." Tel: 444-4401.

Back on Grand Anse Beach, the **Ramada Renaissance** is Grenada's biggest hotel (all 186 rooms of it). Despite its international affiliation, this Ramada is perfectly

Grenadian in atmosphere: Its two stories nestle under tall palm trees, the staff genuinely cares if you're having a nice day, and this may be the only chain hotel in the world suitable for liming—a West Indian expression meaning "just kind of hanging out and relaxing." The beach out front is headquarters for **Dive Grenada** (Tel: 444-4371), an easygoing organization that has all kinds of splashy equipment, day sails, and irregularly scheduled sunset cruises. Newest of the Grand Anse hotels, **Coyaba Beach Hotel** (*coyaba* is the Arawak word for "heaven") is locally built, owned, and operated. Engagingly enthusiastic, it draws an active crowd who willingly sacrifice luxury (the rooms are fairly small and dark) for tennis, water sports, volleyball—and that heavenly beach.

At the end of the beach the **Flamboyant Hotel** has inexpensive hillside rooms, all overlooking the water. Flamboyant's terrace is *the* place for a "sundowner," while watching boats and pelicans heading for a harbor, and for spotting—if you're lucky—the green flash.

Mama's, a laughably underpriced restaurant that epitomizes Grenadian cooking, is on the road to St. George's from the southwest corner, not far from Grenada Yacht Services. The decor—best described as "clean"—isn't much, but the food is unadulterated West Indian, and this is one of the very few places in the West Indies to find it. For years Mama was known for cooking the same things as any other Grenadian housewife—she just served them all at the same meal. Her daughters (and sons, nieces, nephews, and grandchildren) carry on the generous tradition. Therefore, you can count on about 24 dishes, including callaloo soup (made from the dark green leaves of the dasheen plant), stewed armadillo, baked turtle, breadfruit salad, curried chicken, and soursop ice cream. Tel: 440-1459.

St. George's

St. George's is so intent on being functional that it has remained ingenuously unaware that it is one of the prettiest harbor towns in the world. Steep hills and narrow roads (where wide drainage ditches make crossing the street a vaulting experience) climb from the curved lagoon; in the harbor interisland vessels, working skiffs, and a few transport ships engage in man-powered loading and unloading. A few cruise ships and moored yachts add photogenic sophistication. The Carenage, promenade that skirts the harbor, accommodates as many pedestrians as cars—and nothing moves very fast.

An oddly urban vehicular tunnel built in the 1800s connects the Carenage side of St. George's to the market side. On Saturday mornings every farmer, fruit grower, maker of straw hats, and spice dryer in the area comes to market and spreads his or her wares across wooden stalls or on the courtyard cobblestones. One vendor makes rotis, another stirs a fragrant oil-down (a local stew), and the smell of cinnamon and clove hangs in the air. On the other six days of the week the **Marketing and National Importing Board** on Young Street stocks produce and spices—along with a fine selection of hot sauces, nutmeg syrup, guava jam, and honey cookies fresh from the kitchens of local housewives.

In the nonedible department, **Tikal** on Young Street is top choice for Grenadian crafts—calabash bowls, woven handbags, and the ubiquitous spice baskets. Owner Jeanne Fisher found attractive wall hangings and batik patterns in South America and encouraged local artisans to copy them. Techniques mastered, the inventive Grenadians have taken off with designs of their own, which are even more colorful, and less studied, than the originals; Tel: 440-2310. Around the corner **Yellow Poui Art Galleries** features primitive paintings by Canute Caliste (Carriacou's 80-year-old Grandpa Moses) and works by other Caribbean artists; Tel: 440-3001. **Spice Island Perfumes**, on the Carenage, carries locally produced lotions, scents, and body oils, along with batik fabrics, hand-painted tee-shirts, and—yes—spices; Tel: 440-2006.

Grenada's **National Museum**, behind the thick walls of a onetime prison, is what you might call a "hands-on museum"—that is, it contains anything the curators could get their hands on. On display is stuff as varied as farm implements, Amerindian artifacts, early telephones, and Empress Josephine's bathtub. The most popular section is the one that describes, through yellowed news clippings and 8×10 glossies, the Bishop years and the Intervention. Tel: 440-3725.

St. George's is a little short in the haute cuisine department, but that's part of its unpretentious charm. And you can still eat very well indeed. On the **Nutmeg**'s second-floor porch over the Carenage you can have a curry-

flavored roti or a plate of really good fried chicken and a
Carib beer while watching the harbor activities. Tel: 440-
2539. Nearby **Rudolf's** lends a Central European touch to
St. George's, with beer-hall wooden tables and goulash
on the menu. Rudolf also serves gazpacho, stuffed crab
backs, local fish, and a rum punch strong enough to have
anesthetized all of the Hapsburgs. Tel: 440-2241. For one
of those exotic tropical drinks plus a view, **Delicious
Landing** is right down on the water's edge—so close to
those harbor activities you can count the bilge pumps.

If these restaurants had existed in 1961 they would
have had a fine view of the cruise ship *Bianca C.* burning
and sinking in the harbor. Subsequently towed off shore,
the *Bianca C.* is now one of the Caribbean's best "wreck
dives," and all water-sports centers on the island offer
trips to the site.

The West Coast

The sleepy pose of the town of Gouyave (pronounced
"guave"), just north of St. George's, masks furious activity
in the Nutmeg Station cooperative. Amid the drying,
crushing, and grading, women sort nutmegs with light-
ning-fast skill. Nutmegs—along with the mace that clings
to the shells—are Grenada's major exports; 15 minutes
in the station will go a long way toward explaining the
island in a nutshell. At Dougaldston Estates, a banana and
spice plantation up in the nearby hills, women scrape
mace off nutmeg shells in a low-ceilinged barn. They will
pause willingly from this task to describe the bay leaves,
nutmeg fruits, cinnamon, allspice, and cocoa beans—
other Grenadian export items—laid out on a display
table.

Several of Grenada's new bootstrap-economy indus-
tries are also up in the hills above the west coast. North of
St. George's (in what is known locally as the St. Paul's
area), Dunstain and Yvette Holder at **Funtime Products**
(Tel: 440-4771) bottle Sea Moss, a healthful local drink
reputed to be a mild aphrodisiac. "It can move mountains," they say modestly, "but it can't wake the dead."
Nearby, La Grenade Liqueur has been produced by the
same family—using a 200-year-old unwritten recipe—for
a number of years. They also make nutmeg jams, jellies,
and syrup. Tel: 440-3241.

The North Coast

In the 17th century a number of Indians threw themselves to their deaths off the cliff at Sauteurs rather than surrender to the invading French. Today Carib's Leap is overgrown and apparently not as high.

Morne Fendue, a well-maintained plantation house set among well-maintained gardens inland from Sauteurs, is a uniquely personal visitor attraction. Owner Betty Mascoll's living room is cluttered with family photographs and framed press clippings, and her buffet lunches (by reservation only, Tel: 442-9330) are memorable. Her specialties include callaloo soup, pepper pot, and island-vegetable casseroles. Shine, the shy bartender, makes a bold, nutmeg-flavored rum punch and a refreshing lime drink he calls "the Marilyn."

From Morne Fendue swing down the east coast to the **River Antoine** (pronounced "an-twine") **Rum Distillery**. Since 1705 it has produced a rough spirit that could fell a National Football League defensive team with a sip, or defrost a refrigerator in one-half hour. Though replacement parts are obviously difficult to come by, the distillery is still fully functional, operating much as it did nearly three centuries ago. The informal guided tours are interesting (just pick up every third word of the local patois), and a one-quart bottle purchased at the source should make about 3,000 rum punches. Tel: 442-7109.

Grand Etang Forest Reserve

The mountain range in Grenada's center virtually explodes with lushness and fertility. On a hill overlooking Grand Etang Lake (the crater of an extinct volcano), the new national park unit has established a visitor center/interpretive building. The park has cut trails and opened up a wilderness that was formerly accessible only to serious hikers equipped with machetes, pitons, crampons, croutons, and who knows what else.

West of Grand Etang Lake, the pretty 40-foot waterfall at **Annandale** (not exactly Iguassu, but pretty) is surrounded by exotic plants, thickly foliaged trees, and elephant ears that Dumbo would covet. Guides from the welcome center will tell you all there is to know about the medicinal uses of these leaves and roots. At **Bay Gardens**, about 20 minutes to the southwest, trails wend through three acres dense with every fruit, flower, tree, and bush that grows in Grenada. Most are labeled, and knowledgeable guides will identify the rest. Accustomed to nature's lavishness, Grenadians may wonder why visitors are so astounded by it all, but they're pleased by the astonishment and delighted to share all they know about all they grow.

Part of the Grand Etang (but best accessible from the west coast road), **Concord Falls** is well worth the 45-minute, stream-crossing, sometimes slippery, uphill hike. Your reward at the top is cold, pure water tumbling down through a narrow cleft in the rock and into a boulder-formed pool. It is surely what God had in mind at the first thought of water.

Down on the south coast **La Sagesse Nature Center** is another recent effort to preserve and protect Grenada's natural blessings. Explanatory leaflets are available at the guest house or the little beach bar, and lots of trails amble along the shore and inland. Along with nature's bounty, the property includes the ruins of an old rum distillery and a stone foundation, all that remains of the island's first European settlement.

Carriacou

Surrounded by tiny islands, 13-square-mile Carriacou (CARRY-a-koo) is the largest of the Grenadines. This hilly island, a 17-minute plane ride from Point Salines International Airport, is like Grenada but much drier. It is so undeveloped that the sound of a car horn heralds a plane's arrival, warning drivers off the airstrip/road.

Hillsborough, where 18th-century stone-and-shingle buildings hug the narrow roads, is the only town of any consequence on the island—the only town at all, in fact. The settlement of Windward, across the island, harbors aspirations of town status. Right now, Windward is the boat-building center, and local craftsmen construct wooden schooners, scratching the plans in beach sand as they go along.

Not far from Hillsborough, Silver Beach Cottages has recently become **Silver Beach Hotel** by adding a new building with nine rooms upstairs (seven of which overlook the water) and a ground floor entirely devoted to an open-air bar and dining room. It's owned by the Bullen family (an entrepreneurial tribe who own a number of small businesses on both islands) and well managed by Judy Bullen. A young woman of great charm and capability, Judy Bullen could, one suspects, probably handle the entire merchandising department of Bloomingdale's in her spare time. If she suggests conch steak for lunch or dinner, forget every negative thing you ever thought about conch and give it a try. Dipped in herbs and egg batter and sautéed quickly, it tastes like veal with flavor. Follow that with warm bananas with brown sugar, butter, and Jack Iron Rum—one of the island's "slightly overproof" potables. Occasionally Silver Beach presents the Big Drum Ceremony, featuring African tribal dances.

Silver Beach has the island's first on-the-premises dive center, German-run **Dive Paradise**, with excellent instructors and equipment. The 30 dive sites in the immediate area are still relatively virgin territory, unspoiled by previous generations of careless divers. For those who like to make fish-watching a tankless experience, Dive Paradise also rents snorkeling masks and flippers. Fax only: 443-7165.

To escape the fervor of mainland Carriacou, take a red and yellow motor boat from Hillsborough for **Sandy Island.** No more than two clumps of palms and sea grapes connected by a sandbar, this isolated paradise has reefs for snorkeling, a beach for swimming, and shade for napping.

USEFUL FACTS

What to Wear
Conservative sportswear. No jackets required.

Getting In
BWIA flies direct daily from Miami and New York. British Air flies once a week from London. American Airlines has daily flights from San Juan. The best connection is through Barbados via Leeward Islands Air Transport (LIAT), which has several flights a day to Point Salines.

Entry Requirements
Passports required. U.S. and Canadian citizens may substitute two proofs of citizenship (birth certificate, expired passport, driver's license), one with a photograph. There is a departure tax of U.S. $10.

Local Time
Grenada is on Atlantic standard time year-round, one hour ahead of the U.S. east coast except when the east coast moves its clocks ahead an hour during daylight saving time. Then the two keep the same time.

Currency
Eastern Caribbean dollar; U.S. currency is widely accepted. As of this writing the rate of exchange was U.S. $1.00 to E.C. $2.67.

Electrical Current
220/240 volts, 50 cycles; U.S.- and Canadian-made appliances require converters.

Getting Around
Don't rent a car. The new roads are good, but most roads you'll encounter are twisting, unmarked, paved goat paths. Depend on taxis, tour services, or local buses. If you do rent a car, you will need a valid license and U.S. $22 for a local permit—another reason *not* to rent. Driving is on the left.

Business Hours
Monday through Friday, 8:00 to 11:45 A.M. and 1:00 to 3:45 P.M.; Saturdays, 8:00 to 11:45 A.M.

Festivals
Carnival begins the second Monday in August.

For Further Information
Grenada Board of Tourism, The Carenage, P.O. Box 293, St. George's, Grenada, W.I., Tel: (809) 440-2001, 2279, or 3377, Fax: (809) 440-6637; **in the U.S.,** 820 Second Avenue, Suite 900D, New York, NY 10017, Tel: (800) 927-9554 or (212) 687-9554, Fax: (212) 573-9731; **in Canada,** 439 University Avenue, Suite 820, Toronto, Canada M5G 1Y8, Tel: (416) 595-1339, Fax: (416) 595-8278; **in the U.K.,** 1 Collingham Gardens, Earls Court, London SW5 0HW, England, Tel: (71) 370-5164 or 5165.

ACCOMMODATIONS REFERENCE
The rate ranges given here, in U.S. dollars, are projections for fall 1992 through spring 1993, and span the lowest rates in the low season to the highest in the high season. Unless otherwise indicated, rates are for double rooms,

double occupancy. As rates are subject to change, it's always wise to double-check before booking. The telephone area code (within the U.S. system) for Grenada is 809.

▶ **Blue Horizons Cottage Hotel.** P.O. Box 41, St. George's, Grenada, W.I., Tel: 444-4316 or 4592; Fax: 444-2815; in U.S. and Canada, (800) 223-9815 or (212) 545-8469. $80–$135, E.P.

▶ **Calabash.** P.O. Box 382, St. George's, Grenada, W.I. Tel: 444-4334; Fax: 444-4804; in U.S. and Canada, Tel: (800) 223-9815 or (212) 545-8469; Fax: (212) 545-8467; in U.K., (244) 341-084. $190, B.P.–$320, M.A.P.; pool suites, $280, B.P.–$430, M.A.P.

▶ **Coyaba Beach Hotel.** P.O. Box 336, St. George's, Grenada, W.I. Tel: 444-4129; Fax: 444-4808; in U.S. and Canada, Tel: (800) 223-9815 or (212) 545-8469; Fax: (212) 545-8467. $90–$150, E.P.

▶ **Flamboyant Hotel.** P.O. Box 214, St. George's, Grenada, W.I. Tel: 444-4247 or 1463; Fax: 444-1234; in U.S. and Canada, Tel: (800) 223-9815 or (212) 545-8469; Fax: (212) 545-8467; in U.K., (62) 847-7088. $70–$95, E.P.

▶ **Ramada Renaissance.** P.O. Box 441, St. George's, Grenada, W.I. Tel: 444-4371; Fax: 444-4800; in U.S., (800) 2-RAMADA; in U.K., (71) 235-5264. $100–$183, E.P.

▶ **Secret Harbour.** P.O. Box 11, St. George's, Grenada, W.I. Tel: 444-4548 or 4439; in U.S., (800) 334-2435 or (813) 535-1446. $120–$208, E.P.

▶ **Silver Beach Hotel.** Carriacou, Grenada, W.I. Tel: 443-7337; Fax: 443-7165; in U.S. and Canada, Tel: (800) 223-9815 or (212) 545-8469; Fax: (212) 545-8467. $65–$95, E.P.

▶ **La Source.** For rates and opening date, Tel: (809) 450-0119.

▶ **Spice Island Inn.** P.O. Box 6, St. George's, Grenada, W.I. Tel: 444-4423; Fax: 444-4807; in U.S. and Canada, Tel: (800) 223-9815 or (212) 545-8469; Fax: (212) 545-8467. $235–$295, M.A.P.; pool suites, $295–$420, M.A.P.

▶ **12 Degrees North.** P.O. Box 241, St. George's, Grenada, W.I. Tel and Fax: 444-4580; in U.S. and Canada, Tel: (800) 223-9815 or (212) 545-8469; Fax: (212) 545-8467. $115–$150, E.P.

TRINIDAD AND TOBAGO

By Daisann McLane

Daisann McLane's articles about Caribbean culture, food, and music frequently appear in Vogue, *the* New York Times, *the* Village Voice, Caribbean Travel and Life, *and* Rolling Stone, *for which she is a columnist. Under the name of Lady Complainer, she spent several years singing calypso in Trinidad.*

A great genetic experiment." That's how one traveller described Trinidad when passing through in the fifties. There are few places in the world where so many different kinds of people have mixed and mingled their blood, their ways, and their cultures. This "mix" is Trinidad's main attraction, and what sets this nation of a million people apart from other Caribbean islands.

Trinidad's intriguing culture does not easily reduce to a 3 × 5 postcard, or to a one-week package getaway; this island, a Connecticut-size rectangle just seven miles off the Venezuelan coast, takes time—at least two weeks, if possible. The petroleum-rich nation is off the beaten track, and hasn't been that interested, until recently, in developing its tourism industry. Here you won't run into busloads of pink-skinned vacationers—far from it. You will be surrounded by amiable Trinidadians. The island attracts travellers, not tourists, intrigued to learn more about its unique cuisine and culture, and its celebrated

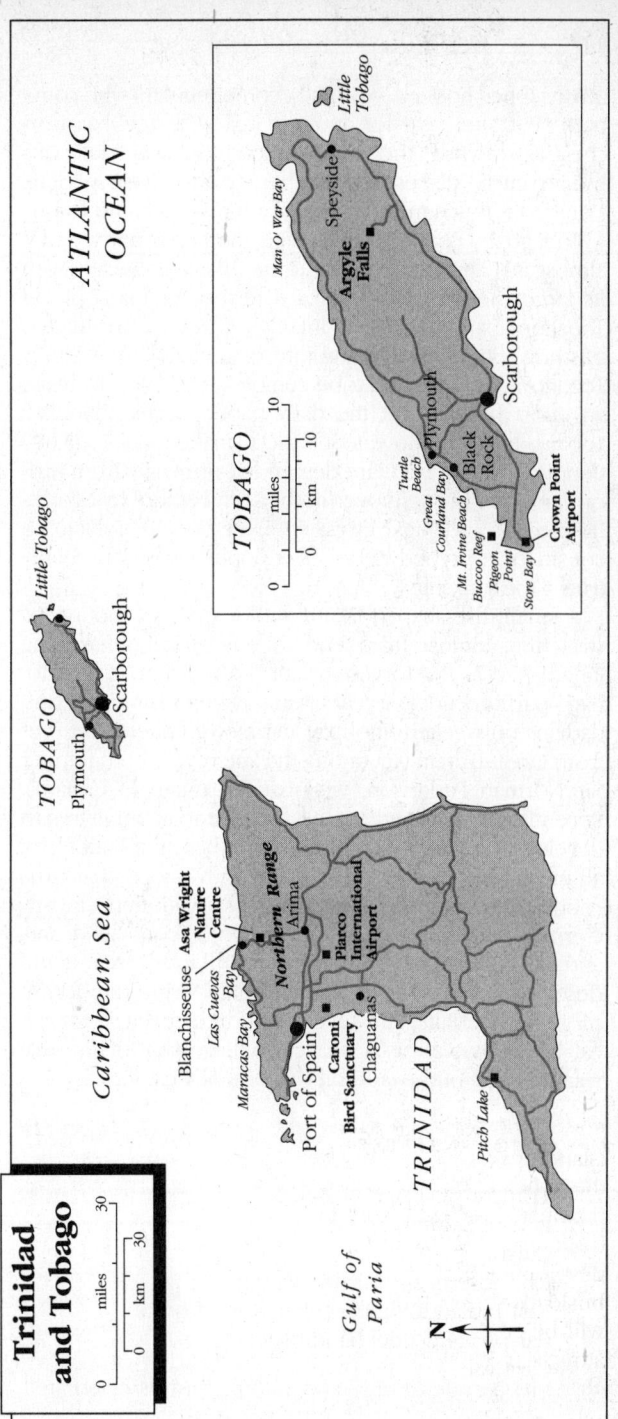

Trinidad and Tobago

ATLANTIC OCEAN

Caribbean Sea

TOBAGO
Little Tobago
Plymouth
Scarborough

TOBAGO

Little Tobago
Man O' War Bay
Speyside
Argyle Falls
Scarborough
Plymouth
Black Rock
Turtle Beach
Great Courland Bay
Mt. Irvine Beach
Buccoo Reef
Pigeon Point
Store Bay
Crown Point Airport

miles 10
km 10

Gulf of Paria

Blanchisseuse
Las Cuevas Bay
Asa Wright Nature Centre
Northern Range
Arima
Maracas Bay
Piarco International Airport
Port of Spain
Caroni Bird Sanctuary
Chaguanas
TRINIDAD
Pitch Lake

N

miles 30
km 30

music. Once hooked, visitors become regulars who come back year after year for another "fix"—of steel-band orchestras, calypso, the world-famous Carnival, delicious Indian curry dishes, the exuberant and lively people. Trinidad is much more than a vacation: It's a compulsion.

Tobago, by contrast, seems like another country, and it almost is. (The island chose to link itself politically with its larger neighbor in 1888, a date that for many proud Tobagonians still lives in infamy.) Whereas Trinidad is bustling with highways, nightlife, businesses, and people, Tobago is tranquil and a bit remote—you have to make an effort here to get the daily paper. Unlike Trinidad, Tobago has a homogeneous racial makeup. The 45,000 people who live here are descended primarily from African laborers brought over in the 18th century by Scotch-Irish cocoa and sugar growers. "Everybody in Tobago's a cousin of everybody else" is a popular—and probably true—local saying.

A small, fish-shaped island with a spine of mountains stretching almost from end to end, Tobago has long languished as the forgotten half of the Trinidad and Tobago partnership. For years it was visited mainly by Trinidadians on weekend holiday and by well-heeled retirees from Great Britain (including the late royal photographer Sir Norman Parkinson, who had an estate in Castara). Recently the government has been encouraging resort development, and Tobago currently boasts a handful of all-inclusive beach hotels, each with more than 100 rooms. However, the latest influx of vacationers (mostly German and Italian) has been a gentle, controlled one, and hasn't disrupted Tobago much. Still intact are miles of deserted beaches, acres upon acres of virgin rain forest, magical waterfalls, and several hundred species of tropical birds, as well as a peaceful village way of life that retains some of the cultural richness of West Africa.

MAJOR INTEREST

Trinidad
Port of Spain
Cuisine
Rain forests and bird-watching
East Indian temples, culture, and festivals
Calypso and steel-band music
Carnival

Tobago
Get-away-from-it-all atmosphere
African culture
Diving, snorkeling, and Buccoo Reef
Rain-forest trails and bird-watching

TRINIDAD

History and geography account for Trinidad's unique flavor. Located at the very end of the chain of eastern Caribbean islands, Trinidad sits in the mouth of Venezuela's Orinoco river, part of what was once a peninsula linked to the South American mainland (Trinidad's flora and fauna resemble that of the Amazon rain forest). Trinidad's relative remoteness from the prized centers of New World treasure made it uninteresting to colonizers; for hundreds of years it remained a West Indian backwater, never aggressively exploited by the European powers. Plantation slavery didn't reach the level of intensity it did in islands like Barbados or Jamaica. Nor was slavery a way of life in Trinidad for very long compared to other places in the West Indies. As a result, Trinidad's Africans have held on to much of their African heritage. The Yoruba religion—called Shango—remains a potent force on the island to this day.

Columbus passed by Trinidad on his third voyage in 1498, naming it "the Trinity" after a trio of mountains he spotted on the south coast, before moving on. For the next 300 years Trinidad slept. The Spaniards who followed Columbus were more interested in the quantities of gold they imagined lay beyond in South America than in this small island; they killed off most of the native Arawak Indians and established a rough outpost where Port of Spain now stands, but never developed it into more than a settlement.

In 1787, when the Spaniards opened up the island to outside settlers, French planters came with their slaves, and the pace of Trinidad began to pick up. Among other things, the French introduced Carnival to the island, a custom that was quickly adopted and imitated by their African slaves. The French built plantation houses in the country and laid in crops of cocoa, coffee, and sugarcane.

The population swelled. Ten years later British troops captured the island, and in 1803 Trinidad officially became British when the Spanish ceded it in the Treaty of Amiens.

The Africans deserted the plantations after the passing of the Emancipation Act in 1834, an action that left the British with a dilemma. They wanted to develop sugar as the island's main crop, but they had no one to work the plantations. So they recruited nearly 150,000 East Indians as indentured laborers to come and work the cane fields covering Trinidad's vast central plain. Most of the workers stayed on the island after their contracts expired and settled on small farms. Today more than half of the Trinidad population can trace some or all of its roots to India.

PORT OF SPAIN

Brash, sassy, hopped-up, uncompromising, quirky, street-sharp, a jumble of faces and races from Africa to India, China to Lebanon, Port of Spain isn't anything like what you imagine as a picture-postcard Caribbean town. Instead of the usual dreamy village of palm trees nestled by a turquoise bay there's a Third World urban confusion of concrete and corrugated iron sprawling alongside a hazy, pea-green gulf. (The waterfront on the Gulf of Paria is not visible from the city streets and accessible only with difficulty; Port of Spain is a seaport that turns its back on the sea.) Much as it may be lacking in obvious charms, however, Port of Spain is a fascinating, complex, culturally rich metropolis.

An hour or two spent wandering along **Frederick Street**, the main downtown shopping area, is a good way to get into the swing of Port of Spain. Here, vendors line the sidewalks offering newspapers, small take-away snacks, fresh bananas (called figs here), and orange pawpaws the size of footballs. Listen and watch and you'll begin to notice the African rhythm of the city: in the flourish with which the ice cream seller hands his wares to a small child; in the casual grace of the slender fellow leaning against the wall by the rum shop; in the cadence of the market woman's voice as she haggles with a customer over the price of a *sapodilla* (the furry brown fruit with flesh like a spoonful of cinnamon sugar); in the pulse of the *soca* music blasting from the storefronts. The **Frederick Street Mall** souklike is a warren of little shops

tucked into a vacant lot smack in the middle of downtown. Here, young businessmen hawk everything from
fresh spices to clothes, from classic old calypso records to
delicious vegetarian lunches. Across the street is
Woodford Square, Trinidad's own Hyde Park. At lunchtime speakers of all persuasions mount soapboxes and
hold forth to crowds of curious listeners (this is how the
political career of Trinidad's most distinguished states-
man, the late Eric Williams, got started).

By five in the afternoon downtown is dead, and the
action moves a half mile north to the **Queen's Park Savannah**, a grand stretch of open green and racetrack that is
Port of Spain's Central Park. Walking and jogging around
the Savannah's perimeter at dusk is a favorite Port of
Spain ritual (go when there's a crowd, not alone after
dark). Those looking to lose excess poundage, however,
will be daunted by the line of food vendors along the
western end; the *phuloorie* (scrumptious deep-fried balls
of chick-pea batter served in a hot mango sauce) will
tempt even the strong-willed.

Along the western end of the Savannah you'll encounter Port of Spain's grandest architecture, a string of turn-
of-the-century buildings known as the "Magnificent
Seven." Beginning with **Queen's Royal College**, a rose-
colored Rococo Georgian fantasy with clock tower (and
the top boys' academy in the nation), the Seven line the
Savannah like old, slightly wacky dowagers, architecturally so eclectic—full of turrets and gingerbread and
gargoyles—they're almost comical.

Two roads lead north from the Savannah, up steep hills
and into Port of Spain's most well-to-do and gracious
suburbs, **Maraval** and **St. Anns**. Most visitors to Port of
Spain choose to stay in one of the hotels or guest houses
in these two quiet, garden-filled neighborhoods, away
from the hot, flat downtown area but within easy cabbing
or walking distance from all the action. Because Trinidad
traditionally has drawn tourists only at Carnival time, the
top-end hotels here are geared to business travellers and
may disappoint if you're used to the luxurious resort-type
places commonly found in other Caribbean cities. With
that in mind, you may find the home-style warmth, delicious local breakfasts, and personal attention of a guest
house like **Monique's**, in Maraval, a better holiday value
than a room in one of the large chain hotels.

The **Trinidad Hilton** is without a doubt the best of Port
of Spain's upscale accommodations, located just at the

base of the St. Ann's Road, with a grand hillside view of the city and the harbor beyond. The Hilton's advantage—besides hot and cold water, good phone service, and tennis facilities—is that it functions as an important social meeting ground for Port of Spain's business class. Stay here and you'll bump into the most interesting people in town by the poolside or at the **Aviary** bar, with its sweeping view of the city. (Try an elegant nightcap of the local rum punch, garnished with freshly grated nutmeg.)

Following the St. Ann's Road you'll come to **Hotel Normandie**, smaller and more intimate than the Hilton but a similar level of comfort. Its 53 rooms open to a garden patio and swimming pool, and the hotel adjoins a tiny shopping mall of crafts shops, art galleries, and restaurants, including Port of Spain's best Italian, **Il Giardiano**. Farther up the hill the charming **Alicia's House**, a 13-room guest house in a converted private home covered with vines and flowers, seems to be clinging for dear life to the side of the hill. Up still another steep offshoot (Carib Way) of the St. Ann's Road you'll find the restaurant **Wazo Deyzeel** (Tel: 623-0115), a secret hideway for a group of lively young Trinidadians in the arts and theater. Specialities include nouvelle versions of local Creole dishes and the view: At night Port of Spain looks like a carpet of twinkling rhinestones from this vantage point.

No matter where you stay, a stroll through **Woodbrook**, located west and south of the Savannah, is a pleasant way to spend the cool early evening. A district of old white wooden houses with steep, red-iron corrugated roofs and intricately latticed eaves, Woodbrook is home to Trinidad's most "in" restaurant, **Veni Mange**, at 13 Lucknow Street (lunches only). Two beautiful sisters, Alyson Hennessey and Rose Hezekiah, preside over Creole feasts of *accra* (fried fish fritters), *callaloo* (a sort of spinach and crab soup), and fresh fish. Because Alyson is a popular local TV hostess, the crowd here is hip and media oriented; anything important going on in Port of Spain can be gleaned during a visit to Veni Mange.

Continuing west along the Western Main Road out of Woodbrook, you'll run into **St. James**, a neighborhood made famous by its former resident, writer V.S. Naipaul (his first book, *Miguel Street,* was set here). A polyglot neighborhood of East Indians and Africans, St. James is known to locals as "The City That Never Sleeps." At just about any hour of the day or night, even when the rest of

Trinidad is shut down, you can come here to "lime" (Trinidadian for "hang out") and eat.

To visit Trinidad without tasting the endless varieties of local cuisine, the most eclectic in all the Caribbean, is like going to Italy on a diet. Take-away is the Trinidadian passion. You'll find all the local cuisines, from Chinese to Indian to Creole, available in the clean, well-run spots by the roadside in St. James. The street vendors and small shop owners here sell some of the best *roti* (curried meat, vegetable, or shrimp sandwiches wrapped in flat Indian bread) on the island; few locals, however, can agree whether **Dolly's** (she's on the south side of Western Main Road) or **Molly's** (across the street on the north) is the best. For a more formal eating experience, **Seabelle** at 27 Murcurapo Road (Tel: 622-3594), a St. James favorite, serves fresh fish marinated in local herbs, grilled or fried, and accompanied by Trinidad's searing-hot pepper sauce (the stuffed crab here is spicy and delicious).

St. James stays open all night because plenty of Trinidadians demand roti at dawn. Port of Spain's nightlife tends to stagger into the following morning, especially, but not exclusively, around Carnival time. The hub of the action is not casinos (there's no legalized gambling in Trinidad) or tourist discos, but giant, outdoor parties with live soca bands (rock groups with brass instruments playing dance versions of calypso). The parties, called "fêtes," can be held anywhere, anytime, but some of the most popular venues include the **Queen's Park Cricket Oval** in St. James and **Soca Village**, a massive fenced-off field across the street from the Holiday Inn downtown. The well-written daily newspapers, *Trinidad Express* and *Trinidad Guardian,* are the best guides to the fête scene (watch for the large ads). An important part of Trinidad life, fêtes are attended by Trinidadians of all races, ages, and classes—you need not worry about wandering into an uncomfortable scene, but if there's a doubt, ask your host or hotel concierge.

OUT ON THE ISLAND

Because of the government's lack of interest in tourism, Trinidad remains a sanctuary of unspoiled wonders, both natural and cultural. There are few "organized" attractions here, but time, serendipity, and an easygoing manner will pay off in extraordinary experiences and vistas. Local contacts, from your guest-house host to the new friends you've met at the fête, are your best introduction to this hidden Trinidad. Rent a car, buy a map (sold in the Hilton pharmacy), and head out in any direction from Port of Spain.

North and East

No, Trinidad's beaches are not the best in the Caribbean. But not a single big resort hotel clutters its empty miles of coastline. As you drive through a cathedral of palm trees on a near-deserted road, you will be alone with the wind, the roar and tumble of the ocean, and the staccato songs of a thousand different birds.

Trinidadians' favorite beach is **Maracas Bay**, located a dramatic 20-minute drive on Saddle Road (which becomes North Coast Road) from Port of Spain. To get there you ascend to the crest of Trinidad's Northern Range on a twisty but well-paved road built by the U.S. Army in the 1940s. These mountains, which extend the full length of Trinidad's north, are covered with virgin rain forest. Depending on the season, the green forest-covered hillsides will be dotted with a rainbow of white, yellow, or flame-orange sprays of *poui* and immortelle blossoms. Fresh springs cascade from the rocky mountainsides. You'll want to drive slowly and stop often, as every winding turn opens into another fabulous vista of jungle and water. At the crest of the range the road opens into a parking area overlooking the splendid, horseshoe bay below.

Maracas is a social beach; Trinidadians come here to see and be seen, to frolic in the surf (be careful, it can be rough), play soccer in the sand, and eat "shark and hops" fish sandwiches spiced with pepper sauce and ketchup. If this isn't your idea of a day at the beach, continue along the coastal road to the next cove, **Las Cuevas**, for undisturbed sand and sea. Or better yet, keep going about another mile until you reach Blanchisseuse, a tiny fishing village on the north coast. **Surf's Country Inn** here is a not-yet-discovered jewel of a restaurant set on a hillside overlooking the pounding Atlantic. Shimmy down a trail to swim from a private beach while you wait for lunch (maybe huge red snappers smothered in a delicious, peppery coriander sauce) served on an outdoor terrace.

Blanchisseuse is the end of the coastal road; from here you must either retrace your route through Maracas—or continue south for one of the most spectacular, albeit difficult, drives in all of Trinidad (allow an hour and a half). This road, even narrower and more twisting than the previous one, threads precariously through a narrow gorge in the Northern Range and endless rain forest. Sometimes the forest, thickly carpeted with enormous ferns and lush with flowers like the bright red *balisier,* seems to swallow you up in shadow; then, suddenly, you break through the hills into a sunny opening that allows a view of the immense valley a thousand feet below. About halfway through the forest you'll come upon the **Asa Wright Nature Centre**, mecca of international bird-watchers (Trinidad is home to rare species, including the nocturnal oilbird, found nowhere else in the world). The simple but comfortable 22-room hotel here is a popular stop on the international birding circuit, and even for nonbirders Asa Wright deserves a look. A short stroll through this dark, almost spooky antiques-laden 18th-century plantation house will take you back in time to the days of Trinidad's colonial past.

As you may discover for yourself, even during the dry season (December to May) it rains often in the rain forest. In fact, the town you'll come into as you exit the forest, **Arima**, means "rain" in the language of Trinidad's first inhabitants, the Arawaks. In Arima traces of Trinidad's indigenous people endure; to get a glimpse of Indian life (including a demonstration of how to make cassava bread, the main food staple of the Arawaks), pass by the **Carib Cultural Center** museum in town. The Spanish colonial presence in Trinidad centered in Arima, and Spanish is still spoken by some people here. At Christmastime groups of guitarists and singers stroll the streets playing *parang* (Spanish carols).

From Arima you can pick up Trinidad's main east–west highway—a relief after hours of narrow mountain roads. The return portion of this loop back to Port of Spain takes about 30 minutes.

The South

The central part of the island, flat and covered with sugarcane fields, presents a distinctly different Trinidadian personality. Heading south via the Princess Margaret Highway, you'll notice the change immediately. Even the houses are different here: two-story concrete dwellings perched on columns. In front of every house is an array of flags on bamboo poles, announcing the homes of faithful Hindus. These banners, called *puja* flags, symbolize ceremonies of devotion. Near the center of the island and south is where the majority of Trinidad's East Indians live and work. Stepping into a village here, where white-domed mosques compete for attention with exuberantly decorated Hindu temples, is like being transported to the Ganges Valley.

The first stop on any trip into central Trinidad is the **Caroni Bird Sanctuary**, the wetland home (15 minutes south of the capital) of Trinidad's national bird, the scarlet ibis. This is one area where an organized-tour guide comes in handy, because the flocks of reddish-pink beauties are accessible only by hired boat. Winston Nanan (Tel: 645-1305) or David Ramsahai (Tel: 663-2207) will take you out at sunset to watch the ibis' graceful nightly return to their nesting grounds among the mangrove swamps.

South from Caroni along the highway, the cane fields stretch on and on like corn in Kansas. Depending on the time of year they will be lush and green or yellowish-brown and burning. Once you've inhaled the thick, sour-sweet smell of burning cane you'll never forget it. After about 5 miles (8 km), turn off at the exit for **Chaguanas**, the capital of Trinidad's East Indian heartland. Try to time your travels to pass through on a weekday morning when the **Chaguanas Market** is underway; bumping shoulders with ancient white-haired women in saris and little girls with dark velvet eyes wearing heavy gold jewelry, you'll wonder if you've taken a wrong turn and ended up in Bombay. Right on Chaguanas's main road you can pay homage to Trinidad's most famous native son, V.S. Naipaul. His childhood home, called **Lion House** because of its leonine gargoyles, now houses a grocery.

Continuing south from Chaguanas, head right on the Waterloo Road to find a special place even most Trinidadians don't know about: the mysterious **Temple on the Sea**. The tiny earthern dome, painted with Hindu symbols, sits about 100 feet off the coast in the Gulf of Paria, connected to the shore by a homemade bridge made of earth. It was built about 60 years ago by a faithful Trinidadian Hindu who had a vision of it in a dream. He was so poor he couldn't afford to buy land, so he carried buckets of earth out to the sea, one by one, until he'd created his own land—the tiny island you see—upon which he built the temple. Trinidad's Hindus consider this a holy place.

Standing at the silent water's edge, watching the sun set over the little island, the bustling Carnival scene of Port of Spain seems not fifteen, but a million miles away.

Carnival

Trinidad Carnival is the Christmas, New Year's, and Independence day of the island, unique in the Caribbean and in the world. Mardi Gras in New Orleans is more expensively large scale. Carnival in Rio is bigger, more exotic and glamorous. But Trinidad (where the Carnival tradition began in this hemisphere) is the great people's carnival, still quite uncorrupted by commercialism and hype. Here, anybody—even the first-time tourist—can join in the celebration, put on a costume and dance in the Carnival parade, or "play mas." For many, Trinidad Carnival is the single most important reason to come to the island.

The six- to eight-week calypso season, which begins in early January, is Carnival's warm-up period, an entertaining prelude to the big street festivities. Unfortunately, visitors usually miss it by dropping in only for the final countdown days to Carnival Monday and Tuesday. A shame, because the calypso tents (the indoor and outdoor theaters where calypso is performed) provide real insight into what's underneath all the glitter and paint of Carnival. In their rhythmic, witty, and sexy songs, the calypsonians (each tent features about 30 of them) analyze the major issues of Trinidadian life. Tragedy is transformed into comedy, and the future hit tunes of the upcoming Carnival become imprinted on the public consciousness. As described by a Trinidadian writer, "These are the songs that announce in this season the new rhythms for people to walk in." Each tent is headed by one of Trinidad's grand master calypsonians. The lineups, and the tent names and venues, change every year (check the newspaper ads), but you'll usually find a good show in the **Spetakula Forum** on Henry Street downtown, and at **Lord Kitchener's Calypso Revue**, located in a union hall on Wrightson Road, across the street from the Holiday Inn.

Also in January, Trinidad's world-renowned steel-band orchestras begin nightly rehearsals in preparation for their joyful dawn assault on the streets of Port of Spain on "J'Ourvert morning" (Carnival Monday). The steel drum, that familiar Caribbean instrument fashioned from discarded oil containers, was invented here in the city's predominantly African neighborhoods of Laventille and East Dry River. A visit to a steel-band rehearsal area (panyard) is an integral part of any Trinidad experience. Dozens of panyards dot Port of Spain, but the most popular are the yards of the champion **Amoco Renegades** on Charlotte Street near the corner of Henry, and their rivals, the **Desperadoes**, located "up the hill" on Laventille Road.

The third pre-Carnival activity, besides calypso and pan, is mas, the masquerade. Mas camps are the workshop-headquarters for the thousands-strong bands of parading Trinidadians. Each band has a theme, and its costumes are designed by a leading artist. You can visit the camp, take a look at the drawings of this year's costumes tacked to the wall, and take your pick. For a fee of between U.S. $50 and $300 (depending on the costume and the band), you too can take part in Trinidad's national festival. There are literally hundreds of bands, big and small, with camps in the Port of Spain area, but the most popular with visitors are **Edmund Hart's** and **Peter Minshall's** (camp addresses are listed in the *Trinidad Express*).

By the time you've visited a mas camp, a panyard, a calypso tent, and a couple of fêtes, Carnival itself may begin to seem like an afterthought. But when the parade of revellers begins to stream out of the fêtes on Carnival Monday morning, and the steel bands start to beat their siren call, you'll change your mind. Nothing really can prepare you for Trinidad Carnival, the peak of the year, the moment of national catharsis. When it's over and the dust settles on Ash Wednesday, the whole island seems to collapse in an exhausted heap. Then Trindadians—and visitors—begin to lay their plans for the *next* celebration.

TOBAGO

The giant frogs begin hooting at dusk. Soon they're joined by a chorus of a million birds, each one chattering and whooping its own song in counterpoint. Sitting on the beach under a canopy of almond and sea-grape leaves, you watch pelicans dive and soar as the sun drops into the Caribbean Sea. Gentle, peaceful, soothing Tobago remains one of the last true retreats in the Caribbean, a tiny (only 116 square miles) tropical garden teeming with every kind of life—except the tourist variety.

Legend has it that the island of Tobago was the setting for the novel *Robinson Crusoe*. Though the real Tobago is far from a deserted isle, it does have a "swept away" feeling that recent attempts at tourist development have not dispelled. It is still possible to bring your own tent and camp on the beach here, surrounded by all the natural splendor the Caribbean has to offer. For those not into roughing it à la Crusoe, Tobago offers comfortable accommodations at all price levels—from a room in the home of a village family or a friendly bed and breakfast to a suite in an all-inclusive resort-type hotel or a private rented villa.

Tobago's peace and quiet, like Trinidad's multiethnic bustle, is a product of its history. Discovered by Columbus in 1498, the tiny island was all but ignored thereafter. In the 17th century Tobago received some attention as a pawn in the shifting power plays of the English, French, and Dutch empires. It changed flags several times, and its many bays and coves often sheltered pirate ships on the run. In the early 19th century England took Tobago, imported slaves from Africa, and began to develop a small plantation economy of sugarcane and cocoa. The collapse of the world sugar market in 1888 led to the political annexation of Tobago by its larger colonial neighbor, Trinidad. Tobago has been part of the Trinidad and Tobago nation ever since.

Tobago's relationship to its more prosperous partner is a matter of expedience, not of shared identity. Tobago's people, unlike Trinidad's, share the same ancestors as descendants of the West Africans brought over in the 19th century. Because the island's plantation economy was rather loosely developed, Tobago's Africans were able to hold on to quite a bit of their culture. As a result, the folklore here is rich in West African music and beliefs—including *obeah,* the island's magical religion; Tobago's *obeah* men and women, who practice the arts of conjuring and hoodoo, are famous throughout the Caribbean. Walking down an empty Tobago road in the dark of night, you may begin to feel the island's special power. You may even spot a *jumbie* (spirit) dancing at the crossroads.

Nature and a Garden of Eden serenity are Tobago's main lures, followed closely by diving and water sports. The tiny island boasts over 200 species of birds and an extraordinarily rich marine life; divers will find themselves surrounded by rainbows of parrotfish, butterfly fish, turtles, and queen angels. Tobago's environmentally conscious leaders seem to understand that this natural beauty is the island's greatest treasure. More than half of the island's superb virgin rain forest is protected as part of a national forest reserve.

THE SOUTH END

Tobago is shaped like a long, narrow fish, its southern "tail" the "busy" end, with the airport, the best hotels and beaches, and lots of people. (This part of Tobago was the first to be developed, as a popular weekend getaway for Trinidadians.)

Arrival at the newly refurbished Crown Point Airport is easy and hassle free. Cabs and car rentals await outside the baggage area. But before heading to a hotel, you may want to begin your Tobago visit, as many newcomers do, with a post-landing breakfast of succulent flying fish and homemade coconut bread on the verandah at **Woods' Castle Resort** (Tel: 639-0803). The "resort" is actually a restaurant and no-frills hostelry 300 yards north from the airport in an old, peaked-roof wooden house that almost looks Nordic (this may explain why it is frequented by groups of young Scandinavians).

Tobago's most popular accommodations center on the Caribbean Sea coast around Grafton Road, also shelter to some of the nicest fishing villages on the island. First among these properties is the **Mt. Irvine Bay Hotel and Golf Club**, the grand dowager of Tobago resort hotels, perched atop a manicured hill spilling over with pink and fuschia bougainvillaea. With 52 deluxe rooms, 26 private cottages, a swimming pool, tennis court, and, of course, an 18-hole pro golf course, the Mt. Irvine is Tobago's oldest and most toney all-inclusive resort. It tends to attract an older crowd of British and Canadian families; there's a "last days of the empire" atmosphere at the Mt. Irvine, where the dining room is built in the ruins of an old sugar mill. Even if you don't stay here, taking afternoon tea and biscuits on Mt. Irvine's stately patio with its view of the sea and sunset is a lovely and gracious way to end a Tobago day.

Nearby is the new **Grafton Beach Resort**. German-owned and -managed, the all-inclusive 112-room hostelry perches right above Stone Haven Bay—you can all but tumble out of your room into the sea. The casual, wood-and-palm-thatched Grafton is an informal, action-oriented counterpoint to Mt. Irvine's traditionalism. With its own restaurants, disco, water sports, and dive shop, the Grafton is usually jumping with boisterous groups of holiday-making Germans and Scandinavians. Just a half mile farther along the coast is the **Turtle Beach Hotel**, boasting the same facilities as the Grafton but smaller and quieter. Families and couples seem to prefer its toned-down atmosphere and romantic location on a half-mile crescent of lonely beach facing Great Courland Bay.

The appearance of these three hotels has stimulated the economy of the Grafton Road area; ten years ago the nearest village, **Black Rock**, was a struggling little settlement. Now the villagers, while not rich, do a good business renting out rooms to travellers who settle in and become part of the landscape (for information on lodging, ask around for Bertie). In the evening Black Rock is busy with Swedes on bicycles saluting Rastas with knapsacks. Thriving, too, are a scattering of fine new restaurants. Joleen Decle's **Howling Coyote Café** (Tel: 639-8694), located in a tiny pink house on stilts and decorated with cacti and other reminders of the American Southwest, can't be beat for charm or for adventurousness in cooking. The menu includes deliciously fresh versions of local dishes, like roti, as well as Tex-Mex favorites (try the sizzling *fajitas*). Besides her eclectic culinary talents, Joleen, a Trinidadian actress who used to live in Southern California, is a licensed massage therapist (talk to her at dinner, and she'll arrange a soothing half-hour rubdown for you the next day).

Plymouth, at the end of Grafton Road, is home to a few hundred Tobagonians, and the largest village on the north coast. Pass through on a Saturday night and you may wander into an impromptu street party on the main street, with locals and foreigners enjoying music, boiled corn, and barbecued chicken. Many of the visitors will be staying at Plymouth's **Cocrico Inn**, an unassuming little concrete hotel that manages to hit all the right notes for a traveller seeking to catch the Tobago vibrations. With its comfortable, big, breezy rooms (with hot and cold water) set around a swimming pool, the Cocrico is the perfect choice for the budget traveller looking for a people-to-people, not a resort, experience. Two more pluses: The Cocrico has one of the best restaurants in the area, and friendly American owners, Nick and Bev, who'll arrange anything you need, from bicycles to a fresh lobster fest.

The island's loveliest beaches begin at the southern tip

of the "tail" (near the airport). The brown-sand cove of
Tobago's most commercial strand, **Store Bay**, lies at the
base of a short flight of stairs down a rocky hillside. Above
the lively scene of bathers and Tobagonians who come to
"lime" and hawk their tee-shirts and crafts, Store Bay
supports a thriving business of local food vendors selling
lunch from simple wooden huts. You can't really say
you've "done" Tobago until you've worked your way
through a mountain-high plate of **Miss Jean's** (Tel: 639-
0563) curried crab and dumpling—the island's most famous dish.

Follow the shoreline northward about a half mile (or
drive—the road runs parallel to the water) to **Pigeon
Point**, the white-sand stretch of beach that is Tobago's
finest. Here, on the Caribbean side of the island, the blue-
green water is warm and gentle, just perfect for lazy
floating or swimming. From Pigeon Point brightly painted
glass-bottom boats leave for **Buccoo Reef**, the coral garden that for many years has been one of Tobago's most
famous attractions. Although the chartered tourist boats
and divers have taken a toll on this delicate natural environment, you'll still see plenty of technicolor fish darting
in the sun-speckled aquamarine pool, especially if you
don snorkeling gear and jump into the water off your
boat. Buccoo makes a perfect afternoon break from the
beach/sun/lunch routine—and if you don't go you'll end
up having to explain yourself to all the Trinidadians
whose first question when you tell them you've been to
Tobago will be "Did you like Buccoo?"

If it's Sunday afternoon, take a drive east from the airport
along the newly built Claude Noel Highway (named after
the champion middleweight boxer who was born here),
and turn left on Buccoo Road. A stop at Buccoo Village's
"Sunday school" is mandatory—but not for Bible classes.
The "school" is actually a weekly day-long party where
locals and tourists alike down quantities of rum while dancing to recorded calypso and soca music.

SCARBOROUGH TO SPEYSIDE

The center of Tobago's commercial activity, bustling Scarborough on the south coast, has little to tempt the
tourist—except banks, markets, car-rental outlets, and
real-estate offices (check **Duval** or **The Tobago Villa Experience** for information on economical beachside apart-

ment or house rentals). However, if you happen to be in town, you may want to wander up the twisty hill road (the drive is referred to as "going to heaven") to **Fort King George**, Scarborough's main historical attraction. On a clear day, from the heights of this 19th-century fortress you may even spot Trinidad on the horizon.

If you'd like, linger over lunch at one of Scarborough's two fine restaurants. **The Old Donkey Cart**, on Bacolet Street, is a French colonial–style house now noted for its excellent wine cellar and light lunches of salads and open-face sandwiches made with home-baked bread, as well as more substantial gourmet fare. **The Blue Crab**, on the corner of Main and Robinson streets, specializes in fresh-from-the-briny wahoo, dolphinfish (not dolphins), and flying fish prepared in traditional Creole ways. For cocktails, delicious local dishes served in a fine setting, and a mellow view of the Atlantic-washed Bacolet Point, head to **Roussels**.

The main route, Windward Road, heads east from Scarborough along the Atlantic Ocean side of the island, a coastline of splashing seas and black-sand beaches that makes for dramatic photographs—and dangerous bathing. Bring sturdy shoes, not swimsuits, and allow a full day (out and back) for the spectacular trek to Tobago's deserted eastern area, where lush rain forest shelters flocks of exotic birds and every little stream winds back to a mountain waterfall. The drive itself is not for the timid and not to be attempted after dark. Once you get past the outskirts of the capital, Windward Road becomes an obstacle course of steep hills and hairpin turns, and when rain is heavy, portions of the road often tumble down the hillside. But the intrepid will be rewarded with "I can't believe it" vistas around every bend, as bright green forested mountains plunge into the azure blue Atlantic.

About 45 minutes along, a left-hand turnoff leads to the **Tobago Forest Reserve** and **Argyle Falls**, the best marked of the nature areas (and the only one accessible to vehicles other than four-wheel drive). After a few hundred feet along this dirt road you'll come to a parking area; proceed on foot along the rocky riverbed trail to the 450-foot, three-tier falls that suddenly appear like a hallucination, majestic and cascading, in the dark cool forest. After the hike the icy riverpool at the base of the waterfall looks inviting enough to jump in, and many do.

For a deeper trek into the reserve, a guide (with four-wheel drive) is necessary. The dean of Tobago naturalists,

David Rooks (Tel: 639-4276), seems to know the name of every bird, plant, and lichen in the jungle; he'll take you out for the day, or for half a day, into the mountainous spine of the nature preserve (the price for a carload day trip hovers around U.S. $75, depending on the route).

At the end of the road, sitting in the "mouth" of Tobago's "fish," is **Speyside**, a sleepy village of fishermen and, lately, a mecca for scuba divers. If you're not staying the night, a stop for lunch at **Gemma's** provides ample fortification for the two-hour ride home. Perched on a platform in a tree that juts out dramatically over the bay, you'll feast on huge platters of fresh fried fish, hearty rice and peas, and steaming, rich callaloo soup.

Speyside's **Blue Waters Inn** wins the prize as Tobago's most "get away from it all" hostelry. Many hotels bill themselves as hideaways, but the Blue Waters truly is one. There are no phones to disturb the magic serenity of this 29-room jewel tucked away in a little cove past Speyside, on its own private beach at the edge of 46 acres of rain forest. At night you'll be lulled by the rolling surf (all rooms face the sea), and in the morning a celestial choir of birds will awaken you. Excellent diving spots abound in the area, nature trails meander for miles, and excursions are available to nearby **Little Tobago** (a.k.a. Bird of Paradise Island), a 128-acre nature preserve and former home to a flock of those rare beauties until they fled after a hurricane. (After two days in the seductive arms of the Blue Waters, you'll wonder why they left.)

USEFUL FACTS

What to Wear
Bring comfortable summer sportswear (preferably cotton), plus long trousers and sturdy canvas shoes if you plan on trekking the rain forest. There's no need for ties, evening dresses, or formal attire—the nightlife on both islands is very casual. However, during weekdays in downtown Port of Spain dress tends to be rather conservative: skirts and blouses (no shorts or slacks) for women, tailored trousers and short-sleeved shirts for men. A small folding umbrella is useful as a sunshade in the dry season and a lifesaver during sudden tropical cloudbursts.

Getting In
Piarco International Airport in Trinidad, a half-hour drive east of Port of Spain, is the main point of entry. It is now

possible to fly directly to Tobago on BWIA from New York City. Otherwise, you must transfer at Piarco to one of the several jitney flights BWIA operates to Tobago's Crown Point Airport. Be advised: The 15-minute flights are always overbooked. You should remember to confirm reservations in advance by phone, then show up at least one hour before flight time.

Major airlines serving Trinidad are BWIA from Miami, New York, Toronto, Boston, Baltimore, London, Frankfurt, Jamaica, San Juan, and Barbados; Air Canada from Toronto and Montreal via Toronto; British Airways from London via Antigua or Barbados; United from New York via Caracas; American via New York; KLM from Amsterdam via Caracas; ALM from Atlanta, Miami, Haiti, Santo Domingo, Aruba, San Juan, St. Martin, Bonaire—all connecting via Curaçao; and LIAT from Grenada, Barbados, St. Vincent, and St. Lucia.

Ground transport from Piarco Airport and Crown Point Airport is provided by approved taxi services supervised by a dispatcher. Standard fares to hotels and other principal destinations are available on request from the dispatcher or from a tariff board displayed at each terminal. Taxis at Crown Point Airport are operated by the Tobago Taxicab Coop Society (Tel: 639-2707 or 7042) and other appointed operators. The average cost from Piarco to, say, the Trinidad Hilton is U.S. $25 one way. PTSC Bus service is available, at very low cost, from Piarco Airport to Port of Spain and from Crown Point Airport to Scarborough.

Entry Requirements

Passports must be valid for a minimum of six months beyond date of entry; no visa required for British Commonwealth or U.S. citizens, but all must possess an ongoing or return ticket. At immigration the official will ask you for a local Trinidad address and how long you will be staying in the country; if you are uncertain as to the exact length of your stay, add a few extra days to your maximum departure date, because whatever date you tell the official will be stamped in your passport and visa extensions are expensive and time-consuming to obtain. There is a departure tax of about U.S. $12, which must be paid in local currency (TT $50); if you don't have enough in hand, you'll have to change it (at a bad rate) at the airport bank, a real challenge when you're trying to maneuver yourself and your luggage through the non-air-conditioned front area of Piarco.

Local Time

Trinidad and Tobago are on Atlantic standard time year-round, one hour ahead of the U.S. east coast except when the east coast moves its clocks ahead an hour during daylight saving time. Then all keep the same time.

Currency

The monetary unit is the Trinidad and Tobago dollar; as of this writing the rate of exchange was U.S. $1.00 to TT $4.25. Most purchases and transactions are handled in local currency, although sometimes U.S. dollars are accepted. Traveller's checks are accepted almost everywhere, and major credit cards are honored in an ever-increasing number of hotels, shops, and restaurants.

Electrical Current

Same as elsewhere in the United States and Canada: 110–120 volts AC, 60 cycles.

Getting Around

If you feel comfortable driving on the left side of the road, a rental car is convenient around Tobago and in highway-happy Trinidad, a wise investment (unless you've come specifically for Carnival and intend to spend your entire visit in downtown Port of Spain). Rental cars are available at Piarco and Crown Point airports, and at outlets throughout Port of Spain; a valid driver's license is required, plus a credit card (or enough cash for a deposit, usually around U.S. $300). Reliable companies include **Singh's** (at the airports and in Port of Spain, Tel: 809/625-4247) and **Amars** (in Woodbrook on Roberts Street, Tel: 809/628-5516). During Carnival season rental cars are as scarce as sleep in Trinidad; it's best to arrange well in advance. Rates range from U.S. $300 to $400 a week, or U.S. $45 to $60 dollars a day. Gas is plentiful and very cheap, but be aware that on Sundays many of the state-owned service stations are closed. Trinidad's roads are among the best in the Caribbean. (Trinidad's Pitch Lake produces 75 percent of the world's asphalt!).

Even if you decide to rent a car, take a trip on one of the island's colorful "maxi taxis" if you want to experience an important ritual of daily Trinidadian life. Their sound systems pumping soca and calypso music, maxis pick up passengers along regular routes between Port of Spain's neighborhoods, and between Port of Spain and the rest of the island. Despite the high-decibel levels, the maxi taxi is a center for gossip, jokes, and the animated back-and-forth that Trinidadians call "ole talk." A ride on these mobile cultural wagons—so important a part of Trinidad that calypsoes are written about them—costs between TT $2 and TT $10, a set rate depending on the route.

Business Hours

Businesses, shops, and markets open from 8:00 A.M. to 4:00 P.M. and close at noon on Saturdays. Banks are usually open from 9:00 A.M. to 2:00 P.M. daily, with extra evening hours from 3:00 to 5:00 P.M. on Fridays, although several banks have recently expanded evening hours on Thursdays. Malls and hotel shops stay open later on evenings and Saturdays. Sunday is a day when the whole of Trinidad seems to be snoozing in a collective hammock; very few establishments of any sort stay open, not even the roadside food stands.

Festivals

Because of its multiethnic heritage, it's almost impossible to come to Trinidad when there *isn't* some sort of festival going on. Besides **Carnival** (always the Monday and Tuesday before Ash Wednesday), there are many celebrations in the East Indian community. **Hosein** (ho-SAYN), a three-day-long Muslim festival in July or August (dates vary according to the Islamic calendar—check with the Trinidad Tourist Board), features exuberant parades and competitions among the island's top Indian-style *tassa* drummers. **Divali**, the Hindu Festival of Lights, usually takes place in November (again, dates vary). During this celebration honoring the goddess Lakhshmi, central Trinidad twinkles with a galaxy of thousands of tiny clay lamps set out along roads and yards, and even on roofs. **Phagwa**, or **Holi**, is a springtime Hindu celebration marked by music and a lively parade (participants, mostly young boys, toss buckets of red-dyed water at each other).

Tobago celebrates a scaled-down, laid-back version of Trinidad's Carnival. In January Mt. Irvine plays host to the Johnny Walker Pro Am Golf Tournament. For a taste of Tobago's rich African culture, take your holiday during the Tobago Heritage Festival (July 15–August 1) so you can hear Tobago's haunting folk music. Played on drums and fiddle, Tobago's may be the only music in the world to blend Scotch-Irish and African influences.

For Further Information

Trinidad and Tobago Tourism Development Authority, 134–138 Frederick Street, Port of Spain, Trinidad, Tel: (809) 623-1932 through 1934, Fax: (809) 623-3848; **in the U.S.,** 25 West 43rd Street, Suite 1508, New York, NY 10036, Tel: (800) 232-0082 or (212) 719-0540, Fax: (212) 719-0988; **in the U.K.,** 8A Hammersmith Broadway, London W67 AL, England, Tel: (81) 741-4466, Fax: (81) 741-1013.

ACCOMMODATIONS REFERENCE

The rate ranges given here, in U.S. dollars, are projections for fall 1992 through spring 1993, and span the lowest rates in the low season to the highest in the high season. Unless otherwise indicated, rates are for double rooms, double occupancy. As rates are subject to change, it's always wise to double-check before booking. The telephone area code (within the U.S. system) for Trinidad and Tobago is 809.

Trinidad

▶ **Alicia's House.** 7 Coblentz Gardens, St. Ann's, Port of Spain, Trinidad, W.I. Tel: 623-2802; Fax: 623-8560. $50, E.P.

▶ **Asa Wright Nature Centre and Lodge.** P.O. Box 10, Port of Spain, Trinidad, W.I. Tel: 667-4655; Fax: 667-0493; in U.S. and Canada, Tel: (800) 426-7781 or (914) 273-6333; Fax: (914) 273-6370. $142–$182, A.P.

▶ **Bed and Breakfast Association of Trinidad and Tobago.** P.O. Box 3231, Diego Martin Post Office, Trinidad, W.I. Tel: 637-9329; Fax; 627-0856.

▶ **Cornetta's House.** 28 Scotland Terrace, Maraval, Trinidad, W.I. Tel: 628-2732; Fax: 628-7717. $50–$60, C.P.

▶ **Hotel Normandie.** 10 Nook Avenue, St. Ann's, Port of Spain, Trinidad, W.I. Tel: 624-1184; in U.S. or Canada, Tel: (800) 223-9815 or (212) 251-1800; Fax: (212) 545-8467. $90–$100, E.P.

▶ **Monique's Guesthouse.** 114 Saddle Road, Maraval, Trinidad, W.I. Tel: 628-3334; Fax: 622-3232 (wheelchair accessible). $40–$50, E.P.

▶ **Trinidad Hilton.** Lady Young Road, P.O. Box 442, Port of Spain, Trinidad, W.I. Tel: 624-3111 or 3211; Fax: 624-3211, ext. 6133; in U.S., (800) HILTONS; in Canada, (800) 268-9275; in U.K., (800) 289-303. $132–$174, E.P.

Tobago

▶ **Blue Waters Inn**. Batteaux Bay, Speyside, Tobago, W.I. Tel: 660-4341; Fax: 660-5195. $64–$104, E.P. (A.P. available).

▶ **Cocrico Inn**. P.O. Box 287, Tobago, W.I. Tel: 639-2961; Fax: 639-6565; in U.S. and Canada, Tel: (800) 223-9815 or (212) 251-1800; Fax: (212) 545-8467. $45–$55, E.P.

▶ **Duval Real Estate**. Scarborough, Tobago, W.I. Tel: 639-4276; Fax: 625-6452.

▶ **Grafton Beach Resort**. P.O. Box 25, Grafton, Tobago, W.I. Tel: 639-0191; Fax: 639-0030. $195–$220, E.P.

▶ **Mt. Irvine Bay Hotel and Gulf Club**. P.O. Box 222, Scarborough, Tobago, W.I. Tel: 639-8871 through 8873; Fax: 639-8800; in U.S., (800) 223-5695; Fax: (914) 833-3308. $140–$350, E.P.

▶ **The Tobago Villa Experience**. P.O. Box 301, Tobago, W.I. Tel: 639-8737; Fax: 639-8800.

▶ **Turtle Beach Hotel**. P.O. Box 201, Scarborough, Tobago, W.I. Tel: 639-2851; Fax: 639-1495. $65–$150, E.P.

BONAIRE

By Robert Grodé and Sharon Jaffe Dan

Sharon Jaffe Dan travels the islands extensively as an editor of Caribbean Travel and Life *and* Latitudes South. *She is the former editor of* Trade Wind. *Robert Grodé is the contributor of the chapters on Statia, Guadeloupe, Dominica, and Martinique.*

Much of the activity on 112-square-mile Bonaire takes place not on land but among the reefs and shoals that curve along the western shore of this tiny island just 50 miles off the coast of Venezuela. Snorkeling and scuba diving through the crystalline waters occupy most of the daylight—and often many of the nighttime—hours for most island visitors. But nondivers need not worry: There are a number of above-the-sea attractions to enjoy, from unspoiled beaches to a flamingo sanctuary and a national park teeming with wildlife. A small-town atmosphere prevails in Bonaire, and the local population, which numbers only around 11,000, welcomes visitors with enthusiasm. Simple roads and the absence of a single traffic light make exploring the island not only easy but fun.

MAJOR INTEREST

Scuba diving and snorkeling
Bird-watching along salt ponds
Washington/Slagbaai National Park

Like Curaçao and Aruba, Bonaire was sighted by an expedition headed by Amerigo Vespucci in 1499, but the Spaniards, visions of El Dorado dancing in their heads, dismissed the barren trio as *islas inutiles.* It wasn't until 1634 that the Dutch, always on the lookout for economic

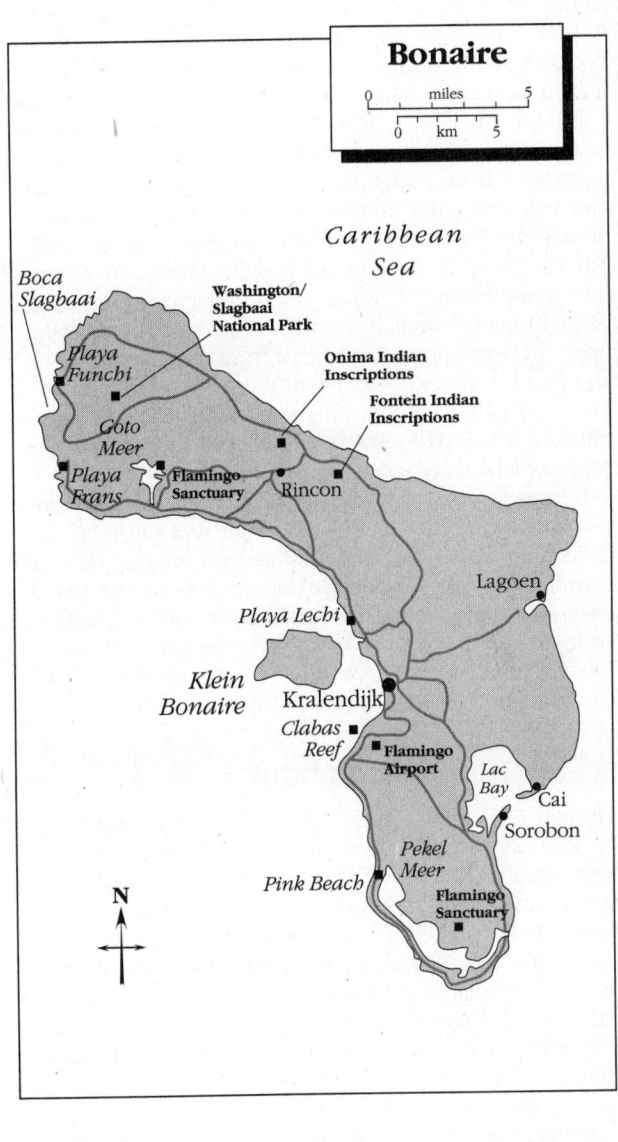

Bonaire

miles 0 — 5

km 0 — 5

Caribbean
Sea

Boca
Slagbaai

Playa
Funchi

Washington/
Slagbaai
National Park

Onima Indian
Inscriptions

Fontein Indian
Inscriptions

Goto
Meer

Playa
Frans

Flamingo
Sanctuary

Rincon

Lagoen

Playa Lechi

Klein
Bonaire

Kralendijk

Clabas
Reef

Flamingo
Airport

Lac
Bay

Cai

Sorobon

Pekel
Meer

Pink Beach

Flamingo
Sanctuary

N

reward, noticed Bonaire's shimmering salt flats and set about turning them into a saline gold mine. Salt harvesting was the island's major industry until tourism began taking off in the 1950s, and it is still a major source of income; the pink and lavender salt ponds with their flocks of resident flamingos have become a tourist attraction in their own right.

But it is the abundant sea life that really draws tourists. Realizing this, the government has declared the surrounding waters from high-tide mark to a depth of 200 feet a national park—the **Bonaire Marine Park**—and has prohibited the breaking off of even a single branch of coral. The launching of a number of farsighted programs assure diving enthusiasts of an unspoiled underwater world for generations to come. A network of permanent mooring buoys prevents potential damage from dive-boat anchors, and free buoyancy control workshops for all visiting divers keep flying flippers off the coral. Bonaire has also initiated a U.S. $10 annual Marine park diving fee, proceeds of which are spent on reef conservation.

Because of its calm, clear waters, where visibility can reach 140 feet, and its abundance of reef life near the shore, few spots are as well suited for snorkeling—or learning to dive—as Bonaire. Most hotels on the island have dive shops that offer both resort and certification courses, and many nondivers who come to the island for the first time happily leave Bonaire in possession of a "C" card, certified initiates to the underwater world.

Kralendijk

Though Kralendijk (Dutch for "coral dike") happens to be Bonaire's capital, there is little of the bustle usually associated with a seat of government in this drowsy seaside town. Careful development in the past few years has brought the pink-and-white Harbor Side Mall and new shops and restaurants, yet the town's laid-back air prevails. Kralendijk is a cluster of handsome, if somewhat salt-scarred, government buildings, restaurants, bars, and a handful of shops offering the usual variety of tourist items—china, jewelry, souvenirs, and infinite tee-shirts singing the praises of Bonaire.

Surprising for such a small island, Bonaire has a wide variety of restaurants, most of which are in town. For elegant Continental dining, visit the **Eetcafé Lucille** (Tel: 8003), at Calle L.D. Gerharts 4, where freshly caught fish or prime U.S. beef are expertly prepared in classic French style and served in an indoor dining room or out on a terrace. South of town on the main road to the airport, **Richard's Waterfront Dining** (Tel: 5263) is a trendy open-air restaurant with a seaside terrace and coral bar, a lively spot for sunset happy hour or a dinner of seafood (try the grilled conch in garlic sauce), pasta, or steak. Another satisfying choice for seafood is **Den Laman Seafood Restaurant** (Tel: 8955) on the beach at Playa Lechi.

Two favorite gathering places for island expatriates are the disarmingly funky **Mona Lisa Bar and Restaurant** (Tel: 8718), whose lively taproom at Calle Grandi 15 is festooned with yachting caps, and the **Rendez-Vous** (Tel: 8454), at Calle L.D. Gerharts 3, operated by the ebullient Marcel, something of an island institution himself. Famished divers in need of a pizza fix should visit **Cozzoli's**, in the Harbor Side Mall, also handy for subs on home-made bread and gyros. Cozzoli's seaside terrace is a popular evening hangout, especially on Saturday nights when there's a live band; Tel: 5195.

One of the most popular hotel choices for both dive enthusiasts and those who can't tell a face mask from a flipper is the **Divi Flamingo Beach Resort & Casino**, stretching along the coastline at the edge of Kralendijk. With 105 oceanfront and garden-view accommodations, two swimming pools, a handkerchief-size beach, tennis courts, a cheerfully informal bar, shops, "the world's first barefoot casino," and a pair of dining rooms overlooking the sea, the Divi Flamingo offers an activities-crammed roster of holiday pleasures. A fully equipped dive operation provides seemingly unlimited options for both experienced and novice underwater aficionados, though groups tend to be on the large side.

Adjacent to the Divi Flamingo is the 40-room **Club Flamingo**, a hotel/time-share complex boasting accommodations with screened, gingerbread-trimmed galleries and a separate dive operation.

Playa Lechi

Many other hotels lie along the shore, a 10- or 15-minute walk north from town. The **Sunset Beach Hotel**, on **Playa Lechi**, one of the island's finest beaches, is popular with divers who want to combine underwater adventures with improving their tans—not a bad idea; it's hard to get that bronzed look in a wet suit, after all. Facilities include a scuba center, water sports, two nightlit tennis courts, a beach bar, and a restaurant. Also on Playa Lechi is the posh, new **Harbour Village Beach Resort**, 72 luxurious suites and spacious rooms, all with such tropical touches as cool white-tile floors, louvred French doors leading out to patios or terraces, ceiling fans, and bright tropical prints. Activities include sunning and swimming on the dazzling palm-lined beach (with gazebo bar), water sports, boating, scuba, and deep-sea fishing. The restaurant here, **Kasa Coral**, is one of Bonaire's best.

For a self-catering vacation, **Sand Dollar Beach Club** is an excellent choice. This oceanfront community on Playa Lechi has 85 attractively furnished studios, one-, two-, and three-bedroom units with red-tile roofs, patios or terraces, and fully equipped kitchens, with a small grocery nearby. The tropically landscaped grounds lead down to the friendly **Green Parrot Restaurant**, where feeding the parrotfish breadcrumbs off the dock is a daily pastime. Sand Dollar boasts the only PADI five-star dive operation on the island; nondivers can loll by the pool or play tennis on one of Sand Dollar's two nightlit courts.

Other small properties along Playa Lechi include **Captain Don's Habitat**, a relaxed and relaxing dive resort made up of 59 cottages and villas with a restaurant and bar. Its namesake, burly expat Captain Don Stewart, has spent more than 30 years in Bonaire, during which time he is credited with opening the island's first hotel and dive operation and being the first to promote and fight for the protection of Bonaire's valuable underwater assets.

Next door is the posh new **Coral Regency Resort**, 33 suites equipped with kitchens and a full-service dive facility on the premises.

Out on the Island

Getting acquainted with Bonaire takes just two or three days, after which even first-time visitors begin to feel like old hands. On the southern end of the island restored slave huts front the salt pans south of Kralendijk, and, just beyond the nearby Antilles International Salt Company lies **Pekel Meer**, a lake designed as a flamingo sanctuary in 1968. During breeding season (March to May) Bonaire's pink flamingo population can reach 15,000, making it one of the largest such colonies in the world. Approaching the birds is forbidden, but from observation towers visitors can watch the flamingos feed in the lake and take off in the evenings for the 50-mile flight to Venezuela, where they supplement their food supply.

On the northern end of the island, the 13,500-acre **Washington/Slagbaai National Park** should be on everyone's agenda. In addition to flamingos the area teems with blue pigeons, darting yellow breasts, screeching parakeets, and more than 100 other species, including the indigenous lora parrot. Immense cacti break the line of the horizon, and you can observe iguanas sunning themselves on the rocky waterfront cliffs. You could easily spend a day exploring the scenic routes within the park, winding past secluded bays, lakes, and coves—some great for swimming and sunning, others for snorkeling and diving. **Boca Slagbaai**, with its restored colonial-era structures and bracing surf, makes a splendid spot for a beach picnic, as long as you don't dwell on the fact that its name means "slaughter bay" (the sunny yellow structures here reportedly were once departure points for hapless goats bound for market).

Just outside of Slagbaai, the picturesque lake, **Goto Meer**, is another prime flamingo-spotting location; bring a zoom lens if you want to capture them on film. **Rincon**, the island's oldest settlement (inland east of Slagbaai), has a peaceful, bucolic air about it. Laundry waves in the breeze and goats and chickens outnumber people in its quiet streets. The homemade ice cream at **Prisca's** makes a stop here worthwhile—try the coconut. Nearby at **Onima** and **Fontein** you may want to pause to examine the Arawak Indian rock inscriptions, said to be half a millennium old.

Sleepy Bonaire comes to life late Sunday mornings at **Cai**, a remote spot located across from Sorobon on **Lac Bay**, on the southeastern coast. At a typical Bonairean Sunday "brunch" here, a local band heats up the seaside scene with lively merengue, islanders cook up the chicken, fish soup, and conch, and the Amstel flows. This impromptu fête attracts a wide mix of visitors and locals, most of whom come to dance and "dine" before retiring to idyllic **Pink Beach** for an afternoon siesta.

For vacationing in the buff, try Lac Bay's 16-room **Sorobon Beach Naturist Resort**. Chalet-style rooms, a casual restaurant, and a private beach make a clothing-optional vacation at Sorobon Beach a pleasant possibility for those who prefer life *au naturel*. Guests from other hotels are welcome to share the Sorobon facilities for a small daily fee.

For a break from diving and snorkeling, visitors can try their hand at a number of other water sports on Bonaire. Lac Bay, actually a protected lagoon with clear, waist-deep and steady 15- to 25-knot winds, is home to **Windsurfing Bonaire** (Tel: 5363), which offers classes and equipment rentals. Water skiing can be arranged at the **Dive Inn** (Tel: 8761) in Kralendijk. Sunfish rentals are available at the Dive Inn as well as the **Bonaire Scuba Center** on Playa Lechi (Tel: 8978). You can sign up for day sails at most hotel activities desks. Deep-sea-fishing expeditions can be arranged through the Divi Flamingo Beach Resort; the Bonaire Scuba Center; or by contacting either Chris Morkos at **Piscatur Charters** (Tel: 8774), or **Dive Bonaire** (Tel: 8285).

USEFUL FACTS

What to Wear
Even describing the dress code on the island as "casual" may be an understatement. Beachwear is the order of the day and most of the nights. No bathing suits on town streets or in restaurants, however.

Getting In
ALM Antillean Airlines serves Bonaire from Miami and Atlanta. Other carriers serving Bonaire are Air Aruba from Newark, Avensa from New York (via Caracas), and KLM from Amsterdam.

Bonaire has no public buses, so you'll have to rely on taxis or a rental car to reach your hotel. Taxicabs are unmetered, but typical fares from the airport are U.S. $5 to Kralendijk, U.S. $4 to the Flamingo Beach Hotel, and U.S. $8 to the Sunset Beach Hotel.

Entry Requirements
U.S. and Canadian citizens must have a passport or other proof of citizenship, such as a birth certificate or voter-registration card. British subjects must have a British visitor's passport. Passports are required for all other travellers. All visitors must have a confirmed room reservation and a return or ongoing ticket. There is a departure tax of U.S. $10.

Local Time
Bonaire is on Atlantic standard time year-round, one hour ahead of the U.S. east coast except when the east coast

moves its clocks ahead an hour during daylight saving time. Then the two keep the same time.

Getting Around
Major car-rental firms operating in Bonaire include Budget, Tel: (599-7) 8300, ext. 225; Avis, Tel: (599-7) 5795; and Dollar, Tel: (599-7) 8888. You'll also find several local companies, including ABC Car Rental, Tel: (599-7) 5410, and Sunray, Tel: (599-7) 5600, ext. 34. Driver's licenses from all countries are valid; driving is on the right. Taxis can be identified on the street by a "TX" designation on the license plate. Stores and restaurants will order taxis for you.

Language
Dutch and English are the official languages; Papiamentu (a local dialect endemic to the Netherlands Antilles) and Spanish are also widely spoken.

Currency
The Netherlands Antilles florin (a.k.a. guilder) is tied to the U.S. dollar and fluctuates in relation to other currencies. U.S. dollars are widely accepted. As of this writing the rate of exchange was U.S. $1.00 to NAf 1.77.

Electrical Current
127 or 220 volts, 50 cycles AC. Adaptors and convertors are necessary for U.S. and Canadian-made appliances.

Business Hours
Stores are generally open from 8:00 A.M. to noon and 2:00 to 6:00 P.M., Monday through Saturday. Stores may be open for a few hours on Sundays when cruise ships are in port. Banks are open from 8:30 A.M. to 4:00 P.M., Monday through Friday.

Festivals
The biggest annual events in Bonaire are Carnival, with festivities taking place over the weekends prior to Ash Wednesday, and the week-long Annual Sailing Regatta, with top-class sailing and windsurfing races in October. For a week in mid-June the focus is on underwater photography, with the Nikonos Shoot-Out competitions (sponsored by Nikon), which offers a variety of prizes.

For Further Information

Tourism Corporation of Bonaire, Kaya Simon Bolívar #12, Kralendijk, Bonaire, N.A., Tel: (599-7) 8322, Fax: (599-7) 8408; **in the U.S.**, The Carriage House, 201 1/2 East 29th Street, New York, NY 10016, Tel: (800) U-BONAIR or (212) 779-0242; **in Canada**, 512 Duplex Avenue, Toronto, Ontario MR4 2E3, Tel: (416) 485-8724.

ACCOMMODATIONS REFERENCE

The rate ranges given here, in U.S. dollars, are projections for fall 1992 through spring 1993, and span the lowest rates in the low season to the highest in the high season. Unless otherwise indicated, rates are for double rooms, double occupancy. As rates are subject to change, it's always wise to double-check before booking. Note that nearly all the properties listed below offer dive packages. The telephone country code for Bonaire is 599-7.

▶ **Captain Don's Habitat.** P.O. Box 88, Bonaire, N.A. Tel: 8290; Fax: 8240; in U.S., (800) 327-6709 or (305) 373-3331; in the Netherlands, (70) 644-938. $145–$160.

▶ **Club Flamingo.** J.A. Abraham Boulevard, Kralendijk, Bonaire, N.A. Tel: 8285; Fax: 8238; in U.S., Tel: (800) 367-3484 or (305) 633-3484; Fax: (305) 633-1621. $100–$185.

▶ **Coral Regency Resort.** P.O. Box 380, Bonaire, N.A. Tel: 5580; Fax: 5680; in U.S. and Canada, Tel: (800) 327-8150 or, in Florida, (305) 359-0065; Fax: (305) 359-0071. $130–$285 (suite).

▶ **Divi Flamingo Beach Resort & Casino.** J.A. Abraham Boulevard, Kralendijk, Bonaire, N.A. Tel: 8285; Fax: 8238; in U.S. and Canada, Tel: (800) 367-3484 or (305) 633-3484; Fax: (305) 633-1621; in U.K., (453) 835-801. $80–$200.

▶ **Harbour Village Beach Resort.** P.O. Box 312, Bonaire, N.A. Tel: 7500; Fax: 7507; in U.S., Tel: (800) 424-0004 or (305) 669-0646; Fax: (305) 669-0842. $135–$395 (suite).

▶ **Sand Dollar Beach Club.** P.O. Box 262, Bonaire, N.A. Tel: 8738; Fax: 8760; in U.S., Tel: (800) 345-0805 or (609) 298-3844; Fax: (609) 298-3849. $125 (studio)–$195 (one-bedroom suite).

▶ **Sorobon Beach Naturist Resort.** P.O. Box 14, Bonaire, N.A. Tel: 8080; Fax: 5363. $95–$145.

▶ **Sunset Beach Hotel.** P.O. Box 333, Bonaire, N.A. Tel: 8448; Fax: 8118; in U.S. and Canada, Tel: (800) 223-9815 or (212) 545-8469; Fax: (212) 545-8467. $65–$145.

CURAÇAO

By Robert Grodé and Sharon Jaffe Dan

Curaçao reveals its European origins in its architecture, its food, and the cosmopolitan nature of its people. The Punda district of the island capital, Willemstad, is a tropical version of Amsterdam or Rotterdam, its closely packed buildings painted in pastels and overlooking not icy canals but the warm Caribbean Sea. True, Curaçao boasts the beaches, the year-round temperate climate, and the shopping bargains that characterize many other West Indian destinations, but it's the Old World atmosphere that distinguishes this 180-square-mile enclave 35 miles north of Venezuela.

For centuries Curaçao has been famed as one of the world's busiest mercantile centers. The island's strategic location and port (the seventh largest in the world) assured its place as a major trading hub. The harbor still rings with the blast of horns as ships seem to float right through the heart of town, and the shops brim with products from around the globe.

MAJOR INTEREST

Dutch food, atmosphere, and architecture
Historic Willemstad
Curaçao Underwater Park
Curaçao Seaquarium
Christoffel Park

Treasure-seeking Spaniards first claimed the island in the 15th century. The Dutch took it over in 1634. Peter Stuyvesant was governor during the early years before moving on to the then-sleepy hamlet of New Amsterdam, later called New York. Early on, the island became a

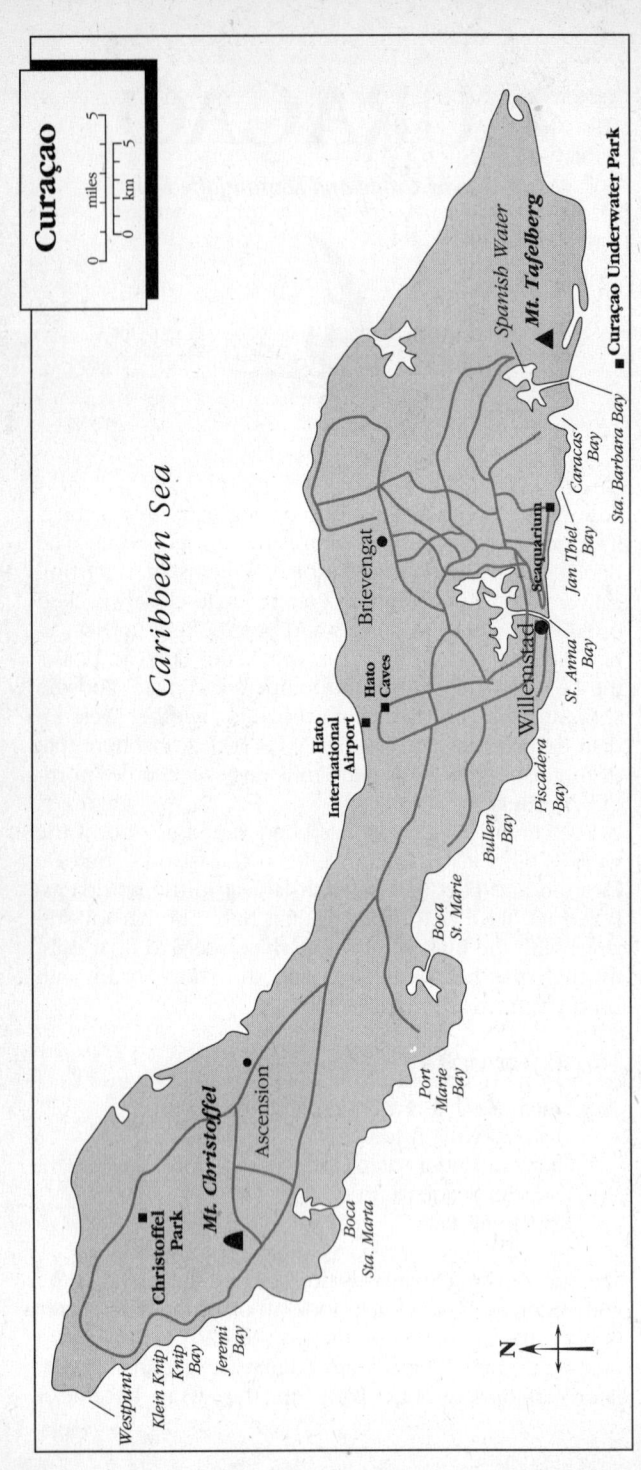

haven for descendants of Sephardic Jews whose ancestors had fled Spain and Portugal during the Inquisition for more tolerant lands. With Dutch blessings these Jewish merchants opened the island to trade and soon prospered. By the mid-1700s it was not uncommon for a hundred ships to pass through Curaçao in a single day. Except for brief periods, the Dutch ruled Curaçao until 1954, when it achieved autonomy as a member of the Netherlands Antilles. Curaçao is the seat of government of the five-member group that also includes Bonaire, Sint Maarten, Saba, and St. Eustatius.

Willemstad

Curaçao's colorful capital straddles both sides of St. Anna Bay. The two sections of the town, Punda on the eastern shore and Otrobanda (meaning literally "other side") on the western, are linked by the Queen Emma pontoon bridge, which swings open 20 to 30 times a day to admit tankers and cruise ships into the inner harbor. You can cross the floating bridge or, when the bridge is open, take one of the small ferryboats to the other side. There was a time when those wearing shoes were charged a few pennies to pass over the bridge, but today there's no need to slip out of your Nikes to save money; the Queen Emma Bridge is free.

Curaçao's remarkable architecture is a legacy of the island's original Dutch settlers, from the town homes and shops in Punda to the elaborate mansions built on the outskirts of town. Willemstad is home to some of the world's finest examples of colonial Dutch style, its buildings replete with red-tile roofs, belly-shaped pillars, and curly white gables. The houses are painted a riotous palette of yellows, oranges, and blues, thanks to a 19th-century governor who blamed his frequent migraines on the glare from all the whitewashed houses in town. He summarily ordered all the houses in Willemstad to be painted a darker color, and the whimsical effects of his decree remain today.

Perhaps the most frequently photographed scene in Curaçao is the **Handelskade**, the waterfront street in Punda lined with some of the most charming façades, including the famous **Penha building**. Built in 1708, this yellow shop with its curly gables and Rococo design has served visitors to Curaçao for almost 300 years. When Dutch settlers outgrew Punda in the 18th century, many built homes across the bay in Otrobanda. **Old City Tours,** led by resident architect Anko van der Woude, offers excellent guided walking tours of this historic district, conducted in English and Dutch; Tel: 61-35-54.

One of the island's most evocative landmarks is the **Mikve Israel-Emanuel Synagogue,** located at 29 Hanchi Snoa near Columbusstraat in Punda. The handsome structure, dedicated in 1732, is the oldest synagogue in continual use in the Western Hemisphere. Inside the hushed sanctuary, with its white walls and mahogany pews, pale sunlight gleams on the antique brass chandeliers. The sand-covered floor recalls a custom dating back to the Inquisition, when Jews went to great lengths to muffle the sounds of their worship for fear of discovery. All are welcome to attend services and visit the adjacent **Jewish Historical and Cultural Museum** (Tel: 61-16-33), which displays centuries-old ritual objects and memorabilia along with reproductions of historic gravestones from the island's Bet Chayim cemetery.

Another sight that should not be missed is the **Floating Market**—among the most colorful in the Caribbean—located between the Plaza Jo-Jo Correa and the Queen Wilhelmina Bridge. Boats from Venezuela loaded with produce moor along the canal, and the stalls are stacked high with bright red tomatoes, fiery hot Scotch bonnet peppers, rosy ripe mangoes (in season), and exotic spices. Overhead, awnings of purple, scarlet, and parrot green flap in the breeze. Housewives haggle with the market men, while members of the crew loll in string hammocks on deck, waiting for the voyage home.

Most of Curaçao's shops and boutiques are clustered in a six-block area of Punda. Among the best stocked in fine crystal, glassware, and jewelry are **Little Switzerland** and **Spritzer & Fuhrmann;** for a dazzling selection of imported perfumes and cosmetics, try **Penha & Sons** or **The Yellow House** on Breedestraat. **Palais Hindu** offers good buys on camera equipment and electronics. A small shopping complex, **Waterfort Arches,** has boutiques and alfresco restaurants and bars tucked away in the sea-swept ramparts of an old prison fortification. After sundown the Arches is a popular spot to meet for dinner or drinks as the waves crash against the centuries-old stone walls below.

Staying and Dining
In and Near Willemstad

Gazing down on all this is the **Van der Valk Plaza Hotel and Casino**, the tallest building in town and one of the few hotels anywhere that carries marine collision insurance because of its waterfront location. The hotel is popular with commercial travellers and large tour groups from Europe. The facilities include a seawater swimming pool, a pool bar and terrace restaurant, cocktail lounges, nightly entertainment, and a casino.

If you are seeking a more intimate vacation setting, the newly renovated, 85-room **Avila Beach Hotel**, a five-minute drive east from town, provides a house-party atmosphere in what was formerly the residence of one of the island governors. Some rooms face the pretty sweep of private beach; others overlook the central courtyard, where the outdoor dining at **Belle Terrace** restaurant ranks among the best on Curaçao. Service is charmingly personal at this favorite gathering spot for both locals and visitors. A few steps away is the **Octagon House Museum**, originally the home of Simón Bolívar's sisters and now a repository of memorabilia of the Liberator's 1812 visit to Curaçao.

Another five-minute drive along the shoreline east of Willemstad is the 205-room **Princess Beach Hotel and Casino**. Preferred accommodations here are in the recently constructed "Pelican" and "Flamingo" wings. Though a bit farther from the center of activity than the other rooms, these three-story wings offer greater privacy, and each includes its own bar area and stretch of beach. This hotel is the site of the annual International Windsurfing Competition every May. Among the amenities are a seawater swimming pool, tennis courts, sauna, dive shop, nightclub, casino, and lounge.

Also in the area, the 72-room **Lions Dive Hotel and Marina**, a sea-green and pink hostelry ringed with balconies, sits amid well-tended gardens. The open-air bar/restaurant **Rumours** features a variety of seafood dishes, and is a popular spot for *après*-beach socializing. At the adjacent Curaçao Seaquarium, the Italian **Baffo & Bretella** restaurant provides another dining option. Lions Dive has a pool, private beach, and weight room; the staff is knowledgeable and eager to please. Dive packages are offered at Seaquarium's Underwater Curaçao dive shop, a stone's throw away from the hotel (see below for the Seaquarium).

Offering a lively resort atmosphere, the **Curaçao Caribbean Hotel-Casino** is large (200 rooms) and replete with diversions: a private beach on Piscadera Bay just west of Willemstad, a pool, tennis courts, water-sports facilities, restaurant and outdoor dining room, shopping arcade, and casino. For trips into the city the hotel provides free shuttle-bus service throughout the day. This is a good choice for families and couples who want a full range of vacation activities.

Dining on Curaçao runs the gamut from Continental, at the romantic **Bistro Le Clochard** (Tel: 62-56-66), located in what were formerly the cells of Otrobanda's Rif Fort (creamy fondues and chocolate mousse are among the Swiss culinary touches on the menu), to the exotic **Rysttafel Indonesia** (Tel: 61-26-06) on Mercuriusstraat west of town. The best place in Curaçao to sample Indonesian cuisine, Rysttafel Indonesia serves the traditional "rice table," a smorgasbord of 16 to 25 different courses along with spicy sauces and condiments.

Other intriguing dining spots are the cozy, eight-table **Wine Cellar** (Tel: 61-21-78), on Concordiastraat, near the intersection with Scharlooweg a few minutes' drive east from the center of town, and **De Taveerne**, in the Landhuis Groot Davelaar, a stately old estate house furnished with heirloom antiques next door to the Promenade Shopping Center on Schottegatweg Oost; Tel: 37-06-69. The **Cactus Club** (Tel: 37-16-00) is a popular Tex-Mex place known for hearty burgers and *fajitas,* at Van Staverenweg 6, a 10-minute drive east of town. A popular spot for cocktails and *tapas,* the open-air **Rum Runners** (Tel: 62-30-38) in the newly restored Koral Agostini complex in Otrobanda, overlooks St. Anna Bay—a great place to watch the ships go by.

Antillean specialties include *erwtensoep* (a savory pea soup flavored with meat), *keshi yena* (Dutch cheese stuffed with meat or fish and baked), and *funchi* (a hearty cornmeal accompaniment to meats and stews). A good spot for sampling local dishes is the no-frills **Golden Star** (Tel: 65-47-93), located at Socratestraat 2 in town. Try the *carco stoba* (conch stew) over rice for a real island treat. Beer is the most popular drink on the island, and the locally brewed Amstel should be your choice. And after dinner there is, of course, the locally produced Curaçao liqueur, made from the skins of local oranges.

Out on the Island

For snorkelers and scuba enthusiasts, a visit to the **Curaçao Underwater Park**, established in 1983, is a must. Stretching more than 12 miles along the southeastern shore, the park protects more than 1,500 acres of coral reef teeming with ocean life. Visibility ranges from 60 to 80 feet, and can even reach 150 feet on an exceptionally clear day. An underwater nature trail is a favorite for snorkelers, while experienced divers may opt for the 20 official dive sites, 16 of which have permanent mooring buoys installed to protect the reef against anchor damage. The park is an easy 15-minute drive east from Willemstad.

The nearby **Curaçao Seaquarium** (Tel: 61-66-66), a cluster of low buildings, houses 75 aquariums containing more than 400 species of sea creatures. Fuchsia and gold royal grammas and black-and-yellow striped angelfish flit like butterflies through the tanks. Stingrays, sharks, and barracudas roam natural holding pools. All displays are labeled in English, Spanish, Dutch, and Papiamentu, the local dialect blending Dutch, Portuguese, Spanish, English, French, and African. The complex also offers facilities for swimming and windsurfing and a complete dive center for trips to the Curaçao Underwater Park. Nondivers may explore the briny depths aboard one of Seaquarium's regular glass-bottom-boat tours.

A new attraction on the island, the long-awaited **Hato Caves**, opened near the airport in late 1991. Hourly guided tours of the caves offer a fascinating glimpse of stalactites, stalagmites, and well-preserved fossil coral formations, not to mention an underground waterfall and domed "cathedral"; Tel: 69-32-11.

The northwestern end of Curaçao is the site of the 4,500-acre **Christoffel Park**. Various walking and driving tours traverse the rolling countryside, and wildlife (including wild goats, the seldom-seen Curaçao deer, and a wide variety of birds and lizards) abounds. The flora is equally unusual; two varieties of rare orchids, divi-divi trees, gnarled and bent by the prevailing winds, and sabal palms add to the Old West flavor of the desertlike landscape. For the strong of wind and limb, there is a three-hour climb to the crest of 1,239-foot Mount Christoffel.

A trip to Christoffel Park or one of the western beaches (see below) is not complete without a meal at **Jaanchie's Restaurant**, on the main road in Westpunt. Amid a flurry of yellow bananaquits (a.k.a. sugar birds), Jaanchie serves up some of the most authentic Krioyo (Creole) food on the island. Fresh fish is a guaranteed winner and well worth the wait even on a busy weekend. No credit cards; Tel: 64-01-26.

A visit to one of Curaçao's plantation estate houses—here called *landhuizen*—should also be included in your itinerary. Maybe you've already dined at De Taveerne, mentioned above, in Landhuis Groot Davelaar. For a tour, one good choice is **Landhuis Brievengat** (Tel: 37-83-44), an 18th-century cattle ranch that has been restored to its former grandeur, complete with antique mahogany furniture and mementos of plantation life. A 15-minute drive north of town, it is open to the public daily. Another is **Landhuis Ascension**, in the village of the same name, a few miles southeast of Christoffel Park. This Landhuis is used these days as a rest-and-relaxation center for Dutch sailors, and the friendly tars host an open house the first Sunday of every month.

The best beaches on the island lie in the west, stretching from Westpunt along the southern coast toward Willemstad, and include Jeremi, Boca Santa Marta, Port Marie Bay, and Boca Sint Marie. Of the 38 beaches on the island, the most popular public beaches are Westpunt and nearby Knip and Klein Knip. Changing facilities are limited. Around Willemstad, where most of the hotels are located, there is excellent swimming at Piscadera bay to the west, and at Jan Thiel and Santa Barbara bays to the east.

A marvelous way to see Curaçao's beaches, or its dry, rugged *cunucu* (countryside), is on horseback. **Ashari's Ranch** offers trail and beach rides for equestrians of all levels; Tel: 68-62-54.

USEFUL FACTS

What to Wear

Light, casual clothing is acceptable almost everywhere on the island; visitors who plan to frequent some of the more elegant restaurants and night spots will want to bring along somewhat more formal clothing.

Getting In

The major airlines serving Curaçao include ALM Antillean Airlines from Atlanta and Miami; Air Aruba from Newark and Miami; and KLM from Amsterdam.

Taxicabs provide the easiest means of getting from the airport to most of Curaçao's hotels; the cost usually ranges from U.S. $10 to $15. To call the airport taxi stand Tel: 68-12-20; the central number is Tel: 61-67-11.

The numerous car-rental companies on the island include Budget, Tel: (599-9) 68-34-66; National, Tel: (599-9) 63-61-82; Avis, Tel: (599-9) 68-11-63; and Caribe Rentals, Tel: (599-9) 61-30-89.

Entry Requirements

U.S. and Canadian citizens need proof of citizenship (passport, birth certificate, or voter-registration card). British subjects need a British Visitor's Passport (available at any post office), but not a regular passport. Visas are not necessary for stays of less than three months, but all visitors must present an ongoing ticket to a destination outside the Netherlands Antilles. There is a departure tax of U.S. $10.

Local Time

Curaçao is on Atlantic standard time year-round, one hour ahead of the U.S. east coast except when the east coast moves its clocks ahead an hour during daylight saving time. Then the two keep the same time.

Currency

The Netherlands Antilles florin (or guilder) is tied to the U.S. dollar. U.S. currency is widely accepted throughout the island. As of this writing the rate of exchange was U.S. $1.00 to NAf 1.77.

Electrical Current

Same as in the U.S. and Canada—110 or 130 volts AC, 50 cycles.

Getting Around

Public transportation is reliable and remarkably inexpensive on Curaçao. The buses are clean, the drivers helpful, and the service frequent, at specially marked bus stops. Tel: 68-47-33 for schedule information. Most coaches take off and return to the De Ruyterkade station near the market in Willemstad. The views along the various routes are almost invariably intriguing, and, should you for some reason tire of the passing scene, you can attempt to translate the 16 regulations posted in Papiamentu just behind the driver. One will inform you that passengers attempting to smuggle live animals on board risk *big* trouble.

Taxis are unmetered, so you should come to an agreement with the driver before embarking on a trip. Most hotels offer complimentary shuttle buses into central Willemstad.

Language
Dutch and English are the official languages; Papiamentu (a local dialect endemic to the Netherlands Antilles) and Spanish are also widely spoken.

Business Hours
Banks are open from 8:00 A.M. to 3:30 P.M. on weekdays. Stores are generally open Monday through Saturday, 8:00 to noon and 2:00 to 6:00 P.M. When cruise ships are in port, some shops also open on Sundays.

Festivals
Curaçao's version of Carnival, at the beginning of Lent, is the largest and most raucous festival on the island, with a parade and much music and revelry. Thanks to Curaçao's constant 12- to 22-knot trade winds, the island plays host to a number of races and regattas throughout the year. In the spring the Curaçao Regatta attracts sunfish, sailboard, and catamaran sailors from around the world. In late May there is the International Windsurfing Competition; the Simón Bolívar Regatta between Venezuela and Curaçao is held in August. And in November the Curaçao Caribbean Jazz Festival features top jazz and Latin music performers.

For Further Information
Curaçao Tourist Board, Pietermaai #19, P.O. Box 3266, Curaçao, N.A., Tel: (599-9) 61-60-00, Fax: (599-9) 61-23-05; **in the U.S.**, 400 Madison Avenue, Suite 311, New York, NY 10017, Tel: (800) 332-8266 or, in New York, (212) 751-8266, Fax: (212) 486-3024.

ACCOMMODATIONS REFERENCE
The rate ranges given here, in U.S. dollars, are projections for fall 1992 through spring 1993, and span the lowest rates in the low season to the highest in the high season.

Unless otherwise indicated, rates are for double rooms, double occupancy. As rates are subject to change, it's always wise to double-check before booking. The telephone country code for Curaçao is 599-9.

▶ **Avila Beach Hotel.** 130–132 Penstraat, Willemstad, Curaçao, N.A. Tel: 61-43-77; Fax: 61-14-93; in U.S., Tel: (800) 448-8355 (except Nebraska) or (402) 498-4300; Fax: (402) 398-5484. $120–$145.

▶ **Curaçao Caribbean Hotel-Casino.** J.F.K. Boulevard, P.O. Box 2133, Willemstad, Curaçao, N.A. Tel: 62-50-00; Fax: 62-58-46; in U.S. and Canada, Tel: (800) 223-9815 or (212) 545-8469; Fax: (212) 545-8467. $132–$210.

▶ **Lions Dive Hotel and Marina.** Curaçao, N.A. Tel: 61-16-44; Fax: 61-82-00; in U.S. and Canada, Tel: (800) 223-9815 or (212) 545-8469; Fax: (212) 545-8467. $110–$120.

▶ **Princess Beach Hotel and Casino.** Dr. Martin Luther King Boulevard 8, Willemstad, Curaçao, N.A. Tel: 61-49-44; Fax: 61-41-31; in U.S., Tel: (800) 327-3286 or (305) 441-8951; Fax: (305) 441-9266. $95–$235.

▶ **Van der Valk Plaza Hotel and Casino.** Plaza Piar, P.O. Box 229, Willemstad, Curaçao, N.A. Tel: 61-25-00; Fax: 61-65-43; in U.S. and Canada, Tel: (800) 223-1588; Fax: (212) 644-6840. $100–$130.

ARUBA

By Robert Grodé and Sharon Jaffe Dan

If Aruba's daytime dazzle is found along the island's shimmering white-sand beaches and sun-sequined waters, her nighttime glitter shines in a setting of action-filled casinos and after-dark shows. Rapidly becoming one of the Caribbean's most popular vacation destinations, Aruba offers an array of pleasures that range from fine dining and shopping to folkloric festivals and colorful street markets.

MAJOR INTEREST

Some of the finest beaches in the Caribbean
Nightlife/casinos
Friendly people
International cuisine

Aruba first fell under European eyes in 1499 when Alonso de Ojeda, having landed at Cape San Román in Venezuela, spotted the island floating on the horizon a mere 18 miles offshore. When they eventually settled the island, the Spaniards did little more than use it as a source of Arawak Indian slaves to work the gold mines of Hispaniola. The Dutch took over the island in the mid-1700s and have retained control ever since, except for a brief period of English hegemony in the early 19th century.

On January 1, 1986 Aruba, which had been a member of the Netherlands Antilles, separated from her five sister islands — Curaçao, Bonaire, St. Maarten, Saba, and St. Eustatius — and became a quasi-independent entity within the Kingdom of the Netherlands. With her newfound status, Aruba is enthusiastically promoting her tourism industry, and there is a sense of excitement in the air. Construc-

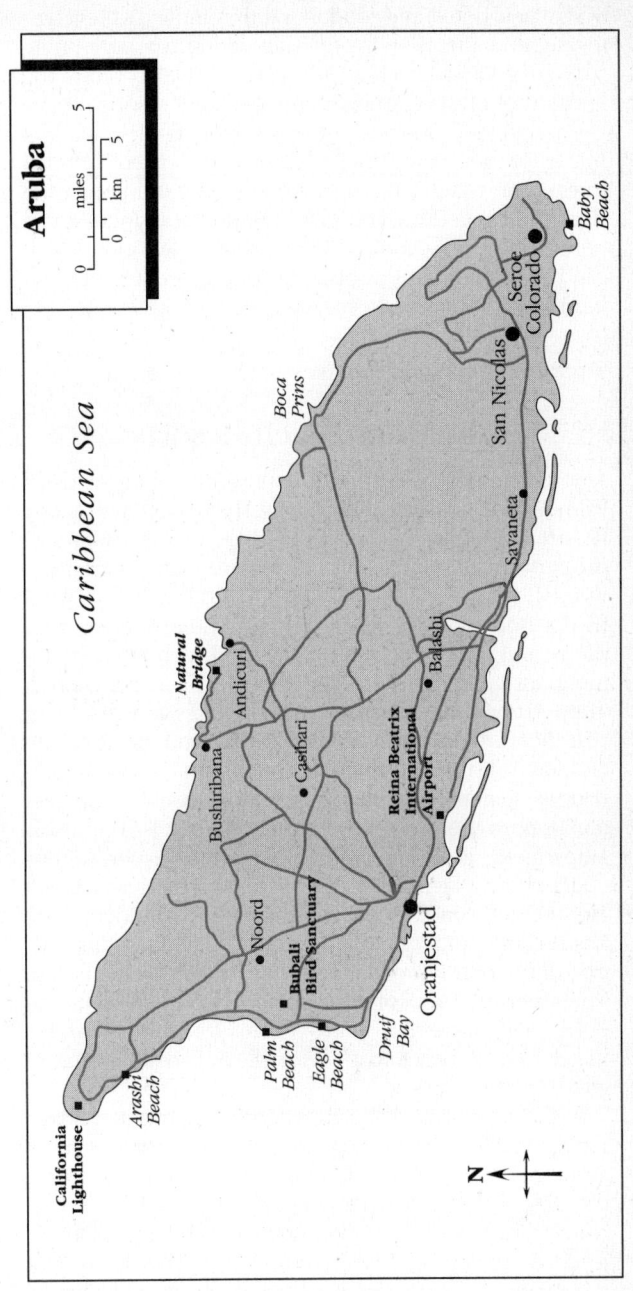

Aruba

Caribbean Sea

California
Lighthouse

Arashi
Beach

Palm
Beach

Eagle
Beach

Druif
Bay

Noord

Bubali
Bird Sanctuary

Oranjestad

Reina Beatrix
International
Airport

Balashi

Bushiribana

Natural
Bridge

Andicuri

Casibari

Boca
Prins

Savaneta

San Nicolas

Seroe
Colorado

Baby
Beach

N

miles   5

km   5

tion of new hotels and condominium complexes is evident throughout the island, especially along the seven-mile stretch of Palm Beach at its western end, presently the location of most of Aruba's high-rise hotel resorts.

Though the landscape greeting visitors is rather stark—immense boulders, prickly cacti, and twisted divi-divi trees—the island's beaches are among the finest in the West Indies, and are the main reason vacationers come here. The island is cooled by persistent trade winds, which can prove daunting on occasion but generally keep the humidity low and pesky insects at bay.

The Palm Beach Resorts

Among the hotels that line the powdery white sands of Palm Beach is the spanking new **Hyatt Regency Aruba Resort and Casino**. The centerpiece of this 360-room property is its multilevel pool replete with waterfalls, a waterslide, and a saltwater lagoon teeming with tropical fish. A host of water sports, tennis, a fitness center with sauna and steam room, a casino, and nightly entertainment are other features. Nearby is the 378-room **Golden Tulip Aruba Caribbean Resort**, the island's very first high-rise hotel. Popular with Europeans and groups, the Golden Tulip provides spacious, comfortable accommodations that happily avoid the assembly-line sameness apparent in more recently constructed hotels. The lushly landscaped grounds include a sports center, tennis courts, fitness facilities, and a pool. The **Americana Aruba Hotel and Casino**, on the other side of the Golden Tulip, has recently undergone an extensive face-lift and is now one of the prettiest of the larger properties on the island. The Americana, too, offers a casino as well as a swimming pool (with Jacuzzis), tennis courts, restaurants, and a thatched-roof beach bar—as well as a daily roster of children's activities.

A short stroll up Palm Beach, the ziggurat-style **Playa Linda Beach Resort** offers time-shares as well as hotel accommodations. On an island noted for its "go-go" pace, the 194-suite Playa Linda stands out with its nonstop round of activities. Even poolside sunbathing here seems to be done with intense determination. The decor is of the Atlantic City/Las Vegas school of design, the service friendly if somewhat frenetic.

Other Resorts

Far more laid-back is the atmosphere at the venerable **Best Western Talk of the Town Hotel** near the island capital of Oranjestad. Low, Spanish-style buildings surround a freshwater swimming pool and a garden shaded by almond trees. The hotel restaurant enjoys an island-wide reputation for the excellence of its Continental cuisine. The **Divi Divi Beach Resort** on Druif Bay, halfway between Oranjestad and Palm Beach, also offers a slower-paced vacation style. The service is attentive and the amenities include such civilized details as fresh-cut flowers and discreet room service. A newcomer to Eagle Beach, just south of Palm Beach, **La Cabana All Suite Beach Resort and Casino** is a 441-suite property with studio, one-, two-, and three-bedroom accommodations, each with fully equipped kitchenettes and private Jacuzzis. Suites are clustered in four-story wings surrounding the two-story atrium lobby with its huge stained glass window centerpiece of Venezuelan design. A state-of-the-art fitness center and tennis, racquetball, and squash courts keep guests on the move, providing they can resist the Royal Cabana Casino, touted as the largest in the Caribbean. Other amenities include a pool, minimarket, and shopping arcade.

Facilities, equipment, and instruction for a variety of water sports are offered by most of Aruba's resort hotels or by concessionaires on the property. If your hotel doesn't offer your sport of choice, chances are that the staff will be happy to make appropriate arrangements for you. Visibility in the waters off Aruba ranges up to about 100 feet; several sunken freighters just off the coastline make for excellent diving. And the strong tradewinds contribute to the challenging windsurfing conditions that draw aficionados of the sport from all over the world. Anglers can arrange for charter boats from any of a number of operators on Aruba; typical catches include tuna, bonito, marlin, kingfish, sailfish, and barracuda.

If you want to sample what may very well be the Caribbean's best nightlife, a visit to the **Alhambra Casino and Bazaar** is highly recommended. The casino is an Edwardian extravaganza of stained and etched glass, the shops in the bazaar offer a wide range of interesting items, and the Aladdin Theatre puts together an array of revues and Broadway revivals. For big-name entertainment, top billing at La Cabana's 600-seat **Tropicana Showroom** has gone to Regina Belle, Celia Cruz, Johnny Mathis, and the ultimate Caribbean crooner himself, Harry Belafonte.

Oranjestad

Oranjestad's main street, Nassaustraat, is a fairly predictable melange of tourist emporiums featuring jewelry, china, crystal, linens, perfumes, and other *articles de luxe*. Though shopping is not technically duty-free, bargains can be found. **Spritzer & Fuhrmann, Penha, Little Switzerland, Colombian Emeralds**, and **The Yellow House** rank among the most enticing stores.

On the waterfront in Oranjestad, **Seaport Village Mall** features more than 85 designer boutiques, shops, and restaurants, as well as the splashy Crystal Casino. Part of the complex, the new **Sonesta Hotel, Beach Club, and Casino** has ingeniously made the best of its downtown location by creating a canal between the sea and the hotel's soaring atrium lobby. Here, vacationers board launches for a ten-minute trip across the harbor to the hotel's private 40-acre Sonesta Island, where two beaches, a restaurant and bar, and a full complement of water-sports facilities await them. The Sonesta's imaginative design makes it one of the Caribbean's most unusual caravanserais. **Wharfside Village** faces the hotel across the square, a recently constructed enclave of bright pastel Dutch colonial shops, whose scallops and plaster curlicues prompted one recent visitor to dub them "architectural petits fours."

More authentic examples of traditional Aruban architecture are scattered along Oranjestad's back streets. One of the most interesting examples is **Fort Zoutman**, with its blue and red clock tower. The fort, dating from 1796, now houses the **Museo Arubano**. Within thick walls nestles a typical Aruban cottage, its rooms filled with exhibits of tools, musical instruments, household items, and furniture. Every Tuesday evening the Bonbini Festival takes place from 6:30 to 8:30; the courtyard facing the house echoes with traditional Aruban melodies and the air is fragrant with the aromas of well-loved island dishes. Dancers and singers add to the festive atmosphere. The admission charge is little more than a dollar; Tel: 260-99.

A block or two down Zoutmanstraat is Aruba's **Archaeology Museum**, located on the second floor of another time-mellowed building. The small rooms, opening onto a breezy gallery, are filled with artifacts created by the island's original Arawak inhabitants—shell ornaments, burial jars, and even the skeleton of one of these gentle Indians. Just around the corner on Wilhelminastraat stands the island's original Protestant church. Unused for many years and now locked and shuttered, it is still worth a brief visit if only to examine the unique gesso decorations on its stubby tower. Another museum worth browsing is the **Numismatic Museum** on Irausquinplein. The collection boasts ancient and rare coins from some 400 countries, including Egypt, Syria, and Greece.

Dining is varied on Aruba, a legacy of the island's mixed heritage. For superbly prepared Italian fare and a romantic Mediterranean atmosphere, take a trip to **Valentino's** (Tel: 647-77) in the Caribbean Palm Village near the village of Noord, north of the city and east of Palm Beach. The delicately herbed seafood and meat dishes feature light sauces, and the pastas are scrumptious. For *rijsttafel* (the multicourse Indonesian feast) Oranjestad offers either **The Bali Restaurant** (Tel: 206-80), romantically set in a curved roof, batik-draped houseboat moored at the foot of Schooner Harbour, or the cozy **Warung Djawa** (Tel: 348-88) on Wilheminastraat. **Papiamento** (Tel: 245-44), housed in an impressive Aruban mansion in downtown Oranjestad, and **De Olde Molen** (Tel: 220-60), a venerable windmill brought to the island from Holland and set up outside town in the Palm Beach area, are popular with celebrating Arubans. The menus at both restaurants are classic French. For a taste of Dutch cooking with a bit of Caribbean dash, sample the *keshi yena* (Dutch cheese stuffed with chicken, raisins, and herbs) at the rustic **Bon Appetit** (Tel: 652-41), within easy reach of the major hotels in Palm Beach.

If you are especially interested in sampling classic Aruban dishes, a visit to the seaside village of **Savaneta**, a 20-minute drive east along the southern coast, will prove highly rewarding. There you'll find **Brisas del Mar** (Tel: 477-18), an unpretentious little restaurant whose menu includes *sopito* (a hearty fish soup); *kerri-kerri* (another spicy fish creation); a variety of lovingly prepared seafoods; *pan bati* (the traditional island bread); and *funchi* (a polenta-like side dish that is an island staple).

Out on the Island

Visitors need not stray far from the Palm Beach strip to take in Aruba's flora and fauna. Inland from Palm Beach just south of De Olde Molen restaurant lies the **Bubali Bird Sanctuary**, home to some 300 different species of birds. Within the sanctuary a man-made lake (actually recycled water from the local sewage treatment plant and the only body of fresh water on desertlike Aruba) provides an oasis for herons, frigate birds, pelicans, terns, parrots, and dozens of other plant and bird species found nowhere else on the island. Visitors can easily glimpse feathered friends from the road that rings the preserve or from the dry paths traversing it.

Island sightseeing, though low on most beach lovers' list of priorities, does offer some worthwhile rewards. **De Palm Tours** (Tel: 245-45) makes morning excursions to many of the island sights, but you might be happier renting a car for a day and taking off for an afternoon's exploration on your own. The problem with the organized tours is that several tour buses converge simultaneously on the various attractions, forcing the passengers to dart out of range of other travellers' cameras and to peer over the shoulders of the assembled multitudes.

Santa Ana Church, near the village of Noord just east of Palm Beach, sits in the middle of a vast sun-baked parking lot. Either the congregation is immense or the lot has been extended to accommodate the herds of tour buses that rendezvous here. Inside, the ornately Gothic-style altar (dating from 1860) is the work of Dutch artist Van Geld. Note especially the 18th-century stations of the cross. You may want to wander among the colorful family crypts in the cemetery next door. Whenever a family member is interred, the walls of the crypt are given a spanking new coat of paint.

Continuing east toward the center of the island, you'll find at Casibari a gigantic rocky outcropping, worth a visit if only for the sweeping views of the surrounding countryside and the silhouette of Haystack Mountain. On the north coast of the island the landscape takes on a lunar quality, swept bare by the prevailing winds. Ruined stone walls are all that remain of the smelters erected here during Aruba's mini gold rush during the 1800s. On this rugged coast you'll discover Aruba's most famed sight, the **Natural Bridge**, carved from the coral rock by the pounding sea—a good spot to pause for a cooling drink.

Farther east, near Boca Prins, you can explore caves embellished with Arawak wall paintings. Don't confuse these with the modern examples worked into the walls by a French film crew a few years back. Tempting as a dip in the sea may be here in this arid region, treacherous currents make bathing inadvisable. (For safe swimming outside the Palm Beach area try shallow, calm **Baby Beach** on the southeastern tip of the island or **Arashi Beach** on the northwestern tip. **Eagle Beach**, between Palm Beach and Druif Bay, is a favorite spot for picnicking.)

On the way back to your hotel, a detour to the far northwestern tip of the island will take you to the abandoned **California Lighthouse**. On a hilltop, the spot offers a panoramic view of the desolate, boulder-strewn landscape.

Another option for exploring the island is by renting a horse at **Rancho El Paso**, located near most of the island's hotels. You can arrange for either a two-hour beach ride or a one-hour guided canter through the countryside (the *cunucu*)—a pleasant alternative to the water-oriented pastimes that are Aruba's primary preoccupations; Tel: 233-10.

USEFUL FACTS

What to Wear
Lightweight, casual clothing is suitable for most occasions and recommended for comfort. Those planning to visit the fancier restaurants and casinos should bring along some dressy clothes as well.

Getting In
The major airlines that serve Aruba with direct flights (check with the airlines or a travel agent for information on other routes available with connections) are: Air Aruba from Newark and Miami; ALM Antillean Airlines from Atlanta, Miami and Curaçao; American from New York and San Juan; BWIA from Miami; Viasa from Houston; and Aeropostal from Orlando and Atlanta. KLM serves Aruba from Amsterdam; from Canada, there is service on Air Canada in addition to frequent charter flights.

Entry Requirements

U.S. and Canadian citizens must have a passport or other proof of citizenship, such as a birth certificate or voter-registration card. British citizens do not need passports, but must have a British Visitor's Passport. Visitors from other countries must have passports. Everyone entering the country must have a return or ongoing ticket. There is a departure tax of approximately U.S. $9.50.

Local Time

Aruba is on Atlantic standard time year-round, one hour ahead of the U.S. east coast except when the east coast moves its clocks ahead an hour during daylight saving time. Then the two keep the same time.

Language

The official language is Dutch; Papiamentu (a local dialect endemic to the Netherlands Antilles), English, and Spanish are also widely spoken.

Currency

The Aruba florin; most hotels and the larger shops accept traveller's checks and major credit cards. U.S. currency is widely accepted. As of this writing the rate of exchange was U.S. $1.00 to AFl 1.77.

Electrical Current

Same as in the U.S. and Canada—110 volts AC, 60 cycles.

Getting Around

Rental cars are available from Hertz, Avis, Dollar, Budget, National, Interent, Pelican, Marcos, and JM Car Rental. Driving is on the right. You may operate a car on Aruba with any valid foreign license or with an international driver's license; you must be 21 to rent a car.

Taxis are not metered, so travellers should negotiate rates before embarking on a ride. The approximate cost from the airport to Oranjestad is U.S. $7; to the hotels on Palm Beach, approximately U.S. $12. (The taxi dispatch office can be reached at Tel: 82-21-16.) Airport buses also service the hotels, but you must have a prepaid travel coupon (available through your travel agent). Public buses run between Oranjestad and the hotels on Eagle Beach and Palm Beach. Car rentals are also available at the airport.

Business Hours

Most shops are open Monday through Saturday from 8:00 A.M. to to 6:30 P.M. If a cruise ship is in port, some shops open Sunday mornings. Banks are generally open from 8:00 A.M. to noon and 1:30 to 4:00 P.M. weekdays.

Festivals

Annual events include the boisterous Carnival celebration, culminating with a big parade on the Sunday before Lent; Queen's Day, on April 30, with parades and sporting events; the Aruba Hi-Winds Pro-Am Windsurfing Competition in late May; the Aruba Annual Marathon and the Aruba Jazz and Latin Music Festival in June; the International Fishing Tournament, the first week in November; and the Pan American Race of Champs, a drag race scheduled for the second week of November.

For Further Information

Aruba Tourism Authority, L.G. Smith Boulevard 172, Aruba, Tel: (297-8) 237-77, Fax: (297-8) 347-02; **in the U.S.,** 521 Fifth Avenue, 12th Floor, New York, NY 10175, Tel: (800) TO-ARUBA or (212) 246-3030, Fax: (212) 557-1614; **in Canada,** 86 Bloor Street West, Suite 204, Toronto, Ontario M5S 1M5, Tel: (416) 975-1950, Fax: (416) 975-1947.

ACCOMMODATIONS REFERENCE

The rate ranges given here, in U.S. dollars, are projections for fall 1992 through spring 1993, and span the lowest rates in the low season to the highest in the high season. Unless otherwise indicated, rates are for double rooms, double occupancy. As rates are subject to change, it's always wise to double-check before booking. The telephone country code for Aruba is 297-8.

▶ **Americana Aruba Hotel and Casino.** L.G. Smith Boulevard 83, Palm Beach, Aruba. Tel: 245-00; Fax: 231-91; in U.S., (800) 223-1588; in Canada, (800) 531-6767. $160–$310.

▶ **Best Western Talk of the Town Hotel.** L.G. Smith Boulevard 2, Oranjestad, Aruba. Tel: 233-80; Fax: 324-46; in U.S. and Canada, Tel: (800) 223-1108; Fax: (914) 763-5362. $83–$140.

▶ **La Cabana All Suite Beach Resort and Casino.** L.G. Smith Boulevard 250, Oranjestad, Aruba. Tel: 390-00; Fax: 354-74; in U.S. and Canada, Tel: (800) 835-7193 or (212)

251-1710; Fax: (212) 545-8467. $85–$355 (one-bedroom suite).

▶ **Divi Divi Beach Resort.** L.G. Smith Boulevard 45, Oranjestad, Aruba. Tel: 233-00; Fax: 340-02 or 342-30; in U.S., Tel: (800) 367-3484; Fax: (305) 633-1621; in U.K., (453) 835-801. $120–$295.

▶ **Golden Tulip Aruba Caribbean Resort.** L. G. Smith Boulevard 81, Palm Beach, Aruba. Tel: 335-55; Fax: 232-60; in U.S., Tel: (800) 344-1212 or (212) 867-3838; Fax: (212) 867-3867. $90–$250; suites, $765.

▶ **Hyatt Regency Aruba Resort and Casino.** L.G. Smith Boulevard 85, Palm Beach, Aruba. Tel: 312-34; Fax: 354-78; in U.S. and Canada, Tel: (800) 233-1234; Fax: (402) 593-4030. $180–$370.

▶ **Playa Linda Beach Resort.** L.G. Smith Boulevard 87, Oranjestad, Aruba. Tel: 310-00; Fax: 252-10; in U.S., Tel: (800) 346-7084 or (201) 617-8877; Fax: (201) 617-7579. $110–$300.

▶ **Sonesta Hotel, Beach Club, and Casino.** L.G. Smith Boulevard 82, Oranjestad, Aruba. Tel: 360-00; Fax: 343-89; in U.S. and Canada, Tel: (800) SONESTA; Fax: (617) 421-5434; in U.K., (800) 898-410. $100–$230; suites, $640.

INDEX